Doing
Oral
History

A Practical Guide

SECOND EDITION

Donald A. Ritchie

OXFORD
UNIVERSITY PRESS

OXFORD
UNIVERSITY PRESS

Oxford New York
Auckland Bangkok Buenos Aires Cape Town Chennai
Dar es Salaam Delhi Hong Kong Istanbul Karachi Kolkata
Kuala Lumpur Madrid Melbourne Mexico City Mumbai Nairobi
São Paulo Shanghai Singapore Taipei Tokyo Toronto

Copyright © 2003 by Donald A. Ritchie

Published by Oxford University Press, Inc.
198 Madison Avenue, New York, New York 10016
www.oup.com

Oxford is a registered trademark of Oxford University Press

Library of Congress Cataloging-in-Publication Data

Ritchie, Donald A.
Doing oral history : a practical guide / Donald A. Ritchie.—2nd. ed.
p. cm.
Includes bibliographical references and index.
ISBN-13 978-0-19-515433-7 (cloth : alk paper)—ISBN-13 978-0-19-515434-4 (pbk. : alk. paper)
1. Oral history. 2. Oral history—Methodology. 3. Historiography.
I. Title.
D16.14.R57 2003
907'.2—dc21   2003009205

Designed by Nora Wertz

5 7 9 8 6

Printed in the United States of America
on acid-free paper

To Anne Ritchie

Doing
Oral
History

SECOND EDITION

Contents

Doing
Oral
History

SECOND EDITION

Most human affairs happen without leaving vestiges or records of any kind behind them. The past, having happened, has perished with only occasional traces. To begin with, although the absolute number of historical writings is staggering, only a small part of what happened in the past was ever observed. . . . And only a part of what was observed in the past was remembered by those who observed it; only a part of what was remembered was recorded; only a part of what was recorded has survived; only a part of what has survived has come to historians' attention; only a part of what has come to their attention is credible; only a part of what is credible has been grasped; and only a part of what has been grasped can be expounded or narrated by the historian.

Louis Gottschalk, *Understanding History* (1950)

Introduction and Acknowledgments

So many new developments in oral history emerged over the last decade that revising this manual caused some trepidation. How much of the original advice remained valid? How much had grown obsolete? In what new directions was the methodology moving? What technological advances had occurred? What advice, given the rapid innovations in sound and video recording, would remain relevant the longest?

Fortunately, the fundamental principles of preparing, conducting, and processing oral history interviews had held firm, although an abundance of new examples and literature could be cited to support those functions. What changed most was the breaking of the Third Wave over oral history. In 1980, the futurist Alvin Toffler contended that having passed through agricultural and industrial stages, the world was entering an electronic era that would revolutionize production, education, government, and communication. Since then, the proliferation of personal computers, e-mail, and Internet web sites has verified Toffler's forecast. Since oral history owed its existence to mechanical equipment, from tape recorders to transcribers and video cameras, its practitioners moved speedily toward the new digital era. Their willingness to employ new technology improved interviewing, processing, and disseminating their work, to make people more aware of their own history.

The digital revolution has impacted every chapter of this new edition. It required deleting many references to "tape" since recordings are now as likely to be made on disk or on digital video cameras. As a policy, this book refrains from recommending specific equipment or software programs since they are likely to grow dated. However, it tries to raise issues that need to be taken into consideration when acquiring any new technology. An important off-shoot of the digital revolution was the creation of the H-Net lists, in which specialists in many fields communicate with each other via an e-mailed list service. I owe much gratitude to all those oral historians who contributed to the H-Oralhist list, sending in questions, suggestions, announcements, warnings, and solutions, with much pragmatic advice drawn from their own experiences that I have incorporated into *Doing Oral History*.

The Internet has been both a godsend and a vexation for oral historians. After struggling to find ways to bring their interviews to the attention of more researchers and to the general public, oral historians found the Internet ideally suited for disseminating collection catalogs, interview transcripts and sound recordings, along with related illustrations and memorabilia. Researchers now pay virtual visits to far-flung archives and read entire transcripts online or do word searches for specific topics. Students have particularly made use of the new medium, and the number of "hits" that interviews receive on the Internet far exceed the traffic that they sustained in traditional archives. But the Internet also generated new ethical and legal issues and new debates among oral historians about the appropriate way to proceed. Both the rewards and the pitfalls of putting oral histories online became recurring themes of the new edition.

Beyond digital technology, a growing interest in memory has placed the work of oral historians and public historians more squarely within the mainstream historical scholarship. Grappling with issues of public memory—from official histories, parades and reenactments to public monuments and designated landmarks—historians have examined how people have constructed the past to make it useful to them in the present. As they gradually recognized how collective memory can preserve or distort a community's past, scholars grew more appreciative of oral history. How, what, and why people remember and narrate the past is, after all, the primary business of the oral historian. This convergence of interests is reflected in the number of oral history programs that have added memory to their titles, from the Oral History and Community Memory Institute and Archive at Monterey Bay, California, and the Center for the Study of History and Memory in Bloomington, Indiana, to the Centre for Popular Memory in Cape Town, South Africa.

The appearance of Institutional Review Boards on college campuses has also significantly affected oral historians. Established to review medical and psychological research on human subjects, the boards have spread into the social sciences and humanities, often misapplying criteria designed for questionnaire-based, quantitative methodologies to oral historians' open-ended qualitative interviewing. It is a troubling issue with which the Oral History Association and the American Association of University Professors have grappled to devise means of preserving academic freedom in oral history research.

A more positive trend has been the globalization of oral history. Whereas past centers of oral history lay primarily in North America and Western Europe, the digital revolution together with sudden political and social changes have shifted much of the dynamic of oral history around the world to include the former Soviet bloc, Asia, Africa, South America and the South Pacific. The inadequacy of written documentation from previous regimes and colonial powers has accelerated the need—and even the demand—for oral history. From the local to the national level, governments have come to see the value of oral history and have mandated and funded specific projects. At the same time, the democratic impulse of oral history has convinced many practitioners that it is "time to hand the mike to the people." Oral historians are increasingly training students and community members to collect interviews themselves. Since the first appearance of *Doing Oral History*, the International Oral History Association has held meetings in Sweden, Brazil, Turkey and South Africa, each meeting producing multiple volumes of conference proceedings. Much of the new material in the book reflects projects under way around the world. Despite differences in the subjects being studied in their diverse places, oral historians share many commonalities in methods and techniques. Universally, they have encountered the tendency of oral history to confound rather than to confirm their assumptions, confronting them with often conflicting viewpoints. Oral history derives its value not from resisting the unexpected, but from relishing it. By adding an ever wider range of voices to the story, oral history does not simplify the historical narrative but makes it more complex—and more interesting.

"Oh, you do that vocal history," someone once said, trying to fathom oral history. That identification was half-right, since oral history thrives on talking, largely by the interviewee. The interviewer's task is to do thorough research beforehand, then ask meaningful questions, suppressing the urge to talk and listening instead. Yet it always seems amusing that oral historians, who have disciplined themselves to be silent during interviews, behave so loquaciously when they gather at professional conferences. The truth is that oral historians love to talk. As the only historians who deal exclusively with the living, they have to be convivial enough to establish rapport with interviewees, to put them at ease and encourage candor. Practitioners of the craft of posing questions, oral historians also find themselves constantly questioning their own concepts, methods, and applications of new technology. Those who collect the voices of history make their own voices heard on how to do and use oral history.

It is impossible to pinpoint a place on the globe where people are not now doing oral history. Since the appearance of the first recording devices, from wax cylinder to wire recorder to reel-to-reel, cassette, videocassette, and digital audio tape, and mini-disk recorders, interviewers have questioned politicians and protestors, indigenous peoples and immigrants, artists and artisans, soldiers and civilians, the sacred and the secular. Oral historians have recorded the reminiscences of survivors of the Nazi Holocaust, the Japanese-American internment, and the Soviet Gulags. Interviews have also captured the everyday experiences of families and communities, whether in inner cities, satellite suburbs, or remote villages. When historians came to realize that women and racial and ethnic minorities were missing from the pages of most history texts, oral historians recorded their voices to construct a more diverse and accurate portrait of the past.

Archives of oral history interviews exist throughout the world and in every state and territory of the United States, ranging from a few tapes housed in the local history collection of a neighborhood public library to thousands of transcripts preserved at major university libraries. Inside the federal government, oral historians have collected testimony about national parks and historical sites, diplomatic maneuvering, military strategies, intelligence activities, space flights, and social security and welfare programs. Over time, this information has been returned to the public in countless books and articles, museum exhibits, folklife festivals, radio programs, documentary films, and web sites—indeed, the development of the Internet has permitted the worldwide dissemination of oral history transcripts and sound recordings.

The real impact of the oral history movement may not be fully realized until well into the future. Although the earliest recorded memories date back into the nineteenth century—one transcript at the Columbia Oral History Research Office contains firsthand recollections of the bloody New York City draft riots of 1863—most of the collected interviews have been with contemporary figures discussing recent events. Individual researchers do not always need to wait for archival oral history collections to release interviews; armed with their own tape recorders, they can go forth themselves to question whoever is willing to answer. But as generations pass and participants in historic events are no longer living, future researchers will have to depend on what earlier interviews collected, processed, and deposited in archives. How will these future researchers judge our work? How much of today's oral history will be considered an important supplement to the written documentation of our time, or dismissed as superficial and superfluous? How much of what we do will be preserved, and how much will be lost? Oral historians need to look beyond their own immediate needs to consider the corpus of work they will leave for the future.

Doing Oral History raises many questions and provides answers that address the range of current practices and considerations. Its question-and-answer format is intended not as a catechism of the true faith but as a dialogue between the reader and the author, similar to that of an oral history interview. Questions ranging from the open-ended ("What is oral history?") to the specific ("Should transcripts reproduce accents and dialects?") are intended for those conducting group projects, working as individual researchers, establishing oral history archives, videotaping, teaching, and seeking to make use of oral histories in various forms of public presentation. These questions have repeatedly been asked at oral history workshops, particularly by those just entering into oral history. The answers offer realistic and practical advice while maintaining the standards that oral historians have collectively devised and promoted. Some questions come from more established practitioners who are reevaluating their methods and missions midway through their projects. The answers seek to be as serviceable to veterans as to novices.

Early in the oral history movement, the director of Columbia University's Oral History Research Office, Louis Starr, lamented the absence of manuals for interviewers but wondered how useful any single book would be, since every interviewer would have a different personality and style and every subject would have its distinctive requirements. Subsequently, manuals and fieldwork guides have appeared in profusion, reflecting the many disciples that employ the interview technique and differing according to the standards, practices, and technology at the time they were written and the backgrounds and interests of their authors. Historians, archivists, librarians, folklorists, anthropologists, educators, journalists, linguists, and gerontologists have contributed to the burgeoning literature. This book draws from that body of scholarship as well as from my personal experience: as a historian, I use interviews as part of my research, and I conduct an archival oral history program for the U.S. Senate Historical Office. Although my work has been largely in political and public history, my contacts with the many state, regional, national, and international oral history associations have given me opportunities to view the far reaches and creative diversity of the field.

From 1988 to 1991, I coordinated the efforts of the Oral History Association (OHA) to revise and improve its professional code of principles and standards and its evaluation guidelines. In such a fluid and dynamic field, these fundamentals plainly needed reexamination after a generation in use. Several appointed committees addressed interviewing, processing, videotaping, teaching oral history, the roles of independent researchers, and ethical issues. The committees discussed and debated every conceivable aspect of oral history and presented their findings at two consecutive OHA meetings, where the members further debated, amended, and eventually adopted the new guidelines.

Numerous disagreements occurred during this process, raising eyebrows and voices over this or that practice, because oral historians represent many fields that often have different objectives and terminology. But a consensus finally emerged from this process, the findings of which are incorporated throughout this book (and are reprinted in appendix 1).

Not every oral historian will agree with every point made here, since there is no uniform way of doing oral history, and unconventional approaches may sometimes work well. The principles and standards were established for good reasons, but for every rule there has been an exception that works. Oral historians welcome innovation and imagination. Rather than seek to make all interviewers march like soldiers in cadence, this book aims to help them first think carefully about what they are doing and to be aware of potential consequences.

The questions and answers that follow deal with so many principles and potential pitfalls that they may intimidate some beginning oral historians. But awareness of the issues should not paralyze the process. Oral history interviewing may not be easy, but it can be enormously satisfying and rewarding to meet and engage in dialogue with memorable individuals and to make sure that otherwise neglected aspects of the past will be preserved for the future.

Most oral historians learn by doing, and our understanding of the theories of interviewing and our interpretation have more often followed than preceded our interviewing. *Doing Oral History* seeks to provide practical advice and reasonable explanations for those planning to conduct and collect oral history interviews. Its emphasis is on doing; planning is essential for the success of an oral history project, but I have seen project directors fret for years without actually conducting any interviews. They worried about raising money, about what types of questions would be legitimate, about whom to interview, and additional problems that other projects were capable of solving. My recommendation is always to stop worrying and actually do some interviews. Projects can begin small and grow as funds become available and personnel gain experience. Finishing just one interview gives a project something tangible to show for its efforts, something to present to funders and to use as a mode for volunteer interviewers. Even a poor interview offers mistakes from which a project can learn. Lengthy deliberations and delays run the risk that desired interviewees will die before they can be interviewed, for oral historians are in a perpetual contest with the actuarial realities.

Because the costs of doing oral history vary widely and the technology associated with it changes rapidly, this book does not give estimates for operating budgets, such as the cost per hour for interviewing or transcribing, nor does it endorse particular equipment. Anything so specific would become out-of-date almost upon publication. Readers planning to launch an oral history project would be better advised to contact other projects in their locality for cost estimates and equipment recommendations. There are also no mechanical descriptions here of how tape recorders or video cameras work, since the author boasts no mechanical skill other than being able to turn on a tape recorder and check periodically to make sure it is functioning properly. Nor should this book be taken for a cookbook of recipes that specify the precise measurements of ingredients and instructions to guarantee satisfying results. Instead, it offers a wide-ranging discussion of the methods of oral history, with notes and a bibliography that can lead those with specific queries to more specialized sources.

Each chapter presents a different role related to oral history: starting a project, doing interviews, processing interviews, using interviews in independent research, videotaping, preserving interviews in libraries and archives, teaching, and presenting the material to various publics. Few oral historians are involved in all of those phases, and most will specialize only in a few aspects. But rather than confine themselves to a single niche, readers should examine the complexity of oral history. Interviewers need to understand thoroughly what archivists want from the process, and vice versa. Teachers and students should consider aspects of public presentation, and audio interviewers should have at least some curiosity about videotaping. The various chapters offer glimpses of each area and suggest further reading.

More useful than any written sources, however, were the many oral historians with whom I have talked and compared experiences over the years. I owe special thanks to Terry Birdwhistell, who prompted me to write this book and whose advice and editorial judgment I depended on throughout its writing. Martha Ross introduced me to oral history as a research tool and to the network of oral history associations. Richard Baker gave me the opportunity to create an oral history project at the U.S. Senate and the exceptional experience of uncovering the Senate's history through the observations of senators and career staff.

Oral History Association presidents Ronald Marcello and Lila Goff commissioned and supported the revisions of the OHA's principles and standards and evaluation guidelines. In coordinating those efforts, I received extraordinary assistance from committee chairs Sherna Gluck, Linda Shopes, Pamela Henson, Barry Lanman, George Mehaffy, and Terry Birdwhistell, and from all the other committee members. The exchange of memoranda, draft reports, and conference calls and the face-to-face meetings that went into the project constituted my complete reeducation as an oral historian.

Many colleagues and friends have generously read and wisely commented on various portions of this book, among them Frank Clearfield, Maygene Daniels,

Barry Lanman, David Mould, John Neuenschwander, Mary Kay Quinlan, Terri Schorzman, Brien Williams, and Mark Zadrozny. Charles T. Morrissey, a prolific writer on oral history methods and proficient trainer of interviewers, submitted his helpful editorial impressions on tape. Cullom Davis, Michael Devine, Ronald Marcello and John Neuenschwander provided welcome breaks during spring-training baseball seasons, where oral history was discussed between innings. My able editor at Oxford, Nancy Toff, conducts her own oral histories with flutists. This book is dedicated to my wife, Anne Ritchie, who does oral history interviewing for the National Gallery of Art in Washington, D.C., and whose companionship, advice, and keen memory I rely upon daily.

CHAPTER 1

An Oral History of Our Time

What is oral history?

Memory is the core of oral history, from which meaning can be extracted and preserved. Simply put, oral history collects memories and personal commentaries of historical significance through recorded interviews. An oral history interview generally consists of a well-prepared interviewer questioning an interviewee and recording their exchange in audio or video format. Recordings of the interview are transcribed, summarized, or indexed and then placed in a library or archives. These interviews may be used for research or excerpted in a publication, radio or video documentary, museum exhibition, dramatization or other form of public presentation. Recordings, transcripts, catalogs, photographs and related documentary materials can also be posted on the Internet. Oral history does not include random taping, such as President Richard Nixon's surreptitious recording of his White House conversations, nor does it refer to recorded speeches, wiretapping, personal diaries on tape, or other sound recordings that lack the dialogue between interviewer and interviewee.[1]

To avoid repeating common mistakes, oral historians have created standards for doing interviews, and established principles for dealing ethically with their interviewees. But oral history is too dynamic and creative a field to be entirely captured by any single definition. For every rule, an exception has worked. Imaginative interviewers are constantly developing and sharing new methods and uses of oral history. Any definition of the oral history process, or any method of interviewing, must reflect the goals of the specific project, the resources available, and other practical considerations.[2]

When did people begin collecting oral history?

As distinct from oral traditions—stories that societies have passed along in spoken form from generation to generation—oral history *interviewing* has been occurring since history was first recorded. Three thousand years ago, scribes of the Zhou dynasty in China collected the sayings of the people for the use of court historians, and several centuries later, Thucydides interviewed participants in the Peloponnesian wars. Skepticism of oral testimony dates back equally as far. Thucydides complained that "different eye-witnesses give different accounts of the same events, speaking out of partiality for one side or the other or else from imperfect memories."[3]

During the European conquest of the Americas in the sixteenth century, Spanish chroniclers relied on oral sources to reconstruct the history of the indigenous people, from the Aztecs to the Incas. To assist in both colonization and conversion, they collected the testimony of survivors of these once great civilizations, concentrating on their social, economic, and religious traditions. Although strongly colored by the colonizers' cultural assumptions, these histories remain important sources for the new world's pre-Columbian history.[4]

In 1773, when Samuel Johnson argued against the proposition that an impartial history could not be written in the lifetime of those who had experienced the events, he reasoned that "a man, by talking with those of different sides, who were actors in it and putting down all that he hears, may in time collect the materials of a good narrative." Johnson admonished that "all history was at first oral" and noted that this was how Voltaire had prepared his histories of the French kings. Indeed, Voltaire wrote that he had questioned "old couriers, servants, great lords, and others" and recorded only "those facts about which they agree." Jules Michelet studied the French Revolution, a half century after it took place, by contrasting the official documents with the recollections of "peasants, townsfolk, old men, women, even children; which you can hear if you enter an evening into a village tavern."[5]

Soon after the battles of Lexington and Concord launched the American Revolution in 1775, a Congregationalist minister named William Gordon interviewed the participants, among them Paul Revere. Gordon's recounting of Revere's elaborate preparations contradicted efforts to portray the battles as unprovoked attacks by the British, and revolutionary leaders managed to suppress the story. Two centuries later the historian David Hackett Fischer declared Gordon's essay drawn from Revere's interview "remarkably full and accurate." In the 1870s the California publisher Hubert Howe Bancroft compiled his seven-volume *History of California* (1884–90) by sending students out to collect the papers and the reminiscences of nineteenth-century Mexican military governors and *alcaldes* (civilian officials) and of the first American settlers.[6]

It seemed reasonable to consult oral as well as written sources until the late nineteenth century, when the German school of scientific history promoted documentary research to the exclusion of other, less "objective" sources. Leopold von Ranke asserted that documents created at the time historical events occurred are the most reliable form of historical evidence; Ranke's followers helped turn history from a literary form into an academic discipline dependent on the rigorous use of evidence. They trained historians to scrutinize documents in their search for truth and dismissed oral sources as folklore and myth, prized only by well-meaning but naive amateurs and antiquarians. They deemed oral evidence too subjective; shoddy memories told from a biased point of view.[7]

Ironically, historians turned away from oral sources just as other professions and disciplines were embracing the interview. Journalists made interviewing a mainstay of their craft around the time of the American Civil War. In 1859, when New York *Tribune* editor Horace Greeley went west to conduct a highly publicized interview of Mormon patriarch Brigham Young in Salt Lake City, he launched a trend in newspaper interviews. By 1868, President Andrew Johnson, facing impeachment by Congress, sought to present his side to the public by giving the first presidential interviews for attribution. "I want to give those fellows hell," Johnson told the reporter who was interviewing him, as he gestured towards the Capitol, "and I think I can do it better through your paper than through a message, because the people read the papers more than they do messages." Interviews quickly became so popular that clever politicians took to preparing their own question-and-answer dialogues, which obliging journalists published as news.[8]

In the 1890s, the U.S. Bureau of Ethnography dispatched researchers to record on wax cylinders the songs and stories of Native Americans. During the Depression of the 1930s, the Works Progress Administration (WPA) hired unemployed writers to chronicle the lives of ordinary citizens. Especially valuable were the WPA's interviews with former slaves. Four decades later, when historians finally accepted these records—comprising more than 10,000 pages of interviews they helped to alter fundamentally the historical interpretation of American slavery.[9]

When the United States entered World War II, President Franklin D. Roosevelt ordered all military branches and civilian agencies of the government to prepare records of their wartime experiences. Planning not only a postwar history, but a series of morale-boosting "American Forces in Action" booklets, the U.S. Army dispatched historians into the battlefields, armed with heavy wire recorders. Directed by Lt. Col. S. L. A. Marshall, a World War I veteran and journalist turned army historian, they pioneered in the post-combat interview, debriefing soldiers immediately after the battle to reconstruct the events of the day. Sgt. Forrest Pogue spent D-Day interviewing wounded soldiers who had been evacuated to a hospital ship anchored off Normandy Beach. Recalling concerns that his bulky wire recorder might attract sniper fire, Pogue noted that the army wanted live history "and live historians."[10]

Although the term had been used earlier, not until the 1940s did "oral history" attach itself to interviewing. A Harvard-educated Greenwich Village bohemian and flophouse denizen, Joseph Gould, otherwise known as "Professor Sea Gull," wandered around Manhattan collecting what he called "An Oral History of Our Time." Joseph Mitchell's profile of Gould that appeared in the New Yorker in 1942 drew attention to his crusade to record the stories of average people. "What people say is history," Gould insisted. "What we used to think was history—kings and queens, treaties, inventions, big battles, beheadings, Caesar, Napoleon, Pontius Pilate, Columbus, William Jennings Bryan—is only formal history and largely false. I'll put down the informal history of the shirt-sleeved multitude—what they had to say about their jobs, love affairs, vittles, sprees, scrapes, and sorrows—or I'll perish in the attempt." The quest garnered many a free meal for Gould, but his oral history proved to be a figment of his imagination. When Gould died he left nothing behind but the name.[11]

Another journalist-turned-historian, Allan Nevins, created the first modern oral history archives at Columbia University in 1948. A decade earlier, in his book The Gateway to History, Nevins had proposed to reinvigorate historical study in America by making "a systematic attempt to obtain from the lips and papers of living Americans who had led significant lives, a fuller record of their participation in the political, economic and cultural life of the last sixty years." Recognizing that modern communication and transportation were making letter-writing and diary-keeping obsolete, Nevins founded the Columbia Oral History Research Office. This new effort raised complaints from those who considered "Oral History" either too imprecise or too Freudian. But by the 1960s Nevins's successor, Louis Starr, could point out that the term had so worked its way into the language that newspapers were referring to it in the lower case. "Oral history, like it or not, is here to stay," Starr declared. "It's gone generic."[12]

The University of California at Berkeley launched a similar oral history program in 1954, as did UCLA in 1958. The Harry S. Truman Library inaugurated the first presidential library oral history program in 1960. The John F. Kennedy Library began interviewing shortly after Kennedy's assassination, before the library was constructed. Oral history soon became standard practice for building presidential collections. By 1967 the Oral History Association was founded, gaining membership throughout the United States and abroad. Oral history projects developed on every continent, and national oral history organizations formed from Mexico to New Zealand. In 1972 the Imperial War Museum in London established a Department of Sound Records to collect and preserve oral testimony of those servicemen and women who "for lack of inclination, opportunity, or literary skill" would leave no other record for history. A 1987 meeting in Oxford, England, established the International Oral History Association, which meets biannually around the world.[13]

Worldwide political and social changes during the last decades of the twentieth century confronted historians with the inadequacy of archival documentation, which often reflected a discredited government rather than the resistance against it. Newly emerging nations in Asia and Africa found that the written documents reflected the views of former colonial masters and used oral history to revive buried national identities. When the Soviet Union dissolved, Russian and Eastern European oral historians' efforts began immediately to reexamine and rewrite that region's discredited official history by collecting personal testimony suppressed under Communist regimes. In Brazil and Argentina, oral history projects have focused on periods of military dictatorship to record the experiences of those brutalized by state terrorism. South Africans similarly turned to oral history in their search for truth and healing in the post-Apartheid era. Interviewers in many nations have found interviewing a critical tool when confronting issues of repression and reconciliation.[14]

Who is being interviewed?

In the United States the first oral history archives studiously avoided Joe Gould's "shirt-sleeved multitudes." Allan Nevins was a political historian who interviewed the major players in government, business, and society. Long after Nevins's retirement, Columbia continued to interview people of the stature of judges, cabinet members, senators, publishers, business executives, and civic leaders. By contrast, European oral history projects from the start were the domain of social historians who sought to record the everyday lives and experiences of working-class people.

Not until the 1970s did a new generation of American historians begin writing history "from the bottom up." Lacking the abundant manuscript resources and formal documentation available on the elites, they turned to oral sources. Encouraging these efforts were the best-selling books of Studs Terkel, a Chicago radio talk-show host and former WPA interviewer whose books, such as *Hard Times* (1970), *Working* (1974), and *The Good War* (1984) captured the voices of everyday people in a compelling manner. Alex Haley's *Roots* (1976) similarly inspired people, especially African Americans, to collect their own family histories through interviews. The availability of convenient and relatively inexpensive cassette tape recorders and video recorders further helped to popularize oral history.[15]

For years oral historians argued the respective merits of "elite" versus "nonelite" interviewing. As the debate tapered off, oral history projects grew more all-inclusive. The more that interviewers studied their practice, the more they realized that no one group had an exclusive understanding of the past, and that the best projects were those that cast their nets wide, recording as many different participants in events or members of a community as possible. Once a military oral historian was questioned about the possibility of using oral histories to reconstruct the social acculturation of barracks life. He responded coolly, "I only interview generals." Since then, oral history has changed, even in the military, where historians now conduct interviews with all ranks of enlisted personnel and officers, in garrison and in combat, to build important research collections.

When journalists interview, are they doing oral history?

Journalists usually interview subjects for very specific purposes having to do with the newspaper story, magazine article, or news broadcast they are preparing. Working on short deadlines, reporters depend heavily on oral rather than written sources. They may corner someone in a corridor or phone them to ask highly focused questions; often they have no time to elicit or listen to lengthy elaborations. Only a few short quotations may appear in their articles or as "sound bites" in their broadcasts. Journalists frequently interview without attribution, collecting "off-the-record" responses simply for background information with no intention of revealing these sources in their stories. Sometimes their interviews are recorded—especially if intended for broadcast—but, after the story appears, journalists do not retain the original interviews and notes for long. The record that journalists leave for the future consists primarily of their published articles or tapes of their broadcasts. Journalists rarely expect to deposit their interview tapes or notes in a library of archives where other researchers might examine them.

In this regard, journalists are not unlike scholarly researchers who conduct interviews to provide documentation for their articles or books without planning to open the interviews for general research. Usually they only excerpt the interviews in their books, rather than reproduce their full notes or transcripts. After the book is published, these documents most often languish in the author's files, packed away in a basement or attic.

An interview becomes an oral history only when it has been recorded, processed in some way, made available in an archive, library, or other repository, or reproduced in relatively verbatim form for publication. Availability for general research, reinterpretation, and verification defines oral history. By preserving the tapes and transcripts of their interviews, oral historians seek to leave as complete, candid, and reliable a record as possible.[16]

Regarding daily news reporting as the "first rough draft of history," many journalists have applied their talents to writing history, for which they instinctively turned to oral sources. Drawing on their skills as interviewers, they produced some notable works of oral history, such as Howell Raines's *My Soul Is Rested: Movement Days in the Deep South Remembered* (1977), and Wallace Terry's *Bloods: An Oral History of the Vietnam War* (1984). Two of Lyndon Johnson's leading biographers are Robert Caro, an investigative journalist turned biographer, and Robert Dallek, a professional historian. When asked to explain the differences in their approaches to the same subject, Caro pointed to the extensive interviews he conducted with key participants, by comparison to Dallek, a university professor who relied more on manuscripts than interviews. To this, Dallek rebutted, "I'm not a journalist."[17]

What does it take to become an oral historian?

Oral history has always been multi-disciplinary. While many professional historians conduct oral history, a degree in history has never been a prerequisite for entering the field. Well-established scholars sometimes make poor interviewers, and those who are part of the community or profession being interviewed, if properly trained in conducting oral history, have advantages in establishing rapport and in prior knowledge. Law students have interviewed judges, women coal miners have successfully interviewed other women coal miners, and members of a community have conducted oral histories with their neighbors. In Alaska, a portrait artist conducted interviews with the people she was painting to gain a deeper understanding of the personalities she was trying to capture on canvas. In Japan, a physician interviewed his elderly patients in a fishing community that was rapidly disappearing. He wrote the resulting book from his office overlooking a new expressway built on the riverbed. "That vanished river, that water's edge, once rang out with the shouts of men hauling in their net as couples on houseboats waited among the reeds for night to fall. It wasn't so very long ago, and yet that era, that scenery, and the life-breath of those people have all vanished liked phantoms," the doctor wrote. The oral histories he collected stood as a tribute "to the too-swift passing of time."[18]

Saying that a Ph.D. in history is no requirement for doing oral history does not mean that anything anyone records is oral history. The Oral History Association has developed principles, standards, and guidelines to raise the consciousness and professional standards of all oral historians. There are interviewing skills to be learned. There are right and wrong ways to conduct an oral history. There are great differences between useable oral history and useless ones, and there are far too many of the latter.

Oral history has room for both the academic and the layperson. With reasonable training, through oral history courses, workshops, or manuals, anyone can conduct a useable oral history. Oral history conferences are notable for the variety of participants, among them radio and video documentary makers, museum curators, archivists, journalists, gerontologists, anthropologists, and folklorists. Regardless of their diverse objectives, they share many common methods of interviewing. "If an interview goes well, then we say it's magic," the Canadian investigative reporter John Sawatsky commented. "But it's not magic. It happens for an understandable reason. It's rational. It's a skill. It's easy to teach someone skills."[19]

How reliable is the information gathered by oral history?

"The most naive policeman knows that a witness should not always be taken at his word . . . ," wrote the French historian Marc Bloch. "Similarly, it has been many a day since men first took it into their heads not to accept all historical evidence blindly." Oral history is as reliable or unreliable as other research sources. No single piece of data of any sort should be trusted completely, and all sources need to be tested against other evidence. The historian James MacGregor Burns, who was trained under S. L. A. Marshall to interview American soldiers during World War II, found that the interviews generated some spurious information (about how frequently infantrymen fired their rifles in combat) and also some startling insights (about how many troops were killed by friendly fire). Burns concluded that "such interviews were a most valuable contribution to military history, but only if used in careful conjunction with more conventional sources, like documents and enemy records."[20]

Although archival documents have the advantage of not being influenced by later events or otherwise changing over time, as an interviewee might, documents are sometimes incomplete, inaccurate, and deceiving. For instance, researchers have found more than one occasion of a local newspaper ignoring an entire event, such as a strike against one of its major advertisers. Until the 1960s, most general circulation newspapers ignored news from black communities. As a result of such blind spots, oral history can develop information that might not have appeared in print. As the novelist Gore Vidal has commented: "Since I have been written about perhaps a bit more than most historians, I am not as impressed as they are by what I see in print, no matter how old and yellow the cutting."[21]

Scholars have accepted correspondence, diaries, and autobiographies as legitimate documentation, although their authors may be biased or incorrect. Politicians have kept diaries with publication in mind, designing them to present themselves in the best possible light. Oral history interviews are often conducted years after the event, when memories have grown imprecise, but they have the advantage of being conducted by a trained interviewer who can raise questions and challenge dubious answers. As any researcher can attest, letter writers and diary keepers do not always address all the issues that scholars are researching. Autobiographers are often unaware of all the issues that interest researchers. Well-trained interviewers can coax interviewees into areas of concern to researchers that the interviewees might never have thought of discussing otherwise.

Then why are some historians still skeptical about oral history?

The skeptics distrust eyewitness accounts as being too subjective. When historians describe evidence as "objective," they mean not only unbiased but also unchanging, such as documents that remain the same over time even if interpretations of them shift. "Subjective" suggests a partial and a partisan point of view, less reliable because it is subject to alteration over time. When the oral historian Alessandro Portelli wrote of the need for broadly based interviewing that would "tell us not what people did, but what they wanted to do, what they believed they were doing, what they now think they did," he was criticized for passivity and "unsystematic" reasoning. Some social historians have accused oral historians of swallowing whole the stories that informants tell them. They argue that a truer "people's history" must be based on statistical analysis and other objective data rather than on subjective individual testimony.

The correlated assumption that the historian, with hindsight and thorough research, perceives past events more clearly than those who lived through them. Or, as David Lodge asserted in his autobiographical novel *Out of the Shelter* (1989), history is the verdict "of those who weren't there on those who were."[22]

Others express skepticism of the accuracy of human memory—a view sometimes shared by researchers who were themselves part of the history they study. After Abraham Lincoln's death, two of his private secretaries, John Nicolay and John Hay, collaborated on writing his biography. They naturally anticipated a great advantage in having access to Lincoln's closest confidants, but as Hay commented: "we ascertained after a very short experience that no confidence whatever could be placed in the memories of even the most intelligent and most honorable men when it came to narrating their relations with Lincoln." Nicolay likewise regarded most reminiscences of Lincoln as "worthless to history," and so the pair relied almost exclusively on written documents. Ironically, their preserved interviews have appeared more convincing to later scholars. Nicolay and Hay had rejected testimony that reflected poorly on Lincoln, especially those personal observations of Lincoln's bouts with depression and his troubled marriage. Other sources subsequently corroborated the stories that the protective secretaries chose to suppress.[23]

At the Russian and Eastern European Institute at Indiana University, scholars engaged in a dispute over the validity of oral sources. Two members of the faculty had been mining statistics and documentary evidence to determine why Russian women continued to have fewer children even after Stalin outlawed abortion. One day they looked at each other with a common thought: "Why don't we just ask them?" After conducting a hundred interviews, they came to the conclusion that peasant women, whose mothers had often borne ten to twelve children, many of whom had died in infancy, simply ignored official orders and had illegal abortions. Another member of the same institute, dissented from this conclusion on the grounds that Russian peasants "tended to rely on rumor, so the reliability of their stories is not as interesting as their meaning." Yet even the dissenter agreed that the oral sources "may not tell you much about what Stalin was doing, but they are terribly useful in telling you about people's minds."[24]

Should the interviewer be an objective—or neutral—observer?

Oral historians have debated how much an interviewer should intervene in the interview. Initially, some argued that independent researchers (those doing interviews for their own research) were too biased to conduct oral histories, and that archival oral historians would be better interviewers because they had no vested interest in any interpretation. In the type of oral history Allan Nevins pioneered at Columbia, the interviewer was envisioned as a neutral, objective collector of other people's reminiscences; this concept was carried to such extremes that the questions were eliminated entirely in Columbia's early transcripts. The interviewee's responses were rendered as an uninterrupted narrative. Although Columbia soon adopted the question-and-answer format for its transcripts, many books featuring oral history testimony continue to expunge the interviewer. Studs Terkel, for example, has disclosed only a few of the questions that elicited such compelling replies from his interviewees.[25]

Other oral historians rejected the image of the neutral questioner and saw their role as that of an active agent in the process. The codirector of the Duke University Oral History Program, Lawrence Goodwyn, insisted that interviewers who remained passive surrender too much of their professional capacity. Goodwyn acknowledged, however, that more active interviewers risk distortion of their interviews by intruding their own cultural assumptions and political perspectives. Accepting subjectivity as inherent in the process and impossible to avoid, the advocates of a more active, scholarly interviewer believed that the interviewer's questioning actually involved "a first interpretation" of the interviewee's narrative. Influenced by trends in anthropology, literary criticism, and social history, they examined not only what was said, but what was left unsaid, and they speculated about the lapses in historical memory. The more methodologically oriented oral historians criticized the uncritical acceptance of oral testimony, called for more thorough research and higher standards in conducting interviews, and lamented that the lack of scholarly analysis, by both interviewers and interview users, had turned oral history into "movement without aim."[26]

Since the 1970s a proliferation of methodological studies has added not only "aim" but increasing depth and sophistication to oral history. Still, a difference remains between analyzing oral evidence *after* it has been collected and suggesting that theorizing *precede* the interview. An interviewer must always be prepared to abandon carefully prepared questions and follow the interviewee down unexpected paths, always helping the interviewee by questioning, guiding, coaxing, and challenging. Michael Frisch has offered a middle ground in his book, *A Shared Authority* (1990), whose clever title promotes the notion that both participants in an interview are responsible for its creation and share its authorship. Interviewers may believe they are more than an equal partner in this shared authority, since their questions shape the responses and they are extracting the raw material of memory for use in scholarship. But interviewers are actually less than an equal partner in the sense that the ultimate value of oral history lies in the substance of the interviewee's story. Nor does the interpretation of the interview rest exclusively on the interviewer's side of the microphone, for interviewees are constantly reinterpreting and analyzing their own motives and actions as they recall and describe them.[27]

Discussions of oral history practices have been enriched by new applications of communications theory, feminist interviewing, and psychological studies of memory. Beginning oral historians should not be discouraged by the complexity of hermeneutics (the principles of interpretation), discourse analysis (language in use) or deconstruction (hidden and unspoken information in a narrative). Rather than start by trying to put any particular theory into practice, a new oral historian would be better advised to adopt the more pragmatic approach of "putting practice into theory." First gain some experience in conducting interviews before plunging too deeply into theoretical issues. Doing interviews actually raises curiosity about methodological debates, since it soon becomes apparent that the interviewer is more than collecting "just the facts."[28]

These debates over theory and methodology go back to the first oral history colloquium in 1966. In a review of the proceedings of that meeting, Herman Kahn noted that the participants spent much time worrying about the nature and validity of oral history. All their self-questioning reminded him of an adolescent peering into a mirror and wondering, "What am I?" and, "Why am I not better known and more popular?" Introspection will and should continue, but Kahn urged oral historians to get on with their job of interviewing: "They will need to cultivate patience, acquire self-assurance, and be content to leave the proof of their pudding to the scholars who are its ultimate consumers."[29]

If doing an oral history is a shared responsibility between the interviewer and the interviewee, which one is the oral historian?

Both participate in the oral history, and neither one's role should be minimized, but for all practical purposes the oral historian is the one who schedules, prepares for, conducts, processes, and interprets the interview. The interviewer participates in the give-and-take of an interview by questioning and following up on the interviewee's responses and by providing names, dates, and other commonly forgotten information. But interviewers—especially when doing life histories—should never forget whose story is being told.

What's in a name? Some oral historians reject "interviewee" for its passive sound and have embraced more active designations like "informant," "respondent," "oral author," and "narrator," the latter term often used by folklorists and social scientists. The weight assigned to the two terms is reflected in the index to a collection of essays on oral history, whose various authors used both "interviewee" and "narrator." The index listing for "interviewee" is divided into "abandonment of," "apparent contradiction of," "deception of," "manipulation of," and "misinformation by." The index terms for "narrator" included "free expression and," "power of" and "in negotiation with researcher." The role of both is the same; only the nomenclature differs. Such vocabulary concerns aim to make oral historians more aware of how inequalities in the interviewer-interviewee relationship can influence the interview. In drafting its evaluation guidelines, the Oral History Association chose to retain the familiar triangular relationship of interviewer and interviewee producing the interview. Whatever terms employed, keep in mind that an oral history is a joint product, shaped by both parties.[30]

MEMORY AND ORAL HISTORY

Isn't oral history limited by the fallibility of human memory?

Dealing with memory is risky business, and it is inescapably the interviewer's business. Every interviewer has a story about someone interviewed too late, when memory had lost its sharpness, begun to dim, or faded almost entirely. Such disappointments are balanced by experiences with interviewees who possess remarkable recall, who remember individuals and incidents clearly, and whose accounts can be corroborated in other evidence. As one of the interviewers who collected oral histories with immigrants for the Ellis Island museum noted, elderly interviewees "might not remember their daughter's phone number. But they do remember what it was like when they got off the boat."[31]

Motivated by the death of baseball legend Ty Cobb in 1961, Lawrence Ritter set out to interview as many of the surviving pre-World War I baseball players as he could find. Traveling thousands of miles, he tracked down a group of elderly men who shared a remarkable storehouse of memories and an ability to articulate them vividly. "Many of the people I talked to had to think longer to get the names of all their great-grandchildren straight than they did to run down the batting order of the 1906 Chicago Cubs," he observed. But they were not garrulous old men chewing over oft-repeated stories. "Well, this is more than I've talked about in years, and it's good," said "Wahoo Sam" Crawford, who had played for the Detroit Tigers at the turn of the century. "I don't see many people, and even when I do I don't talk about baseball too much." As a skeptical researcher, Ritter went back to the old newspapers to verify the stories he heard, and almost without exception found that the events had occurred just as the old-time players had described them, embellished only occasionally "to dramatize a point, to emphasize a contrast, or to reveal a truth."[32]

The study of memory by psychologists has concentrated largely on short-term memory rather than on the long-term recall of a life span. Short-term memory studies that evaluate the accuracy of an individual's perception of events are of little help in explaining the uncanny preciseness with which some interviewees recall events that took place decades ago, or in understanding how interviewees who had reached obvious senility—forgetful even that they had scheduled the interview—can still speak authentically about events far in the past. Long-term memory has been less thoroughly explored, although the phenomenon has often been commented upon. The Confederate leader Jefferson Davis, for instance, on his deathbed began recalling scenes from his youth as a West Point cadet. "I seem to remember more every day," Davis marveled.[33]

The gerontologist Robert Butler has postulated that all people, as they grow older and perceive that they are approaching death, undergo a mental process of life review accounting for depression and despair in some, and for candor, serenity, and wisdom in others. The past "marches in review," permitting the elderly to survey and reflect especially on moments of unresolved conflict. Older people will review their lives whether anyone asks them about their memories or not, either mulling over their thoughts silently, or regaling family, neighbors, and visitors. In this process, the elderly may reveal details of their lives, and characteristics about themselves, previously unknown to their families and friends. Butler concluded that memory "serves the sense of self and its continuity; it entertains us; it shames us; it pains us. Memory can tell our origins; it can be explanatory; and it can deceive."[34]

Oral history is an active process in which interviewers seek out, record, and preserve such memories. Knowing that with age most people find it difficult to recall names and dates, oral historians conduct preparatory research to assist interviewees, give some context and structure to the dialogue through their questions, and mutually address any seeming misstatements and contradictions in the testimony.[35]

What should interviewers take into consideration about memory?

People remember what *they* think is important, not necessarily what the interviewer thinks is most consequential. An oral historian studying Texas teachers who made the transition from the one-room schoolhouse to modern consolidated schools found that white teachers said almost nothing about racial segregation or the details of the integration process. Blacks, Hispanic Americans, and disabled students remained largely "invisible" in their memories. African American teachers by contrast recalled the days of integration vividly because it affected their own lives so personally.[36]

Regardless of the project's worthy objectives, a good oral history will always leave room for interviewees to speak their own minds, and will not try to shoehorn their responses into a prepared questionnaire or mind-set. Since people remember best what was most exciting and important to them, their most vivid memories are often of the earliest days of their careers, when events were fresh and invigorating, even if their status at the time was relatively insignificant. By the time they had risen in stature and assumed more important positions, daily events had actually become more routine, making details of later life harder to isolate and identify during an interview. One interviewee summed up her three decades on the U.S. Senate staff by observing that when she began work, she was young and the senators were old; when she retired, she was old and the senators were young. As is often the pattern, her descriptions of her youthful experiences were lengthier and richer in detail than her recollections of more recent events.[37]

After the Second World War, when Congress investigated the Japanese bombing of Pearl Harbor, the chief of naval operations, Adm. Harold Stark, could not recall where he had been the night before the Japanese attacked on December 7, 1941. By contrast, Stark's flag lieutenant, H. D. Kirk, remembered precisely that they and their wives had gone to see a performance of *The Student Prince*, and then returned to the admiral's home, where Stark received a telephone call from President Roosevelt. One of the investigating senators asked Kirk how he could remember the occasion so well, considering that Stark could recall nothing. "Because I was a small fish, and great things were transpiring," Kirk replied, "and you don't forget that sort of thing."[38]

People regularly reevaluate and re-explain their past decisions and actions. Just as historians rewrite history to incorporate new evidence and fit different theories, individuals use the insights gained from current events to reshape them and make new sense out of past experiences. There is nothing invalidating about this reflectivity, so long as interviewers and researchers understand what is occurring and take it into account.[39]

Memories start with the initial perception. Interviewees speak from their own points of view, and no two will tell a story exactly alike. Not everyone had a clear picture of what happened, understood what it meant, or felt self-assured enough to accept responsibility. The contradictory tales told in the classic film *Rashomon* (1951) represented the tellers' differing impressions, self-images and self-delusions, but not poor memories. In combat, generals in the rear may see the broad sweep of the battle, and battlefield troops will have a more microscopic view of the action. As LTJG John F. Kennedy wrote from the Solomon Islands during World War II: "Frankly I don't know a god-damned thing, as my copy of the *Washington Times-Herald* arrives two months late, due to logistical difficulties, and it is pretty hard to get the total picture of a global war unless you are sitting in New York or Washington, or even Casablanca. I understand we are winning it, which is cheering, albeit hard to see, but I guess the view improves with distance. I know mine would."[40]

Those at the center of events can well recount their own accomplishments, but those on the periphery are often better able to make comparisons between the principal actors. Perceptions that were originally flawed will produce distorted memories. Distant and second-hand information is more susceptible to distortion. By contrast, direct, dramatic, and emotional situations tend to produce more fixed and lasting memories. For these reasons, oral history projects attempt to collect a wide range of interviews, to piece the puzzle together from various points of view.[41]

Not every perceived event is retained in memory. When the radio and television newscaster David Brinkley wrote *Washington Goes to War* (1988), about the years when he first came to the capital as a young broadcaster during the Second World War, he was surprised to find so much in the old newspaper files that had faded from his memory. "I've always thought I had a good memory. Now I know I don't," Brinkley commented. "Things I knew very well and in fact stood and watched and interviewed people about, I'd totally forgotten. That was the startling thing—how much I'd forgotten." Once meaningful information can become irrelevant or insignificant by comparison to later events. Since Brinkley continued to absorb current news as a journalist, the more events grew distant from the latest headlines, the less likely he would think about or retain them.[42]

The passage of time enables people to make sense out of earlier events in their lives. Actions take on new significance depending on their later consequences. Certain players grow more important in the story, and others diminish over time. People's memories may take on a more mature, mellow, or disillusioned cast according to their mood and condition of the time of the interview. Community members who share a common experience, such as the trauma of a flood or tornado, will talk about it among themselves for years, reinforcing the memories. By the necessity of availability, oral historians interview "survivors," those who lived through it, stuck to it, stayed behind, or otherwise succeeded—all factors that shape how and what they remember.[43]

Interviewers have to consider how creditable their interviewees are as witnesses. Were they in a position to experience events firsthand or are they simply passing along secondhand information? What biases might have shaped their original perceptions? Have interviewees forgotten much of their past because it was no longer important to them or because the events were so routine that they were simply not memorable? How differently do interviewees feel now about the events they are recalling? What subsequent incidents might have caused them to rethink and reinterpret their past? How closely does their testimony agree with other documentary evidence from the period, and how do they explain the discrepancies? None of these considerations would disqualify an interviewee from giving testimony, but answering these questions as completely as possible helps the interviewer and future researchers to assess the value of the information recorded.[44]

The memories of direct participants are sources far too rich for historical researchers to ignore. Interviewers must be aware of the peculiarities of memory, adept in their methods of dealing with it, conscious of its limitations, and open to its treasures.

Don't peoples' memories tend to become nostalgic?

In his typically tart manner, President Calvin Coolidge once reflected that the folks of his hometown of Plymouth, Vermont, "remember some of the most interesting things that never happened."[45] Coolidge was referring to how history can be inflated by retrospective associations. It is similarly common to encounter rosy reminiscences about "the good old days," considering that oral historians interview older people about their youth, when even disappointments can be remembered as adventurous incidents. Dissatisfaction with present conditions makes the past look far better; and people's very survival can convince them that the hard times were not so bad after all. "It's not easy remembering the past," said ninety-one-year-old Evelyn Bailey Wahl when asked to recall her community's evolution from rural to urban over her lifetime, where endless shopping strips and apartments replaced the meadows and farms of her youth. "Sometimes I try not to think about it." Many interviewees will talk about the pain and suffering in their lives, about humiliation, harassment, and discrimination, about disappointments and losses, but others have blocked out the most negative aspects of the past or rewritten their own histories, consciously or subconsciously. It is the oral historian's task to move the interview away from nostalgia to confront the past candidly and critically. If things were different in the past, what were they like? When did they change? How did they change? Why did they change?[46]

In the reaction against the elitist practice of interviewing only famous people, many oral historians changed their focus to community-based "people's history." But after letting the people speak, historians examining community history projects soon realized "that 'the people' weren't speaking unadulterated truth." Linda Shopes, who interviewed for the Baltimore Neighborhood Heritage Project, has argued that: "So many people want to do oral histories in well-intentioned but extremely naive ways: to get interesting stories, to get the anecdotes, to get the colorful stories, to get the cute things. People don't want to confront the fact that history is . . . not a happy little story of days gone by." Quite often people do not want to talk about difficult issues, such as the changing ethnic and racial composition of a community or one generation's rejection of another generation's values. Interviewers must be prepared to ask questions about painful and embarrassing subjects—although they must also respect people's right not to answer such questions, if they so choose.[47]

Nostalgia is hardly limited to social history. Political historians have observed that the longer politicians are out of office, the more highly people rate them, a phenomenon that has been characterized as the "law of rising recollections."[48] Presidents still in office are compared to their predecessors; out of office they are measured against their successors. The uncertainty of today's headlines sometimes turns past anxiety and turbulence into images of happy days. It becomes more of a challenge for interviewers recording the reminiscences among members of a presidential administration, or associates of some other retired or deceased high-ranking official, to keep them from mentioning only the most positive aspects of their former leader—the side they too often assume is all that the interviewer wants to hear about.

Whole groups may blank out unpleasant memories. When the Southern Oral History Project interviewed the men and women who worked in southern cotton mills during the 1930s, they encountered mostly silence about the General

Strike of 1934, "a kind of social amnesia, born of defeat and of the failure of trade unionism to take root in a living tradition." One mill worker explained: "You see, after we come back and got out of the union and got back to work, why that was a thing of the past. . . . You forget about things in the past, 'cause you don't think about them, you don't talk about them, and that leaves your mind." The lack of oral testimony sent the researchers back into the documentary evidence of these events, even if current memories suppressed them.[49]

Oral historians documenting traumatic events of the past have found that many survivors will refrain from talking about those events, even to their own children. Researchers point out that the first stage of grief is shock, and the second stage is denial. People can stay in denial for a very long time. But as they grow older, and as others who shared the experience die, the survivors will grant interviews as a way of reconciling a haunting record, and also of ensuring that future generations do not forget. J. Robert Slaughter was part of the first regiment of American troops sent ashore at Omaha Beach on D-Day, which suffered appalling casualties. He and other survivors had great difficulty in readjusting to civilian life. In the 1970s, a British television crew tried to interview him for a documentary, but he could remember nothing, having blocked out the painful memories. Not until the 1990s was he able to confront them. "For a long time nobody wanted to think or talk about all that and what it cost," he commented. "For a long time nobody cared. I began to have nightmares that we'd have to do it again someday." Researchers of the Holocaust hear a similar refrain from victims: "I kept quiet for many years, but soon I will be gone and now I must tell my children."[50]

What is "public memory"?

By contrast to individual memories of personal experiences, public memory represents a society's collective conceptions about the past. Public memory involves symbols and stories that help a community define and explain present conditions according to how it remembers (or wants to remember) the past. These can take the form of parades, reunions, reenactments and celebrations, or in monuments and landmarks that often serve to represent reconciliation and healing after a war or tragic event. Such commemorations often have a political connotation, the historian John Bodnar has observed, designed to "stress the desirability of maintaining the social order and existing institutions."[51]

Since individuals experience events differently and maintain different social objectives, they will hotly contest issues of public memory. Arguments predictably erupt over the design and location of monuments and the inscriptions placed upon them. The dispute over an appropriate Vietnam Veterans Memorial, for instance, invoked earlier controversies as groups who had differed over fighting the war now disagreed over how to portray it. Politics lies behind every public monument and also explains the absence of monuments and memorials to people and events that communities would prefer to forget. Public memory can also influence personal memory, since people within a community absorb the public debates and internalize particular positions. Interviewers need to be conscious of a community's collective beliefs and try to move beyond public memory to the personal experiences of those they interview.[52]

Recognizing that what people remember can be shaped by their social environment, scholars have analyzed the ways in which communities construct and use their collective memory, and what they pass along to succeeding generations. The folklorist Alessandro Portelli conducted interviews in the Italian town of Terni, where he gathered several versions of the death of Luigi Trastulli. A twenty-one-year-old steel worker, Trastulli had died in a clash with police. Contemporary newspaper accounts placed the date of his death in 1949, when steelworkers walked out of their factory to attend a Communist-sponsored rally against the Italian government's joining the North American Treaty Organization. But as time passed, the townspeople collectively altered the story to give it epic form. One interviewee after another shifted the date and context of Trastulli's death from the anti-NATO rally to the street fighting that followed a massive layoff of steelworkers four years later. Wondering why so many people got it "wrong," Portelli concluded that the community had been unable to accept Trastulli's death as an accidental shooting in a minor scuffle over a fleeting political issue. Instead, people had relocated the event to a far bigger dispute that involved their basic livelihood. As transfigured, Trastulli's death helped to heal the community's wounds and to instruct the next generation: "He died for you."[53]

What's the difference between oral history and folklore?

Oral historians and folklorists both use interviews to collect information, but not necessarily the same type of information. The two practices have been described as opposite ends of a continuum: oral historians concentrate on recording the personal experiences of the interviewee, and folklorists collect the traditional stories, songs and other expressions of the community, fact or fiction. An oral historian would most likely interview a husband and wife separately, seeking to identify the unique perspective of each spouse. A folklorist, being as interested in the way a story is told as in its substance, would interview the couple together to observe the interplay as one begins a story and the other finishes it. The folklorist Barbara Allen has observed that historians "tend to see oral historical sources as mines of raw data from which historical evidence can be extracted," while folklorists are more concerned with "recognizing identifi-able patterns" in the way people shape their narrative.[54]

Sharing an interest in interviewing, oral historians, folklorists, ethnographers, cultural anthropologists, sociologists, and linguists, each have different objectives that influence their methodology. "Field-oriented" disciplines rely on participant observation and may not even take notes in the presence of those they are study-ing, waiting to write up their notes later from memory. Unlike historians, who seek concrete evidence of what actually happened and to document it as fully as possible, folklorists, ethnographers, and anthropologists are often less interested in verification of facts and see folk tales and folklore as no less legitimate than other stories. Linguists will often be more concerned with the manner of telling a story than in its substance. Despite the distinctive way that these assorted dis-ciplines analyze and use interviews, the intersection of their methodological techniques has permitted collaborative, cross-disciplinary oral history projects on a range of community, racial, ethnic and immigration issues.[55]

Can storytelling be considered oral history?

Diverse cultures depend on storytelling to pass along knowledge and under-standing. The storyteller might be a parent teaching a child, a tribal elder recall-ing communal traditions, a preacher illustrating a point in a sermon, an Old Salt spinning a yarn, or anyone else able to recount past experiences in a manner entertaining enough to hold a crowd. Folklorists find that tales passed down, fam-ily lore, and community legends have value as much for their form (how they are told) as for their content. Such stories are often communal in nature, tran-scending the individual experiences they describe. Recurring stories within a community that emerge in oral history collections also reveal what people con-sider to be the key aspects of their historical experience.[56]

In those cases where storytelling takes place without an interviewer who can pursue issues raised in the stories by questioning the narrator, it does not fit the standard definition of oral history, but its study illuminates some significant issues facing oral historians. Most storytellers aim not so much to preserve a per-manent record as to inform and influence their immediate audience. Although the storyteller usually controls the performance, the particular setting and audi-ence can affect the story's presentation. Telling a story in a new setting, to a new audience creates new meanings. Storytelling reminds us that all oral presenta-tions involve a degree of performance, and that the audience (even an audience of one, as in the interviewer) can affect that performance. Stories told in an inter-view often involve a re-telling of something the interviewee heard from some-one else or has previously told to others. As the "audience," the interviewer can affect in subtle or even striking ways the content of the story. The process continues even after the interview is completed. The oral historian William Schneider has pointed out that "once the narrator stops talking and the recorder leaves with the tape, the teller no longer knows who will hear it and how they will understand what he or she said." Some sensitivity to the nature of storytelling is therefore essential to the management of oral history collections. To be fair to participants, Schneider advises, "we have to be mindful of a wide range of considerations, not the least of which is the oral tradition from which the narrator may have built the telling and from which the audience derives its background for understanding what has been shared."[57]

Is it better to interview immediately after an event or wait until years later?

There are advantages and disadvantages to each course of action. The military pioneered debriefing interviews with soldiers immediately after a battle or after returning from a combat tour of duty. Memories of details will be sharper the closer to the actual events that the interview occurs. But interviews conducted long after the events benefit from the interviewee's reflections that better enable them to weigh the events and sort the significant from the trivial. Debriefings tend to be shorter and more focused interviews. Later oral histories, especially life review interviews, tend to be more extensive.

The day after the bombing of Pearl Harbor in 1941, Alan Lomax contacted other folklorists around the country to collect "man on the street" reactions. Recordings of interviews that ranged from janitors to physicians, cab drivers, housewives, students and soldiers were then sent to the Library of Congress and used to create a radio documentary program for national broadcast and distribution to schools. Sixty years later, within a week of the terrorist attacks on September 11, 2001, oral historians began interviewing witnesses and survivors. The Columbia Oral History Research Office, together with the New-York Historical Society and other New York museums, quickly launched a project to interview those who had escaped the World Trade Towers, families of victims, police and fire fighters, rescue and relief workers, and members of nearby Muslim communities. Underwritten by the National Science Foundation, the project not only conducted initial debriefings but planned additional interviews in later years to examine the durability of memories of traumatic events. At the Library of Congress, the American Folklife Center initiated a "September 11, 2001 Documentary Project" to record the thoughts and feelings of citizens across the country. Historians for the National Park Service and the Red Cross taped interviews with eyewitnesses to the tragedies, while historians for the military services interviewed those who experienced the plane crash at the Pentagon. The Senate Historical Office conducted interviews concerning the evacuation of the Capitol Building on September 11th and of the anthrax contamination that closed the Hart Senate Office Building for three months. "Down the road, researchers also will use newspaper accounts, videos and film, government documents and mementos culled from the destruction to study that day. There will be intelligence reports, declassified years from now, to add to the record," the *Wall Street Journal* noted. "But it is the oral histories that are most likely to help researchers understand what it felt like to be under attack on that late summer morning."[58]

What distinguishes a "life history" from other interviews?

Gerontologists refer to the "life review" process of the elderly, and oral historians speak of conducting "life histories," by which they mean full-scale autobiographical accounts that allow interviewees to relate their entire life, from childhood to the present. Social scientists may concentrate on a series of shorter interviews with members of a group in a particular community or environment, such as workers on a shop floor. Oral historians call these "episodic" interviews. Shorter interviews conducted with members of a group soon after they shared a mutual experience are referred to as "debriefings." Conducting life histories usually means selecting fewer interviewees and devoting more time, and multiple interview sessions, to each one. Life histories give the interviewee enough time to relate what both the interviewer seeks and the interviewee wants to tell. The oral historian conducting even a subject-oriented project should seriously consider expanding the scope of its questions to record as much as possible about each interviewee's life. Broader questioning establishes links that neither interviewer nor interviewee may have considered in a more narrowly focused interview session.[59]

When the Oregon Historical Society launched an oral history of the federal court system in its state, it focused on the people who conducted the court rather than the institution of the court itself. Following a full biographical approach proved especially useful when dealing with the appointment of judges. An institutional approach might also have included questions about a judge's appointment, but interviewers found that the meaning and significance of the responses were enhanced when told within the context of the judge's full life history.[60]

The first presidential library oral history projects concentrated almost exclusively on the interviewees' relationships with the president or roles in the administration. This produced a large number of relatively short interviews. In later years, some of the libraries returned to re-interview the key players in more depth. In this second round of interviewing, the oral historian at the Lyndon B. Johnson

Library conducted thirty-six hours of interviews with Lawrence O'Brien (who served as congressional liaison and postmaster general), and sixty-four interview sessions with Joseph Califano (who was special assistant to the president for domestic affairs). Although this level of in-depth interviewing lies beyond the budget of most oral historians, other projects should aim, at least on a selective basis, to do fuller life histories. Even individual researchers need to look beyond their immediate interests when interviewing. The American Historical Association has advised that, "to the extend practicable, interviewers should extend the inquiry beyond their immediate needs to make each interview as complete as possible for the benefit of others."[61]

PUBLIC HISTORY AND ORAL HISTORY

What is the role of oral history in "public history"?

Public history was once defined exclusively in terms of historians' activities in public agencies and as private consultants outside of the university. But the definition has expanded beyond place of employment to include the audiences that historians try to reach. Public historians aim for an out-of-school public audience, which might be officials in the government agency, corporations, union, philanthropic organization, or professional association that employs the historian or the library-using, documentary-viewing, museum-going general public. Other professional historians, for whom the bulk of historical literature is intended, account for only a small portion of the public historian's audience.[62]

Public history is an organized effort to bring accurate, meaningful history to a public audience, and oral history is a natural tool for reaching that goal. The oral history and public history movements share a natural affinity, both having attracted practitioners and audiences different from those for more traditional history writing. Both oral and public history have experimented with videotape, slide-tape, and even interactive videos, in museum exhibits, dramatic performances, and other applications outside of the classroom and in publications.[63]

How pervasive is oral history within government?

Governments at all levels have come to appreciate the utilitarian aspects of oral history. Government agencies hire historians on staff or on contract to use oral history as a tool for collecting and presenting information relating to that agency's operations. When the Washington-based Society for History in the Federal Government conducted a survey, it found oral history projects in all branches of the military, the intelligence agencies, many cabinet departments,

Congress, the federal courts, the Smithsonian museums, and independent agencies from NASA to the National Institutes of Health. The National Park Service has the most ongoing oral history projects, with historians and rangers across the country collecting interviews for use in documenting the sites and producing visitor orientation materials.[64]

Perhaps the most common programs interview the staff of the sponsoring agency, who discuss their careers and evaluate the political appointees, policy making, and institutional changes they have witnessed. Retired staff members, whose obscurity and anonymity masked the often significant roles they played within their agencies, offer recollections that can explain and unravel the voluminous, impersonal, and unrevealing written records of the modern bureaucracy. Public historians possess several advantages in conducting these staff interviews. As employees of the same agency, they have a better chance of obtaining access to agency files, whether open or classified. They share a familiarity with arcane agency procedure that helps not only in preparing questions but in establishing rapport and obtaining candid responses.

Most often, oral history is a component part of a government historical office rather than its primary mission. Periodically, however, Congress has appropriated funds specifically for an oral history. In 1998, when Congress directed the National Park Service to establish a historic site in Tuskegee, Alabama, that would memorialize the World War II African-American pilots known as the Tuskegee Airmen, it earmarked funds for an oral history with the survivors. Their experiences dated to the era when both training and combat assignments had been racially segregated. Two years later, Congress authorized the American Folklife Center at the Library of Congress to establish a nationwide Veterans History Project to encourage citizens to conduct and donate to the Library audio and video oral histories with war veterans from World War I to the Persian Gulf war.[65]

Local governments have also delved into oral history, to promote a community anniversary or some other significant event, or to document the workings of the government. Projects have ranged from the New York Transit Authority's collection of interviews with transit workers for a history of the city's subways, to the Minnesota Department of Natural Resources sponsorship of a video history of the state's park, forest, and wildlife management. On a worldwide basis, local councils from Sydney to Southampton have funded oral history to record events of significance to their communities.

How have oral historians marketed their services?

The public presentation of oral history has generated a number of independent enterprises. Oral historians have set up business to conduct family interviews, and they work as freelance interviewers for corporations, charitable trusts, scientific organizations, and various other government and private agencies. Charles Morrissey, who has made a career as a freelance oral historian in fields ranging from politics to biomedical research, commented, "To my total amazement, once my availability evidenced itself to others, the number of clients seeking help from me as an oral historian became formidable."[66]

Independent interviewers work on both specific projects and long-term contractual arrangements. Joel Gardner, as head of Gardner Associates, specializes in conducting oral histories for corporations and other organizations, and his clients include the Robert Wood Johnson Foundation, the Philadelphia Fire Museum, the Union League of Philadelphia, and the Pew Charitable Trust. One of Gardner's projects resulted in a book, *Seventy-Five Years of Good Taste: A History of the Tasty Baking Company* (1990), based on interviews with thirty-five employees. Noting that corporate executives were increasingly attuned to the value of preserving their historical records, Garner helps create corporate archives and libraries. When doing oral histories, he seeks unlimited access to records, documents, and employees. Gardner urges his corporate sponsors to make the oral histories available to the public, but he notes that some of his clients turn to him because they feel uncomfortable with university-based oral history programs and prefer to keep the interviews within their own archives. In suburban Maryland, near Washington, D.C., Philip Cantelon founded History Associates, which has done oral histories for the federal government, for MCI, and for the American Furniture Hall of Fame. The Amfac Land Company contracted with the Center for Oral History at the University of Hawaii to interview longtime laborers and managers at its former sugar mills and plantations in the islands, a century-old way of life that is ending. Such projects have been remarkably successful, but as one independent interviewer noted, "When your funding depends on grants, as mine does, I spend more time writing reports and applying for grants than I do interviewing."[67]

When the president of Atlantic Richfield Company (ARCO) concluded that the corporation was losing the knowledge of its "epochal events" because employees and manager with firsthand knowledge of those events were dying, he commissioned Enid Douglass to conduct oral histories that would produce both an oral history archival collection and a written history of the company. The book was intended to make the company "more human and real" to the public, as well as to help ARCO employees better understand and thereby identify with the company so that they would become "more loyal and dedicated employees." Management used the oral histories to develop case studies on decision-making process and for workshops to train potential corporate executives.[68]

In contrast to these corporate activities, oral history has also been used for public-interest projects. In the Southwest, anthropologists, historians, legal scholars, lawyers, folklorists, and oral historians worked together to assist citizens in fighting for land and water rights. The New Mexico-based Center for Land Grant Studies was particularly concerned with protecting the rights of Native Americans and Mexican Americans who lacked the traditional types of ownership documentation to their lands. Representatives of the center used oral history as part of their courtroom testimony, a use that required proper techniques for gathering oral evidence and a greater need to assess the reliability of the oral testimony.[69]

What are the potential drawbacks of doing corporate oral history?

Oral historians hired for corporate projects report that many corporate executives and policymakers do not understand how historians work or how they use oral histories and that they need to be educated about the methods of historical research. Managers and other corporate executives often do not value or use their corporate archives and fear the consequences of allowing outsiders to see their records. They will not open records even for the historians they hire. They assume that oral historians, like journalists, can interview anyone, anytime, without extensive research. Oral historians have to explain their needs to see records to prepare adequately for their interviews. Sometimes, however, these records will not be forthcoming. In the 1960s, for instance, interviewers for the John F. Kennedy Library were initially denied access to Kennedy's records.

Charles Morrissey has observed that corporate managers tend to select prospective interviewees depending on their rank in the corporate hierarchy, whereas oral historians want to interview those who actually shaped the issues being studied, "even if they are obscure figures in the structured bureaucracies and do not command power or deference within their institutions." In fact, these seemingly anonymous members of the institution may have drafted the letters and speeches of higher executives and may have proposed the policies that the hierarchy adopted. They often have the least biased perspective on the institution. Lower-level staff members may actually have a clearer view of how policies evolved, be better able to evaluate people and programs, and have not only more detailed memories but a greater "willingness to impart what they remember."

Interviewers should try to align with one of the senior members of an organization, such as the chairman of the board, the chief executive officer or the director of a public agency, who can open doors for the project and get access to records. The interviewer should brief top policymakers about the project as it

evolves, giving them an idea of what methods are being employed and what information is being collected. Public historians are not public relations specialists
and should not be required to tailor their work to reaffirm the picture of itself
an institution may promote to the public. To be useful to clients, a historical study
has to be honestly critical. The public historian's need to maintain professional
standards works both ways: not only must historians be honestly critical, but they
must also be willing to keep information confidential according to the policies
of the organization that hired them.[70]

What will future historians want from our oral histories?

Researchers will want to hear the first-person observations of events great and
small, and to learn what sense those people made out of the events in their own
lives. Motivations and objectives are especially important. Other sources can usually provide the who, what, when, and where of history; interviews can offer better insights into the how and why. The historian's job is to pull together a
multitude of evidence from documents, objects, interviews, and other resources,
weaving them together to create a narrative that makes sense of all of the often
conflicting evidence.

Not all human activity is coherent and purposeful, the historian Elie Kedourie
pointed out; it is more often a complex of choices producing unpredictable
effects. Kedourie defined history as an account of people "in the peculiarity, idio-
syncracy, and specificity of their personalities, outlooks, capacities, and positions,
confronting or dealing with other [people] differently placed in respect to these
things, and confronting or dealing with them in situations different from one
another at least in respect of time and place, initiating, originating, taking meas-
ures, parrying, responding, reacting; the vocabulary we use to describe all this
amply indicating that here are present and involved purpose and choice, mind
and will." Or, as Ecclesiastes 9:11 instructs, "The race is not to the swift, nor the
battle to the strong... but time and chance happeneth to them all." Oral history
records both the purposeful and the accidental. Interviewers who allow people
a chance to assess why they did what they did will most likely capture the peculiarities and idiosyncracies of the history of our time.[71]

Historians writing a dissertation or a book, planning an exhibit or scripting a
documentary, will have their own set of questions they want to ask but may not
have the opportunity to ask those questions personally. I first used oral history
while writing a biography of a man who had died ten years earlier. Fortunately,
he had given a lengthy oral history to Columbia University just months before
he died. It was a thoroughly detailed, in-depth life history, amounting to seven
hundred pages of transcripts. As I could no longer question the man, Columbia's

interviewer served as my surrogate. Today's oral historians are doing the pre-liminary work of tomorrow's biographers and researchers, hoping they will not have to agonize too often over the questions we failed to ask.[72]

Oral history is about asking questions. While researching the history of Methodist camp meetings in Southern Mississippi, Charles Sullivan sought to visit every campground still operating. One day he mentioned to a student each of the camps that he had identified. "Yes, and Mt. Pleasant, too," the student responded, explaining that it was a black Methodist campground established after emancipation from slavery. Astonished, Sullivan wondered why no one had mentioned this camp before. "Probably because you never asked," came the reply. That is the reason for doing oral history: to ask the questions that have not been asked, and to collect the reminiscences that otherwise would be lost.[73]

CHAPTER 2

Setting Up an
Oral History Project

How do you begin an oral history project?

Start by determining your objectives. Not all goals need to be attempted at once, but they can be reached incrementally. For instance, having identified the likely pool of interviewees, oral historians will usually interview the oldest and most significant individuals first, while planning to move to younger or secondary figures later, depending on financial resources, available interviewers, and processing capabilities after the interviews are conducted.

After organizing a project, plan to start with a few well-conducted, in-depth interviews and then process them fully. The result will be something tangible to show when seeking additional funding. By concentrating on a few interviews, project organizers can establish a pattern of management and paperwork— from preparing and conducting the interviews to processing and transcribing them—that can expand along with the project. Similarly, projects may begin with only a few interviewers, paid or volunteer, who later can help train new recruits.

Always balance your objectives with your resources. Limited resources can frustrate ambitious objectives, and too many projects have ended with little to show for their efforts except boxes of tapes, unidentified, unprocessed, and unusable. Other well-intentioned projects have been stretched too thin; trying to interview too many people can produce superficial interviews that will not satisfy research needs.

What kind of goals should an oral history project set?

Decide what kind of a record you want to create, and for what purpose. Oral history should be collecting not what is already known but information, observations, and opinions unavailable elsewhere. Oral history projects are often designed to supplement existing archival material, filling in gaps in paper sources with the contributions of people who did their business instead in person or on the phone. An oral history project may record a piece of community history that the local newspaper ignored or inadequately covered. Oral history projects have been designed to determine the contributions that individuals made to a movement such as the civil rights movement or to trace the impact of a movement on individuals and communities. Projects have been focused on various professions, ranging from journalism to architecture, medicine, and the law, recording recollections of pioneers and other practitioners and tracing professional trends. Above all, oral history projects, by recording history in the words of those who lived it, can tell future researchers how people lived and how they perceived the events of their time.

A project may aim to record the history of a church, a school, a business or a philanthropic foundation, interviewing a cross-section of people associated with that institution. Project interviewers might follow members of a state legislature from session to session, capturing their versions of how legislation was enacted or defeated. An oral history project might be concentrated on a neighborhood or a particular ethnic group within the community. Oral history is appropriate not only for looking at the broad sweep of a community's history but for examining it at a specific time, say during the Second World War or during the 1960s. An event (an election, a strike, the construction of a monumental building) or catastrophe (a hurricane, a flood, a major accident) can be its organizing theme. Or the subject can be the history of a group, such as women, African Americans, or Hispanic Americans, or a sub-group such as immigrant women, African American teachers, or Hispanic American entrepreneurs. Some oral history archives focus their collections on the city, state, or region where they are located; others have built broad national and even international collections.

During the course of conducting interviews, it may be desirable to change or reevaluate the project's goals. Interviewers may find that some of the original objectives are impractical or that new avenues open up as additional interviewees are identified. Goals are often time-determined. Some oral history projects are ongoing, but others may work on a year-to-year, grant-to-grant basis and must regularly do a certain amount of interviewing to ensure continued funding.

An oral history project will be judged on the significance of the goals its organizers set and the substance of the information they collected. Researchers will measure projects according to whom they interviewed, what questions they asked, and how they processed the recordings and transcripts. Users will also scrutinize oral history projects for new and different or at least colorfully quotable information on the subjects they are studying.

Should a project set a goal of how many people it intends to interview?

Trying to calculate in advance an exact number of individuals to interview puts unnecessary pressure on an oral history project. Rushing to meet numerical objectives causes both the depth of interviewing and a reasonable pace of processing to be sacrificed. Once interviewing begins, it will be discovered that some interviewees have much more to say than others, are more perceptive and cooperative, and have sharper memories. These are the interviewees to whom it is worth devoting more time. For reasons of age, health, or general disposition, other interviewees will have little to say of enduring value. Often not until an interview begins can the interviewer determine whether the interviewee is able to make much of a contribution. Sometimes a very old interviewee has a surprisingly sharp recall, and even more stamina than the interviewer; sometimes not. Preliminary contact can help the interviewer to get a better sense of the abilities of the interviewee to gauge how much time to budget for a session or a series of interviews. One oral historian went to considerable effort and expense to bring a crew to film an interview only to discover too late that the interviewee was distressingly senile.

Oral history projects invariably receive recommendations to interview the local raconteur, whom everyone says has a story about everything. Although more than willing to talk, this person may be unable to move beyond a store of set stories. Correspondingly, the most famous individual identified with an event may offer only a garbled, self-centered account. The most forthcoming interviewee may turn out to be a lesser-known, secondary figure who keenly observed what was going on and remembers it vividly. To do interviews of equal length with these varying individuals makes little sense. Remain flexible enough so that you can spend less time with those who have little to say and more time with those whose contributions are substantial.

In designing a project and in seeking funding, set the number of hours of interviews or sessions you intend to conduct rather than the number of individuals to be interviewed. A project that budgets for one hundred hours may spend one hour with one interviewee and ten hours with the next, giving each of them sufficient time to exhaust the subject to the best of their abilities.

Is there an optimal number of hours for interviewing each person?

An interview session is usually best limited to an hour and a half to two hours to avoid exhausting both the interviewee and interviewer but there is no ideal length for an entire interview. Each interview depends on how much of value to the project that the interviewee has to say, and whether the project is conducting a life history or concentrating on a smaller segment of a person's experiences. Whenever interviewers have to travel any great distance they will have to estimate the number of hours of interviews in advance without knowing if that time will be sufficient. A second trip may be necessary, budget permitting.[1]

Be careful not to overschedule interviewing trips, forcing the interviewer to rush from one appointment to the next, and cutting interviewees short regardless of what they have to say. Interviewees still actively engaged in their careers may set rigid limits on the amount of time for an interview, while retired people tend to be more tolerant about giving longer, open-ended interviews that may or may not include lunch or other time diversions. Interviewers need to use their judgment in deciding when an interviewee has become fatigued and is no longer thinking clearly. Good interviewers frequently find the interview situation more stressful for themselves than for their interviewees, and their own ability to pay attention and interact diminishes the longer an interview lasts.

FUNDING AND STAFFING

How much does it cost to do an oral history?

How much can you afford to spend? Oral history can be expensive, but its costs are containable. The price tag may include research preparation and interview time, equipment, travel to and from the interview, lodging and meals if the interview is conducted out of town, transcription, indexing, cataloging, photocopying, postage for correspondence, and other overhead costs.

Some projects pay their interviewers, others rely on unpaid volunteers. Some purchase or rent their equipment, others make use of equipment, services, and personnel of their parent organization, whether a church, library, corporation, university, or government agency. A project can include the work of transcribing, or recordings can be sent out to professional transcribers, who are paid by the page, by the number of hours of recording, or by the number of hours worked. Some choose to abstract and index rather than transcribe. Using volunteer typists with access to word processors can reduce costs, but volunteers have to be trained and their work needs to be reviewed and edited. Rates for rental equipment, transcribing services, salaries, and overhead will also vary according to the geographic location of the project and the available labor pool.

If experienced oral historians are used, the budget will have to include pay for their services as interviewers and cover their research, travel, and processing expenses. Patricia Pilling, who does family interviews, has had clients question why her oral histories cost what they do when anyone can turn on a tape recorder and ask questions. She asks whether they can cook; if they say yes, she replies, "But can you make a gourmet meal?" Her analogy makes most clients see the value of professional expertise.[2]

How do oral history projects get funded?

Funding comes from an array of sources. More fortunate projects are based within institutions that provide them with office space, equipment, salaries, and travel expenses. Some institutions will meet part of those needs, such as office space and equipment, but expect the oral history project to raise the rest of its funds for salaries and expenses. Private granting agencies and many state humanities councils have long supported oral history projects. These often cover the conducting and processing of all or part of the planned oral histories, including interviewing, processing, and overhead. Some projects have done their interviewing and then turned to state humanities councils or other agencies for grants to transcribe the best of the interviews. Local governments, municipal libraries, and state legislatures have funded various components of oral history as a public service. The Mississippi legislature, for instance, funded the University of Southern Mississippi's effort to post its civil rights interviews on the Internet.

Seeking funds for an oral history project needs to be a creative effort. Volunteer groups have successfully sponsored receptions and other exhibits of their material as fund-raising events. If direct funds are unavailable, projects also seek such "in-kind" support as the loan of equipment and secretarial, printing, photocopying, and transcription-binding services.

Projects focused on a specific issue, such as women's rights or environmental policies, have often received support from individuals and organizations that support or promote the issue. The Washington Press Club Foundation's oral history project on women journalists, for instance, received funding from an array of media sources that included the Gannett Foundation, the Sulzberger Foundation, and Time Warner, Inc. For a project centered on the career of a specific individual, such as a prominent politician retired from office, approach contributors to the politician's campaigns. A dinner in that person's honor could well serve as a fund-raiser for the oral history project. In addition, businesses, trade associations, and labor unions have funded oral history projects related to their field. Families have underwritten interviews and whole oral history projects about an illustrious member.

Funding may determine who is interviewed. Corporate funding and support by wealthy individuals has accounted for much of the "elite" interviewing done by oral history projects in the past. Public and private funding agencies have supported community-based oral history projects, but these funds have fluctuated widely, depending on the financial or political climate. Although interviewee selection should be conducted separately from fund-raising, some project organizers have identified interviewees based on the likelihood of their financial contribution to the project or to the parent institution, slighting others whose interviews would have made a more significant contribution. Economic realities may be inescapable, but oral history projects should include as wide a range of interviews as possible and not be limited to those who can pay for it. Care must be taken not to allow funding sources to inhibit the choice of topics or interviewees.

How does an oral history project apply for a grant?

Granting agencies range from the Ford and Rockefeller Foundations and the Pew Charitable Trust, and the National Endowment for the Humanities (NEH), to a plethora of less-known, family-based and issue-oriented foundations. The NEH through its research, education, and preservation and access divisions, has frequently funded oral history, although an enormous investment in time and effort is required to prepare NEH proposals, the competition is intense, and only about 20 percent of all proposals receive funding. The larger foundations require more information (a sixty-page application to the NEH is not unusual), whereas the grant process is less onerous at smaller foundations, whose smaller staff may limit grant proposals to a few pages. If a foundation asks for only four pages, submit four pages, since it may not read larger proposals. Some smaller foundations do not accept unsolicited applications, in which case a project might tap one of its advisory board members or seek an introduction from a well-regarded member of the community to help arrange for an invitation to submit a proposal.

Before approaching a foundation, a project should have a clear notion of what it wants to accomplish and what public benefit will result from its work. Granting agencies will want to know about the capacity of the project's organization and staff, and about the public accessibility of the finished product. What is the value of the project? Who will care about it? Will there be public outreach in the form of a publication, a web site, or performances in schools, nursing homes, and other public places? Will students working on the project acquire skills and return something to the community? A good method of determining what a foundation wants is to review the lists of projects it funded in the past. Funding agencies will also be interested in any additional institutional support a project has gotten, including in-kind contributions, loans of equipment, and volunteers who will donate time and effort.

It is important to know the specific requirements of the foundation to which you are applying. Consult the *Chronicle of Philanthropy*, and check the granting agencies' web sites for their guidelines. Carefully note their time lines and deadlines, and always allow some extra time to cope with unexpected delays. If a foundation rejects your proposal, ask to see the readers' comments, and consider resubmitting a revised version. It may take several proposals to narrow in on what a particular foundation wants. If possible, visit the foundation and make contact with its project officers. Although grants are usually made by an agency's board, the project officers prepare the paperwork and have good ideas about what boards will accept. Seek the project officer's opinion and then try to follow it. Grant organizations often appreciate collaborative projects, in which several organizations pool their efforts, and where others will match the funds they are giving. Some institutions will provide in-kind support, such as teaching reductions and office space. The first grant application usually takes a great deal of time and effort, but once a project has received one grant, it usually becomes easier to convince other foundations. Even a small grant from a prestigious foundation serves as a form of accreditation for a project that gives increased confidence to other potential funders.

How large a staff does an oral history project need?

There is no set number. Many projects are one-person operations, and others rely on a crew of volunteers or paid staff. Each project needs a manager or coordinator, who may also double as an interviewer or transcriber. The project managers prepare grant proposals, set up an advisory committee, recruit interviewers, identify likely interviewees, acquire equipment, handle correspondence, create the necessary filing system and other documentation (including legal release forms), arrange for transcriptions or abstracts to be made, organize workshops or training sessions for interviewers, and ensure that the interviews are deposited in a library or other institution where researchers can use them. The project manager may also handle publicity for the project or supervise the use of the interviews in publications, exhibits, and other forms of public presentation.

The pool of interviewers available to a project will influence the number of interviews that can be conducted. More interviewers can do more interviews but require more equipment and more processing time. Volunteers especially enjoy interviewing but are not as eager to do the less glamorous job of processing the interviews. Avoid doing more interviews than can reasonably be processed, to prevent large backlogs and delays in producing transcripts. Once processing begins to fall behind, it becomes increasingly arduous to catch up. If promises have been made to give copies of the recording or transcript to interviewees, long backlogs create embarrassing delays.

In most projects, the interviewer is responsible for researching, conducting, and editing the interview. Sometimes a project will offer assistance with research, but the interviewer has to be thoroughly versed in the subject matter and cannot rely solely on prepared questions. An interviewer must be prepared to deviate from the outline at any moment and follow up on unexpected information from the interviewee. In some larger projects, interviews are contracted out for a set fee, which includes the interviewer's preparation of a finished transcript.

Depending on funding, trained interviewers are paid a salary or a fee per interview. Fees may be set for the entire interview or by the hour, with reimbursement for any costs incurred in traveling to the interview. If using inexperienced volunteers, project organizers should ensure that interviews are properly conducted and processed by arranging for an oral history consultant to run workshop training sessions for interviewers and transcribers and to review their work periodically. The project manager may double as the oral history consultant. Consultants usually charge fees, but university oral history archivists will sometimes provide advice to smaller projects in their vicinity as a pro bono service.

Should a project appoint an advisory committee?

An advisory committee can help a project determine its goals, review proposals, suggest potential interviewees, assist in fund-raising, and offer general support to the interviewers. If the project is part of a larger institution, such as a library, archives, or university, whose administrators may not fully recognize all of the project's requirements, a wisely selected advisory committee can offer a strong network of support.

Select advisory committee members who are likely to be respected by the host institution or by the chief funding agency and who have the time and the interest to attend occasional committee meetings. Keep the committee small enough to facilitate communication and meetings, but diverse enough to provide different areas of assistance. Potential members are scholars in the particular subject area (who can advise on the interviewing process), prominent members of the community being studied (who can help make contact with potential interviewees), and perhaps fund-raising experts (who can help keep the project going).

Many funding agencies prefer some form of advisory committee, and grant proposals usually include funds to pay honoraria and sometimes travel expenses for advisory committee meetings. Some projects have blue-ribbon advisory panels that were created as showcases to appease funding agencies and whose members rarely convene meetings or are kept informed. This is a self-defeating practice. Any project can benefit from the experienced advice of advisory committee members, especially during the initial stages of design and development.

How should potential interviewees be identified?

The project advisory committee can often suggest the most likely interviewees. If a project is part of a larger organization, its leaders and members may have their own recommendations. Research into the subject will also identify those who were involved in the events at the time, and *Who's Who*, professional directories, phone books, pension lists, and other references can help locate those potential interviewees who are still living.

Interviewees from particular groups or communities can be found through advertising in local newspapers, on radio or television stations, in the newsletters of companies, unions, churches, and civic organizations, in alumni magazines, and on the Internet. But mass appeals run the risk of stimulating massive responses, overwhelming the project with volunteer interviewees. Rather than disappoint people by not interviewing them, projects can limit their initial appeals to informal networks before going public through the media.

How should a project select interviewers?

Look first for those with previous interviewing experience, those who have already done interviews or taken an oral history course or workshop. Ideally, interviewers should have some competence or experience in the project's subject matter. Occasionally, interviewers who fit both categories can be found, but usually the project organizers settle for one or the other qualification. Experienced interviewers coming into a new field need to do extensive research in the subject matter. Those already familiar with the subject material but who have not yet done any interviewing need training in interview techniques.

Inexperienced interviewers should attend training sessions conducted by an experienced oral historian, who can be located through the state, regional, and national oral history associations or through nearby universities and historical societies. It is essential that all interviewers be fully informed of the project's objectives, as well as of the ethical and legal considerations, before they begin interviewing.

Volunteers often come from the community or group being interviewed. Being part of the community gives them an advantage in researching the subject matter and in establishing rapport with interviewees. The disadvantage of using "intimates" lies in their reluctance to probe unpleasant topics and in interviewees' hesitation to disclose candid information to another member of the community. The "clinical" interviewer from outside the community may be seen as more neutral and discreet. Outside interviewers will take less for granted and encourage interviewees to talk over subjects that may be well known within the community but less recognized and understood beyond its boundaries. Be aware also that interviewers who share similar experiences will usually have their own stories to tell and may not be able to stop themselves from interrupting and injecting themselves ("Oh, yeah? Let me tell you what happened to me") into the interviews. To forestall these temptations, it may be advisable to interview the interviewers. Let them tell their stories on tape first. Being interviewed will also serve to further familiarize volunteer interviewers with the process.

Regardless of whether they are paid or volunteer, all interviewers should prepare written records of their preparation and methods, and the circumstances of the interview. Interviewers should write a brief biographical statement about themselves to include with the recordings and transcripts. Future researchers will find this information valuable in understanding the dynamics of the interview and will want to consider how the background of the interviewer might have affected the interview. Biographers will consider how the oral history itself became an incident in the interviewee's life, a time when he or she had the opportunity to reflect on past successes and defeats. They will want to know where and under what conditions the interview took place. Interviewers as well as interviewees deserve appropriate acknowledgment for their work in the recording and transcript and in all subsequent forms of citation or usage.[3]

How can the work of a variety of different interviewers be coordinated?

Maintaining consistency in the quality and standards of the oral history project is an issue when a number of interviewers, whether volunteers or paid, are used. Once again, a workshop for interviewers can be helpful, particularly at the beginning of a project to help them not only get some training but to appreciate the scope of the project and have a chance to compare experiences and concerns. A core of common questions may emerge from these workshops or group meetings. Interviewers should be encouraged to read each other's transcripts, to measure their own work against the group's, and to offer some peer review. When many interviewers are employed over a protracted period of time, it is advisable to prepare a project handbook, with both general oral history procedures and information specific to the project. Model handbooks include *Working Womenroots: An Oral History Primer* (1980), designed for interviewing women trade union activists, *Oral History Techniques and Procedures* (1992) for army historians; and *Oral History in the National Park Service* (1984) for National Park Service interviewers. Numerous oral history web sites on the Internet also provide guides aimed at both general and specific projects.[4]

Better-funded, institutional projects have sponsored "memory-jogging" conferences to bring together a field's key people to discuss the topic and to fill in the gaps that scholars have found in the record. At these conferences, interviewers conduct preliminary interviews with both individuals and groups to determine how the attendees participated in the events being studied and to plan priorities for full-scale interviews. Memory-jogging conferences have been held, for example, to examine NATO's nuclear strategies during the cold war and the Cuban Missile Crisis.[5]

What credit should interviewers get for the work they have done?
Interviewers deserve full credit for their work. Display the name of the interviewer on the recording and the transcript. Whenever possible, cite the interviewer in any references to the interview in publications, exhibits, and other public presentations. Although the point of doing the interview is to collect the interviewee's story, it would not exist without the interviewer and might have emerged very differently if conducted by someone else. Increasingly, books heavily drawn from oral history interviews have cited the interviewer on the title age through phrases such as "with the assistance of. . . ," "as told to . . . ," and "based on an oral history with . . ."[6]

EQUIPMENT

What basic equipment is needed for an oral history project?
Necessarily dependent on technology, oral historians have adjusted constantly to introductions of new equipment. Fortunately, technological progress has resulted in lighter, easier-to-operate, and more affordable recorders. Dean Albertson, Allan Nevins's assistant at the Columbia Oral History Research Office, recalled purchasing Columbia's first wire recorders: "Instead of a reel of tape, they had a magnetic recording head through which passed a spool of fine wire. A more devilish machine was never invented. Quite apart from the fact that they weighed about forty pounds was their propensity for jamming and spewing immense coils of wire all over the floor."[7]

Subsequently, oral historians moved to belt, reel-to-reel, and cassette tape recorders, digital audio tape, compact discs and mini-disk recorders, as well as videocassette and digital cameras. Transcribing equipment has also advanced, from typewriters to word processors. Oral historians need to keep current with the latest and best equipment, being careful to adopt only those devices that adequately record and preserve high-quality sound. Pocket dictating machines, for instance, serve their own purposes but make poor recordings for oral history.

Purchase or rent the best that your project can afford. You need reliable equipment that will record clearly. Professional sound-quality reel-to-reel recorders were long the best, but also the most expensive and least practical for interviewing. Most projects use good-quality, reasonably priced, portable cassette tape recorders and mini-disks. Some interviewers use earphones to monitor what is being recorded. Other useful accessories on the recorder are a signal to indicate when the tape is about to run out (enabling the interviewer to change the tape with minimal interruption to the interview) and a register to indicate the strength of the sound recording (to alert the interviewer that batteries may be wearing down).

Electrical power is more reliable than batteries for recording, even though it may require some extra time or furniture rearranging to position the recorder near an outlet. Bear in mind, however, that the physical setting of the interview cannot always be determined in advance, and that you occasionally may need some mobility, say, to follow a craft worker through various stages of production in different locations. Always bring a supply of batteries to meet such contingencies.

Use only high-quality tapes. For cassette tapes, the recommended length is sixty minutes, although many prefer ninety-minute tapes because they entail fewer interruptions to the narrative. Anything longer than ninety-minute tape will be much too thin and likely to tangle and break. With digital recorders, look for larger memory storage capabilities. Unlike tape recorders in which an interview is interrupted momentarily to change tapes, digital recorders with limited memory must be downloaded to a computer or compact disc before they can begin recording again.[8]

Charles Hardy, whose work on radio documentaries has made him keenly attuned to sound quality, finds that DAT (digital audio tape) recorders provide the best sound quality for the money, but that basic, inexpensive consumer model mini-disks will work just as well for most oral history projects, and sound much better than most analog tape recordings. The money saved by using less expensive mini-disks can be applied to purchasing better microphones and headphones.[9]

Whatever the type of recording, good microphones are critical. Never use a recorder's built-in microphone; it will pick up all of the machine's operating noises. Many interviewers prefer to use lavaliere mikes, which attach to a lapel or other item of clothing and assure clear recording, especially if both the interviewer and interviewee have mikes. Lavalieres are a great advantage when interviewing soft-spoken people, the type who swallow their words, mumble, or unconsciously cover their mouths when they talk. If only one lavaliere mike is available, it should be used by the interviewee.

Table microphones should be placed close to the interviewee. Always test microphones in advance to make sure that the interviewee and interviewer can be heard clearly. Remember that most microphones have their own batteries that need testing and replacement periodically.

For transcribing, a separate transcribing machine is advisable. A foot pedal on the transcriber allows the operator to stop, reverse, and play back portions of the recording automatically while typing, since it may be necessary to listen to a phrase several times to ascertain the exact wording. Transcribing machines also permit the recording to be slowed down or speeded up to match the operator's typing speed and to help decipher muffled or slurred words. When outside transcribing services are used, transcription equipment is an option for a project, although a foot-pedal-equipped transcriber can assist in audit-editing the transcripts.

Word processors have immensely advanced oral history transcriptions. Before the advent of the word processor, typists prepared a rough draft of the interview, on which the interviewee would make editorial changes, and then typed a clean copy. In fact, the principal transcript in some projects was the rough copy with handwritten corrections; this practice had the advantage of showing researchers where changes had been made, but the disadvantage of sometimes difficult-to-read handwriting that tended to reproduce poorly on microfilm and photocopies. Word processors speed typing time and allow editorial changes to be made more efficiently. Copies can be preserved on disk for instant retrieval and reprinting. Word-processing programs also check spelling and make the job of indexing faster and more comprehensive. Text-searching software is providing greater control and access for extensive oral history collections.

For any equipment, bargains can often be found by ordering equipment via catalog. But the economy can be a false one if the equipment cannot be repaired nearby and must be shipped away at additional expense and for protracted periods of time. Work with reputable dealers and keep files on all warranties and guarantees.

What type of recording lasts the longest?

No sound or video recording will last forever. The National Archives has long recommended one-quarter-inch open-reel audiotape as the best medium for preservation, but once most oral historians used cassette rather than reel-to-reel recorders, archives began accepting good-quality cassette tape for preservation. As consumers' music-buying shifted overwhelmingly to compact discs (CDs), it was essentially the commercial market for books on tape that kept manufacturers producing standard cassettes. With even talking books going digital, analog tape may soon become a relic of the past.

Archivists remain uncertain about the long-term preservation of digital data, oral history projects using compact discs, digital audio tape, and mini-disk recordings sometimes copy digital recordings onto analog tape for archival purposes. Regardless of what technology is used, a master copy of every interview should be made for preservation. Transcriptions and research use should be limited to copies, never the master.

Preservation of tapes requires that they be kept under relatively constant temperature and humidity conditions, avoiding extreme heat and cold, excessive moisture, and dust and atmospheric pollutants. Tapes should be rerun every year or two to prevent blurring of their sound. Unfortunately, many projects do not have the facilities or the budget to maintain these conditions for their tapes or to go through the time-consuming process of regularly rewinding thousands of tapes.

Anyone who doubts that sound preservation is a problem should listen to tapes made a decade or two ago. These tapes often sound so muddy that both the questions and the answers have become indistinct. Although some tapes can be restored and digitally enhanced, documentary makers, after discovering that the sound quality of many oral history tapes has made them unusable, have been forced to use actors to re-create the interviewees' voices. These problems of long-term preservation highlight the need for oral history projects to transcribe their tapes and deposit master tapes in archives experienced in handling sound and video recordings, where they can be preserved for future use. The project can still retain copies of its tapes for its own ongoing uses.[10]

What sort of documentation should be kept on each interview?

The more interviews there are, the more control will be needed over the paperwork. The processing of each interview should move forward at a reasonable pace, and a "history" of each should be retained. The project manager should keep a log, or master project list, for each interview, including who was interviewed, by whom, for how many hours, on what dates, using how many reels of tape, whether the interview has been transcribed, whether it is open for research, what restrictions may have been placed upon its use, and whether a microfilm or microform copy is available.

A file for each interview should include whatever biographical information has been collected, letters arranging the interviews, and an abstract of the interview that briefly summarizes (a single paragraph may suffice) the subjects covered and the names of the people most frequently discussed. This file should contain a copy of the deed of gift (the legal release form from the interviewee) and explanations of any restrictions on the interview. For ease of referral, it should note the libraries or other repositories where interested researchers can see copies of the interview.

Files should also be maintained on each interviewer, with such basic information as home and work addresses, phone numbers, areas of expertise, interviews completed, and interviews scheduled. Keeping lists of potential interviewers and interviewees for later stages of the project is also helpful.

Where should interviews take place?

The location usually depends on the interviewee. Some people are so busy they will grant interviews only at their own office. This locale presents the problem of shutting out distractions and interruptions: a ringing phone, a secretary at the door, and all the reminders of the next item on the day's agenda will divert the interviewee's attention. Similarly, at an interviewee's home the phone, a spouse, children, the family dog, even noisy appliances, can interrupt the flow of the interview and create unacceptable levels of background noise. Too much commotion makes transcribing difficult and limits the eventual use of the recording for media or exhibits.

Try to conduct the interview in a quiet place away from everyday distractions. If not at the project office or the interviewer's office, then choose a room, or even a portion of a room, that the interviewee does not normally use. Get the interviewee away from behind a desk and sit in chairs at the other side of the office or in a conference room down the hall. Or conduct the interview at the dining room table. Politely request others in the home or office not to interrupt while you are recording. Shut the door if there is one.

Having the interviewee come to the interviewer allows for better control of the equipment and placement of the tape recorder or cameras and microphones. When going to the interviewee, allow enough time to set up the equipment. Not knowing where electrical outlets may be located, the interviewer should carry batteries or an extension cord. Always bring more tapes than you can expect to use in case the interviews goes longer than scheduled. Test the equipment just before the interview. The farther interviewers must travel to an interview, the less they can afford a malfunctioning piece of equipment. Murphy's Law applies to oral history: if it can break down, it will—precisely when needed.

What happens if the equipment fails?

Without any backup equipment, the interviewer will have to apologize and schedule another interview. Even worse is to conduct the interview and only later realize that the equipment failed. In addition to testing equipment before the interview, an interviewer must keep watch on it throughout the interview. I once had to call an interviewee to report that nothing could be heard on the tape but static. "Maybe that's all I gave you," the interviewee responded. That interviewee graciously agreed to do another interview, but repeat sessions are rarely as spontaneous and detailed as the original interview.

Failed equipment is the bane of the interviewer. The Oral History Association once invited veteran interviewers to testify to their "worst moments" in doing oral history. Tales of disaster included the absence of electrical outlets, tape recorders that picked up radio transmissions from passing police cars, tape that unraveled to fill an interviewer's car, and a long list of calamities. It is reassuring to know that one is not alone, but such horror stories from experienced interviewers should encourage every project manager to test equipment regularly and be prepared to help interviewers meet any eventuality.

Is it ever appropriate to interview a group of people together?

The best oral history interview is generally done one-on-one. That way, the interviewer can focus exclusively on one person, whose stories will not be interrupted. Yet sometimes it is impossible to avoid having another person in the room, perhaps the interviewee's spouse or grown child, who may interrupt to contradict, correct, or supplement the testimony. Such interruptions can derail the interview, but they can also help by providing forgotten information and otherwise supporting an uncertain interviewee.[11]

Group interviews increase the potential for trouble. Facing a group, the interviewer becomes a moderator, trying to give everyone a chance to respond and ensuring that no one monopolizes the discussion. Transcribers have great difficulty identifying who is speaking in group situations, since all voices begin to sound alike. This problem is alleviated only if during the interview someone other than the interviewer (who has enough to do) keeps a sequential list of each speaker. Videotaping the group session can also facilitate identification.

Although more difficult, group interviews can gather fruitful information. Interviewees remember common incidents when sitting in a group that they might not have thought of by themselves. Self-exaggeration may also be tempered in a peer group situation. The John F. Kennedy Library conducted several successful group interviews with journalists who covered the president and with the chairmen that Kennedy appointed to head the independent regulatory commissions. Nevertheless, group interviews should be considered chiefly as supplements to individual interviews, not as replacements.

Can a team of interviewers conduct an interview together?

Using more than one interviewer distorts the one-on-one relationship that tends to work best for oral history. The anthropologist Michael Kenny warned that a group of interviewers, though it can sometimes work, holds a potential for disaster: "Illuminating as this technique can be, it can also turn into the worst type of press conference, wherein the informant is either thoroughly cowed or offended, and rightly so."[12]

But there can be advantages to using more than one interviewer. Younger students, nervous about the experience, often interview in pairs or are accompanied by a parent or teacher. Novice interviewers may similarly take along a partner for moral support. Some research projects have been done entirely by teams. For one project on racial violence in the South, a black interviewer conducted most of the interviews with white southerners but took the precaution of going as part of a team with a white interviewer. One team member may be better versed in a particular subject and can take the lead in questioning about that area. But in team situations, one interviewer usually serves as the principal interviewer, asking most of the questions and gaining the interviewee's primary attention. Accompanying interviewers should try not to interrupt, except perhaps to interject a follow-up question that the primary interviewer might have missed.

What are the differences between recording events that are still taking place and recording those that are long past?

Most oral history projects look back, but some have conducted "history while it's hot," in the words of Forrest Pogue, the World War II combat interviewer. Military historians since then have carried tape recorders to question troops from Vietnam to the Persian Gulf. During Eugene McCarthy's campaign for the Democratic presidential nomination in 1968, an oral history project recorded interviews with the candidate and many of his staff. Oral historians at corporations and university archives have conducted ongoing interviews with their presidents and other high-level administrators, to review the past year's events and debrief the players in recent major events.

Scheduling is perhaps the biggest problem with interviewing as the events are occurring. The key players are often too busy or too likely to feel interrupted. They make and break appointments at a frustrating pace. Interviewers have to be patient and ready to take advantage of whatever opportunity comes along. Finally, when the subject matter is a current event, take it for granted that almost everything will be closed for some period. For the interview to be anything more revealing than a radio talk show, the interviewer must guarantee absolute confidentiality and allow the interviewee to seal the recordings and transcript for a safe period, until the events have passed into history.

PROCESSING

Must all our interviews be transcribed?

The deteriorating sound quality of audio and visual recordings over time is just one of the many incentives for transcribing oral history interviews. Even with the best recording devices, listeners will find it hard at times to understand interviewees, especially older people whose voices have grown faint, or those who speak with a pronounced accent or in a regional dialect. Others mutter and stumble over words. Background noises may obliterate the speaker's words. If the interviewer, who was present, finds it difficult to understand and transcribe all that was said, imagine the problem future researchers will have interpreting the recording. Transcribing enables both the interviewer and interviewee to review the interview and ensure that the transcript reflects what each intended to say.

Given a choice, researchers invariably prefer transcripts over recordings. Eyes can read easier than ears can hear. Transcripts can be scanned and photocopied. Information can be retrieved even more easily if the transcripts are indexed or if text-searching computer software is used. The recording will provide sound for television documentaries, radio programs, and exhibits, or for biographers, folklorists, and others curious about the speaking voice, dialect, hesitations, and other verbal mannerisms. But archivists note that very few researchers ask to listen to the recordings if transcripts are available.

The Internet has provided opportunities to reunite spoken words with their transcription and helped preserve the "orality" of oral history. Believing it vital for researchers to hear as well as to read interviews, some archives have posted sound recordings along with transcripts, photographs, and other documentation, on their web sites. In the case of non-English-speaking interviewees, such as Native Americans using tribal languages, the transcripts can also provide translations. Since sound files are very big, and consume much time and space for downloading, many projects will provide only excerpts from the sound recordings online. They also seek to keep the transcript verbatim to match the sound recordings if their interviewees agree to refrain from editing their remarks.

If a project cannot afford transcripts, what are the alternatives?

If transcribing is not possible, a project's work should at least include abstracting and indexing the recordings. A summary of the main individuals and subjects discussed, with notations of where they can be found chronologically on the tape, will enable researchers to find the portions they seek. The TAPE (Time Access to Pertinent Excerpts) system has been designed to prepare such abstracts. Oral history project managers must maintain control over their collections as they grow if they want to access portions easily in the future. Whether you transcribe or abstract, it is also essential to process as you go, to avoid creating overwhelming backlogs, which can paralyze a project.[13]

Voice recognition software offers the promise that someday computers will transcribe recordings automatically. While some advances have been made, the technology is not yet adequate for oral history transcription. Existing voice recognition programs are generally geared to understand a single voice, and even that takes much time and effort to establish. The systems make numerous errors, which are compounded by multiple voices, accents, mumbling, and all the other obstacles that even human transcribers must surmount.

Should you transcribe your own recordings or contract them out?

Transcription is by far the most expensive and time-consuming part of an oral history project, requiring an estimated six to eight hours to transcribe each hour of interview as well as more time to audit-edit the transcripts (a form of audio proofreading in which you play back the recording while reviewing the transcript, making sure the two are consistent). Some projects' staffs transcribe their own recordings; in other projects, professional transcribing services are hired. In selecting transcribers, look for someone with previous oral history experience. Typing speed is far less critical for transcription than typing for comprehension. The estimated cost of transcribing should also include making corrections on the first draft of the interview. Request the transcript on computer disk as well as in a hard-copy version. It is advisable to continue with the same transcription service for all of your interviews to ensure consistent stylistic treatment of idiosyncratic vocabulary, acronyms, geographic names, regional dialects, and any number of other factors that might hinder speedy and accurate transcriptions if the interviews pass through too many hands.

In some projects, interviews are transcribed after additional funds have been raised. Funding agencies, such as state humanities councils, have occasionally underwritten the transcription of already completed interviews, since the exact cost can be calculated and a finished collection guaranteed. The longer a project waits, the more difficult the transcription process becomes, owing to the deterioration of tapes and to the possibility that interviewees will die before having a chance to correct the transcript.

What issues need to be worked out in advance with a transcribing service?

Transcribers want recordings that are clear and distinct, with little background noise. Provide a list of any proper and place names and technical terms that are mentioned in the interview, to reduce the chance of error and the time necessary for proofreading and editing. Label recordings with the name of the interviewee, date of the interview, and sequence of the tapes (Interview no. 1, Tape no. 1, Tape no. 2, and so on). As an added precaution, and for ready identification later, at the beginning of the recording, interviewers should introduce themselves, their interviewees, and the date of the interview. This formal preamble can be done before the meeting with the interviewee to avoid jeopardizing rapport. Always retain the master recording and send only a copy to the transcriber.

Agreements should be made in advance with transcribers on the desired format of the transcripts, including spacing, type size, margins, and speaker identification. Make sure that the transcriber uses compatible computer equipment and software so that you can edit the disks and use them to produce copies as needed. Determine whether the transcriber will prepare the index, and what index terms are most important. Caution the transcriber about possibly confidential material on the recordings. (Some transcribers provide notarized assurances that the transcripts will remain confidential.) Make the transcriber aware of whatever deadlines the project is operating under. Report any problems with the transcripts to the transcriber, especially at the beginning of the process before patterns have been established, to keep the final product consistent.[14]

Which is the oral history, the recording or the transcript?

Tape and transcript are two types of records of the same interview. Archivists generally consider the tape, being the original and verbatim record, the primary document. Looked at another way, the tape records what was said, and the transcript represents the intended meaning of what was said. Even the most slavishly verbatim transcript is just an interpretation of the tape. Different transcribers might handle the same material in different ways, including punctuation, capitalization, false starts, broken sentences, and verbal obstacles to presenting spoken words in print. Interviewers and interviewees should edit the transcripts, correcting errors, whether misspoken or mistranscribed. During the editing, interviewees may add material that was forgotten during their interviews, or may remove comments that they have had second thoughts about.

Those disciplines particularly the behavioral sciences more interested in the study of actual speech warn against taking transcripts "too seriously as *the* reality." Viewing transcripts as only a partial rendering of the recordings, they note the importance of such additional features as pitch, stress, volume, and rate of speech, as well as facial gestures and body movements, which are not captured on audio tape. These disciplines often design particular modes of transcription to illustrate some aspect of speech they consider important, such as measuring the pauses in an interviewee's responses. Some have devised symbols to express significant nonverbal responses. When folklorist Henry Glassie interviewed the Irish at Ballymenone, he used a diamond-shaped symbol to signify a "smile in the voice, a chuckle in the throat, a laugh in the tale," suggesting humor visually but not verbally.[15]

In the United States, the transcript rather than the recording has generally served as the primary research tool. Created and directed by historical researchers, the pioneering Columbia Oral History Research Office during its early years produced transcripts and then, because of its limited budget, recorded over its tapes. As often happens, practical policies become elevated to the status of principle. Columbia noted that most researchers asked to use only transcripts and that only folklorists, linguists, and ethnomusicologists wanted to hear the sound recordings. Columbia thus felt justified in its de-emphasis of the tape and spoke authoritatively on this matter. Many oral history projects followed its model.

Canadian oral historians, by contrast, adopted "aural history" and created impressive sound archives, often with no transcripts at all. Similarly converting a practice to a principle, some oral historians rejected transcripts as a distortion or corruption of the interview. To be accurate, they argued, every word, sound or false start should be put down on paper. When the Oral History Association met in Canada in 1976, heated arguments erupted as to whether the tape or the transcript was the "real" oral history. In later years, oral historians generally accepted both tape and transcript as different but equally legitimate records of the same event. Computers have also made transcribing easier and more cost-effective, and transcribing services have blossomed for those who do not want to do it themselves. The advent of the Internet has encouraged advocates of "aurality" to stream their audio tapes online so that more researchers can hear the actual voices of the interviewees, but such procedures need not preclude posting the transcripts as well.

Too great an emphasis on transcribing has caused too many oral historians to ignore the quality of their sound recordings, so that many tapes are of such poor quality that they cannot be used for broadcasting or museum exhibition. Transcripts and high-quality sound recordings (and video recordings) involve considerable expense, and oral history projects have often been forced to take one path or the other. Still, tape and transcript should not be seen as an either-or choice but as mutual goals.

Does editing of transcripts change and distort their meaning?

Editing is usually necessary to make sense of the spoken word when it is put down in writing. As David Crystal has written in his encyclopedia of the English language: "Extracts of informal spoken conversation look weird in print because it is not possible to show all the melody, stress, and tone of voice which made the speaker sound perfectly natural in context." Moreover, the transcriber may have made errors, garbled names, or been unable to distinguish exactly what an interviewee said. The interviewee may have given the wrong name or date or some other unintentionally misleading information. Speakers often do not complete sentences. The listener can get the gist of their meaning, but in written form these fragmented sentences can be unclear and a source of frustration.[16]

Some historians and linguists regret the practice of editing out speakers' hesitations, repetitions, and unfinished thoughts, and encourage transcribing practices that will "convey the cadences of speech as well as its content." They question why we should expect interviewees to speak in complete sentences, when sentence fragments and exclamations are common and readily understandable in everyday conversation. Linguists especially strive to create transcripts that faithfully reproduce human speech, employing systems that range from phonetics to meticulously defined notations, sometimes even counting the seconds that elapse when the speaker pauses. While such exercises honor the oral nature of interviewing and serve particular scholarly purposes, they can never fully replicate the tones and rhythms of the recorded voice and run the risk of obscuring the substance of the interview by leaving unfinished thoughts that could have been clarified through judicious editing.[17]

Oral historians are not the only people who edit transcripts. Members of Congress edit their remarks in the daily *Congressional Record*, and administration witnesses revise the testimony they have given before congressional committees. In his oral history, Carl Marcy recalled how during the 1940s he edited Secretary of State George C. Marshall's congressional testimony:

Secretary Marshall called me to his office one day. He was very austere. He looked at me with a transcript in front of him that I had corrected. He said, "Marcy, you in charge of this?" I said, "Yes sir, I did that." He said, "Well, I don't know what it is, but I feel when I'm talking to the senators that I'm making sense and they understand me. But when I look at the uncorrected transcript it doesn't make much sense." But, he said, "After you fix it up, it looks all right. You keep on doing it."[18]

There are advantages in having interviewees edit their own transcripts. Interviewees know what they said, or meant to say, better than anyone else. They can often spot misspelled names and mistranscribed sentences. Whether a word should appear at the end of one sentence or at the beginning of the next can affect the meaning of both sentences. Dropping a *not* can dramatically reverse the meaning. Words that sound alike, and may make sense in context may not be the words the interviewee used. Transcribers have heard *assumed* instead of *as soon*, *block aid* for *blockade*, and the *Duke of Wellington* instead of *Duke Ellington*. One transcript contained an astonishing comment about two Supreme Court justices: "Brandeis was concerned about marrying Frankfurter." The speaker had actually said that Louis Brandeis was worried about the health of Felix Frankfurter's wife Marion. Another transcript contained a mysterious reference to "I.C. Sping, head of the transition team." Replaying of the tape revealed that the interviewee had actually said: "I ceased being head of the transition team."

Some interviewees will defer to the interviewer to make whatever corrections seem necessary. Others, especially professional people, feel chagrined at seeing their syntax set down in print. They will correct tenses, change "yeah" to "yes," and otherwise make themselves appear as literate as possible. Interviewers need to remind their interviewees that an oral history is a spoken record, and that it is best to keep the verbal rhythms and flows rather than convert the history into a more formal text. Writers of fiction are always trying to re-create believable human dialogue; oral history is human dialogue. The vernacular is accessible and attractive to wide audiences. Too much tampering with the transcript compromises the qualities that make oral history so compelling. Some oral historians insist that any changes in the verbatim transcripts be put in brackets. Others, seeking to avoid even the temptation of making alterations, prefer not to give the transcript to the interviewee for editing. Unless interviewees have already signed releases, however, their dissatisfaction or embarrassment may keep their interviews from being opened for research. Although such issues can be negotiated, the ethics of oral history and the laws of copyright dictate that an interviewee's wishes be honored.

Some changes add to a transcript, as when interviewees realize that they did not finish a story on tape and left out related material, which can be inserted in the final transcript. More problematic are relations of stories or commentary because interviewees have had second thoughts after completing the recorded interview. Rather than eliminate this material, interviewees should be advised to restrict its use for a safe period of time.

Transcripts may be edited, but the original recording should be left exactly as spoken. Interviewers should inform interviewees that no changes or deletions can be made to the master copy. Interviewees may choose to set a longer restriction on use of the unedited recording than they do on the edited transcript, or to require listeners to quote solely from transcripts. Edited copies of the master recording may be released for research pending the lifting of any restrictions on portions of the original.

If a project intends to post both sound recordings and transcripts on its web sites, there should be more incentive to keep the transcript as close to the spoken word as possible, so that listeners can more easily follow the written text. At the same time, there will be less need for transcribers to attempt to reproduce non-verbal cues, such as facial expressions, laughter, sobs, and protracted silences that will be evident on the recording.

What is the interviewer's responsibility for reviewing and editing the transcript?

Oral historians should audit-edit the transcripts of their interviews. Having sat through the interview, the interviewer knows the material better than anyone except the interviewee. Sometimes interviewers transcribe their own recordings, but more often the interviewer serves as editor of the transcript. Listening to the recording, the interviewer reads the transcript to correct spelling errors, fill in words the transcriber could not discern, and generally make sense of what the interviewee said.

During the interview, the interviewer should note any unusual proper names and place names and afterwards ask the interviewee for the correct spellings. Some interviewers do this in the course of the interview, but others strongly prefer not to interrupt the interview and wait instead until the session is over. These interview notes will facilitate the transcriber's job.

Listening to the recording while editing the transcript can also be an important and excruciating learning experience for interviewers, who thus get to listen to their own mistakes. Note the sound quality. Did you take into account the air conditioner or grandfather's clock or the open window when you set up the recorder and microphone, and can you hear how these noises obscure the spoken word and make transcribing difficult? Did you interrupt before the interviewee was finished answering? Did you fail to follow up your initial question or leave an important question unaddressed? Did you pursue new leads in the interview or unwisely force it back to your prepared questions? Every editing session teaches interviewers more about their techniques and better prepares them for future interviews.

Should transcribers also edit?

The responsibility of transcribers is to reproduce as closely as possible what they hear on recordings. Transcribers should never rearrange words or delete phrases for stylistic purposes. Some projects permit a transcriber to remove "false starts," which are sentences that begin one way and then end abruptly as the interviewee changes gears. ("First we went. . . we started . . . well, actually, even before we went," might be tightened to, "Actually, even before we went.") But some false starts reveal something about mental processes, Freudian slips, and attempts to suppress information. Nor should transcribers try to correct ungrammatical constructions. A transcriber should leave the editing to the interviewer and the interviewee and only note those places in the transcript that were difficult to understand and any questions about spelling or syntax.

Working on a particular interview, a transcriber will soon become familiar with the speaker's verbal punctuation. Frequently, interviewees will use a word like *and* to start a new sentence, or a phrase like *and so* to begin a new paragraph. If transcribed literally, the interview will read like one long run-on sentence. Instead, transcribers are justified in replacing such constantly repeated cues with punctuation and paragraph breaks.

How should a transcript indicate sounds and gestures other than words?

Both the transcriber and the interviewer can add in brackets any additional descriptions such as "[laughs]," "[snaps fingers]," "[uses hands to suggest height]" that will help the reader understand what was happening, and what the interviewer intended to express. Humor and sarcasm sometimes do not translate well and may be taken too seriously unless the laughter of the interviewer or interviewee is also recorded. The transcript should also elucidate otherwise unexplainable shifts in the dialogue by noting any break in the tape, mechanical failing, or prolonged lapse in the interview. In all of these cues, however, reasonable discretion and good sense should be employed. Their purpose is to assist the researcher, not to embarrass the interviewee.

Similarly, transcripts should be edited to provide in brackets the full name and any relevant title of individuals when first mentioned, such as "[Senator Hillary Rodham] Clinton," or "President [George W.] Bush." When a city or town is mentioned, the state should also be added in brackets such as Springfield [Missouri] or Springfield [Illinois] unless a series of communities in a single state are under discussion. For stylistic questions about numbers, abbreviations, and so on, transcribers should consult the *Chicago Manual of Style* or whatever style manual the project chooses to employ.[19]

Transcribing is more of an art than a science. The Regional Oral History Office (ROHO) at the University of California at Berkeley once experimented by having four experienced individuals transcribe the same ten-minute segment of a recording. The result was four strikingly different transcripts that ranged from slavishly verbatim to highly polished, with a wide variety of editorial interventions indicating sounds and actions other than words. Each of the versions was a legitimate interpretation, but their extreme variations serve as a reminder that interviewers and project managers need to work with transcribers to set the desired style of the final product. As more projects put their sound recordings on the Internet, they will likely want less-edited transcripts that will resemble the spoken word most closely, including all of the flaws of unrehearsed speech.[20]

Should transcripts reproduce accents and dialects?

If the interview is intended for folklore studies or other purposes for which regional speech patterns are important, then rendering regional dialect in a transcript might be desirable. But dialects are tricky business that should be handled carefully.

Educated interviewees who say "yeah" will insist on altering the transcript word to "yes." They are sorely displeased when transcripts show them saying "gonna" or "talkin'" and would prefer to see their spoken words reproduced as they would write them. If oral historians allow these interviewees to correct their transcripts, they owe the same courtesy to those who are not used to seeing their words set down in print. As the Appalachian Oral History Project concluded, transcribing phonetically gives a pejorative cast to the speech and can "unintentionally demean the speaker." The Appalachian project discovered that its transcribers—student workers from the same area—were unaware of their own dialect's peculiarities (such as pronouncing "our" as "air") and therefore spelled the words correctly. Only transcribers from outside the mountain culture tried to capture on paper what they imagined to be authentic-looking dialect. The Appalachian project trained its transcribers not to correct grammar, but also not to respell what was said to the approximate dialect. That way they kept the flavor of the speaker's style without indicating pronunciation.[21]

The historian Nell Irvin Painter came to the same conclusions about her oral history of Hosea Hudson, a southern black labor organizer and Communist Party member. "Adapting Hudson's spoken language to the printed page meant abandoning its sound, for Hudson does not speak as I have rendered his words," Painter explained. A phonetically reproduced transcript would have been "condescending and difficult to read." She chose to use standard English spellings and to avoid apostrophes in words that showed variations from standard style, "because apostrophes and dialect in literature have long singled out characters that readers need not take seriously, ignorant folk who cannot speak correctly. With black people, the usage is centuries old." Yet as much as possible she preserved Hudson's vocabulary and such unique phrases as "howbeitsoever," to retain the spirit of the words without belittling the man.[22]

What should the transcript look like?

The word processor has revolutionized oral history transcripts and made obsolete many of the previously recommended styles of transcripts. At one time, corrections were either handwritten directly on the transcript or the entire transcript had to be retyped. Using typewriters, oral historians used triple-spaced lines and elaborately wide margins for making correction. All of these techniques became unnecessary with the computer's easy means of correction and reproduction.

Use common sense in setting margins. The practices of early oral historians led to so few words to the page that researchers complained about the inflated photocopying costs. On the other hand, too small a margin causes problems if the transcript is bound. Small type face and single-spacing will also make the transcript difficult to read when it is microfilmed.

Earlier, the anonymous Q and A were used to indicate questions and answers, but the word processor makes it easy to insert the interviewer and interviewee's last names each time that they speak. If the interview extended over several sessions, the transcript should indicate at the beginning: "Interview no.1 with Jane Jones, Wednesday, October 18, 2002," and at the end: "End of Interview no. 1." Begin the next with "Interview no. 2. . ." The title page should list the interviewee's name, the name of the oral history project, the interviewer's name, and the dates of the interviews, and their location.

Introduce the transcripts with a brief explanation of the oral history project and an outline of the interviewee's life and career. Some projects will use a data sheet on each interviewee instead. A brief biographical statement for the interviewer will also be useful for future researchers, since different interviewers (historians, political scientists, folklorists, community members) will ask different questions. Put the deed of gift up front to establish the copyright and research use of the interview. Interview transcripts may also contain relevant documents as appendix material. Some projects include one or more photographs of the interviewee and of people and events described in the interview. An index will also greatly enhance an interview's research use.

Why is an index necessary?

It does not take long before even the interviewer has trouble remembering who said what in which interview. Collecting information is only the first step; retrieving it comes next. Word-processing programs now make indexing so much easier that there is less excuse for not creating them. At minimum, indexes should include all names cited. Subject indexes are trickier but no less important. The program manager and interviewers should work out a general list of important terms for indexing purposes. Indexes help both interviewers and researchers. As interviewers prepare for future interviews, they will want to review pertinent portions of past interviews to prepare their questions. Researchers often do not want to read an entire transcript, but only those portions dealing with their particular subject. Text-searching software has also become a boon to users of oral histories, but since the transcript will often stand alone, particularly if it has been microfilmed, a separate index will still be useful.

Cross-referenced indexes add immeasurably to the research use of a collection. Since 1948 Columbia University has maintained a name index of all of its interviews. Researcher have found this massive index to be a rich resource, since it identifies not only the major players in their subject but also the minor figures whose interviews they might not otherwise have consulted but who often offer the most perceptive observations and analysis.

Should the project director review all transcripts?

Someone other than the interviewer ought to review the transcript before releasing it for research. Depending on the size of a project, a project director or editor may read all interviews or may delegate some to members of the advisory board as reviewer/evaluators. The decision depends on whether the interviews are ready to be opened and therefore can be reviewed by an advisory board member, or whether confidentiality needs to be maintained and revising should be limited to the project director. The project director should review the materials to determine whether the interviewer is following the project's guidelines, asking appropriate questions and follow-up questions, not interrupting, and collecting worthwhile material. Directors can use the review process to advise interviewers on recommended changes in style, or they may decide not to continue to use interviewers whose work is unsatisfactory. Project directors will also want to be sure that a consistent style is followed in the processing of the different interviews in a project.

LEGAL CONCERNS

Journalists do not use legal release forms for their interviews; why should oral historians?

People who respond to journalists' questions assume that their words will appear in print unless they stipulate that something is "off the record" or otherwise not for attribution. Many journalists take notes rather than record their interviews and generally use only brief excerpts from interviews in their stories. Few journalists retain their notes for posterity. Oral historians face different considerations.

Federal copyright laws grant copyright automatically to anyone whose words and ideas are recorded in any tangible form, for a period lasting until fifty years after that person's death. That is, even without registering the copyright with the Copyright Office, interviewees retain the copyright on anything that they have said in an interview. If the oral history project or any researcher publishes excerpts from their interviews beyond "fair use," a relatively small number of words without a deed of gift or contact that permits such use, then the interviewee could sue for copyright infringement.

For this reason, archives require a deed of gift or contact before opening an oral history for research. Similarly, publishers want to be sure that the copyright concerns have been addressed before they publish interviews in a book. To avoid headaches later, interviewers should collect deeds of gift when the interview is conducted, or at least by the time the transcript has been prepared and edited.

The deed of gift establishes who owns the copyright in the interview and what may be done with it. Interviewees may retain the copyright and require that they or their heirs be consulted before anyone uses or publishes excerpts from the interview. This requirement makes the process complex and should be avoided if possible. Other interviewees will assign the copyright over to the interviewer, the oral history project, or the repository but will stipulate that all or parts of the interview must remained closed for a period of time, sometimes until the interviewee's death. Too stringent a time restriction should also be avoided, as archives do not want to store materials for protracted periods if they cannot be used.

A simple deed of gift can turn the copyright over to the interviewer, or the oral history project, to use as they see fit, and to deposit in an institution of his or her choosing. Some deeds jointly assign the copyright to the public domain, that is, both the interviewer and the interviewee waive the right to copyright the material. Assigning copyright to the public domain vastly simplifies administration but offers little control over uses of the material. With the increasing likelihood that projects will post at least some of their interviews on the Internet, deeds of gift should be drawn broadly enough to cover electronic and other forms of reproduction.

Projects should develop a standard deed of gift or contract that offers enough flexibility to meet the requirements of different interviewees. Interviewers should explain to interviewees ahead of time the potential uses and planned deposit of the interviews so that the interviewee knows fully what to expect. Usually, these explanations are outlined in the initial correspondence or conversation between oral historians and interviewees. Should the interviewee die before signing a deed of gift, the verbal agreement on the recording may serve as an oral contract. Otherwise, the oral history project will have to seek out the next of kin to sign the deed. (Sample deeds of gift are reprinted in appendix 2.)[23]

Must the interviewer also sign a deed of gift?

Because the interview is a joint product, the interviewer as well as the interviewee should sign a legal release. Projects that use volunteer or paid interviewers should require them to sign *before* they do any interviewing, to avoid any misunderstandings later on. By signing such releases, interviewers agree to assign whatever copyright they might have to the project, to the interview repository, or to the public domain (see the appendices).[24]

When hiring contract interviewers, the basic agreement should include the names of the project and the interviewer, the interviewer's specific responsibilities, a payment schedule, the assignment of rights for the interviews, the assignment of responsibility for obtaining deeds of gift from interviewees, the procedures for terminating the contract, and dated signatures of both parties.[25]

Do interviewees have the right to close their interviews for a long time?

Before beginning an interview, when interviewees often feel nervous, interviewers will explain their right to close portions or all of an interview for as long as necessary. At the outset, more than one interviewee has announced, "Well, this is going to be hot, and will have to be kept closed for a long time. I don't want to embarrass anyone." By the conclusion of the interview, however, the interviewee usually feels more relaxed, the information elicited rarely turns out to have been salacious, and it has become evident that the people discussed are usually long since retired or deceased and that the "hot" information has cooled down considerably. At this point, the interviewer should point out what a valuable research tool the interview will become, and what a shame it would be to keep it away from researchers for long. Quite often the interviewee may decide to open the interview within a short time, if not immediately. A little flattery and reassurance generally goes a long way to encourage early release.

What rights do interviewees have to publish their own interviews?

Interviewees may want the right of first use. That is, they may want to close the interview while they write their own book. The oral history may provide the outline and the core of what they are writing. Unless the project has its own deadlines for a publication, exhibit, or other public presentation of the material and thus needs to negotiate a mutually beneficial release date, there is no reason why the interview should not be kept closed for a reasonable period that will give the interviewee the chance to publish a book, or abandon the attempt. The book will most likely depart from the interview in many respects, or it may not use all of the interview material. In either case, researchers will benefit from the additional first-person material. Nevertheless, given your oral history project's investment of time and funds in the interviews, and recognizing that some interviewees will never be able to turn a transcript into a publishable book no matter how long they work on it, do not permit open-ended restrictions on interviews that give the interviewees exclusive use and fail to set a definite time when other researchers can gain access.

The *New York Times* noted that when the pilot Chuck Yeager first read the manuscript of his autobiography prepared by his collaborator, he exclaimed, "Hell, it's just like me talking." As it happened, the collaborator had drawn much of the book from forty hours of taped interviews that Yeager had done with the Air Force Oral History Program. The Senate Historical Office interviewed George Tames, who had photographed Washington people and events for forty years for the *New York Times*. Although never a member of the Senate staff, Tames had spent nearly every working day of his career on Capitol Hill, getting into the backrooms to snap his photographs. In his interviews, Tames gave vivid descriptions of the senators he captured on film and seemingly had a story for every photograph he took. When his interviews were complete, Tames dictated his own further reminiscences, which he published as *A View of Washington: Six Presidents Who Have Known Me.*[26]

Future researchers may also find it useful to compare the original spoken interview with the polished publication. For example, the University of Kentucky Library contains the uncorrected transcript of the long series of interviews that Sidney Shalett conducted with the former senator and vice president Alben Barkley and used to produce Barkley's memoir, *That Reminds Me* (1954). The transcripts reveal a more hot-tempered, opinionated Barkley than appears in his genial autobiography, and the differences between the two versions offer useful insights for researchers.[27]

What if someone demands the recordings and transcripts be returned?

Very rarely, an interviewee has second thoughts about an oral history and may refuse to sign a deed of gift or even ask to withdraw the interview from a collection. This unfortunate situation has also occurred when an interviewee dies without signing a deed of gift and the next of kin demands to have the interview back. It is necessary to impress upon these individuals the time and cost that it took to do the interview, and the breach that its removal would cause to the collection. Try negotiating a longer restriction on the interview rather than its removal. Sometimes the interviewee just needs a little reassurance that the interview is a valuable document and does not sound foolish. But if the interviewee is adamant, the recordings and transcripts must be returned. After a reasonable interval, a project can contact those who have removed their interviews, or their next of kin, provide some information on the continued progress of the collection, and encourage them to resubmit the interviews so that the story will not be lost.

Can something said in an oral history ever be considered libelous or defamatory?

Unfortunately, yes. Individuals whom interviewees may libel or defame can sue not only the interviewee but the interviewer and the repository that holds the interview. Such instances are exceedingly rare, but even the threat of a libel suit can be unpleasant. Use common sense. If an interviewee states something extremely negative about the character of a living individual, something that is not widely known or previously published about that individual, and especially if the individual is not a public figure, then simply restrict that material for a period of time until the possibly defamed individual is no longer around to sue. The dead cannot be defamed.

Rather than close the whole interview because of one potentially libelous story, restrict that portion for a period of time until the closure can be safely lifted. It may be disappointing not to be able to open a juicy story immediately. But as a lawyer once advised an oral history project: "You could probably win a libel suit in court, but you wouldn't want to see the legal bills that would be the result."[28]

ARCHIVING AND THE INTERNET

What should be done with the finished interviews?

If the oral history project is not part of a library, archive, historical society, or other institution that deals with researchers, then its recordings and transcripts should be deposited somewhere that is capable of preserving the interviews and of making them available for general use. Public libraries are usually eager to gather materials about a community, its longtime families, churches, and schools for their local history sections. Archives will be pleased to receive copies of interviews relating to any person for whom they hold manuscript collections. University libraries often collect interviews done by students and faculty members. Larger oral history offices are willing to take in donated collections on a wide array of topics.

Each interview's deed of gift should indicate that the interviewee knows, and approves, the interview repository. Supply the repository with basic information about the interviews, project goals, sponsorship, and funding and make sure that all interviewers have documented their preparation, methods, and interview circumstances.

As oral history recordings and transcripts are easily copied, it is not necessary to limit the deposit to a single institution. Put copies of your oral histories wherever researchers are more likely to use them: in different libraries in a community, in archives that have the papers of the interviewee, or with institutions closely associated with the interviewee. In addition, plan to give at least one if not several copies to the interviewee. Even in inexpensive loose-leaf or spiral binding, transcripts make treasured gifts for family members. Retain at least one copy, or disk, for the oral history project's own future reference.

How do you let people know where to find your project's oral histories?

Having gone through all the steps of conducting, processing, and preserving oral history interviews, it can be a source of immense frustration when researchers fail to use them. Your oral history project is really not over until you have made an effort to publicize the existence of the collection. Send announcements to professional organization newsletters or H-Oralhist and other Internet listservs for historians and other disciplines whose researchers are likely to be interested in the subject. Consider writing a brief article, drawing from the interviews, for publication in a newsletter or local newspaper. Oral histories can be included in library catalogs. Archival projects also report their collections on the Research Libraries Information Network (RLIN) or the Online Catalog Library Center (OCLC). Some microfilm publishers also reproduce and distribute oral histories, with the permission of the oral history projects.

In addition to scholarly researchers, you should also make the interviews available to the community from which they came. The library or archive where the interviews are deposited may be willing to mount an exhibit based on them. Local newspapers and broadcasters may draw from the collected materials for articles, programs, and documentaries. Pamphlets and other publications can be planned to give the material a wider distribution. Documentaries, slide-tape productions, and radio and theatrical performance have all tapped into the abundant resources of oral history.

Should oral histories be posted on the Internet?

Given the democratic impulses of the oral history movement, it would be contradictory for oral historians not to avail themselves of the most universal and cost-effective means of mass communication and dissemination ever devised. As the Internet became widely available in the 1990s, scores of oral history projects from high schools to presidential libraries began posting excerpts and entire transcripts of interviews. Some sites included portions of the audio and videotape, along with photographs and other illustrations. Collections of interviews grouped around a similar subject can be linked for easier reference, and can be "hot linked" to related web sites. The Internet helps return oral histories to the community, and expands the boundaries of our definition of community. It is especially attractive for reaching students who prefer to browse the Net than to explore libraries, or who cannot afford to travel much distance to visit an archives. Interviews will usually record more "visitors" in a single month on the Internet than in all the years they sat on archive shelves combined.

Some oral historians have expressed reservations about putting interviews online, ranging from the need to protect interviewees' privacy to the danger of misuse and manipulation of sound recordings and transcripts, and the "unmonitored access" of the Internet, which would result in a loss of archival control over the interviews. They question whether deeds of gift that had not anticipated electronic reproduction and distribution would permit the posting of interviews on the Internet without the express permission of the interviewees or their next of kin. It is imperative that oral historians grapple with the ethical issue of the Internet and avoid exploitation of their interviewees. But the solution is not to avoid the Web, for fear of stepping into a minefield. On the contrary, those projects that do not avail themselves of the Internet run the risk of being ignored by the next generation of researchers.

Downloading an oral history is not the equivalent of publishing it. The Internet is a distributor rather than a publisher (Congress specifically defined it that way to protect it from libel suits), and oral history transcripts are raw data rather than books. In practice, the Internet has not proved conducive for reading book-length manuscripts but does best with screen-sized chunks of information. Online magazines generally feature short essays with eye-catching graphics. The ideal text for easy reading on a computer screen runs about the length of a newspaper column. Longer texts are available on line, including books from the Bible to *Moby Dick*. They are easy to scan by word and key phrase for ready reference, but awkward to read at length. The probability is that most interviews will attract researchers seeking to locate specific information rather than casual readers who will peruse the entire document.

Researchers who consult interview transcripts online will want the product to resemble as much as possible the original document, including the pagination. Although researchers can scan the text by word on the screen, they will need page numbers for their citations as well as to make use of the prepared indexes if they print out a copy of the entire interview. Oral historians themselves will use the Internet when doing research needed to prepare for their interviews, from genealogical data to newspaper articles, alumni news, and background material on organizations and communities with which interviewees were associated, and even maps and driving directions to their homes.

The World Wide Web will not replace oral history archives, which will continue to house the original records and preservation copies of tapes and transcripts. Instead, it can extend archives' user services from their immediate locations to the furthest reaches of the globe. It can make the next generation of researchers more aware of the panoramic scope of oral history already conducted, and more likely to use those interviews. Wider scrutiny could also lead to increased peer review of interviews, with greater attention to issues of evidence and content, and even more rigorous methodological standards.[29]

What needs to be taken into consideration before putting interviews on the Internet?

Projects should build the Internet into their operating plans, informing participants in advance and letting them know their options, drafting deeds of gift that specifically permit digital electronic reproduction of the interviews, and preparing transcripts in formats convenient for downloading. For established oral history archives the task of digitizing a large collection might appear so daunting as to paralyze. A reasonable strategy would be to start by making finding aids available on the Internet. That will alert researchers as to what exists where. As many interview transcripts are already available on microfilm or through interlibrary loan, researchers can obtain copies without traveling to distant collections. Projects can next turn to interviews already transcribed on disk, or scan older transcripts, and post a sample of their interviews to display the richness of their collection. Researchers will pay virtual visits to the collections, searching the finding aids, reading transcripts, listening to some of the recordings, and consulting with the archivists electronically.

Making oral history interviews available on the Internet can be labor-intensive and time-consuming, particularly when audio and visual materials are included in the presentation. They can often tap student help, but the turnover in staff requires regular training and close monitoring for quality control. Web sites may be planned as a group project, but experience strongly suggests that one person should have the final say over content and style. As web sites expand with content over time, to keep them manageable, it is advisable to stick to clear and consistent formats. Unlike a book, where users will generally start at the beginning and flip through to the desired section, web browsers may approach a site at any point, and therefore need to be informed where they are, and be provided with ready links to the project's home page. "Users want ease of access and use," notes Tamara Kennelly, university archivist at Virginia Tech. "They want to navigate easily around a site." Remember that flashy presentations may slow the downloading time for home users.[30]

Projects planning to use audio and video clips from interviews on their web sites should make clear to browsers their copyright status to prevent illicit reproduction and rebroadcast. Some have redesigned their deeds of gift to stipulate whether the interviewee wishes to be consulted before any commercial broadcast or electronic publication of the interview. By the same token, projects should take care in reproducing film or sound clips for which they do not hold copyright or permission from the holder. Even a nonprofit educational organization can be sued for copyright infringement. Libel and defamation are areas of concern on the Internet, just as in archives and publication. Interviewees, interviewers, and projects remain liable for spreading malicious untruths. Internet servers, by contrast, cannot be held responsible for the content of an interview. Congress has defined the Internet not as a publisher but as a distributor, the functional equivalent of a newsstand.[31]

It is imperative that oral historians grapple with the ethical issue of the Internet and avoid exploitation of their interviewees. Beyond revising their deeds of gift for current interviewing, projects should notify living interviewees before placing their interviews online (although it seems excessive to track down next of kin for permission, as their intentions may conflict with those of the interviewee). Give demonstrations to older interviewees who have never used the Internet or provide them with a printout of selections from their interview as it will appear. Oral historians need to honor the wishes of those who find the possibility of worldwide access to their interviews during their lifetimes either threatening or invasive of their privacy. But as most interviewees hope to leave something of themselves for posterity, where their memories might be published, exhibited, and otherwise not forgotten, they will generally be pleased to have their interviews widely accessible.

CHAPTER 3

Conducting
Interviews

What qualities make a good interviewer?

For Studs Terkel, the trick to interviewing successfully is "engaging in conversation, having a cup of coffee." His interviewing style is unobtrusive, straightforward and sympathetic, but challenging when necessary. One interviewee described him as easygoing: "He doesn't ask particularly *probing* questions, and yet he's able to get people to open up and tell these marvelous little stories about themselves. He's a good listener." Similarly, Bob Edwards, who conducts hundreds of interviews annually for National Public Radio's *Morning Edition*, describes himself as "a relaxed, easygoing guy, and I hope people are relaxed with me. They're more forthcoming if they're comfortable." All interviewers need to put their interviewees at ease, to listen carefully to what they have to say, to respect their opinions, and to encourage candid responses. Listening skills do not come automatically, and interviewers have to work hard to achieve these results.[1]

Interviews are partly performance. Not only do interviewers want to handle themselves well, but interviewees often feel nervous about their ability to recall and describe events long past; they also want to do well. No one wants to sound forgetful or inarticulate. Interviewers should become a partner in the process, helping interviewees become as forthcoming and accurate as possible. Interviewers need to guide without leading, providing names, dates, and other information to keep the dialogue moving. A critical task is to move interviewees beyond reluctance to an honest and perhaps self-critical evaluation of the past.[2]

Fundamental rules and principles apply to all types of oral history interviewing: do your homework; be prepared; construct meaningful but open-ended questions; do not interrupt responses; follow up on what you have heard; know your equipment thoroughly; promptly process your recordings; and always keep in mind the practice and ethics of interviewing.

PREPARATION FOR THE INTERVIEW

How should an interviewer get ready for an interview?

Familiarize yourself with whatever information is available about the general subject matter and about the people to be interviewed, their families, communities, jobs, successes, and failures. Interviewers first get acquainted with the outline of interviewees' lives and then allow them to fill in the details. Read any published sources, such as family histories, histories of the town or institution, and histories of the events that the individual experienced, to understand and formulate questions.

Back issues of newspapers and magazines, published and unpublished genealogies, and other sources likely to be found in the local history section of a library or on Internet web sites are natural beginnings for your research. Some interviewees have deposited their papers in a library, although most still have their papers, scrapbooks, and other memorabilia in their closets, attics, and basements. Ask them to make these records available prior to the interview. Others bring relevant memoranda, letters, and photographs to the interview. When all else fails, ask interviewees to give brief descriptions of themselves and to suggest what other sources you might consult.

An especially helpful way to begin your preparations is to read or listen to other oral histories. Investigate other interviews from your project or the recordings and transcripts deposited in a library. Techniques vary, even from interview to interview, depending on the interviewer's expertise and the interviewee's cooperation and loquaciousness. Analyzing different types of questions, and ways of asking them, will help you construct your own questioning style. During the 1970s, Former Members of Congress, Inc. interviewed more than 100 former senators and representatives and gave the tapes and transcripts to the Library of Congress. A number of interviewers participated, and their transcripts reveal a variety of styles and approaches: historians asked questions that fit a mostly biographical framework; political scientists asked organizational questions about seniority, staff, committee assignments, leadership, and other aspects of congressional group behavior.[3]

When preparing a budget, count on doing as many as ten hours of research for every hour of interview conducted. Usually, only the initial interview sessions will require so much advance research. Subsequent interviews will build on the original research and require less preparation time. The cost of preparation decreases when several interviews can be conducted from a single investment in prior research.

Is so much research really necessary?

Yes. It is the only way to determine what questions to ask. The more an interviewer knows about the individual and the subject matter, the easier it is to
build rapport and conduct the interview. Interviewees become impatient with
interviewers whose questions show they do not know the subject matter.

Research also helps an interviewer supply information that the interviewee has
forgotten. As they backtrack through their lives, few people remember names
and dates accurately. An interview can come to a standstill while the interviewee gropes for a forgotten name ("that tall man, you know, what's his name, the
economist, who smoked a pipe"). If the interviewer can provide the name ("Do
you mean John Kenneth Galbraith?"), the interviewee, with great relief, will
continue as if uninterrupted. If you do not know it, promise to look up the name
later to fill in the transcript. Many interviewees, especially older people, lack confidence in their own memories and tensely view an interview as a test.
Interviewers should try to put them at ease. Dates are also significant, since
people will often jumble the chronology or merge events that took place at different times. By interjecting, "Didn't that happen in 1960 rather than 1970?" the
interviewer can help the interviewee get back on track.

Interviewers need to be sufficiently prepared to know both what to expect and
what not to expect from an interview. If interviewees make claims that conflict
with other accounts, encourage them to explain further. Interviewees may bring
up some entirely new matter that was not part of the original research. Explore
this new topic by saying, "I didn't know about that. Can you tell me more about
it?" Although interviewers work hard to prepare questions in advance, they must
be willing to deviate from them sometimes to follow the interviewee's detours,
which may provide valuable information.

How many questions should be prepared for each interview?

It is safer to have too many questions than too few. Some interviewees talk at
great length in response to a single question. During a soliloquy, they may anticipate several questions on the interviewer's list and discuss these issues without
being prompted. Others answer briefly and need several follow-up questions to
draw them out. Whenever Senate Majority Leader Mike Mansfield appeared on
"Meet the Press," the program's interviewers prepared twice as many questions
as for other guests because the senator habitually abbreviated his responses to
"Yep" and "Nope." If an interviewer has prepared more questions than time permits, another interview session would be in order.

Avoid asking the type of question that elicits a brief answer, such as: "You grew
up in Grand Rapids?" "Yes." "And you went to public school there?" "Yes, I did."

Instead of simply verifying your research notes, ask: "What was Grand Rapids like when you were growing up there?" and, "Tell me about the schools you attended." Transcripts that show a string of single-sentence answers indicate poor interviewing techniques. Oral historians seek broader, longer, and more interpretive answers.

Do not ask more than one question at a time; most interviewees would address only one of them. Either the interviewer has to repeat the other half of the question later or it is simply forgotten in the flow of the narrative.

How many times should one person be interviewed?

Single-session oral histories are like "audio snapshots." Depending on the objectives and budget of your project, try to conduct more than one interview with each person. It often takes more than one interview just to break the ice. Repeated visits help establish an intimacy that encourages candidness. Both interviewer and interviewee need some time together to develop the rapport necessary to ask difficult questions and to give honest answers. One interviewee began his fourth interview session by saying, "Up till now I've been giving it to you sugar-coated," and went on to discuss his most disagreeable professional relations. It took the first three interviews to gain his confidence before he lowered his guard.

Interviewees do not necessarily hold things back deliberately; it takes time for anyone to remember all the relevant details. Most minds do not work in a precise and orderly manner, and most of us cannot call forth recollections in perfect chronological order, grouped together logically. An interviewee may talk at length about President Harry Truman's administration and seem to have completely exhausted the subject, until a later session when a question about John F. Kennedy elicits the response, "Kennedy handled that differently than Truman." The interviewee then recounts an aspect of the Truman years that had not come to mind earlier.

Some interviewees just do not have much to say. They may suffer from "mike fright" and become tense. They may not have been very perceptive. Their memories may be clouded. One interviewee in a nursing home drifted off to sleep twice during his interview, awakening each time the interviewer began to pack up the equipment and continuing the interview as if uninterrupted. There was no second session. Other interviewees will surprise you with their volubility, the depth of their recall, and their articulateness. In these cases, it is best to return for several sessions until the interviewer feels they have exhausted the subject matter.

But beware of the lonely interviewee who seeks to prolong interview sessions unnecessarily. Some interviewees have few visitors or are not taken very seriously by their families, and they revel in an audience. Take care to be sensitive to the needs of older interviewees, but remember that you are not a psychiatrist offering free and unlimited therapy sessions.

How long should an average interview last?

Unless you are traveling and have a tight schedule that requires lengthier, even full-day sessions, plan each interview session for no longer than two hours. Longer sessions often have a "narcotic" effect on the interviewee, who can become fatigued and distracted. The interviewer will also have trouble listening to what is being said. If prolonged sessions are necessary, arrange for several short breaks to give both parties a rest.[4]

SETTING UP THE INTERVIEW

Who should be interviewed first?

Logically, you should start with the oldest and the most significant players in the events or community that you are pursuing. For any number of reasons, some people develop more influence, respect, and standing with an organization, profession, or community. A significant player may have been the one who held a critical post, had a warm and caring personality, or served as the institution's unofficial historian and record-keeper. If interviewed early in the process, they can help identify and locate other potential interviewees and help persuade them to be interviewed. Called the "gatekeepers" by oral historians, their assistance is often indispensable. The gatekeeper may have been a longtime employee who still communicates with former colleagues, or a surviving spouse, other relative, or close friend of a key figure in the events. Others often wait until the gatekeeper has sanctioned the interviews. While trying to interview Benjamin V. Cohen and Thomas G. Corcoran, the "Gold Dust Twins" who shaped much New Deal legislation, I received no response to my letters and phone calls to Corcoran. But the day after I interviewed Cohen, Corcoran's secretary scheduled an appointment, indicating that I had passed inspection.

Always keep actuarial realities in mind. Planning an oral history project can be so time-consuming that when a project is ready to begin interviewing the best prospective interviewees may either have died or become too ill to give a useful interview. Potential interviewees should be grouped according to age, significance to the theme of the project, and availability in terms of time and location. Save for a later stage of the project those who are younger, more peripheral, and further away. Travel constraints, however, frequently require that interviewees living in a particular location be bunched together. Remember also the practical journalism advice of starting with those "who are most likely to cooperate." Less cooperative subjects require repeated invitations and patient persistence. In the end, they may agree to be interviewed only to keep others whom they opposed, distrusted, or held in contempt from monopolizing the historical record.[5]

How do you locate potential interviewees?

The oral historian has to play detective. Word-of-mouth referrals will unearth many potential interviewees, but quite often oral historians have to hunt for their subjects. If interviewing for a biography, the interviewer who has read the subject's papers will know which people corresponded with the subject and may have their return addresses on their correspondence. Online phone directories can help locate interviewees. When searching the Internet for information on specific people, start by checking their names in a general Web search engine. Government agencies place a wide variety of public records databases on the Internet regarding licensed occupations, from doctors to contractors. Databases like the Martindale-Hubbel Lawyer Locator provide information on attorneys, while Dunn & Bradstreet identifies business leaders.[6]

Certain individuals within a family, or an organization make a point of keeping in contact with other family members, neighbors, and colleagues and can provide current addresses and telephone numbers. Associations and corporations publish newsletters that reach current and retired employees and can carry stories and advertisements about an oral history project. Newspaper advertisements may also locate potential interviewees, but indiscriminate calls for volunteers may inundate the interviewer with an unmanageable number of willing interviewees and not necessarily identify those who can make the most valuable contributions.[7]

What's the best way to initiate contact with an interviewee?

By letter or phone call, state the purpose of the interview and the nature of the project. Explain what will happen to the recordings and transcripts, and describe the legal release the interviewee will be asked to sign. Follow up any phone conversation with a letter to establish a record for your own files. It is especially important for older interviewees to have your name, address, phone number, the purposes of the interview and the scheduled date, in writing.

Sometimes the interviewer plans a preliminary meeting, perhaps over lunch, to get acquainted with the interviewee and to get a better idea of the major subjects that will be discussed during the actual interviews. Being able to have preliminary meetings clearly depends on the time available, for both the interviewer and interviewee, and the project's budget. In some projects, pre-interview sessions are discouraged to avoid losing the spontaneity and candidness of unrehearsed questioning. The television interviewer Brian Lamb complains of having "ruined" some of his interviews by asking questions before the cameras were turned on, since a question asked the second time rarely elicits as fully satisfying a response as it did the first time.

Schedule the interview at the interviewee's convenience, and make sure you arrive on time. With more prominent interviewees, scheduling can pose problems, especially if the interviewer must travel any distance to the interview. Reiterate to the interviewee the purpose of the project, and be sure to mention the difficulty and expense in arranging it. When planning to go to the interviewee's home or office, ask directions on how to get there. Nothing starts an interview more disagreeably than for an interviewer to arrive late and tense after a frantic search for the right address. Interviewers are guests and should act accordingly. Interviews can easily go awry if the interviewer arrives late, smokes, chews gum, dresses inappropriately, or otherwise offends the interviewee's sensibilities.

CONDUCTING THE INTERVIEW

Where should you position the recorder?

Place the recorder where the interviewer can easily see it and periodically check its functioning, but where it is out of the interviewee's direct line of vision, to keep it from becoming a distraction. Equipment sometimes makes people nervous, but after a few minutes most will begin to ignore the recorder if it is not right in front of them. The microphone should be situated near the interviewee, preferably pinned on as a lavalier microphone. Electrical outlets, or their absence, may also determine the position of the recorder. Either use rechargeable battery packs or bring batteries in case there are no convenient outlets or the original batteries wear down. Recorders should never be completely concealed, however, since hidden recording is antithetical to the trust and confidence on which oral history depends. Surreptitious recording is unethical, and in most states illegal.

Become familiar with your equipment, both the recorder and the microphones. Failure to test equipment may cause the entire interview to be lost or so poorly recorded that it is difficult to transcribe. Every interviewer should try transcribing an interview at least once to grasp the critical necessity of good sound quality.

Most interviewers try to set up their equipment in a quiet place where the interview will not be interrupted by children, inquiring spouses, secretaries, ringing phones, open windows, street traffic, air conditioners, loud clocks, and the like. Interviewees will want to be good hosts, but clinking coffee cups and plates, ice twirling in drinks, and other extraneous noises will all be picked up on the recording. The interviewee may be unperturbed by this everyday commotion, but it will distract the interviewer and make the recording more difficult to use for transcribing, editing, and research purposes.

By contrast, folklorists, linguists, and anthropologists will often try to capture the "sound environment" of the interview, including ambient sounds, from church bells to ocean waves. Some noises are undesirable for any purposes. An interviewer once recorded at a table under a bird cage, not noticing the sound until he played back the tape and found that "noises of the parakeet scratching in his cage all but drowned out the interviewee."[8]

What if the recording ends while the interviewee is still speaking?

Keep an eye on the recorder. Some tape recorders have signal lights that flash when the tape is about to run out. As the tape comes close to the end, take advantage of the interviewee's next pause and ask to stop while you change the tape. Always keep a new tape nearby, and remember that there is no third side to a tape! When turning the tape over, let it run a few seconds, long enough to get past the "leader." With a tape recorder, ninety minutes is the longest tape that is safe to use for oral history recording. Mini-disks allow for 148 minutes of recording time in mono, half that time in stereo.

Make a mental note of the subject that was being discussed at the time the recording stopped. Interviewees sometimes have trouble picking up the thread, even after just a short pause, and will need some prompting from the interviewer: "You were saying that. . ."

Should questions be arranged chronologically or topically?

The scheme of interviewing depends on the goals of the project. For some projects the entire life story of the interviewee will be relevant; for other projects, the focus will be on the events in which the interviewee participated. For instance, Andrew Young might be interviewed for his entire life, for his tenure as United Nations ambassador, or for his role in the civil rights movement. Biographical interviews usually proceed chronologically. If the focus of a project is on an event, then the questions will be more topical.

Jumping right into the main question is not the best approach. Avoid making the first question too abrupt and confrontational; instead, build up to the climactic questions by establishing the historical setting and making the interviewee more comfortable with the process. People tend to recall things chronologically. Set the stage with general questions and then follow with more specific, pointed questions. Strictly topical questions may elicit responses that lack depth and context. Topical questions, however, can follow quite appropriately within a chronological framework.

Are open-ended questions preferable to specific questions?

Ideally, interviewers should mix the two types of question. Your first questions should be open-ended, such as "Please tell me about your childhood." Specific questions can follow: "What schools did you attend?" Starting with too specific a question gives the interviewer too much control of the interview. Interviewers should let interviewees explain what they think is most significant before beginning to narrow the questions. "The best oral history is a quasi-monologue on the part of the interviewee," the oral historian Sherna Gluck has observed, "which is encouraged by approving nods, appreciative smiles, and enraptured listening and stimulated by understanding comments and intelligent questions."[9]

Use open-ended questions to allow interviewees to volunteer their own accounts, to speculate on matters, and to have enough time to include all of the material they think relevant to the subject. Use more specific questions to elicit factual information, often in response to something the interviewee has mentioned while answering an open-ended question. Political reporters and courtroom attorneys use this type of mixed questioning in an approach that has been called "funnel interviewing." Their search begins with general questions and then constantly narrows until the subject has difficulty not answering the final, more specific questions. Oral history is a much less adversarial means of interviewing, but the funnel approach remains useful when the subject is controversial.[10]

In framing an open-ended question, the oral historian Charles Morrissey postulates that the two-sentence format often works best. The first sentence should state the problem; the second poses the question: "The records show you were a leader in establishing the zoning laws that shaped this town. Why were zoning laws your objectives?" There are a number of possible follow-up questions: "How did these laws specifically affect your neighborhood?" "What complaints were raised about these laws?" "How effective would you judge these laws to have been?" "Looking back from today, what would you have done differently?" Questions also might relate to specific zoning incidents drawn from newspaper clippings. For such a topic, a map might serve as a good visual prompter during the interview and as appendix material for the transcript.[11]

Keep in mind that interviewers are not restricted to just asking questions. Statements of fact, concise restatements of what the interviewee has said, brief observations and comments can also stimulate responses from the interviewee as well as inject more spontaneity into the discussion. Mixing occasional comments among the questions provides some relief and can prevent the interview from sounding too much like a cross-examination. But interviewers should always use such injections in moderation to avoid skewing the contents of the interview with their own opinions.

The use of open-ended questions has also been cited as a means of "empowering" interviewees, that is, by encouraging interviewees to relate and to interpret their own stories, such questions shift the balance of power from the interviewer to the interviewee. Those who talk of empowerment view the interviewee as an "informant" and the interviewer as a "reporter." The interviewer may be asking the questions, but the interviewee is actively shaping the course of the interview rather than responding passively. These notions have raised the consciousness especially of those sociologists, anthropologists, and linguists who generally do not identify or create fictional identities for their oral sources, and of interviewers who work outside their own cultures and struggle not to impose their cultural assumptions on the people they observe and interview.[12]

Can the framing of a question distort the answer?

Pollsters say that if you can tell from what position a question is being asked, then the question is loaded. "Do you support a balanced budget amendment to end waste and fraud in the government?" is loaded. "Do you support a balanced budget amendment?" is neutral. Journalists will often ask leading and manipulative questions; the preface "Wouldn't you say . . . ." is designed to produce a response that fits a particular hypothesis. Many politicians have regretted letting a reporter put words into their mouths with such questions. Researchers working on a specific book or article similarly ask questions to fill holes in their evidence, usually having in mind the answer that they *hope* to hear. The danger of this approach is that interviewees want to please and will pick up the clues, from the type of question asked to the tone of voice used, as to what type of an answer they think the interviewer wants to hear. The result is the opposite of the way an oral history should proceed.[13]

Start with broad, open-ended questions, allow the interviewee to talk broadly, ranging as far and wide as possible. Listen and make notes as the interviewee speaks, but do not interrupt. When it is clear that the person has exhausted the subject and stopped, go back and ask specific follow-up questions, clarify points of confusion or contradiction, and pursue details.

What if the answers are perfunctory?

Short answers may be a sign that an interviewer is asking too many specific questions and not enough open-ended "how" and "why" questions. Interviewees are not always sure of how much detail interviewers want. They may give answers that are to the point, but are short, unrevealing, and unreflective. Never be satisfied with brief answers and follow up with more detailed questions to draw the interviewee out.

Short answers may also indicate that the interviewer has been too quick to jump in with the next question. It requires some discipline to remain silent after asking a question, and to remain so until absolutely certain that the interviewee has finished answering. Try not to speak immediately after the interviewee stops, since it may just be a pause for a breath of air or for gathering additional thoughts. Silence indicates that an interviewer expects more. Ten seconds can seem excruciatingly long if neither party is speaking, but can encourage the interviewee to give a more detailed response.[14]

Sometimes answers are perfunctory simply because the interviewer has not engaged the interviewee's interest. Try varying the types of questions and the subjects they cover. Studs Terkel has described his interview with the ninety-year-old philosopher Bertrand Russell. Allotted only half an hour, Terkel knew he would be escorted out promptly when his time was up. His first theoretical question elicited only a short reply. He switched to more provocative questions and noted that as Russell became engaged, his answers grew longer. With time running out, Terkel sought "the home run question." "Lord Russell," he asked, "what is the world you envision?" Russell's response summarized his hopes and frustrations, ending with a touch of weariness. Although he might have ended there, Terkel tried for "a parting shot." "You liked Shelley when you were young, in your formative years," he said. "Do you still feel the same way?" That charming, personal question showed that the interviewer knew his subject, and had come well prepared (although it might have been more effective if he had asked it earlier in the interview). The interview succeeded because the fully engaged interviewer was constantly evaluating his interviewee's responses and changed gears to provoke more stimulating responses. Terkel reminds us that every interviewer ought to be looking for the "home run question."[15]

How should you deal with an uncooperative interviewee?

Former Secretary of State Edmund Muskie once greeted an interviewer by pointing out that he had given his papers to an archives so that historians would not bother him. Anyone who expected him to remember and comment on events that happened years ago "must live in the realm of the ridiculous." The interviewer was well aware of his subject's reputed temperament, and had come prepared with a plan. He knew Muskie retained a strong attachment to his home state of Maine, and although the interview dealt with foreign policy, the interviewer asked about the foreign policy concerns of people in this town or that. The questions appealed to the secretary's interests, and he began to speak at length, continuing well beyond the mandated time for the interview.[16]

For many personal reasons, ranging from their state of health to their unhappiness over the way their lives and careers developed, some people will be uncooperative witnesses. Perhaps they disliked or resented the individual whom the interviewer is researching. They may not like "dredging up the past." By preparing as thoroughly as possible for an interview in advance, interviewers should be able to anticipate some of the causes of such behavior and to develop strategies for dealing with them. If one line of questioning elicits bitterness, shift to another approach. Seek areas that the interviewee enjoys talking about before raising the disagreeable questions. Be prepared to justify the need to "stir up those old ashes" after so many years and to explain why scholars are seeking answers to these questions.

Some interviewees will answer evasively. They may be testing the interviewer's knowledge. If the interviewer allows them to respond incompletely or evasively, they will continue to do so. Following up with more specific questions on the same subject, thereby indicating that the answers were insufficient, may elicit more complete or informative responses. If this tack does not work, then clearly and respectfully point out that the interviewee seems to be less than forthcoming. Perhaps the interviewee will make some explanation or finally give a fuller response. If not, the interview should be ended.

How personal should an interviewer get?

The degree to which an interview explores personal matters is something that each interviewer and interviewee will have to work out between themselves. Like the media, historians increasingly want to know about the personal and private side of public figures. The feminist notion that "the personal is political" has also contributed to the merging of the public and personal spheres in historical analysis. Whether individual interviewees will answer personal questions is another matter.

Different people have different concepts of what is personal. When Ronald Steel was interviewing Walter Lippmann for his biography, Lippmann volunteered to cooperate fully, so long as Steel did not ask anything personal. Steel soon learned that Lippmann defined the word quite broadly. Once when Steel asked him what his father had done for a living, Lippmann stared at him silently and then replied,

"I wouldn't want you to make a novel out of this." (Lippmann was not proud that his family's fortune rested on rents from tenement houses.)[17] In fact, Lippmann's lawyer, Louis Auchincloss, did turn a major turning point of Lippmann's private life into a novel, *The House of the Prophet* (1980) in which the protagonist complains: "Biography is a whole new ball game. It is possible now, even in the lifetimes of our very greatest men, to persuade their friends and acquaintances to record on tape their most intimate impressions of these individuals. All you have to do is wave in their faces the sacred banner of history."[18]

The painfulness of recounting highly personal experiences can make an interview uncomfortable for both interviewer and interviewee. Elizabeth Norman, who interviewed American nurses trapped on Bataan by the Japanese during World War II, found it troublesome when the women cried. "I didn't think you could cry over memories that were fifty-five years old," she commented. "That was very difficult for me to watch, because of their sense of loss and they lost a lot in the war. They lost their youth, many, many friends, their physical health, in some cases their emotional health, and they would cry about it. As a human being, that was hard to watch." Interviewers need to measure the level of discomfort they are likely to cause against the relevance of the subject matter and the importance of preserving the story, treat interviewees with dignity and compassion, and pause sufficiently while interviewees regain their composure.[19]

How should you bring up subjects that may be embarrassing?

Having gone to great lengths to put interviewees at ease and to establish rapport, it is often hard to confront them with embarrassing questions. The sociologist John Gwaltney, author of *Drylongso* (1993), an oral history of Newark's inner-city blacks, once chided members of the Oral History Association for being too polite and discreet to "ask the embarrassing question." He argued that with some gentle and persistent prodding, interviewees will talk about difficult subjects. Playing tapes to demonstrate his point, Gwaltney showed that his questions were humorous and playful, but unrelenting. Being blind, Gwaltney also had the advantage of his interviewees wanting him to understand them; they would go on at great length and punctuate their responses with, "Don't you see?"

One way for interviewers to bring up difficult or embarrassing issues is to quote someone else. During the Gerald Ford and Jimmy Carter administrations, the National Archives maintained an office near the White House where they interviewed officials as they left the administration, many of them involuntarily and under some cloud. The interviewees were often agitated and unnerved over their experience and not happy to talk about it. Conducting preliminary interviews for the Ford and Carter presidential libraries, the Archives interviewer had to ask some embarrassing questions but tried to connect them with published sources: "The *Washington Post* reported that you left office because of such and such. Was this a fair assessment?" Since the matter was part of the public record, and the interviewees were being asked to give their own side of the story, they invariably offered their own defense. Having made the focus the newspaper versus the interviewee (rather than the interviewer versus the interviewee), the interviewer needed to be sure to follow up with questions about the subject's self-defense, its inconsistencies, and its contradictions with other accounts.

That was the approach that New York journalist William Inglis used when he interviewed the notoriously secretive oil magnate, John D. Rockefeller, Sr., while preparing an authorized biography. The elderly Rockefeller had agreed to be interviewed only to please his son, who desperately wanted to rescue the family name from the images drawn by the muckrakers. Between 1917 and 1920 Inglis conducted a string of interviews that produced 1,700 pages of transcripts. Although the planned book was never published, decades later another biographer, Ron Chernow, came across the interviews at the Rockefeller Archives. Struck by their extraordinary insights, he made them the core of his own book. As Chernow explained, "Inglis would read passages from Rockefeller's two chief antagonists, Henry Lloyd and Ida Tarbell ... and Rockefeller would refute them, paragraph by paragraph." For years, Rockefeller had refused to read what his critics had written about him, but given the opportunity to confront the most embarrassing and questionable aspects of his rise to power in the petroleum industry he admitted, "now that I've gotten into it I find it interesting."[20]

When confronted with difficult or embarrassing subjects, the interviewee's first response may be brief, defensive, inconclusive. The interviewer should return to the topic later in the interview. The more the interviewee attempts to explain, offers more details, and strains to make the interviewer understand, the more candid and less canned the responses will become. This approach takes time; once again, multiple interview sessions are important.

Some interviewees will stipulate before an interview that there are certain subjects that they will not discuss. Although it is possible to allude to such topics during the course of the interview, the interviewees may break their own rules and venture into the forbidden topic themselves. Ultimately oral historians must accede to an interviewee's request. It is legitimate, however, to note the interviewee's demand in the files for that interview, thereby explaining to future users why certain subjects were not addressed.

Potentially confrontational topics should be deferred until later in the interview, after the interviewer has established some rapport. While working on a history of an abortive plan to use nuclear weapons to dredge a harbor in Alaska, an oral historian arranged to interview the crusty nuclear physicist Edward Teller. Time was limited, and Teller arrived late. Rather than ask his "warm up" questions, the interviewer decided to jump right in with an opening question about the most controversial part of Teller's involvement with the project. "This interview is over," snapped Teller as he got up and left.

To appear interested and sympathetic, an interviewer does not have to act obsequiously. If a point of disagreement is reached with an interviewee, one solution is to try to restate the interviewee's point of view. The interviewee will usually respond by further defining the position, and the dialogue is thus extended rather than terminated. Finally, keep in mind Oscar Wilde's observation that "questions are never indiscreet. Answers sometimes are."[21]

What if the interviewee asks that the recorder be turned off?

An oral history is not a journalistic interview, so there is little to be gained by hearing a story "off the record." Politely but firmly, interviewers should decline to interrupt the interview. Explain that the recording can remain closed until the interviewee is ready to release it, and that the transcripts can be edited. At times, however, interviewees may want to stop the recording to explain their hesitancy about answering a question or to ask the interviewer's advice about the propriety of discussing a person or issue. Interviewers can halt the recording to hear their problems, counsel them, and offer some reassurance before resuming the interview.

How can interviewers get beyond stories that have been "rehearsed" through frequent retelling?

Oral historians are frequently encouraged to interview the favorite storyteller and unofficial local historian. These individuals often have wonderful stories that may have folklore value, and they will tell their stories regardless of how relevant they are to the interviewer's questions. To a lesser degree, everyone tells stories about past experiences, to relive glory days, celebrate shared experiences, or make comparisons with the present. Each telling of the story embeds it firmer in the mind. Columbia has an interview with Ferdinand Pecora about the highly publicized investigation he conducted during the 1930s of Wall Street banking and stock market malpractice. Although he gave the interview forty years after the investigation, his memory was remarkable for its detail and precision. But Pecora's family pointed out that he had been telling these stories for years, and even after the interview was still telling them on his deathbed to the hospital nurses.[22]

Although important for memory retention, rehearsal can create stumbling blocks for interviewers. Every telling of a story embellishes it, thereby moving it further away from reality. Events are telescoped, chronology tightened, order rearranged and edited, drama or humor heightened. Rehearsed stories tend to omit negative events and concentrate on triumphs. Interviewees have not necessarily forgotten old wounds and mistakes. When questioned, they can recall past defeats, even if they do not always feel comfortable talking about them. By the time the oral historian asks the question, the answer may simply be the oft-told story.

The best defense against a well-rehearsed story is a well-prepared interviewer who can spot inaccuracies and gently challenge inconsistencies. But interviewees may have told their stories so often that they cannot remember it any other way. Some interviewees prime themselves for the interview, and others have stories that they will tell anyone under any circumstances. If the interviewer tries to cut them off, they may become confused or, more likely, will simply wait for another occasion to insert the stories in the dialogue. Since these stories have special meaning for the interviewee, it is usually worth giving them the time to tell their set speeches (you will probably find it impossible to stop them). After the supply is exhausted, try to ask questions that will lead down less familiar paths.[23]

Rehearsing a story, through its retelling over the years, also serves as a form of self-interpretation. People not only remember their past but try to make sense out of it, rationalizing it so they can live with it. An interview with a divorced couple will probably elicit two very different versions of the marriage and why it ended. Defeated politicians have similarly reconstructed their pasts. Interviewers need to ask these interviewees to stop and think about what they have said.

Not all stories have been rehearsed mentally or anecdotally. Questions may cause interviewees to recall events long buried in their memories. They often express amazement at their recall of seemingly forgotten memories, then recount them in explicit detail and at surprising length.

How can an interviewer assist an interviewee's ability to recall?

An interviewee once commented that he felt as if his memory was on trial. Recognizing that most people do not readily remember names and dates, interviewers attempt to become familiar with the major players in the interviewee's life and with its basic chronology, not only to keep the interviews moving but to put the interviewee's mind at ease. Oral historians have similarly explored the use of photographs and familiar artifacts to trigger recall. Family photo albums, newspaper clippings, and letters have all served as tools for unearthing otherwise forgotten information. Some interviewers have even experimented with the sense of smell, to see what memories different smells elicit.[24]

Looking through family photographs not only prompts commentary from the interviewee but can provide illustrations for the interviewer's publications. The historian Pete Daniel traveled down the Mississippi River to interview people in the towns along the way, recording their recollections of the great flood of 1927 fifty years after the event. The photograph albums that many interviewees brought out helped sharpen their memories and provided stunning illustrations for his book, *Deep'n as It Come* (1977). By contrast, Andrea Hammer began her research with a set of the New Deal's Farm Security Agency photographs taken in southern Maryland between 1935 and 1943. Decades later, Hammer located many of the subjects who still lived in that region and who could talk about the people and places in the photos. Her object was to reconstruct the social context of the photographs, an exercise that demonstrated again that photographs can be misleading, and misinterpreted, without help from those who were there.[25]

Interviewees who demur in advance that they remember very little can often be put at ease with questions about normal routines of everyday life in the past, in their households or at work. "See, there was a lot more that you remembered," an interviewer for the Center for Oral History at the University of Hawaii commented to Lucy Robello after her interview about life as a plantation homemaker. "Well, you asked me for it, so I had to talk about," said Robello. "Otherwise I don't think that was important at all. . . . It was just normal living." Capturing on tape a way of life that no longer existed was precisely what the project wanted, and information that the interviewee could easily provide, once she gleaned the interviewer's objectives.[26]

Do differences in race, gender, or age between interviewers and interviewees make any difference in the interview?

Interviewees take the measure of interviewers, make assumptions about what they want to ask, and to some degree try to please them by telling what they want to hear. A study of the Federal Writers Project interviews with former slaves, conducted in the 1930s, discovered that an elderly black woman was interviewed twice, once by a white woman and again by a black man. She gave starkly different accounts of her memories of slavery, painting a relatively benign account for the white woman and a much harsher account for the black man. She may well have spoken even more differently to another black woman.[27]

Differences in age, race, gender, and ethnicity may influence both the questions asked and the responses elicited. There are no set prescriptions to overcome such differences. Some may want to match interviewers closely with interviewees, but men and women of different races and ethnicity should be able to interview each other. In seeking to make interviewees feel comfortable, interviewers might reveal a little of themselves—where they live, where they went to school, where they work, what their families do—to establish points of commonality that might cut across some of the barriers between them.

Even without any common reference, the interviewer can compensate by having thoroughly researched the subject and being familiar with names, dates, and events long past. A well-prepared interviewer becomes, for the duration of the interview, the contemporary of the interviewee. "Oh, do you know about him?" the interviewee will say. Or "I haven't thought about that in years." During the interview, older people seem younger and more animated as they relive the past with a sympathetic listener. The Oral History Associations's *Principles and Standards* encourages interviewers to

> work to achieve a balance between the objectives of the project and the perspectives of the interviewees. They should be sensitive to the diversity of social and cultural experiences, and to the implications of race, gender, class, ethnicity, age, religion, and sexual orientation. They should encourage interviewees to respond in their own style and language, and to address issues that reflect their concerns. Interviewers should fully explore all appropriate areas of inquiry with the interviewee and not be satisfied with superficial responses.[28]

Are there any differences in interviewing the famous and interviewing average individuals?

The difference lies largely in the interviewee's previous experience of being interviewed by the media. The average person has not been interviewed and may initially feel intimidated by the recorder and microphone. For the more prominent interviewee, the interviewer's problem will be to draw a distinction between an oral history and a newspaper interview. Interviewees must recognize that what they say will not appear on the front page of tomorrow's newspaper or on the evening news, a revelation that may actually disappoint some of them but that for the most part enables them to speak candidly. They can leave a complete record, but keep it confidential so that it will not damage their careers.

Professional people can also prove difficult to interview. Lawyers, for instance, have been trained not to volunteer information. Even worse are law professors, who seem to be judging questions to see how much the interviewer already knows. If prepared and able to ask probing follow-up questions, interviewers can earn their respect and perhaps a little more of their cooperation. Business executives may need some coaxing to think of the interview as something other than a promotional device. Most professional people and all politicians have been interviewed before as part of their jobs. They are used to responding to questions, and they have developed certain patterns of response. As a result, their answers may be superficial and packaged, and it can be hard to break through their veneer. Some oral histories with politicians sound more like radio scripts than candid interviews.

During the Vietnam War, National Security Advisor Henry Kissinger complained to reporters that "interviewing GIs is the worst way to find out what's going on. . . . The people in the middle of it have the least idea of what is happening." But historians later concluded that the GIs gave the press more accurate accounts of what was happening than did Dr. Kissinger.[29] When interviewing in an organization or among those who participated in a common event, it is just as important to interview the "little fish" as the "big fish." Those on the middle or lower tiers of any hierarchy usually have more time to do interviews, a broader perspective on events, and less ego invested in the operation. Those at the top may be too preoccupied and perhaps too self-centered to provide much new information. If they are still in power, those at the top are often more cautious in responding and may give little more than a press release. Interviewing at the periphery provides information that makes it easier to interview those at the center. Conversely, interviewing the top people early in the project reassures anxious subordinates that management sanctions the project. Interviewers have to take advantage of whatever scheduling opportunities they encounter and develop their own tactics in determining which individuals in any group to interview, how many, and in what order.[30]

Should interviewers use a questionnaire?

When dealing with a group that has a common identity or was involved in a common event or organization, be sure to ask the same core questions to everyone. Especially if different interviewers are working for the same project, you should agree on a common list of themes and certain questions for all to ask. But individual interviewees have their own unique experiences that no questionnaire can anticipate. You must be willing to deviate from the prepared questions whenever something unexpected and interesting develops. Oral history, after all, addresses neglected areas of knowledge. The best items uncovered are often subjects that you were not prepared to ask questions about and perhaps had read nothing about in your research. A good interviewer hears an unexpected statement and follows up with additional questions.

Oral historians deal with individual memory and perception, which are hard to squeeze into a structured format. By contrast, behaviorists have generally preferred to collect data that could be coded and quantified. They dismissed oral history interviews for not being as objective (or true) as questionnaire-based interviewing. But in recent years, many of the social sciences have been rethinking the concept of an objective reality and have confronted the subjective (or biased) nature of all sources of information. Psychologists, sociologists, and other social scientists have reexamined the forms and motivations of verbal expression. As they have embraced their subjectivity, they moved closer to oral history methodology, putting aside their quantitative questionnaires in favor of more qualitative interviewing.

Psychological interviews traditionally required the interviewer to maintain an observational posture that discouraged personal interactions, in order to collect impartial empirical data. Breaking with this pattern, some psychologists have adopted a more interactive manner to stimulate more communication and provide more depth to their interviews. For a project on "Women, Motivation and Success," Joseph T. Chirban discarded his initial questionnaire as an obstacle and wove his previously formulated questions into something that more resembled a conversation. This led interviewees—all nationally prominent women—to move beyond their celebrity status to speak more candidly and offer more self-reflection. Chirban found that his open-ended questions encouraged the comedienne Lucille Ball to elaborate on herself in ways not evident in her previous interviews. "She experienced my openness, respect, and nurturance, qualities that she valued, and that I recognized in her," he wrote. "She responded in kind, which continually deepened the interview." More interactive interviewing, he concluded, would help therapists (as well as other interviewers) to move beyond simple information gathering to a better understanding of interviewees' feelings, values, and concerns.[31]

Nor do all social scientists favor the use of highly-structured, standardized, quantitative questionnaires with anonymous interviewees. Sociologists James Holstein and Jaber Gubrium have argued that by collecting data so impersonally, social scientists have failed to question where their informants' knowledge was coming from and how it was derived. More active, open-ended, qualitative interviewing would transform their "subjects" into collaborators with the interviewer. The interviewer's objective should not be to dictate interpretation through a predetermined agenda but to provide a conducive environment for a conversation that addresses relevant issues. Mary Jo Festle reached the same conclusions when she directed a project to interview lung transplant patients: "When people talk, they can provide clearer, subtler, and fuller explanations than quantitative data permits."[32]

Can follow-up questions be prepared in advance?

Follow-up questions require both prior research and spontaneity. A thoroughly prepared interviewer will sense when the interviewee is being incomplete and will press for a fuller discussion. Research also helps you spot some new information or information that conflicts with other accounts. "I didn't know that, can you tell me more about it?" can often be the best follow-up question, since it encourages the interviewee to devote more attention to the issue and provide more details. Interviewees are often surprised when an interviewer seems to care about a particular subject that they would have mentioned only in passing if interest had not been expressed.

The most important skill in asking follow-up questions is being able to listen carefully to what interviewees are saying. Those who study listening have concluded that people generally hear only a small portion of what is said to them, a phenomenon that every parent and teacher can confirm. Even in an interview situation that is more focused than a normal conversation, the interviewer is keeping an eye on the recorder, concentrating on choosing the next question to be asked, and growing fatigued and distracted as time elapses. Listening to a tape of one of his interviews, Theodore Rosengarten, the author of *All God's Dangers: The Life of Nate Shaw* (1974), realized that he had "set out to question, not to listen." Thinking ahead from question to question, he had allowed the tape recorder to listen for him. "Let the machine record," he admonished, "and you listen!"[33]

Training themselves to remain alert saves interviewers from the embarrassing position of asking a question that the interviewee has already answered—a clear signal that the interviewer has not been paying attention—and helps flag the unexpected revelations that deserve to be followed up. In listening to the tapes after their interviews, even the most experienced interviewers will hear things that eluded them during the interview. These areas can be pursued in subsequent interviews, but not as spontaneously as when they first arose.[34]

How should interviewers react to statements with which they strongly disagree?

The hardest part of listening is having to pay attention to ideas and information with which you may differ. You may be inclined to interrupt and argue, but you need to hear the interviewee out before confronting areas of disagreement. Challenge answers that seem misleading, and pursue responses that seem mistaken. Interviewees may misspeak or poorly express themselves; sometimes they are misinformed or just wrong. But they also may possess a more accurate version of events than the interviewer has seen in other sources and, given the opportunity, may be able to present their version convincingly.[35]

Oral history collects the interviewee's recollections and opinions, not the interviewer's. Interviewers are not responsible for converting interviewees to any true faith, nor do they need to demonstrate that they are purer than the people they are interviewing. A true test of both the interviewer and the oral history project is whether they conducted interviews with representatives of all sides of an issue, including those whom they considered less than admirable.

But what if the interviewer suspects that an interviewee is lying or shading the truth?

Never be too quick to presume that an interviewee is wrong or is lying. Your objective is to record the story from the interviewee's point of view, even if that includes some exaggerated claims or boasting. You need not embrace totally whatever the interviewee is saying. Try to draw interviewees out further on any dubious assertions. Return to troublesome issues at different points during the interview, as a means of prodding interviewees into defending or refuting their previous statements. Do not hesitate to cite contrary evidence in newspaper accounts and other sources. Conflicting information can be attached as an appendix to the transcripts for future researchers to consider. (First, however, be sure to alert the interviewee to the added material.)[36]

Eyewitnesses to memorable events who change their testimony and contradict themselves may be reflecting their initial confusion or the array of other viewpoints they subsequently encountered. It was no conspiracy that individuals in the crowd at Dealey Plaza the day John F. Kennedy was assassinated heard differing numbers of shots and disagreed over the direction from which those shots came. Having gone abruptly from cheering a presidential motorcade to running for cover, their fear and bewilderment contributed to inconsistencies in observations and memories. Their recollections were further shaped by news coverage, conversation, speculation, books, and motion pictures. "I have read and heard so many things, it mixes together," said Danny Arce, who worked at the Texas Book Depository. "You don't know if it's your own memory or it's somebody else's. We all read a lot of things, and sometimes inadvertently adopt things we heard from others. It's hard to separate the two, and can get real confusing trying to figure out what you remember without having your memory colored by everything that has come out."[37]

There is also the possibility that people are lying to themselves. Some people dramatically change their positions but convince themselves of their consistency and correctness. Some may have consciously or subconsciously distorted memories of an unpleasant past. Australian oral historians encountered "organized structures of forgetting" regarding their country's Aboriginal population, for years largely omitted from the white society's collective memory and recorded history. In Germany and Italy, oral historians have encountered mass amnesia about fascism and the Holocaust. In France, interviewers have faced a reluctance to recall collaboration with German authorities during military occupation. "Better to let the dead rest in peace and the living live in peace," commented one of those who declined to be interviewed.[38]

As an oral history interview usually takes place years after the events occurred, it can have a cathartic effect by allowing interviewees to confront long-buried memories. In such cases, the interview serves as therapy as well as to set the record straight. But even a psychiatrist would have trouble getting some interviewees to confront the past honestly. The lie sometimes takes on a mythic significance of its own, and the interview may become valuable not for the story's accuracy but as a means of analyzing the roots of its distortion and measuring an idealized self against less favorable perceptions.

Should an interviewer pay attention to the interviewee's "body language"?

Even interviews that are not being videoed have a visual component. Sitting in close proximity, interviewers and interviewees communicate nonverbally through facial expressions and body movement. Always focus your gaze fully on the interviewee. Looking around the room, staring into space, examining your nails, suggests that you are not paying attention, just as frowning suggests disagreement or disbelief. Interviewees will either interpret such behavior as rudeness or, fearing that they are boring you, begin abbreviating their answers. Except for glancing periodically at the recorder or looking at photographs and other items relating to the interview, maintain eye contact diligently throughout the interview. A smile or a nod signals that you got the point and will encourage the interviewee to keep talking. Quiet signals are preferable to verbal interruptions ("oh, yes," "uh-hmmm," "you don't say"), which sound foolish on the recording and clutter the transcript.

Good journalists have learned to be "people watchers." Understanding that interviewees also send non-verbal cues, they ask themselves what a gesture might mean or why someone looked down while speaking. A person leaning toward the interviewer and pointing a finger projects an aggressive, take-charge attitude; sitting back with crossed legs and arms and leaning away suggests a closed, self-protected attitude. Body language may indicate nervousness about the interview, and topics that make interviewees particularly uncomfortable may cause them to shift in their seats, drum their fingers on a table, and engage in other such noticeable behavior. Some interviewees glance at the interviewer to see how an answer has registered. Amelia Fry reported that when she interviewed former California senator William F. Knowland for a life history, he never looked at her but stared fixedly at the ceiling, "as if he was answering to a higher authority." It later became evident that Knowland was undergoing a crisis in his personal life and found it distressing to reflect on his past. This crisis caused him to commit suicide before she could conduct another interview.[39] In another extreme but still instructive case, an oral historian who conducted a series of interviews with prisoners at the state penitentiary detected that the inmates had "a great deal of practice at perfecting their intentionally deceptive statements." He identified such nonverbal cues as tapping a cigarette and loss of eye contact during specific replies as signals that a statement might be deceptive.[40]

Sounds also play a part in nonverbal communication. Voice pitch, hesitation, emphasis, sarcasm, and muttering of asides provide indications of attitude. When people become emotional, they tend to talk faster and raise their voices. Interviewers need to catch these nonverbal clues, since they are almost impossible to transcribe. A sarcastic inflection, for instance, can completely change the meaning of a sentence. The interviewer might point out a sarcastic response and ask the interviewee to explain the sarcasm.

Is there a role in oral history for what social scientists call "continuing observation?"

Oral historians have rarely shared the interest of social scientists in observation as part of the interviewing process. Historians tend to isolate interviewees from their environment and to put them in a quiet place where they will not be interrupted during the interview, whereas in other disciplines subjects are examined in their natural setting. Anthropologists, for instance, live in communities to record their day-to-day observations along with their subjects' testimony.

Richard Fenno has encouraged political scientists to collect data by "interactive observation," by which he means "following politicians around and talking with them as they go about their work." Fenno accompanied politicians through their home districts, through elections, and through their legislative service:

> Much of what you see, therefore, is dictated by what they do and say. If something is important to them, it becomes important to you. Their view of the world is important as your view of the world. You impose some research questions on them; they impose some research questions on you. That interaction has its costs most notably in a considerable loss of control over the research process. It also has benefits. It brings you extremely close to your data.[41]

Fenno's prescription describes what many social sciences consider effective fieldwork. Although oral historians often travel to the area where their interviewees live and are interested in their environment, participatory observation has not been a major component of the oral history interview. Oral historians frequently interview those who have retired and live in different communities from where they spent their careers. Observing current daily routines would not offer many clues about the past that oral historians seek to capture on tape. Sometimes, however, interviewees want to show interviewers buildings and other sites that played an important part in their past. Oral historians should take advantage of such offers and visit the sites, bringing along their recorders, cameras, and possibly video cameras to supplement the interviews.[42]

CONCLUDING THE INTERVIEW

What's the best way to conclude an interview?

Look for a natural "wrap-up" question, something that causes interviewees to reflect back on their lives, to compare recent events with their earlier years, to draw conclusions about major events, or to look ahead toward the future. Ask the interviewee whether there are any other issues that could be discussed. Occasionally, an interviewee has anticipated a question that the interviewer did not raise. The interview itself may have triggered memories of long-forgotten people and events that the interviewer had not researched. Encourage interviewees to put whatever they consider important into the record.

At the conclusion of the interview, remind the interviewee of how the recordings will be processed and where they will be deposited. Explain what their role will be in editing the transcript and in signing the deed of gift. Sometimes the interviewee is asked to sign a release immediately after completing the recording session and another release later approving the transcript; other times no release is signed until the interviewee has reviewed the transcript. The timing depends on how quickly a transcript can be produced and on whether the interviewee is likely to request that the interview be restricted.

It is customary to present copies of the recording or transcript to the interviewee and to sometimes make additional copies for family members. If the object of the interview is an article or book, try to give a copy to the interviewee. Plan to invite interviewees to exhibit openings or other public presentations based on the interviews.

You cannot simply walk out the door with someone's life story, their candid reflections, and sometimes extremely personal observations. Interviews can be difficult, emotional experiences, and sometimes you need to spend some time to talk with the interviewee after the interview, without the recorder running. Let interviewees know how important their interviews will be to the oral history project, and reassure them that they were helpful. Give them some idea of how long it will take to process the interview, when they can expect to receive copies of the recording or transcript, when they will sign the deed of gift, how you expect the material to be used, and where the interview will be deposited and opened for research.

Should interviewees ever be paid for their interviews?

Most oral history projects work on such limited budgets sometimes depending on volunteer staff that they rarely can afford to pay interviewees. They operate on the valid principle that having one's life story recorded for the future is reward in itself. A very few projects, however, especially those in which the interviews are with musicians and others commonly paid to perform, have recognized some financial obligation to the participants. Blues and jazz projects have further justified their decision to pay on the potential profitability of the interviews. "Since blues is a marketable form of oral history," wrote Walter Liniger of the Blues Archives at the University of Mississippi, "we felt morally obliged to secure the rights of the informants and to pay them a fee for their contributions."[43]

Obviously, any financial arrangement depends on the resources of the sponsoring project or institution. Some projects have written stipends for interviewees into their grant proposals, similar to the honoraria paid to their advisory committee members. But whether or not payments are made, all oral historians have a responsibility to inform interviewees of the anticipated uses of their interviews, whether in publication, radio or video documentaries, the Internet, CD-ROM, or other means of public presentation that might generate royalties or other monetary compensation.

CHAPTER 4

Using Oral History in Research and Writing

Oral history methodology seems geared for large projects; how much of it can the individual researcher apply to interviews for a book or an article?

Individual resources may be more limited than those of a group project, but an individual researcher is no less concerned about making interviews fully usable. Since researchers are the primary users of the information they collect, they ought to set their own standards to at least equal, if not surpass, those of an oral history project or archives. Both projects and individual researchers want to collect oral documentation that is complete, accurate, and reliable, but researchers scrutinize even more intensely than do project interviewers what they hear in the interviews they conduct and apply a higher degree of professional skepticism to them. They seek verification in other sources for information gathered through interviews, and they evaluate contradictory material to draw their own conclusions.

Despite their focused efforts and self-defined goals, individuals doing their own interviewing bear definite professional responsibilities. The American Historical Association has issued the following recommendations for individual interviewers:

1. Interviews should be recorded on tape but only after the person to be interviewed has been informed of the mutual rights and responsibilities involved in oral history, such as editing, confidentiality, disposition, and dissemination of all forms of the record. Interviewers should obtain legal releases and document any agreements with interviewees.

2. The interviewer should strive to prompt informative dialogue through challenging and perceptive inquiry, should be grounded in the background and experiences of the person being interviewed, and, if possible, should review the sources relating to the interviewee before conducting the interview.

3. To the extent practicable, interviewers should extend the inquiry beyond their immediate needs to make each interview as complete as possible for the benefit of others.

4. The interviewer should guard against possible social injury to or exploitation of interviewees and should conduct interviews with respect for human dignity.

5. Interviewers should be responsible for proper citation of oral history sources in creative works, including permanent location.

6. Interviewers should arrange to deposit their interviews in an archival repository that is capable of both preserving the interviews and making them available for general research. Additionally, the interviewer should work with the repository in determining the necessary legal arrangements.

7. As teachers, historians are obligated to inform students of their responsibilities in regard to interviewing and to encourage adherence to the guidelines set forth here.[1]

Why bother to record interviews? Why are notes not sufficient?

After years of scribbling notes during class lectures, many researchers feel perfectly able to take coherent notes during an interview. They consider a recorder an unnecessary expense, a bother to lug about and operate, and a possible barrier to a candid interview—whether with public figures, who may be overly cautious about having their words recorded, or with nonpublic figures who may be intimidated about talking into a microphone. Some researchers consider note taking superior to tape recording. Barbara Tuchman, for instance, complained that tape recorders simply encouraged people to "ramble effortlessly and endlessly." She described note taking as a "crystallizing process" in which the writer automatically distinguishes the significant from the insignificant. Others have cited the risk of the recorder breaking down at crucial moments as their rationale for not recording.[2]

Such responses combine cogent truths and unnecessary rationalizations. Tape recorders are no longer such an expense or a novelty. They can be purchased or rented for a reasonable cost, are easy to operate, and have become so commonplace that few interviewees will be surprised or uncomfortable to see one. More important, tape recorders radically expand and improve any interview. The longer interviews last, the more interviewers tire and miss nuances. Later, when they play back the tape, interviewers inevitably hear more than they did during the interview itself. Note takers may make honest mistakes in what they hear or find their handwriting hard to decipher. Note takers also run the risk of hearing only what they want to hear rather than what the interviewee actually says—a recurring phenomenon to which anyone interviewed by the press can readily attest.

Note taking makes some researchers feel more comfortable, because it helps focus their attention—as they listen to what is being said—on the exact points they anticipate later using. But there is no reason not to record and take notes at the same time. The notes can serve as the recording's index, which is especially useful if a full transcript cannot be made.

Recording is the researcher's best means of self-protection. Interviewees may object to how they were quoted or may not be willing to stand behind statements they made in their interviews. A recording of the interview provides the documentation to defend against such reactions. Some interviewees, especially the more prominent, may be so skittish about being misquoted that they will insist that the interview be recorded. For his biography of Henry Kissinger, Walter Isaacson interviewed former president Richard M. Nixon. Isaacson took notes, while Nixon recorded the interview. When the tape recorder broke down, Nixon commented, "I've never been very good with these things."[3]

What if a potential interviewee refuses to be recorded?

Interviewers operate under ground rules that interviewees set. For an oral history project, such an objection would likely cause that person to be stricken from the list of potential interviewees, as there usually remains little reason to conduct an oral history if it cannot be recorded. But the individual researcher may consider the person a critically important source, regardless of the ground rules. Notes may be inferior to a recording, but they are better than nothing. As soon as the interview session is over, the interviewer needs to write down as full an account as notes and memory permit.

An interviewee may decline to be recorded out of fear or vanity, emotions that can sometimes be overcome by some reassurances and flattery. The late historian Gordon Prange, whose ego matched the monumental books he wrote on the Second World War, refused to be tape-recorded during an interview on the grounds that Gen. Douglas MacArthur had never allowed his interviews to be recorded. The interviewer took notes for a few minutes and then injected, "What a shame that this isn't being recorded, Professor Prange, because my notes will never do justice to your cogent thoughts and beautifully crafted sentences." Accepting that as a point well taken, Prange permitted the tape recorder to run for the rest of the interview.[4]

But why make a recording if you cannot afford to transcribe it?

You can make notes from your own recordings without having to transcribe them entirely. Having the recording allows you to quote accurately, and to pick up nuances you may have missed during the interview. The recording can be quoted, cited, deposited in a library, and referred back to for proof should any queries arise about the accuracy of the material.

Transcripts are costly and time-consuming to create, but they increase the usefulness of an interviewer to everyone, including the original interviewer. Researchers planning to conduct extensive interviews for a dissertation, book, or other project should seek a logical repository, whether it be a university library, a state archives or historical society, or a community library, to which to donate the completed tapes. The repository will most likely have legal release forms that the interviewer can use. If the interviews meet the repository's standards, it may be able to have its own staff transcribe the interviews or join the interviewer in seeking a grant for transcription.

Why should independent researchers make their interviews available to anyone else?

Scholars have a professional obligation to permit access to their sources. A footnote citing "personal interview in the author's possession" leaves much open to question, especially if the interviewee has died. Readers may question how accurately the researcher quoted or paraphrased the interview. Even when a researcher quotes an interview meticulously, in all probability he or she needs to cite only a small portion of it. Future researchers may make different use of the same material.

While writing her doctoral dissertation on the Office of War Information, Holly Cowan Shulman, discovered that another historian had conducted an interview with a key official of the agency. Her graduate adviser, however, dissuaded her from asking to see a copy of the interview, on the grounds that it was someone else's work. Although she complied at the time, she came to feel that it had been wrong not to examine the interview for her research because interviews "were a piece of historical evidence just as much as letters or diaries." Seeking to raise the consciousness of the historical profession on the issue, Shulman has argued:

> When we conduct interviews, we are creating evidence. When the next historian comes along interested in another aspect or interpretation of the same topic, he or she should have access to the interviews we did. This is the very nature of the rules of history. Otherwise, I could hide all of my evidence to protect myself from competition and argument. Or I could make up anything I wanted and assert its truth citing interviews

I supposedly conducted but would let no one else see. In other words, if we historians don't treat interviews seriously, we raise a series of problems which could hurt the profession as a whole.[5]

Must individual researchers get signed legal release for their interviews?

A legal release is essential if the interviewer intends to deposit the recording or transcript in a library or archive. By signing a legal release, the interviewee indicates that he or she understood what the interview would be used for and establishes its ownership. Just having recorded another person's words does not give the interviewer copyright on those words, and making quotations beyond "fair use" length might stimulate a legal challenge. The problem may not come from the interviewee but from the interviewee's heirs, who may seek compensation for the interview's publication.

Unfortunately, graduate advisers have too often assured individual researchers that they were just doing interviews, not an oral history project, and therefore did not need to get releases. This oversight unnecessarily limits the interview's future use. While depositing the interviews in an archives, the interviewer must go back to get signatures on legal releases. Sometimes interviewees have died and their next of kin must be located. It is always easier to have the legal releases signed when the interview is conducted.

Researchers at most colleges and universities must also comply with Institutional Review Boards that will want to see evidence of the interviewee's "informed consent." Standard oral history release forms should suffice, indicating that the interviewee understands and approves of the purpose and intended uses of the interviews. Some Institutional Review Boards further require release forms to stipulate that the interviewee can decline to participate, can choose to remain anonymous, and understands the potential risks involved in participation—factors more applicable to medical and behavioral science projects than to oral history. (See chapter 7 for further issues relating to Institutional Review Boards.)

With limited time and resources, why should independent researchers ask questions beyond their immediate research interests?

Researchers understandably think of interviews as filling in gaps in their work or expanding their own knowledge of the particulars and want to ask questions precisely about that area and nothing else. But this attitude is counterproductive in a number of ways. First, the interviewee's memory may not immediately be able to dredge up the specific information that the interviewer is seeking.

Interviewers need to spend some time establishing rapport, building up to the central issue, and understanding its context in the interviewee's life. Interviewers need to be sensitive to the feelings of interviewees and not to dismiss other areas of their life they may consider relevant to the interviewer's questions.

In the 1970s I interviewed the New Dealer Benjamin V. Cohen about his role in creating the Securities and Exchange Commission in the 1930s. Watergate was in the news when the interview took place, and Cohen wanted to talk about Nixon. But for my dissertation, I needed to hear about Franklin D. Roosevelt. Not willing to follow his tangents, I constantly steered the interview back to my immediate interests. Not until later did I realize that I had missed the opportunity to capture Cohen's thoughts about Watergate and to find out whether the development of the "imperial presidency" had in any way changed his opinion about the expansion of the executive branch during the 1930s.

Within a few years of completion of most oral history projects, many of the interviewees will have died. There is no guarantee that these people will have been interviewed by any other programs. A researcher's notes, recordings, and transcripts of interviews therefore become valuable sources for other researchers, who no longer have access to the deceased.

Does the independent interviewer have any advantages over the oral historian in a group project?

Anyone working on a specific book or article becomes far more steeped in the subject matter and has a much more personal stake in the process. Their interviews lead to publication and promote their professional advancement, perhaps even earn them royalties. Researchers can verge on obsession with their projects, wanting to know *everything*. They press interviewees to go into greater detail than does an interviewer for a more general project. A number of interviewers participated in the Former Members of Congress oral history project, and not surprisingly, one of the lengthiest and most detailed interviews was conducted by an interviewer who was also writing a doctoral dissertation on the senatorial interviewee. The interviewer pressed the senator on any number of issues, even persuading him to sing his campaign song.[6]

Individual researchers may express disappointment with the project-directed interviews they read in oral history archives because the project interviewers did not dig deep enough into the subject. The main themes may have been covered, but not enough of the smaller details are included. Because individual researchers generally are seeking answers to specific questions, they may undervalue the parts of an archival interview that do not directly address their needs. The curse of oral history is failure to pursue details.

Can an independent researcher's interviews be considered an oral history?

There are differences between interviews conducted for one researcher's express purposes and those conducted as oral histories for general use. Oral histories are broadly conceived and conducted, then processed, preserved, and made available to other scholars in archives. Research interviews fill the narrow needs of the individual interviewer, are rarely recorded or transcribed, and generally wind up in the interviewer's file cabinets or in boxes in basements and attics.[7]

These distinctions blur when a researcher's interviews are recorded or transcribed and deposited somewhere so that other researchers can use them. Oral historians have long objected to the use of the term "oral history" to describe every interview, regardless of whether it was recorded or simply handwritten notes were taken. "Historians have been interviewing people for hundreds of years; there's nothing new about that, and I don't think they've been doing oral history," observed Philip Brooks of the Harry S. Truman Library in 1966. "I think there's a *real* distinction here between a researcher who interviews people for his *own* purpose to derive information for *his own* book, and that of what I sometimes call a 'pure' oral historian, who is accumulating a stock of evidence for the use of other researchers, any and all researchers, as we do in an archival agency. I think this is related somewhat to the question of objectivity." More recently, oral historians have conceded that all interviewing—archival or individual—is subjective, and that the earlier distinctions posed a false dichotomy.[8]

Similarly, when the Oral History Association first issued its *Evaluation Guidelines* in 1980, they were directed almost exclusively toward group or archival projects. When the revised guidelines were promulgated in 1992, they addressed the "independent/unaffiliated researcher" as well. Fully half of the guidelines involve the transfer of the independent researcher's interviews to an archives. Some interviews may not be worthy of permanent preservation, particularly if the researcher has not followed other criteria for oral history interviewing, preparation, and processing or has not been sensitive to oral history ethical considerations. Still, in the long run, institutions—whether public libraries soliciting and collecting family history interviews for their local history sections or major research libraries working with authors and documentary film producers to collect oral history project interviews—stand to gain from a closer partnership with individual researchers.

It would be a mistake to define oral history so narrowly that it applied only to large archival collections. But to do oral history, interviewers must live up to its standards and assume its legal, ethical, and methodological responsibilities, including that of making their interviews available to other researchers for verification and further use.

ORAL EVIDENCE

How valid is oral history as historical evidence?

Treat oral evidence as cautiously as any other form of evidence. Documents written at the time have an immediacy about them and are not influenced by subsequent events, and yet those documents can be incomplete, in error, or written to mislead. In 1966 President Lyndon Johnson invited the television critic Jack Gould to meet with him in the Oval Office. A memo from a White House aide later reported to Johnson that Gould had stopped at his office after the meeting and said, "Why doesn't the President appear on television the same way he talked to me—the President is so gracious, affable and well informed." Subsequently, scholars have frequently cited that memo when writing about Johnson and the media. Gould's son, a historian, came across the quote in the mid-1980s, and asked his father about the incident. Gould recalled that he had left the White House immediately after the interview, had not seen the aide, and had not said what was credited to him in the memo. The episode impressed his son as "a cautionary tale about relying on archival material without double-checking the sources used."[9]

A statement is not necessarily truer if written down at the time than if recalled later in testimony. Whether written or oral, evidence must be convincing and verifiable. A federal court jury on which I served was presented with a written statement that the prosecutor described as the defendant's "signed confession." The defense insisted that the prosecution had misinterpreted the statement, whose many grammatical errors obscured its meaning. In the jury room, jurors repeatedly read the statement, trying to decipher exactly what it meant, before concluding that it failed the test of convincing evidence.

Oral history can be unconvincing. Some interviewees' remarks are self-serving; they remember selectively, recall only events that cast themselves in a good light, and seem to always get the better of opponents. Interviewers may be too polite or too timid to ask probing questions about events that did not turn out well. Sometimes interviewees honestly cannot remember. They jumble names and dates and confuse people and places. Sometimes they deliberately recast their past to fit their current self and public image. Whole series of interviews can be faulted for paying attention to only one side of the issue, or for interviewing only

le who would speak positively about the individual who was the sub-
: project.[10]

gh bad oral histories have been done to satisfy the worst suspicions of
malists, and yet enough good interviews have been conducted to validate the process. Properly done, an oral history helps to interpret and define
written records and makes sense out of the most obscure decisions and events.
An interview with a thoughtful participant and perceptive eyewitness can generate new ideas and avenues of inquiry that a researcher might have never
thought of pursuing. Interviews can explore the use of language by subgroup—
such as jazz slang, black English, shop-floor jargon, and even the acronyms of
government bureaucrats—and discover word meanings that might otherwise
have eluded researchers outside the subgroup. Oral evidence does not always
derive from oral history. The French historian Emmanuel LeRoy Ladurie published what amounted to an oral history of a fourteenth-century village in the
Pyrenees, Montaillou. His sources were depositions taken during the
Inquisition by Bishop Jacques Fournier, who interrogated some five hundred
suspected heretics between 1318 and 1325. Scribes copied down the questions
and answers and gave the accused the opportunity to correct the transcripts.
The final copies were deposited in the Vatican archives, where six centuries later
they enabled Ladurie to quote the words of the common folk of Montaillou,
people who stood in stark contrast to the nobles who dominate the chronicles
of the Middle Ages. *Montaillou* (1979) became a best-seller in France and elsewhere, possibly because of its explicit accounts of sexual relations within the
village. Prurient interests aside, the first-person accounts make the book compelling reading for even nonmedievalists.[11]

Similarly, the pension application process for militiamen in the American
Revolutionary War amounted to what the historian John C. Dann has called
"one of the largest oral history projects ever undertaken." In 1832, when
Congress agreed to pay a yearly pension to any militiamen who served for more
than six months in the Revolution, thousands of elderly veterans applied.
Since written records were scarce, the government required them to dictate their
reminiscences to court reporters, giving as many names, dates, and other
details as possible. Government clerks then scrutinized these testimonies to
determine their accuracy. Selecting from a great mass of applications a century and a half later, Dann published the first-person eyewitness accounts of
foot soldiers, runaway slaves, and women who followed their husbands into
combat. Their accounts authentically describe not only combat but everyday
life in the camps, wounds, diseases, and the whole social setting of the
Revolutionary War.[12]

Oral history makes a critical addition to oral evidence: a trained interviewer who can guide an interviewee's recital of events that he or she may not have thought about for years but can recall vividly when asked. Questions prompt interviewees to discuss issues they might otherwise have skipped over. Interviewers can question inconsistencies between the oral account and written documentation. A good oral history can present and preserve convincing evidence and put it in quotable, first-person prose that enlivens historical narratives. But oral history should not stand alone as a single source. Researchers need to seek out available material to substantiate both written and oral evidence. If written and oral information contradict each other, then the researcher must dig even deeper to determine which is more accurate.

While preparing to interview the former chief clerk of the Senate Labor, Education, and Public Welfare Committee, Stuart McClure, I centered much of my research on the National Defense Education Act. In 1957, when the Soviet Union launched *Sputnik,* the first earth-orbiting satellite, McClure wrote a memo to the committee's chairman, Lister Hill, suggesting that the public attention generated by *Sputnik* might help pass the education bill that had stalled in Congress—if they called it a "defense education act." One account of the bill's passage devoted a chapter to the fight between the Senate, which wanted to make the money available as grants in the form of scholarships, and the House, which insisted on making it available as loans. During the interview, when asked why the Senate lost the battle, McClure laughed and replied:

Oh, that was another clever, clever ploy. That was done on the House side. They narrowed the issue. There were millions of dollars for all kinds of other things, but Carl Elliott [the Alabama representative who chaired the House subcommittee on education] and his guys narrowed the issue to whether we should have the federal government hand out scholarships or loans. . . . The House denounced scholarships, it was a waste of money and socialism and all of that. And the minute the damn scholarship issue was done for, dead, the bill swooped through. I don't think anybody had read any other title in it. Oh, that was clever stuff. Carl Elliott was a brilliant strategist, as good as Lister Hill in his way, in different houses.[13]

Here oral history exposed a legislative ploy that not only fooled most members of the House of Representatives but the scholar who had published a history based on official documentation. The debate over loans versus scholarships had been a subterfuge designed to allow the House, which had previously defeated federal education bills, to save face and claim victory. McClure's story has the ring of credibility—first, because it is logical, and second, because Senate staff rarely give credit to House members, except to express sheer admiration for a brilliant legislative strategy.

Do courts accept oral history as evidence?

Without the interviewee being present for cross-examination, courts generally regard the recording or transcript of an oral history as hearsay. Nevertheless they have permitted oral histories to be subpoenaed as evidence and have accepted oral traditions in rendering verdicts. In dealing with land claims of native peoples, courts in several nations have acknowledged the inadequacy of written documents—although legal obstacles to those native claims remain formidable. When those fighting a land claim in Canadian courts argued that oral histories "did not accurately convey historical truth," the chief justice of the Canadian supreme court ruled that "stories matter," and that the legal convention of hearsay could be waived in regard to the oral traditions of Canada's "first people."[14]

When South Africa established a Truth and Reconciliation Commission to examine past government tactics used to suppress resistance to apartheid, critics of the commission argued that the oral history it gathered was unreliable and grossly inaccurate. The stories that victims told were subjective, they charged, telling "their understanding of what happened to them and not necessarily what happened." A minority report asserted that: "Exaggeration is a natural consequence of human suffering." These critics assumed that when the alleged perpetrators took the stand, having been granted amnesty, they would refute the victims' claims of human rights violations. Instead, the perpetrators confirmed the most outrageous of the stories and affirmed the reliability of the oral history.[15]

Can information from an oral history ever be cited by itself, without other supporting evidence?

It depends on the information. A personal description, the expression of an opinion, or the telling of a colorful anecdote would permit citation of the interview as the single source. But the more controversial the subject, the less an interview can stand alone. Critics would question the authority of the interviewee. Was that person in a position to know, or does the interview constitute simply secondhand speculation? When in doubt, employ the journalist's practice of seeking at least two witnesses before asserting a statement of fact—if indeed a second witness is still alive.[16]

Independent researchers can also borrow from journalists the practice of having one interviewee comment on what another has said. A novice reporter, sent to cover a dispute involving a local developer, interviewed the developer and wrote his story. "Did you talk to the architect?" asked his editor. The reporter dutifully interviewed the architect and added his comments to the story, but his editor was still not satisfied. "Take what the architect said back to the developer and get him to respond," the editor instructed, "then take what the developer said back to the architect, and after they've answered each other's charges, then you write your story."

In cultural resource management projects that have included oral history interviews despite the misgivings of archaeologists and others on the team who are not oral historians, efforts have been made to determine the quality of evidence that the interviews gathered. The oral historian Dan Utley has described how, in one project collecting information about a defunct farming community, each interviewee was encouraged to talk at length about the annual hog killing, a universal experience within the community. "The hog killing stories were then compared and used as a rough guide to evaluate the memories, descriptive abilities, and involvement of the interviewees," he explained. "It was not easy to sit through numerous descriptions of the slaughter process, especially after breakfast, but they did provide an important comparative dimension to the overall project."[17]

Isn't most oral history anecdotal?

People naturally recount events and personalities anecdotally, in small self-contained stories that illuminate or instruct. Anecdotes often focus on humorous situations and characteristics and in conversation are designed to stimulate a smile or a laugh. In many ways, the anecdote is a writer's freshest material. The term derives from the Greek word *anekdota,* meaning "things unpublished," and it is often the telling stories taken from interviews that make a book original and different from previously published sources. *Anecdotal* is not synonymous with *apocryphal,* meaning spurious or unverifiable information. Names, dates, and other facts can usually be more reliably obtained elsewhere, but each interviewee has a unique store of anecdotes.

Although scholars sometimes denigrate anecdotes as the antithesis of analysis, these accounts can actually be informative, offering their analysis in a vivid and colorful manner and enlivening a narrative, often with a touch of humor. Good writers have an eye and an ear for a lively and believable anecdote that can make their points both memorably and compactly. Critics also dismiss oral history and other forms of narrative history because anecdotal information, by its nature, is randomly gathered and not statistically significant enough to make generalizations from. Social scientists look to census data, marriage licenses, death certificates, and voting statistics rather than to interviews, unless they are using a standard questionnaire and questioning a large, representative sample. Oral historians tailor their questions for individual interviewees, and time and financial limitations tend to restrict their pool of interviewees.

Although anecdotal information has a personal flavor, the collected stories from a group reinforce each other and show common threads in the lives of the group's members. Mixing anecdotal information with the hard data of statistical abstracts, the skilled researcher and writer can re-create a colorful as well as a convincing portrait of the past.[18]

Can an interviewer argue with interviewees if they seem wrong in what they are saying?

Individual researchers have more liberty than archival oral historians to inject the interviews with their own opinions and to challenge the interviewees. Remember, however, that all interviews are voluntary and last only as long as the interviewee desires. Keep in mind that too forceful an intervention by the interviewer may also distort the interviewee's responses.

Deliberate carefully when trying to decide whether interviewees' stories are accurate, misleading, or erroneous. An individual researcher usually approaches an interview with a thesis to prove and may assume that anything contradicting that thesis is wrong. Give the speaker a fair hearing, and then challenge any inconsistencies in the testimony with other sources. When pressed, the interviewee may be able to provide some additional rationale or even hard evidence to support previously unsubstantiated assertions. An impaired ability to listen can be a dangerous affliction for interviewers.[19]

"Research involves the shedding, not the confirmation, of our preconceptions," the historian Blair Worden has asserted. "If historians go to the archives expecting certain answers to their questions, careful study of the evidence will almost invariably change their minds." Living sources can magnify this condition by looking interviewers in the eye and telling them they are wrong and by revealing unexpected information. Interviewees may see things entirely differently from the researcher, and although interviewees might be biased or just plain wrong, so might the researcher's thesis. The best information to emerge from an oral history is often completely unexpected: a different way of looking at something, turning preconceived notions upside down. An interviewer may want to argue points with an interviewee, but it is self-defeating to seek out people to interview and then ignore what they have to say. Or as Lyndon Johnson used to say, "I ain't never learned nothin' talkin'."[20]

Although interviewers strive to take a neutral role during the interview, neutrality may not be acceptable in its publication. When James Green published his interview with the historian C. Vann Woodward in the *Radical History Review,* it stimulated a series of angry letters to the editor expressing outrage that Green had not rebutted Woodward's critical remarks about the Marxist historian Herbert Aptheker. The opinions had been Woodward's, but Green took the blame for his silence and apologized for not challenging Woodward's assertions. "My purpose in interviewing Woodward for RHR was not, however, to expose our political differences," Green explained, "but to examine his contribution to the Left's understanding of Southern history and to the study of race, class and region in U.S. history."[21]

Is it possible to get a worthwhile interview from someone with whom you profoundly disagree?

The emphasis on interviewing "from the bottom up" has presumed that interviewers at least admire their interviewees even when they do not agree with them. But some researchers record the lives of people whose politics and ideologies they find "unsavory, dangerous, or deliberately deceptive." The sociologist Kathleen Blee, who interviewed former Ku Klux Klan members from Indiana, has no sympathy for the Klan's anti-Semitic, anti-Catholic, and racist politics and violent attitudes. She found it unnecessary to appear empathetic when interviewing Klan members and made little effort to shy away from controversial topics. She anticipated "no rapport, no shared assumptions, no commonality of thought or experience" and expected her interviewees to be too wary of her to reveal their true attitudes. But her expectations proved groundless. Not only did the former Klan members seem at ease during their interviews, but they assumed that she, "a native of Indiana and a white person," had to agree, even if secretly, with their views. "Even challenging their beliefs had no effect on their willingness to talk," Blee noted, concluding that despite profound differences, rapport was disturbingly easy to achieve in an oral history interview.[22]

Won't interviewees try to convince their interviewers to adopt their viewpoints?

A certain amount of intellectual seduction—interviewees trying to make interviewers agree with them—may take place. Sitting down to talk with prominent figures can be a heady experience, and it is all too easy to slip into a false sense of intimacy that can diminish scholarly distance and detachment. The makers and shakers who spend their careers assiduously trying to manipulate the media may treat historical researchers in much the same manner. They want the researcher to see events from their perspective, to validate their positions. Some of them are campaigning for historical vindication just as energetically as they did for public office.

Researchers can also be captivated by less prominent individuals who have lived noble lives, suffered oppression, or been crusading spirits. Empathy helps greatly in conducting interviews. Allan Nevins once said that an interviewer needs *gemutlichkeit,* an "obvious sympathy with the person whom he interviews, friendliness and tact, as well as courage." But researchers must also demonstrate scholarly skepticism. Interviewees may have played a role in the events and often have positions and reputations to defend. Researchers are observers, not players, and must not let personal admiration keep them from weighing the evidence dispassionately and creating a convincing account of people, movements, and past events.[23]

How does a researcher go about finding oral history interviews that have been collected and are open for research?

Although researchers may feel an impulse to grab a recorder and begin interviewing for themselves, the best place to start is with oral histories that have already been collected, transcribed, and opened. Many authors have used these collections and many books have cited them, but only a small portion of these vast resources have been tapped.

Several directories to oral history collections exist, and various states, regions, and individual archives have published catalogs (many listed in the bibliography to this volume). Oral history archives have been collected at Baylor University, the University of California at Berkeley, California State University at Fullerton, Columbia, Cornell, Duke, Radcliffe, UCLA, and the universities of Connecticut, Kentucky, North Texas, and Vermont, and at many other colleges and universities. Presidential libraries conduct their own oral histories, as do many corporate and labor archives. A sizeable portion of these oral histories have been microfilmed and are available in a library's microform division or through interlibrary loan. The Library of Congress, for instance, holds copies of most of the microfilmed oral history collections.[24]

Interview recordings and transcripts are also interspersed through the manuscript collections of both interviewees and interviewers and in numerous agency files within larger archives. A great many of these collections are included in the National Union Catalog of Manuscript Collections, unwieldy as that multivolume guide can be. Oral histories are also cited in the individual bibliographies for such biographical series as the *American National Biography.*

A steadily increasing number of oral history repositories have begun posting their catalogs, and sometimes full transcripts and audio recordings of their interviews on the Internet. These can be located through the major Internet search engines or through "hot links" from other web sites, including archives and national and regional oral history organizations.[25]

Is it legitimate for a researcher to use interviews conducted for someone else's earlier book?

As researchers's periods of study move further into the past and survivors are no longer available to interview, they have to rely more on "second-generation" use of oral history, reexamining interviews that were conducted for other publications. The original interviewer may have cited only portions of the material or may have overlooked significant clues buried in the testimony. Seemingly innocent remarks may take on new meaning in the light of later developments. New trends in historical research may highlight issues that earlier researchers considered marginal or insignificant. Second-generation research potential increases the importance of depositing and preserving interviews in libraries and archives for verification, reinterpretation, and reuse long after the interviewee, and the interviewer, are gone.

When Mark Stoler wrote his concise biography of General George C. Marshall, he worked in the shadow of Forrest Pogue's monumental four-volume biography of Marshall. Although General Marshall had steadfastly refused lucrative offers to write his own memoirs in the 1950s, Pogue persuaded him to give interviews. Eventually, Marshall warmed to being interviewed and left behind a rich, reflective commentary on his impressive career, particularly his earlier years. Since General Marshall died years before Stoler began his research, the historian made use of Pogue's interviews at the Marshall Research Foundation in Lexington, Virginia. Repeatedly, Stoler quoted from Pogue's interviews for Marshall's evaluations of his colleagues and self-assessments of his actions. Although drawing from the same sources that had been available to Pogue, Stoler's book was a fresh interpretation of the material he thus shared with the earlier researcher.[26]

How reliable are an interviewee's reconstructions of conversations with others?

People often recall events in the form of conversation ("so she said to me . . ."). They remember the words of presidents and other famous people they have met; they remember arguments, warnings, humorous and ironic remarks, and beautifully turned phrases. People reconstruct dialogue not only in oral histories but in their letters and diaries; the results can be colorful but treacherous.

Interviewers hear only one party's version of a conversation, generally years after it took place. In evaluating such evidence, think about whether the comments are characteristic of the person to whom they are attributed and whether they make sense in the context of the time and place of the conversation. Be suspicious of interviewees who always managed to get the last word or administer the perfect squelch. They may be recalling what they wish they had said or may be claiming credit for lines spoken to them rather than by them. The humorist Garrison Keillor once confessed in a radio monologue that his childhood reminiscence about an overripe tomato thrown with perfect aim was absolutely true—except that his sister had thrown it at him, not the other way around.

The historian Arthur Schlesinger, Jr., noted that remembered dialogue helps to "impart immediacy to narrative" but warned that such information should only be used when the remarks are "plausibly supported by context or other evidence." He added: "I have extended this tolerance to oral history and employed the literary convention with the same critical caution I hope illustrious predecessors have applied to written documents. It remains a convention."[27]

How legitimate is it to cite anonymous interviews?

Journalists and other writers often rely on anonymous sources. Like Bob Woodward's "Deep Throat," journalists have interviewees whose identities they promise to keep secret and would go to jail rather than divulge. Reporters know they would not get sensitive information if they interviewed only for attribution. Social scientists employ pseudonyms to protect the privacy of the communities they study. Anthropologists, linguists, and sociologists often interview people as representatives of types rather than as identifiable individuals. Their fieldwork techniques permit the creation of fictional identities for people and places. They believe that anonymity encourages interviewees to speak more candidly and that it protects interviewees, their families, and their jobs from retribution.

Oral historians influenced by the social sciences have felt a similarly strong need to protect interviewees' well-being by not revealing their names. They feel that sometimes the general message carries more significance than the particular speaker. For instance, the historian Sherna Gluck regretted that the political climate in the Middle East prevented her from revealing the real names of the Palestinian women she interviewed. "They have made it clear, however, that this personal recognition is less important to them than making their story public."[28]

Yet anonymity clashes with some of oral history's most fundamental objectives. Having sought to give "voice to the voiceless," it is inconsistent to render them nameless. Oral historians conduct life review biographical interviews because they consider interviewees important as individuals and want to record their unique experiences and perceptions. Future historians using those interviews will also expect some verification of sources. They will want to know where the information came from and what biases might have affected the testimony. Just as critics of journalistic practices have complained that unbridled anonymity allows public officials to evade responsibility for their views, oral historians believe that their interviewees should be held accountable for what they say for the record. Nothing based on anonymous sources can be proven, and the evidence remains at the level of rumor and innuendo. "When sources choose anonymity," the oral historian William W. Moss warned, "whether out of privacy, humility, or fear, the record produced not only suffers the loss of user confidence that accompanies any anonymous testimony, but the primary assertion of oral history that the individual indeed matters is also lost."[29]

The issue of anonymity created the greatest single area of disagreement when the Oral History Association revised its principles, standards, and evaluation guidelines in 1991. After protracted debate, the OHA adopted guidelines that ask whether "the Interviewee understands his/her right to refuse to discuss certain subjects, to seal portions of the interview or in extremely sensitive circumstances even to choose to remain anonymous."[30]

By accepting anonymity under dire circumstances, oral historians indicated that it should never be a routine practice. When authors claim that their books are based on hundreds of interviews and cite none specifically, or assert that none of their interviewees chose to be identified, there is a strong suspicion that anonymity was part of the researcher's design and that interviewee's were never encouraged or given the opportunity to speak for the record. The use of blanket anonymity also raises the question of the expiration of that anonymity. Was the promise of anonymity eternal, or can the interviewees' identities be restored to them at some safe point in the future?

One solution for writers seeking to balance their interviewees' anonymity with scholarly verification is to deposit the recordings and transcripts in a library or archives with provisions for identifying the interviewees after a safe interval. The political scientist Richard Fenno has given his interviews with members of Congress to the National Archives. As these interviewees had left public life, they could be identified without fear of political embarrassment, thereby enhancing the future research value of the collection. A history of the U.S. space program drew heavily from interviews with past and present employees of National Aeronautics and Space Administration (NASA), asking about their personal backgrounds, the type of work they did in the space program, and their perspectives on how the agency changed over time. Given that many of the interviewees were still NASA employees, they were assured that their names would not appear next to any quotations used in the published history—which identified each interview only by number—but that the transcripts, linking names to the numbers, would be preserved in the NASA History Office.[31]

PUBLISHING ORAL HISTORY

How much editing of interviews is acceptable for publication?

Transcripts of recordings are edited, and most published oral histories have been further edited, condensing and highlighting remarks and in some cases rearranging testimony for chronological and narrative purposes. But how much is too much? Oral historians have expressed suspicion over the popular books of Studs Terkel, who usually removes his own questions and sometimes reorders his interviewee's answers. When Charles Morrissey questioned some of the Vermonters quoted in Terkel's *American Dreams, Lost and Found* (1980), they objected to the way their remarks had appeared in print. One complained that Terkel "applied his thoughts to my words and came up with the version in his book." Another felt that his words had been rearranged "in such a way that I can't make sense of it."[32]

Some of the best known "oral history" books have been produced by professional writers who lacked training in historical research and handled oral documentation rather loosely. Serious questions were raised about the authenticity of Alex Haley's *Roots* (1976); many felt it was a work of historical fiction more than history. Merle Miller's *Plain Speaking: An Oral Biography of Harry S. Truman* (1974), in a similar fashion, seems to mix Truman's recollections with Miller's own creative writing. Miller did not publish his interviews until after Truman's death, and some of the statements he attributed to Truman strain credulity. Miller's rambling remarks to an Oral History Association meeting in 1975 augmented the audience's worst suspicions. "I don't consider myself an oral historian," Miller later admitted. He then added, "Oral historians don't either. I spoke at their national convention several years ago and they loathed me, detested me, because since I don't know the rules of oral history—and operate as a reporter, which I consider myself—I violate them." After Miller's death, seven hours of his recorded interviews with Truman, conducted in 1961–62, were opened for research at the Truman Library. Historians who reviewed the tapes found nothing in them to support the book's more sensational claims.[33]

Editing and rearranging interviews for clarification and cutting away tangential material are appropriate so long as the original meaning is retained. The goal is to sharpen the focus without putting words in the interviewee's mouth or altering the essence of what was said. For instance, if an interviewee spoke at length about someone's positive characteristics and fleetingly of one negative quality, it would be misleading and unfair to quote only the latter.

In reproducing large sections of oral history interviews for publication, researchers should consider including the questions as well as the answers. Some subjects may not have been discussed simply because the interviewer asked nothing about them. Other subjects came up precisely because that was what the interviewer wanted to know about. By leaving as many of their questions in the text as feasible, oral historians not only show what questions elicited the responses but demonstrate that the interviewee did not necessarily volunteer the information and may even have had to be coaxed to reveal private and potentially embarrassing information. Without the questions, the basic dialogue of an oral history is lost, creating the impression that people raised the issues when, in fact, they were responding to queries. Similarly, when several interviewees focus on a particular trait or make a similar observation, it could be simply because they are all responding to the same question.

Oral history has become fashionable among popular writers and other purveyors of popular culture who are not always careful about its presentation. Cullom Davis, who directed the oral history program at Sangamon State University in Illinois, warned of its "debasement" by those who fail to "observe the canons of our profession." He charged that publication or oral history without interpretation produces little more than a scissors-and-paste scrapbook and a disorganized mass of recollections. "As serious practitioners, whether lay or professional," Davis argued, "we must identify the hucksters and charlatans who exploit oral history's intrinsic appeal for their own shallow, ahistorical and even unethical ends."[34]

Should oral history interviewees speak for themselves, or do they require scholarly interpretation?

The compelling nature of the spoken word, the enjoyment of reading the vernacular, the honesty and humor of so many interviewees, has kindled a strong interest in allowing oral sources to "speak for themselves." This approach, which often involves little interpretation on the part of the compiler, sometimes results in books that resemble collages. The literary critic Elizabeth Hardwick has dismissed "tape recording without an interpretive intelligence" as "a primitive technology for history" designed to relieve the author of the burden of writing. Hardwick insists that a book requires an author's "signature of responsibility."[35]

Reviewing the biography of Robert F. Kennedy by Arthur Schlesinger, Jr., Henry Fairlie dismissed oral history as testimonials of dubious value. It is up to the historian "to do the hard work of sifting," wrote Fairlie. "When we are given the personal words of various actors, that is all we are given, and we have either to take or reject their word that something happened as they say. . . . That is what we have historians for: to take their word that this was so." Historians act as judges, interpreters, and critics, compiling and analyzing sources of the past. Historians are rarely themselves eyewitnesses to the events they write about. They reconstruct events and the temper of the time from a mixture of sources, balancing the reliability of one piece of data against another, arranging them in a coherent pattern to make sense out of what happened.[36]

The very act of editing and arranging interviews shows that the author has not simply allowed interviewees to speak for themselves. Editorial intervention begins with determining whom to interview, what questions to ask, which interviews to include in the volume, in which order, and how much of the original interviews to publish. Even if the editor refrains from adding an overt interpretation, he or she is still deciding which interviewees are most worthy of being recorded and published. Having gone that far then, the editor owes something more to readers. At the minimum, authors of oral history collections should provide some background for their interviews to place the interviewees in context, offering suggestions about why they said what they did and took certain positions and sometimes spelling out where interviewer and interviewee did not agree.

A certain romantic belief has developed that putting a microphone in front of people will miraculously provide the road to truth. In his influential review of oral history literature, Michael Frisch has argued that what historians do—interpreting evidence, weighing, testing, connecting people and events—is still critically important. "And yet, at the same time the exciting thing about oral history is that the process becomes a less exclusive one," he added. The scholar and the subject collaborate: "They come together and provide a good advantage for understanding the meaning of the experience." This is the notion that Frisch calls a "shared authority": "the grounds of authority are very different, and have different meaning, but there is a kind of sharing in the process of the interpretive authority, which is one of the exciting things about doing oral history."[37]

If writers quote from interviews they conducted, do they need to first submit them to their interviewees for review?

Some researchers allow their interviewees to check their quotes before they use them. "I think it's only fair," Arthur Schlesinger, Jr., reasoned, "that when you talk to people, you should give them the same kind of control over an interview as they have over an oral history transcript." Other researchers might chafe over this idea, given that an interviewee might change or delete something entirely. Yet anyone who has ever been interviewed by a reporter and then misquoted in the newspaper article can appreciate how differently the teller of the tale and the listener can hear the same story. Context is essential for accuracy, and even a perfectly quoted sentence can have its meaning altered if taken out of context.[38]

At the same time, interpreting what the interviewees said remains the historian's domain. A researcher and an interviewee may form entirely different opinions about the events being discussed. Even though interviewees were eyewitnesses, their perspectives could be distorted, and their memories incorrect. By collecting evidence from a multitude of sources, the historian may come to a different conclusion. The author's duty is to quote the interviewee correctly and not distort the remarks to fit a thesis. Otherwise, the author is entirely responsible for the finished product.

What do reviewers look for when reviewing oral history books?

Reviewers have been notoriously inconsistent in dealing with oral history. Too often a review begins with an admission that the reviewer knows little about oral history or does not trust oral sources, characteristics that never seem to disqualify them from reviewing the book. They distance themselves from the methodology and consequently add little to our understanding. At the root of their complaints, however, is a fairly common call for the author to assume a more interpretive role. Commenting on the increased appearance of books based on interviews, the novelist and frequent reviewer Diane Johnson asserted, "There does seem in this technique an almost cowardly reluctance to think."[39] In the same vein, Timothy Foote began a review of an oral history of the Second World War by noting: "Anything calling itself oral history probably ought to be approached with deep suspicion. Time is short. There is much to read. We're already awash in ill-chosen words. And though tape recorders are splendid gimmicks, people who present interviews as history are farther from the mark than a cook who insists that a loose collection of eggs, sugar, milk, vanilla, flour, and a few squares of bitter chocolate are in fact a chocolate cake."[40]

Reviewers more experienced with oral history have reacted to the literature through the lens of their own disciplines or tailored their reactions to fit the publications in which their reviews appear. After conducting a survey of oral history reviews, the book review editor Linda Shopes observed that reviewers in the *Oral History Review* generally wanted to know more about the interviewing process and procedures than about the subject matter and particular findings of a project, although the accuracy of the information gathered was often a major touchstone of *OHR* reviews. Reviewers commented on whatever unique insights and perspectives emerged from the interviews but took the authors to task for not testing the accuracy of oral evidence through corroborating sources. Reviews in the more theoretically oriented *International Journal of Oral History* were more likely to be interpretive, focusing on subjectivity and how oral tradition and narratives "can reveal the complex consciousness of a culture." Reviews in the British journal *Oral History* tended to raise questions of a political nature, reflecting the journal's socialist leanings.

Reviewers for general, non-oral history journals express more concern about oral history's substantive contributions to historical knowledge. These reviews emphasize the importance of first-person narrative in conveying a sense of people as historical actors and actresses. General historical reviewers tend to respond best to authors who use a variety of interviewees together with other documentary sources, and who place the data in broad analytical context. The chief conclusion that emerges from this sampling of reviewers is that the author of an oral history volume is inevitably judged as a historian and cannot escape that role by suggesting that the sources "speak for themselves."[41]

How should oral histories be cited as references?

How to cite interviews is a question that touches on how seriously researchers take oral sources. Of all the academic disciplines engaged in interviewing as a research tool, professional historians have devoted the least amount of methodological attention to its problems and potentials. This laxity contrasts sharply with the intense seriousness historians bring to written sources. Authors dutifully list every manuscript collection, book, and article consulted, and then limit the bibliography of oral sources to a few lines acknowledging those who "shared their knowledge" in "conversations" with the author. Footnotes identify the interviews with cryptic initials and often without dates or other information that would tell the interested reader how the interview was collected. Some interviews are not cited at all. Substantial numbers of histories drawn from oral sources give no indication of whether the recordings and transcripts are deposited somewhere, either for other researchers' use or for verification. It remains puzzling why professional historians have accepted on faith the author's reliability in note taking, transcribing, and even interpreting oral information.[42]

Guides to historical writing specify that the standard reference should begin with the name of the interviewee. The title of the interview (if there is one) should be in quotation marks. The citation should include "interviewed by [with the name of the interviewer]" and mention whether the interview is a recording or transcript, and whether it has been published as part of a book or journal article or in any other medium, with standard references to such publication. The citation should indicate whether the interview is in the author's possession or has been deposited in a library or archive. Keep in mind that the purpose of a footnote is to show where the information comes from and to help the reader find the original source. Page numbers for transcripts, or other publications, should be provided. For interviews found on the Internet, cite the archives where the collection is physically located as well as its electronic address.[43]

The following are examples of citations of interviews from oral history archives, from independent research, and from published sources:

Beth Campbell Short, interviewed by Margot H. Knight, April 23–August 17, 1987, transcripts, Women in Journalism Project, Washington Press Club Foundation, Washington, D.C.
http://npc.press.org/wpforal/bcs.htm

Sen. Hugh D. Scott, interviewed by the author, January 27, 1986, tape and transcript deposited at the Senate Historical Office, Washington, D.C.

David Montgomery, interview by Paul Buhle, *Visions of History,* ed. Henry Abelove, et al. (New York: Pantheon, 1983), 169–83.

CHAPTER 5

Videotaping Oral History

Should oral histories be videotaped?

Memories are recounted in more than words. Transcripts can indicate laughter, sobs, finger pointing, or fist shaking. But some expressions and gestures are too complex or subtle to reduce to words. When Richard Sweterlitsch tape-recorded an interview with the Italian-American Sophia Bielli about the granite industry in Barre, Vermont, he realized that her language was not just verbal. "Sophia spoke with her hands punctuating her oral statements, and with her face and eyes she communicated her intensity and reactions to what she was saying," he observed. "It was obvious that I had to document the visual along with the aural."[1]

Transcripts, audio recordings, and videos all impart the same basic information, but video provides an extra dimension to oral history interviews. Transcripts reduce language to written symbols. Audio recordings convey tone, rhythm, volume, and speech patterns. But the facial expressions and body language captured by video reveal even more of an interviewee's personality. A smile, a wink, a frown, a look of perplexity would be missed in an audio interview and convey more than what can be reproduced on the tape.

The setting in which the interview takes place can also add color and context. For many families, videotaped oral histories with elderly relatives are treasured keepsakes. For museums and archives, video interviews expand the potential uses of oral histories as valuable resources for exhibits and documentaries. The Smithsonian Institution used video interviews with zoologists not only to talk about but to show changes in zoo facilities and animal care. History Associates, Inc. conducted a video history of a large Washington, D.C., law firm, producing a videotape that mixes interviews with film footage around the offices and around the capital. Harlem's Schomburg Center for Research in Black Culture videotaped African-American dance traditions. The Museum of Jewish Heritage in New York incorporates a series of ten-minute films combining video oral histories and film footage throughout its exhibitions. Producer Steven Speilberg has underwritten the filming of tens of thousands of interviews for the Survivors of

Shoah Visual History Foundation. San Francisco's Legacy Project videotapes interviews and captures the motions of dancers dying of AIDS.[2]

Video is highly practical when recording group interviews. Anyone who has tried to transcribe an interview with multiple interviewees knows the frustration and helplessness of not being able to tell who is speaking, since voices in a group sound impossibly alike. Speakers will interrupt each other, cut in, and speak simultaneously, all chaotic conditions for the transcriber. One solution is to assign someone to sit in the session and note the order of speakers, but a video provides a much more precise means of distinguishing speakers.

Digital video recording has become the favored medium for capturing oral history visually. Although film is an acceptable alternative, it is infrequently used because of its expense, production complications, and inconvenience. Videotape cameras also required the use of extra lighting, sound equipment, and crew, which encouraged many video interviewers to restrict their work to studios where they could best control sound and light conditions. Digital camcorders, by contrast, perform well in low-light conditions, need only a single operator, and allow interviews to take place in more natural settings.

Why aren't all interviews being videotaped?

Initially, the equipment and personnel requirements made videotaping more cumbersome and costly than audio interviewing. Interviewers worried that cameras and lights would make it harder for interviewers to put interviewees at ease and establish rapport. People might not warm up quickly to the cameras, might become more self-conscious, and might have more trouble speaking candidly. A video interview could also result in hours of visually dull "talking heads." Oral historians also needed to be assured that video had the same recording and preservation capabilities as audio recordings; that the technology had advanced to the point where it was worth the investment; that the video could be considered reliable; that the recording would last; and that the demands of the technology would not impede the interviews.[3]

Behind their pragmatic reasons, the reluctance of many oral historians to try videotaping also suggested a widespread "technophobia," or nervousness about any new technology. Similar fears caused some interviewers to use reel-to-reel tape recorders long after the majority had switched to more portable and affordable cassette recorders. There were good reasons for caution—reel-to-reel tape remains preferable to cassettes for archival preservation—but "we've never done it that way before" was a poor excuse for not exploring and trying new equipment. While veteran oral historians hung back, National History Day judges observed that high school-age students were quick to master the new technologies and that the videos they produced were often impressively polished, professional, and creative.

Some projects videotape every interview, but most use cameras more selectively. There are advantages to conducting audio oral histories first, to collect basic information, and then return to video a portion of the interview, allowing the cameras to illustrate the oral history. The video segment may cover new ground or repeat some questions to recapture highlights of the previous session. Video interviews with artists and craftspeople can be devoted to recording them at work or to having them describe and explain their creations. Having recorded most of the interview on audio gives the interviewer and the interviewee a better idea of what to expect during the video session, making them both a little more comfortable in front of the camera.[4]

Researchers have discovered that the video portions of an interview can be more quotable than the audio portions. If the video interviews serve as summaries of longer series of audio interviews, the interviewees have had some time to think about their responses and, perhaps because they are also more conscious of the camera, tell their stories more succinctly. Interviewees, in a sense, edit themselves the way a film editor might cut a story down to size. Not only does this make for better video, but the transcripts of the video segments are often more compact and articulate than the sometimes rambling versions of the audio recordings.

Documentarians often resort to coaxing an interviewee to repeat a phrase, louder, with different emphasis, or in more complete sentences. The necessity of some staging in video offends those practitioners who believe an oral history should always be authentic and unrehearsed. In fact, there has never been any truth to the adage that "photos never lie." Just as Civil War photographers rearranged bodies on the battlefield to heighten the visual effect, modern documentary makers often choose to meld history with artistry.[5]

If the ultimate objective is to produce a documentary or mount an exhibit, it makes sense to video every session of every interview. But if the objective is an archival collection for all types of research, selective videotaping is more cost-effective. Vivian Perlis, director of the Oral History and American Music Project at Yale University, has described the video component as "the finishing touch" of their oral histories. Initially, the project historians conducted videos of all their interviews at the homes of such interviewees as Aaron Copeland, but they came to realize that some musicians are "more filmic" than others and that the expense of regular on-site interviewing was growing unmanageable. They did subsequent videotaping at a studio at Yale and even then videotaped only major figures rather than all interviewees.[6]

Won't the camera make interviewees
nervous and uncomfortable?

Undeniably, the use of a camera, which sometimes entails a crew, lights, and a studio, may intimidate some interviewees. Video specialists recommend that interviewers explain the equipment to interviewees, demonstrating how it works, making sure that they are seated comfortably, and encouraging them to look at the interviewer rather than at the camera, which should be placed off to one side.[7]

Yet television and home videos have become so commonplace in modern society that interviewees are far less likely to be put off by cameras than might be expected. Video interviews with elderly residents in nursing homes, for instance, show that even people never before videotaped quickly feel at ease and talk naturally on camera. Keep in mind, however, that interviewees can become fatigued and not look their best for the camera. Some video historians have raised the ethical question of what obligation a project has to interviewees who, because they slumped or were nervous or made awkward gestures, are disappointed or embarrassed over their video appearance.[8]

Sometimes the interviewer can be even more nervous than the interviewee on camera. Listening carefully to what is being said and thinking ahead to the next question, interviewers also have to wonder about how they appear themselves (although interviewers may not necessarily be seen in the picture). It takes some practice to switch from audio to visual taping. The Oral History Association once sponsored a debate between a video supporter, who had conducted all of his interviews on videotape, and a video skeptic, who had previously expressed deep-felt reservations that the camera destroys the intimacy needed to establish rapport in an interview. When the debate took place, however, the skeptic announced that, to be fair, he had decided to try doing a video interview himself. To his astonishment, he admitted, it was the best interview he had ever conducted. Not only was he freed from watching the tape recorder and changing the tape, but the crew was unobtrusive and the interviewee had no problem talking on camera. Delighted with the results, the skeptical interviewer had become an enthusiastic convert to videotaped interviews, forcing the video supporter to interject a few words of caution about video's potential problems into his presentation on its benefits.

Should interviewees be prepared in advance of a video interview?

Interviewees should be informed of the purpose of the interview, of any special requirements for videotaping, of their legal rights, and of the need for their signature on a release form. For videotaping on location, the interviewee needs to know about, and give permission for, setting up camera and lights in his or her home. Interviewees should also be reminded of the expense and difficulty of sending a crew to video an interview, to encourage them not to cancel or postpone the interview without sufficient notice.

Some interviewers recommend appropriate dress to interviewees, or at least advise them on the types of colors and patterns to avoid (white or black, and clothes with bold stripes or patterns). Interviewers should be available to talk with interviewees in advance of the interview, to answer their questions and satisfy their concerns. Such information and reassurance often help interviewees feel comfortable with the video medium, encouraging them to speak as candidly as possible.

Does the use of video versus strictly audio recording affect the types of questions that an oral historian asks?

The medium definitely affects the message. Oral historians who work with video report that they have had to reformulate questions to elicit the type of information that makes for better visual presentation. They often have replaced abstract and generalized questions with more specific inquiries, asking fewer "why" questions and more "how" questions. They have asked interviewees to demonstrate how equipment worked or to go through their usual routines, eliciting the type of detail that an audio interview could never approach.[9]

Shifts in questioning become more pronounced when curators, exhibitors, documentary makers, and material culture specialists conduct their video interviews with specific ends in mind. The museum curator might be seeking a video of a worker talking about and demonstrating a mechanical or artistic process, to accompany the actual machinery or display in the museum. The questions therefore would be aimed precisely toward that end. The National Park Service set up lights and cameras in the home of Jimmy Carter in Plains, Georgia, and had Carter conduct a tour of the house and grounds. Although the interview raised questions about Carter's life and career, and particularly about his postpresidential years, the chief focus was on the architecture of the house and an inventory of the Carters' furniture, memorabilia, and other belongings. Eventually, when the house passes to the National Park Service as a historic site, the videos will enable curators to re-create the environment in which the Carters lived. Excerpts from the interviews will be shown at the visitors' center.[10]

Although the type of question may change, the way in which questions are posed should not. However complete their transfer from the aural to the visual medium, oral historians must maintain their professional standards and avoid the temptation to emulate the more aggressive television news interviewers. Interviewees may pose, but oral history interviewers should never play to the cameras.

SETTING AND EQUIPMENT

Should a video oral history be conducted in a studio or in a more natural setting?

Studios are artificial, perhaps even intimidating, settings for interviews. As a result, interviewers often prefer to bring the camera to the interviewee's home or equally familiar surroundings. The natural setting provides a more interesting backdrop and usually an abundance of stimulants for interviewee's memories. The Smithsonian Institution has conducted video oral histories in the laboratories and workshops of its scientists and curators. The Minnesota Historical Society has similarly videoed on location, from farmyards to boat docks, after first completing audio interviews. Once the audio segments are made, several interviewees are selected to retell portions of their stories on camera and to point out places or demonstrate activities related to their testimony.[11]

While more visually interesting, natural settings add to the problems of doing a video interview, including the inconvenience of moving equipment, the obstacles to acceptable sound quality, and the unpredictability of light, sound, and background noise when videoing outdoors. Video interviewers need to know the limitations of the equipment and must be prepared to solve technical problems in the field. They need to prepare checklists so that equipment is not forgotten. Videotaping at an interviewee's home or place of work may require an advance trip to the site to decide how to set up the equipment. Considerations include seating the interviewee away from the glare of a window and avoiding noisy rooms, being conscious of outdoor noise and wind, and watching out for inquisitive neighbors and dogs. When taping outside, the wind may create noise or play havoc with the interviewee's hair, distracting viewer attention. The sun may cast unflattering shadows, and clouds may cause the light to fluctuate during taping.[12]

For quality control, a studio or other indoor setting is preferable for video interviewing. Studio interviews, however, more often result in "talking heads" and lack the variation in images that improves and enlivens a documentary. A reasonable compromise is to conduct part of the interview in a studio and then take a camera to follow interviewees through more natural settings walking around their homes or neighborhoods, at a factory, going down a road by themselves or with the interviewer. These images can later be edited, with the studio audio used as a voice-over. Still photographs also can be interspersed.

After the interview has been completed, a "sweeping pan" can be taken of the room where the interview took place, to capture the interview environment for the historical record. Photographs from a family album can also be videoed at the end of the interview. Known as "cutaways," this additional footage can be interspersed later throughout the interview to vary the visual effects.

If a project has a limited budget, how can it afford to use a studio?

Video oral historians have a number of affordable options to get technical assistance and access to equipment. Numerous community colleges and universities maintain broadcast facilities, often as part of communications departments. These studios, which offer the help of student assistants, can be rented for reasonable costs. The studio managers are often open to cost-sharing proposals to reduce charges further.

Another avenue for low-cost of free use of studios and equipment is the local community-access cable channel. These channels were made possible by the Cable Communications Policy Act of 1984, which entitled communities to require the creation of a community-access channel as part of their franchise agreements with cable television companies. An estimated 1,500 public channels have been established nationwide. Service, fees, and expertise vary widely, but these facilities have been used successfully by oral historians in different regions to produce video interviews and documentaries.

Community-access channels generally provide free use of their equipment, and since they are always seeking new material, they may offer to show the resulting programs and documentaries. For a nominal fee, the channels usually offer training for individuals or groups in the use of video cameras, lighting, audio mixing, scripting, directing, and producing. The studios may provide free tape stock for the programs they air but probably will charge for any duplicate tapes. Oral historians who must travel to do their interviews can look for a local resident to sponsor their use of the local community access studio. To identify community-access channels, contact the local cable programmers or the Alliance for Community Media.[13]

How large a budget is necessary to do video oral history?

Digital and other video cameras are relatively affordable, but a full-fledged, good quality video oral history is not an inexpensive process. Costs range widely, but basically include fees for the interviewer's preliminary research, interview time, travel and transport expenses, and editing of the interviews. A crew may need to be hired, and equipment leased for the day, at the going rate where the interview takes place. The crew may also incur transportation, lodging, and meal expenses. Supplies must be purchased.

When the interview is completed, transcribers or indexers are needed. Duplicate recordings must be made for archival preservation and use, and sometimes copies of the recording or transcript must be given to the interviewee. General office expenses and supplies cannot be overlooked. Those costs all mount up. When applying for grants to do video histories, it is essential not to underbudget, or operating expenses will evaporate well before the project is completed. In fact, most granting agencies and foundations have acquired a good sense of the financial requirements of video oral history and dismiss applications that are underbudgeted as a sure sign of the applicant's inexperience.

Is a camera crew necessary?
What is wrong with the interviewer simply
setting the camera on a tripod to run itself?

Before the advent of digital cameras, video producers considered it a grievous mistake for the interviewer to try to play camera operator. Interviewers need to concentrate fully on the give-and-take of the interview. Running a tape recorder offered distractions enough, but the camera, lights, and sound requirements of a video interview required trained technical assistance.

Digital cameras can operate with an automatic focus and without additional lighting. Those with remote monitors allow the interviewer to see what the camera is recording, and to adjust the camera angles accordingly. Experienced video interviewers who once insisted on the necessity of a crew have found that digital cameras enable them to operate entirely on their own. But less-experienced interviewers should keep in mind that video complicates the interviewing process, and that amateur filming will diminish the ultimate utility of the video images.

Although cameras have built-in sound recordings capabilities, it is always advisable to audio record the interview separately. A boom mike produces good quality sound recordings without intruding on the picture. Operating that equipment, including changing audio and videotapes when necessary, makes it harder for the interviewer to focus full attention on the interview. Having someone else handle the equipment relieves the interviewer of potential distractions and improves chances of a better product. Those operating the equipment should be fully aware of the project's objectives, of the mood it is seeking, and of any of the interviewee's mannerisms to be recorded. The video interview is therefore a collaborative effort, not only between the interviewer and the interviewee but between the interviewer and the technicians responsible for the quality control of the video recording.

How many people are necessary to run a video oral history project?

Numbers vary according to project budgets, but the functions that have to be handled are the same, regardless of the size of the staff. In better-funded projects, these functions are divided among several staff members; the staffs of smaller projects wear many hats. All oral history projects, audio or visual, need a director who will set the agenda, raise and administer funds, handle contracts, maintain the paperwork, and supervise the rest of the personnel.

A video oral history project requires a producer (who may be the project director or the interviewer doing double duty) to choose the interviewees, the times and the sites of the interviews, and the crew to conduct the interviews. The director (who may also be the producer) supervises the technical crew and the setting of the lights and cameras and maintains the general aural and visual standards of the day's taping. The camera operator (who may also be the director) composes the shots, tapes the interview, and keeps the interviewer informed of when the tape is running out. Larger projects may employ a sound operator to handle the microphones and monitor the audio recording levels, and a "grip" or assistant, to set up and take down the equipment before and after the interview. It is also beneficial to have a production assistant present at the site of the interview to take care of the paperwork, get release forms signed, handle the master tape, and deal with problems as they arise. All of those functions may devolve to the oral historian, who from necessity acts as interviewer, camera operator, and paperwork handler, but more help assures better quality control.[14]

What kind of video equipment should be acquired for an oral history project?

The better the quality of the equipment, the better the video interview. The initial consumer video recorders were not appropriate for long-term preservation and use in exhibits or documentaries, which required professional-quality cameras and studio videotapes. Digital video has been easier to use, reproduce, and edit. Digital video also offers greater resolution than previous video camcorders. Digital video is sometimes copied onto VHS tapes for preservation in that format, or transferred to DVD and CD-ROM.[15]

Cameras are only as good as their lenses. Use a lens wide enough for video recording in close quarters. A zoom ratio from telephoto to wide-angle of at least 8:1 is recommended. For sound recording, many use a "boom mike" that extends close to the speaker. A lavaliere mike, pinned unobtrusively onto a scarf, necktie, or lapel, also promotes good sound quality. To be safe, record the interview on a tape recorder or minidisk recorder as a backup system. The audio recording can be used for transcribing and archival purposes. Work with reputable dealers, and while taking advantage of whatever discounts are available for equipment, make sure that you understand the warranties and guarantees.[16]

Digital video technology has been a boon to documentarians who shoot with only a single camera. Editing interviews creates "jump cuts" that are usually masked by inserting other images between the breaks. "You've got to think reverses, b-roll and graphics, something to cut away," the filmmaker William Gazecki commented. "How are you going to string this together when you're using bits and pieces later on." The more seamless the editing, the less distracting it will be for viewers. Digital technology offers filmmakers "all of your post-production tools at your fingertips in one room." But while digital technology affords low-cost access to production, Gazecki reminds us "it's really just a tool. The real meat is in the idea, in the concept."[17]

What's the optimal way to set up the cameras for an interview?

A video oral history needs a competent camera operator who knows how to frame and light a picture properly. Poor camera work can make even the most interesting interview dull. If you have gone to the trouble of using the visual medium, you need to be conscious of the picture you are getting. Although oral historians interview to gain information, video offers the observer an array of new insights. The aim is to present the picture so that it does not overwhelm or distract viewers from the substance of the interview but enhances the meaning of what is being said.

Video documentaries are almost always viewed on television-sized screens, and television is a close-up medium, in which head and shoulder shots predominate. In framing the picture, it is important to give the speaker adequate "head room" and "look space." Balanced head room prevents the head from appearing too close to the top of the frame or sinking below it. Eye room similarly suggests the amount of space from the face to the side of the frame. For variety, the camera can move in for a close-up that shows the face only from the eyes to the mouth. Viewers mentally complete the picture. The video specialist David Mould also notes that "the human body has certain natural divisions at the neck, at the waist, at the knees," and he warns against framing an interview so that the bottom of the pictures breaks at one of these divisions.[18]

The way a subject is framed can constitute a subtle form of editorializing. The popular television news show *60 Minutes* frequently shoots its interviewees in extreme close-ups, cutting the tops of their heads from the picture and focusing on their eyes. By contrast, when the camera turns to the program's own interviewers, it pulls back to give them full head and shoulders and "lots of visual breathing space."[19] Shooting below or above the interviewee also distorts the picture. A more neutral picture of the speaker is taken at eye level, so that the viewer sees the speaker at the same level. Interviewees should sit at a slight angle to the camera and talk to the interviewer rather than to the camera. The background should be relatively uncluttered to avoid diverting viewers' attention. Interviewers should dress appropriately for the particular interview and should avoid wearing unusually patterned clothing that would clash with the backdrop or otherwise prove distracting.

Camera angles differ when videotaping a group. Video oral histories have experimented with many different arrangements or interviewers and interviewees. A particularly successful arrangement is to place the interviewer, back to the camera, in the open end of a V-shaped table at which the interviewees are sitting. The interviewer can maintain eye contact with whomever is speaker, just as the camera can focus easily on the speakers, either individually or in groups.[20]

Keep in mind the time needed to set up and tear down equipment before and after an interview. Veteran documentary makers urged video historians to "add pad time" to their shooting schedule. You should not expect to begin taping for at least an hour after arriving at a location. Leave time also after the interview to video photographs, maps, and memorabilia.[21]

Is it appropriate to use a zoom lens during a video interview?

Zoom lenses change the picture composition to create more diverse and interesting visual effects, to produce close-ups, or perhaps to capture an artifact of a speaker's expressive hands. But video specialists cringe at "unmotivated" zooming and recommend that the zoom-in or -out take place during the question rather than during the answer. Documentary makers inevitably edit the tape for their particular needs, cutting out false starts, phrases, and whole sentences and paragraphs; they prefer a standard camera angle and position and head size because the speaker's head remains a uniform size when they cut back into the tape. They aim to produce a seamless product, which appears "as if nobody did anything." Ideally, viewers should not even be aware of editing techniques. Editors also favor some variety in shots, however, and suggest that at least two standard framings be used. Video historians must consider all the possible uses of their product and proceed accordingly.[22]

Should both the interviewer and interviewee be seen on camera?

The chief focus should be on the interviewee. The interviewer's questions shape the dialogue, but the reason for doing interviews is to hear what interviewees have to say and, on video, to watch them saying it. When the budget covers the use of only one camera, as is most often the case, focus on the interviewee during the interview. If necessary, the interviewer can be filmed asking questions and reacting (that is, listening quietly) after the interview is over. Television news broadcasts have long employed this technique, which is a pivotal point in the movie *Broadcast News*. As in the motion picture, staged "reaction" shots raise ethical issues and should be handled very carefully.

Some oral historians object strongly to taping only the interviewee. Noting the collaborative nature of an interview, they ask, why video only one party to it? "The integrity of the document may be compromised if only half of the interview 'team' is photographed and recorded," Thomas L. Charlton of the Baylor University Institute for Oral History has written. He recommends using two cameras: one to focus exclusively on the interviewee, the second to focus alternately on the interviewer and on group shots containing both the interviewer and interviewee. Some video oral historians have also used a split-screen technique. Multiple cameras are easier to use in a studio than on location.[23]

PRESERVING AND USING THE VIDEO RECORDINGS

What type of documentation is needed for a video oral history?

Just as with an audio interview, video oral histories require some basic data for research use. At a minimum, documentation should include: the date of the interview; the names of the interviewee and interviewer; a summary statement on the interviewee and the subjects covered; whether there are transcripts of the interview; whether the recording is audio or visual; the running time or length of the interview; and any restrictions on the use of the material.

Are deeds of gift also required for video oral histories?

Federal law specifies that any tangible recording of a person's words is protected by copyright. Interviewees retain ownership of their words until they sign a deed of gift, contract, or release form, which usually transfer intellectual property rights of the interview from the interviewee to the sponsoring institution or documentary maker. Video release forms can be the same as those for audio oral history, with one difference: the use of an interviewee's face as well as voice in a documentary can be unsettling if unexpected, so some video releases include a statement that the interviewee has been notified of the uses to which the material will be put.[24]

What archival considerations should be taken
into account when making video oral histories?

As with sound recordings, archives face the problem of new technology making current video equipment obsolete. Some video interviews have been recorded in formats for which archives have no playback equipment. The recordings have to be converted or they are not usable.

When videotape was introduced, it was found that each time the tape was played the picture quality decreased. As a result, a master video recording was required for preservation. "Dubbing masters" were used to make copies for showing and editing. Archivists recommended the use of "larger, thicker, wider tape" for quality sound and image recording, reproduction and preservation, although they recognized that such high-quality recording required large and cumbersome equipment and considerably higher costs. Moreover, manufacturers increasingly abandoned the one-inch and three-quarter inch videotape that archivists preferred in favor of Betacam and digital formats.[25]

Digital video systems have become increasingly popular because of their ease in recording and editing. Audio and visual recordings are converted into data and can be handled the same as any other electronic data. Computer software programs facilitate online editing of both audio and video, and the product can be transmitted electronically and stored on CD-ROM. Digital audio and visual recordings can also be copied endlessly with little loss of sound and picture quality. But some archivists worry that CDs are an unstable archival medium, and that preservation copies should be made on videotape.[26]

How long will videotape last?

The life span of home videotape, stored at optimal conditions, has been estimated at about fifteen years. Archivists and museum curators who have accessioned older government videos into their collections have opened the cassette only to find a ribbon of clear acetate and a pile of brown powder. According to one report, "the oxide was dropping off videotape like so much dandruff." Heat and moisture will make the tape deteriorate all the quicker, making it even more important to store the tape at temperatures between fifty-nine and seventy-seven degrees Fahrenheit, and at a midrange of humidity.

Video archives must plan to regularly copy their videotapes before the images deteriorate. Each copy is considered a generation, and it is estimated that consumer VHS tape can make it to three generations. To ensure longer preservation, a digital reproduction can be made from the original tapes. Every copy made from the digital master is the second generation that is, as good as the first copy of the original. Digital copies can be preserved on CD-ROM, although they are probably not suitable for long-term preservation and will need to be copied periodically. Another alternative is to consider converting video into film, which has the longest potential lifetime.

The decay of videotape, the fading of color photographs, and the disintegration of highly acidic paper has created the ironic situation, one photographic specialist noted, "that we're becoming the most fully-documented people in the history of the species, yet ours is the epoch most likely to vanish from the record."[27]

Don't television networks already save extensive video interviews?

Network collection and preservation of video has been less extensive, and more recently initiated, than is generally assumed. Nations with publicly owned television networks took the lead in depositing their film and video at their national archives. The Canadian Broadcasting Company's collection at the Canadian National Film, Television, and Sound Archives in Ottawa provides an outstanding example. By contrast, the privately owned American networks went for decades blithely unconcerned about preserving their film and video heritage and either discarded film or routinely erased and recorded over videotape. Universities made the first effort to save broadcast materials; in 1968 the Vanderbilt Television News Archives, for instance, began collecting an extensive backlog of television news programming. The National Museum of Broadcasting in New York has also begun preserving and exhibiting old television programs and news broadcasts. Purdue University houses the C-SPAN archives and the University of Maryland is home to the National Public Broadcasting Archives.

Much video remains uncollected, however, especially interview segments (or "out-takes") that were not used in documentaries or broadcast on the news. In Hawaii, a video producer's "sheer frustration" in seeking resource material led to the creation of the Film and Video Archive Project. Chris Conebeare realized that as soon as a television documentary is finished and goes on the air, its producers go on to other projects, rarely stopping to think that, though they used only three minutes from an interview, the "other twenty-five minutes they didn't use might be very interesting, historically, to people who are scholars, or even just the general public who has a curiosity about history or culture." Those working on the Film and Video Archive Project also realized that because the shelf life of videotape is so short, these out-takes, without proper maintenance, may be entirely lost within a few years.

Supported financially by Hawaii's public broadcast channel and its state legislature, the Film and Video Archive Project began by compiling an inventory of the condition of videotaped interviews in the state. The project also has encouraged groups applying for funding to produce video documentaries to make provisions to archive all of their interviews. As documentary makers usually operate on budgets tight on both time and funds, stopping to preserve the material they do not use in their finished documentaries can be an expensive nuisance. They are more likely to comply with this provision if they have built preservation into their budgets and scheduling from the start. Doing archival work as an afterthought, when the documentary has been completed and shown and new projects are beckoning, is not nearly as successful.[28]

Other oral history archives with extensive audio interview holdings have begun collecting video interviews and out-takes from producers in their region. The University of Kentucky, for instance, has received the interviews done for such documentaries as *Harlan County, U.S.A.* (1976) and *Long Road Back: Vietnam Remembered* (1985). The deposited recordings and transcripts are available for others to research.[29]

What is the difference between a video oral history and a documentary?

A video oral history in itself is not a documentary. Few people would want to watch the many hours of video necessary to conduct a full life review oral history. Instead, the video interview is source material for documentaries and exhibits. One oral history project included 30 hours of video interviews, of which twenty-five minutes appeared in the seventy-eight-minute documentary. But even this product was cut down to "a television hour," or fifty-six minutes, requiring further reductions in the interviews shown. In another project, fifty hours of interviews were condensed into a one-hour program. In any documentary film or video project, an interviewee who speaks for an hour on video usually appears for only a few minutes, or even a few seconds, in the final product.[30]

Video interviews are more than just another source, however; they have profoundly influenced the nature of documentaries. Older documentaries relied heavily on newsreels and television film. "The producer usually centered on some sort of theme like *The Roaring Twenties* or *The Depression Thirties*," noted the pioneer oral historian Dean Albertson. "A snappy narrative against a background of contemporaneous pop music would be provided, and voilà, a history film." Since the 1970s documentary productions have drawn increasingly on oral histories, and the availability of interviews from particular times and places have shaped the subject and focus of their projects. The old-style documentary showed newsreel clips of women working in a World War II airplane factory, with an omniscient voice-over narrative explaining how women went to work during the war. But *The Life and Times of Rosie the Riveter* (1987) quoted the women themselves, reflecting on their own experiences, talking decades after the war, but often seen in earlier photographs.[31]

Oral histories have helped documentaries become more intimate, more compelling, and more complex. Such projects as *Vietnam: A Television History* (1984) and *Eyes on the Prize* (1986 and 1990) appeared on national television and have been far more widely used as educational tools in schools. The textile strike that swept through Southern cotton mills in 1934 had been the subject of books and dissertations, but reached a much wider audience, including current and former textile workers, in a televised documentary *The Uprising of '34* (1995). *From the Earth: The Pioneers of Lander County* (1996) draws on the stories of the diverse community of immigrants who settled in the isolated mining and ranching region of northern Nevada during the twentieth century.

Before the oral history-based video documentary, *Living the Story: The Civil Rights Movement in Kentucky* (2002) was completed, project staff conducted focus group meetings with potential viewers who expressed a strong preference for hearing stories and getting to know the characters, rather than having a narrator tell them what to think. Although the project had conducted 175 interviews with Kentuckians who had been civil rights activists, the documentary makers responded to these focus groups by selecting only fifteen of the interviewees to make recurring appearances throughout the program, and letting them provide the narration. When *Living the Story* aired on Kentucky Educational Television, the producers also organized "viewing parties" that met at community centers around the state to watch the program and then discuss its meaning and the historical events it covered.[32]

Video interviewing requires making choices as to whom to interview. Turning video interviews into a documentary requires further choices as the documentary maker selects material from the interviews. The editing of the interviews also reveals how much documentary makers value the interviewees as interpreters of their own experiences who can provide anecdotes about people and pivotal moments and help re-create the drama of a moment. By minimizing the role of the narrator and allowing interviewees to speak for themselves, some documentaries have carried the message that only those who "were there" are allowed to speak for history. In reviewing the popular documentary series *Vietnam: A Television History,* Michael Frisch complained, "It is as if students of the Pentagon Papers or journalists or historians, over the years, have not learned more about these events than immediate participants can possibly have experienced, much less remembered and willingly discussed, and as if we had not, in the process, arrived at alternative ways of understanding these events."[33]

Academics also have been troubled that documentaries do not fit the generally accepted notions of scholarship. Films and videos had no footnotes or bibliographies, and rarely explained their methodologies for determining what was included and what was left out of the final film. They offered little means of verification or corroboration to written sources. "Perhaps this is one of the reasons why a scholarly book or article seldom if ever cites a video documentary as its source," noted Richard Sweterlitch, an academic who has produced video oral histories. "We simply don't trust productions which lack the critical apparati of scholarship."[34]

To meet such criticism, documentary makers turned to the Internet, establishing interactive Web sites in conjunction with the documentaries. Generally designed for education purposes, these sites contain supplementary background material, additional interview segments, suggestions for further reading, and links to related sources, often to the full text of interviews. For instance, the documentary *The Clinton Years* (2001), jointly produced by ABC's *Nightline* and PBS's *Frontline*, drew on interviews with twenty White House staffers, advisers, and cabinet members. The program's web site contained not only the text of each episode but the transcript of each interview.[35]

Do artistic considerations take precedence over accuracy in video?

Being a visual medium, video makes the picture a primary consideration, a priority that can frustrate those more concerned with the information an interview generates. It is a common complaint among television journalists. The veteran broadcaster Daniel Schorr has commented that whenever a television reporter offers a story, the producer will ask, "What do we see?" Dramatic pictures can blow a story entirely out of proportion on television. The evening news opens with a picture of a dramatic rescue from a burning building, while the next morning's newspaper relegates the same story to a paragraph or two buried deep in its pages. On Capitol Hill, television commentators have complained that they could get better coverage for senators and representatives if they could get them to ride around in fire engines.[36]

At an Oral History Association meeting in 1987, Ken Burns, whose previous documentaries had included *The Shakers: Hands to Work, Hearts to God* (1985) and *Huey Long* (1987), and who was then working on *The Civil War* (1989), discussed the ethical problems of using illustrations to tell the story though they were not always accurate. Burns once decided to use a photo of Huey Long surrounded by uniformed police to illustrate a voice-over explaining that Long traveled with armed bodyguards because he feared for his life. Long's guards dressed in street clothes rather than uniforms, but a photo of plainclothesmen would not have made much of a visual point. Burns selected an untypical picture because it told the story better. To justify his decision, he related the practice of a football coach who would ask an injured player what time it was. If the player could not answer correctly, he would be sent to the hospital for observation unless the coach really needed the player, in which case he would tell him the time and send him back into the game. If an illustration is really needed, Burns advised, use it. Just be careful, he cautioned, not to make cutting such corners an automatic practice.

The video interview presents an unvarnished look at the interviewee; a documentary doctors both the audio and visual to produce a more polished product. The practice of some documentary makers of not always distinguishing between generic and specifically identified photographs raises questions about the integrity of the process. By using illustrations that make the point that the speaker is discussing, but show someone other than the speaker, a video misleads viewers into thinking that they are look at historic photos and film of the speaker. Documentary makers may choose to leave in a statement that, though they know it to be slightly erroneous, is told colorfully by an important source. They may coach an interviewee to repeat a line, over and over, until it is said the way they want it. Even more troublesome is the technological advance in video editing that allows documentary makers to trim and rearrange a speaker's words without the audience being aware that it is not hearing the remarks strictly as spoken. Digital imaging similarly permits editors to alter elements of the picture. Careless or devious editing can make speakers seem to be saying exactly the opposite of what they intended.[37]

How much control does an oral historian have over how interviews are used in a documentary?

Oral historians' control depends on their role in making the documentary, particularly on whether they are producers or consultants. "Consultants are at a disadvantage; they only consult," observed E. John B. Allen, who did interviews and consulted on a documentary on skiing. "The director and cameraman work full time on the film. As the cutting, editing, i.e., the finalizing of the film takes places, it enters on a life of its own." The oral historians as consultant may find that advice previously taken is discarded in the editing process, that misleading, historically inaccurate film footage has been used because of its visual impact, and that the final product does not correspond to the consultant's personal and professional standards.[38]

Historians who have worked as consultants for documentaries are often appalled at the filmmaker's blatant manipulation of people's words and disregard for facts in order to create a more visually exciting product. Documentary makers are eager to attract and appeal to large audiences. They seek to be enlightening and educational, but also entertaining and provocative. Recognizing these dual and conflicting needs, the American Historical Association has promoted standards that encourage historians to "be sensitive to the artistic and dramatic rights of film and video collaborators and seek solutions that respect both historical and artistic-dramatic concerns."[39]

Besides documentaries, how else have video interviews been used?

Museums quickly embraced video oral histories as a means of presenting information in a visually appealing manner. As collectors of objects, museums are always seeking ways of placing them in context and showing how people used them. Oral history reconstructs the context, but audio alone rarely goes into great deal about objects and the ways they were used. Video interviews, however, can be directed far more toward objects.[40]

Video also makes speakers more real, providing them with faces and gestures and emotions. The U.S. Holocaust Museum in Washington, D.C., illustrates its message with both audio and visual interviews. In the stark "Voices of the Holocaust" hall, visitors listen to audio interviews of a series of survivors telling their stories. The disembodied voices have a haunting quality. Later, in a small amphitheater, visitors watched videotaped interviews with concentration-camp prisoners recounting their experiences. A woman recalls sharing her soup with a friend; a man weeps as he remembers talking with his father in the camp barracks; another former prisoner describes a guard with a bulldog-like demeanor who saved her life. Their faces—some stoic, some wretched with emotion, solemn but occasionally smiling—complement the words and capture the audience. Viewers gather in larger numbers and tend to stay longer for the video than the audio presentations. A less emotional topic might need more artistic staging—these films are nothing more than talking heads but tears welling in a speaker's eyes make their point vividly.

At the Boott Cotton Mills Museum in Lowell, Massachusetts, the National Park Service has set up a self-guided tour of the factory with an emphasis on realism. At the shop-floor level, the machinery and other artifacts and authentic background noise help visitors "hear, smell, and feel" what workers experienced. Upstairs, in a more traditional museum setting, an exhibit on the broad history of weaving includes video monitors that present the testimony of retired spinners and weavers about their relations with other workers, salaries, and working conditions. One reviewer noted that "seeing and hearing the interviews of individuals such as Valentine Chartrand, a spinner who witnessed the fatal accident of a co-worker, and Victor Sherbon, who talked about the death of the mill, elicit emotional responses that no label or artifact could match."[41]

What is the potential for individual research in video oral history?
Although researchers prefer transcripts, which can be skimmed and photo-copied, when they turn to the recordings they often learn more than they would from an audio interview. By viewing a film or video, noted one video specialist, the researcher not only hears voice inflections but sees raised eyebrows, hand motions, and unspoken body language, "everything, in short, from clothing to reaction gestures and mannerisms." And gestures combined with words some-times convey very different meanings.[42]

Some researchers have used the video camera themselves to gather material and information for their work. David Seaman videotapes artists in the process of creating. While interviewing West Virginian artist Ruth Rodgers, Seaman showed her meditative process: sitting and visualizing what she wanted to put on the canvas. Then, as she painted, he crawled on the floor and reproduced what she had seen in her meditative state. Seaman found that people who communi-cated in the visual arts—painting, photography, sculpting—also communicated well with words and could provide articulate running narratives for his videos.[43]

Richard Candida Smith at the Regional Oral History Office at Berkeley has engaged a "digital videography" that mixes artists narrating their own lives together with images of them in their work space and samples of their work. "Living History/Performing Narratives" began with an oral history, done in col-laboration with the San Francisco Museum of Modern Art, of a conceptual artist, David Ireland, who turned his entire house into a "developing art per-formance." The use of video allowed for critical examination of the ways in which artists' life stories and artistic creations intersect.

**Do archives face any particular problems
in using video oral histories?**
Those archives that have compiled substantial video oral history collections report increasing use of the interviews by television producers for documentary purposes. That television producers tend to demand material in a rush can be an aggravation for an archivist, but more troublesome are the questions about how the material will be used. With sometimes hundreds of interviews on video-tape, an archives cannot consult with each interviewee about the uses of their interviews beyond whatever the interviewee specified in the deed of gift. Still, it can be disconcerting for interviewees to see themselves unexpectedly in a broadcast. Archives must explain the copyright provisions for their videos and should obtain some written confirmation from the producers concerning their intended use of the material. The Smithsonian archives, for example, initially makes available only a copy of the video interview in half-inch VHS format

with time codes displayed on-screen, which discourages its use for broadcasting. Broadcasters and documentary makers view the video and determine what portions they want, then formally apply for the three-quarter-inch broadcast-quality film.

Like audio interviews, videos may be sealed or otherwise restricted by interviewees for a period of time. In at least one instance, an archival videotaped interview was requested for use in a court proceeding although not subpoenaed and the interviewee agreed to its use in court.

Considering all the expense and problems involved, is videotaping worth the effort?

The video oral historian Brien Williams has commented that even the most poorly produced and wretchedly preserved videotape of Abraham Lincoln would still have enormous value. Arthur Schlesinger, Jr., concurs:

> I think if we had videotaped interviews with Emerson, Socrates, Charlemagne, it would be marvelous. On the other hand, videotaping compounds all the problems of expense, storage, dilapidation, and so on. Obviously it would have to be used selectively. But, for commanding figures, particularly those who haven't been amply documented on television, it would be particularly useful. Eric Sevareid's interviewing of Walter Lippmann, for example, would be invaluable to historians a hundred years from now wondering what Lippmann was like. But only an unusual case would justify the expense. There are not that many Walter Lippmanns.[44]

Some video historians envision a time when all oral history will be videotaped. But many barriers remain to universal videotaping. Because the oral historian cannot always control the location of an interview, audio recording on-site, rather than videotaping, will continue to be the logical choice sometimes, especially when interviewees for whatever reasons of privacy or vanity refuse to have their pictures taken. But if the opportunities are available, the funds are forthcoming, and the subjects are willing, then future researchers and users of oral history may ask why we failed to capture the historical picture as well as the words.[45]

CHAPTER 6

Preserving Oral History in Archives and Libraries

Why are oral history projects so often associated with archives and libraries?

The oral history movement in the United States traces its roots to the archival collections at such prestigious universities as Columbia, Cornell, Berkeley, and UCLA. These collections started not as individual projects to produce specific books but as a means of gathering reminiscences for general research use. At many of these "founding" programs, the staff conducted most of the interviews. Since then, archives and libraries have provided the institutional home for many oral history projects, offering space, services, and sometimes—although not always—salaries for the project staff. Once interviews have been conducted, archives and libraries process and preserve them, prepare catalogs and other finding aids, and make them accessible for research.

This early identification with archives profoundly shaped the conduct of oral history in the United States. By contrast, independent researchers—or sometimes smaller centers of scholars conducting interviews for specific projects—were responsible for the advent of oral history in Europe. Over time, Europeans and others in the international community increasingly acknowledged what Ronald J. Grele, a director of the Columbia Oral History Research Office, called a "sense of collective responsibility, that these are documents made for public use, not just private documents for the private research of those connected with a particular center." American archivists identified oral history as another way of supplementing the letters, diaries, and memoranda in their collections. They sought interviews with the same prominent people who donated manuscripts to their archives, thereby giving oral history its initially "elitist" bent.

Archival oral historians also promoted the ideal of the interviewer as a neutral, objective observer, free from any compulsion to prove a particular thesis. Philip Brooks, who directed the Truman Library, described the "pure" oral historian as someone who was "accumulating a stock of evidence for the use of other researchers, any and all researchers, as we do in an archival agency." Such an archival oral historian was "almost by definition likely to be doing a more objective job than the one who is writing his own book, especially the one that has a case to prove." Given their preference for paper, archival oral history projects championed the transcript rather than the tape as the primary record and ultimate product of an oral history interview. Although oral history has remained closely associated with archives, each of these preconceptions has undergone significant modification over the years, just as archives themselves have changed.[1]

With archives filled to capacity with paper and electronic records, why should they bother collecting oral history?

Some researchers and archivists are convinced that archives have higher priorities than conducting oral history. The popular historian Barbara Tuchman protested that "over-documentation" was causing those who wrote contemporary history to drown in "unneeded information," a problem she believed oral history adds to rather than alleviates. Tuchman charged oral history with producing "trivia of appalling proportions . . . with all sorts of people being invited merely to open their mouths, and ramble effortlessly and endlessly into a tape recorder." In a similar vein, archivists have argued that with paper and electronic records expanding and budgets shrinking, they must set priorities and determine the cost-effectiveness of their various functions. Oral history, being expensive, is therefore more often expendable. Both views are regrettably shortsighted.[2]

Although Tuchman aptly identified the explosion of modern paperwork, she neglected to address the declining qualitative value of that documentation. As the records of government agencies, corporations, and other institutions have multiplied, their worth has decreased. Subpoenas, state open records laws, and the federal Freedom of Information Act have made many officials reluctant to express themselves candidly on paper. Memoranda may disguise what actually happened or try to shift responsibility. Telephones, fax machines, e-mail, and other advances in communications have reduced the reliance on traditional written documentation. As researchers gain access to modern records, they often discover them to be unrevealing and uninformative.

Oral history can be as useful when there is too much documentation as when there is too little. Every presidential administration leaves behind more paperwork than did its predecessor, with the National Archives estimating that every four months the federal government now generates as many records as all those produced between the administrations of George Washington and Woodrow Wilson combined. Scholars trying to trace the development of modern federal policymaking are confronted with more material than they could possibly read in a lifetime. Yet it is nearly impossible to know what documents an official actually wrote or ever saw. A researcher who plowed through the papers of a recent senator complained that the collection consisted almost exclusively of routine correspondence and mass mailings and that he had found almost nothing from the presidents with whom the senator had been closely identified.[3]

Faced with hundreds or thousands of cubic feet of records, usually with limited finding aids, researchers need guidance. Oral history interviews with the principal figures can serve as road maps, suggesting which individuals and what issues should be followed through the manuscript collection. Researchers with limited resources want to make maximum use of a collection in a minimum amount of time. Smart researchers have learned to look first for oral histories; unfortunately, others still leave oral histories to the last.

Being well aware of the limitations of the written record, many archivists have recognized the need for "auxiliary documentation." Oral history is more than a supplement and less than a substitute for other archival materials. As one more type of research tool among many, oral history can be especially helpful in filling the gaps that often obscure the motivations behind individual and institutional actions. Gaps may also exist in what written records can contribute to our understanding of the actions of whole groups of people who, perhaps because of gender, race, class, or ethnicity, have not been represented in the archival collections. The challenge for archivists, James Fogerty has written "is to go beyond their collections to individuals not represented, who have no personal papers or records to donate. This is an unusual activity for an archives but is one way in which the gap between collections and subject areas can be bridged."[4]

Surely it is not an archivist's job to create records?

The reason pained expressions sometimes appear on the faces of archivists when they talk about oral history is that its practice breaks so many of their rules and customs. Archivists have had difficulty agreeing on a terminology for oral history and refer to "collecting oral history" as if interviews, like manuscript collections, were out there waiting to be acquired. But the information exists only in the interviewee's mind, and someone must first record and preserve it in some tangible form. In doing oral history, archivists find themselves creating, not just collecting, a new resource.[5]

Many archivists feel uncomfortable being both curator and creator of primary documents. Oral history is an entirely different type of record from those they normally handle, since it is not an artifact preserved from the past but a present record that attempts to re-create the past and is subject to memory failures and reinterpretation through intervening events. When archivists serve as interviewers who draw out these memories, they also step out of character to become something of a player in the events. The demands of this new role have raised fears that archivists may become advocates of one form of documentation over another, instead of maintaining professional detachment and neutrality. Of course, whenever archivists choose to accession one collection over another, oral history or not, they put their supposed neutrality on the line. Some archivists consider oral history a secondary form of documentation and regard all the planning, conducting, and processing of interviews a diversion from their primary responsibilities. These concerns most likely reflect the increasing identification of archivists not so much as historians as information specialists, records managers, and computer specialists.[6]

Despite these objections, oral history has become an increasingly standard addition to modern archival collections. As a growing number of librarians and archivists handle oral history collections, it is essential that they become familiar with the theory and techniques of oral history research, interviewing, and processing.

How does funding shape an archival oral history collection?

Funding impacts oral history the same as it does other archival activities, affecting the scope and priorities of a project. Conducting and processing interviews can be expensive. Although housed in university libraries, some of the most prestigious oral history archives—such as the Regional Oral History Office at Berkeley—long operated without direct subsidies from their host university and raised their own operating funds to finance interviewing and processing. Many projects have been conducted with individuals, families, corporations, and associations that actually underwrote their own interviews. This fact of fiscal life can produce some outstanding research resources that might not otherwise exist, but it can also skew a collection towards those who can afford to be patrons. Now more than ever before, oral history archivists need to seek alternative sources of funding to ensure that their collection contains a wide representation of voices, and scholarly researchers need to support such broad-based oral history collecting.[7]

Oral history archives have had to be financially creative and flexible. In 1960 the U.S. Navy engaged the Columbia Oral History Research Office to interview high-ranking naval officers. An interviewer was dispatched to Washington to begin a lengthy series of interviews when Columbia discovered that navy regulations prohibited a flat sum payment for a year's worth of interviews. Rather than allow the bureaucracy to defeat them, they instead arranged for the navy to purchase each interview when completed, each payment helping to underwrite the rest of the program.[8]

Grants from such funding agencies as the National Endowment for the Humanities (NEH), the state humanities commissions, the Ford, Rockefeller, and Doris Duke foundations, and Pew Charitable Trust have launched and supported many oral history projects. But the priorities of such agencies go through periodic shifts. In the 1970s, funding agencies were quite generous to oral history of all sorts. In a spirit of democratization, the agencies funded some well-intended but unprepared projects that consumed their grants without producing anything more than boxes of tapes that were untranscribed, undocumented, undeeded, unidentified, and consequently unusable. Concerned funding agencies encouraged the Oral History Association (OHA) to establish standards by which they could judge oral history proposals and completed projects. At an appropriately grant-funded meeting at the Wingspread Center in Racine, Wisconsin, OHA established its first evaluation guidelines in 1979.[9]

During the 1980s, Ronald Reagan's presidency dramatically reduced federal funding for oral history. The NEH, which had enthusiastically supported oral history under previous administrations, abruptly shifted its interests elsewhere. Other funding agencies cut grants for archival oral history programs, on the grounds that they were not cost-effective, and concentrated instead on assisting individual research. Funding agencies would underwrite the costs of a researcher's interviews, but they did not always stipulate that the interviews be deposited in an appropriate archives.

As federal funds became scarcer, oral history projects turned to state humanities councils. Although more limited in the amounts they could grant, state councils remained convinced of the benefits of oral history interviewing. State humanities councils helped underwrite transcriptions of interviews that had already been conducted, a way of marshaling their resources to produce a tangible product—the transcript—for deposit in an archives and possibly for further use in publications and exhibits. The state of Kentucky went a step further in 1976 when it established the Kentucky Oral History Commission specifically to fund interviewing and transcription of Kentucky-related subjects. Kentucky remains unique in this respect, but legislatures in California, Hawaii, Texas, Illinois, and New Jersey have officially funded oral history projects within their states.[10]

By the 1990s, NEH regained interest in oral history and gave support to projects at such organizations as the Lincoln Center for the Performing Arts, the Museum of Modern Art, and the Washington Press Club Foundation. NEH's preservation and access division has shown special interest in the archival preservation and digitizing of oral history audio and video recordings. Competition for federal funding has grown intense, however, and applicants must weigh the limited chances of being funded against the time-consuming application process. Private foundations, corporations, and state and local agencies remain better avenues for support.[11]

Is it appropriate for an oral history archives to charge fees for publication use of its interviews?

Although archives do not, and should not, charge for research access to oral histories, publishing lengthy excerpts from those interviews is another matter. Many library-based oral history collections have enough institutional support to be able to forgo fees of any type, but other oral history archives run on shoestring budgets and are constantly looking for ways to raise funds. One way has been to charge users for any reproduction that goes beyond "fair use." In setting costs, archives need to be reasonable and flexible. If their goal is to disseminate information, then setting fees too high will discourage users. Doctoral dissertation writers are rarely in a position to make a payment. Most publishers will not pay for such costs, which would then become the author's responsibility.

A bigger problem arises when oral history archives sell the reproduction rights to their collections to microfiche publishers and other agents. Such arrangements may initially raise needed funds for the archives, but the terms of these agreements can put unreasonable restrictions on the use of the collection, such as prohibiting researchers from making photocopies. Some archives have sold the literary rights to their interviews to one company, which in turn has sold it to another, which thereafter controls the reproduction fees. In a sense, these archives have lost control of their own collections.

MANAGING ORAL HISTORY COLLECTIONS

Is there any difference between accessioning oral histories and written documents?

In accessioning any form of documentation an archives determines whether the material is appropriate for its collection, takes legal and managerial control over it, and decides how soon and under what conditions it can be used. Except in the case of "exit interviews" or "debriefings" that are done as a requirement of a job, military assignment, or completion of a project for which someone has been paid, most oral history interviews are voluntary efforts and interviewees retain the copyright until they have deeded it to the archives or to the public domain. Like manuscript collections, donors may set conditions on the oral histories they give to an archives. It is the responsibility of the archives to ascertain the donor's wishes, negotiate any mutual concerns, and honor any restrictions the donor has set.

Deeds of gift and contracts can vary widely, from simple to very complex, depending on the legal advice sought. Attorneys naturally want to protect an archives from any contingency, but some interviewees may blanch at the sight of an overly complicated deed. A brief, straightforward agreement engenders less reluctance to sign. On the other extreme, more prominent interviewees may insist on adding stipulations about permission to quote and other potential uses of their interviews. Wherever possible, archives should adopt a simple release form that indicates what restrictions have been set and when those restrictions will expire. Without such releases, archival oral histories are unpublishable beyond "fair use," as publishers will not take the risk of printing material whose copyright is in question. Sometimes scholars who have recorded verbal agreements with their interviewees, giving them control of the interviews, sign an agreement with the library or archives to deposit the collection as a whole, establishing its copyright and making provision for its research use and reproduction.[12]

What kind of data should be kept on each interview?

Archivists want to know the "provenance" of records, by which they mean the circumstances under which the records were created and originally maintained. For oral histories, they want to know who conducted the interview, with whom, when, where, and for what purpose. In addition to the sound recordings and transcripts, archives often retain copies of legal agreements, correspondence with the interviewee, background information used for the interview, photographs of the interviewee, and indexes to the recordings.

Label disks, tapes, and tape containers with the names of the interviewee and interviewer, and the date of the interview. On the container, also indicate the sequence of recordings, if more than one occurred; the location of the interview; the length of interview; and the project title (if there are multiple projects within a collection). For some projects, such information is also recorded on separate data sheets.

Archives often ask interviewers to prepare summary sheets on their interviews, recording their impressions of the interviewee and anything significant that happened during the interview. As the interview itself is an event in the interviewee's life, researchers will be curious about its context. If the interview was never completed or did not deal with certain significant events in the interviewee's life, researchers will want to know why. Did the interviewee cancel sessions? Was the interview terminated earlier than expected? Did the interviewee set ground rules about not answering certain questions? Without some explanation of omissions, the documents will leave the impression that the interviewer neglected important areas of inquiry. Although such administrative files do not require release forms, oral historians should keep interviewees informed as to what sort of material will be made accessible to researchers.

As an oral history archives grows, the need for a general log quickly becomes apparent. Whether done as a file, in a book, or on a computer, the log should contain basic accessioning and labeling information for every interview and collection. By keeping a record of the interviewer's notes and correspondence, from letters setting up the interview to thank-you letters at the end, an archives also has a record of interviewees being kept fully informed of their rights, which is useful if they or their heirs later question or object to the opening of the interview for research or its publication.

It is fairly common for oral history projects to include introductions to individual interviews, summarizing the person's life and providing other background information. Oral historians in general, however, have not been as diligent as anthropologists and ethnographers in noting their personal observations of the interview's circumstance, and not every oral history collection keeps all of this data. Each archives determines what types of records will best serve its researchers. Whatever decisions archives make, consistency is key: archivists should think through the process at the outset to avoid having to go back to re-create information and fill in gaps later.[13]

How should interviews be arranged in a collection?

A government attorney, in all seriousness, once advised a federal historical office against arranging its oral history files alphabetically by name and recommended that the office keep its interviews "in a box at random." The attorney worried that an alphabetical file would constitute a system of records, as defined by the Privacy Act, and would therefore constitute an invasion of privacy. However seriously offered, the advice was ridiculous. Almost any other system of arrangement would make more sense.

Oral histories are most often cataloged by name of the interviewee, individually or as part of a larger collection. Some archives create an alphabetical or numerical accession system for arranging all interviews and accompanying materials. Others divide the interviews according to the specific projects for which they were done. The interviews conducted around a specific community, event, or group of individuals can be filed according to that project name, though arranging by subject becomes more complex unless the project titles were clearly subject-oriented. Specific subjects can be located through indexes and other electronic retrieval systems.

Should an archives prepare its own
oral history processing guide?

Given how many different staff and volunteers might be involved in conducting, processing, accessioning, cataloging and retrieving oral history, any archives with a substantial oral history collection should seriously consider preparing its own procedures manual. A guide would serve as an introduction for newcomers and assure overall consistency. Starting with a mission statement, the guide should suggest general areas for investigation through interviews, and outline procedures for handling the oral histories, from acquisition to conservation, including samples of all forms used and the rationale of the filing system. For instance, records of the actual interview, such as transcripts, indexes, and correspondence may be filed separately from organizational papers such as financial records, internal correspondence, and bills for supplies and equipment. The guide should set standard procedures for transcription, and for cataloging and indexing the interviews to assist in their retrieval for research.[14]

Now that transcripts are routinely produced and stored on computer, processing guides should account for electronic handling of restricted materials. Closed interviews or interviews in progress should not be saved in shared directories, where they might be accessed by unauthorized personnel and researchers.

What types of finding aids are most useful for oral history?

Oral history collections may begin with just a few interviews but can grow so quickly that even the interviewers have trouble remembering who said what. For the purposes of both internal administration and efficient research use, oral history archives must investigate and establish finding aids, such as catalogs, indexes, and computer retrieval systems. Oral historians need to recognize that doing the interviews is not the end but the beginning of the process. With Internet postings of oral history, microfiche editions, catalogs, indexes, and a great deal of communication between archives and their users, archives are better able to attract researchers to use the interviews they have collected.

Researchers, who want to know whether they have seen all the pertinent material on their subject in an archives, have a responsibility to inquire about what records are open, but the institution also has an obligation to ensure that cataloging information about their collections is available. Nothing infuriates researchers more than learning after they have left an archives that they missed important additional information. When dealing with archival oral histories, researchers face three major retrieval problems: learning the location of an oral history with a particular individual or about a specific subject; determining which interviews to consult; and then finding the information within a recording or transcript.

The most common finding aid is a simple, alphabetical list of all the individual interviews within a collection by name of interviewee, whether in a publication, an in-house document, a card catalog, or online. In addition to the name of the interviewee and the date of the interview, the list might include a biographical sketch of the interviewee and identify key subjects and individuals discussed. Finding aids should indicate whether the recordings have been indexed or transcribed and note whether the interview is open, closed, or otherwise restricted, and when the restrictions will end.

Either the recordings or transcripts of interviews should be indexed, ideally by subject as well as by name. From such separate indexes, the archives can construct a cross-reference index. The Columbia Oral History Research Office began a simple card file index for the names of individuals mentioned within its interviews; this index has become an enormous and valuable tool for searching through its thousands of interviews. Creating such a cross-reference index is always easier if started at the beginning of a project and grows with it than attempted after the bulk of material has been collected. Cross-reference indexes uncover fascinating information. (It has often been observed of oral history that the most useful insights come from the least expected sources.) When transcripts have been stored electronically, text-searching programs also make it possible to search an entire interview, or a series of interviews, by names and other key words.[15]

SOUND RECORDINGS

Do oral histories belong specifically in sound archives?

Most archives divide their collections according to physical types, separating photographs, sound recordings, and electronic records from written documents. These divisions may be for managerial purposes, or for the preservation of the audiovisual and electronic materials under the most appropriate temperature, humidity, and storage conditions. Specialists in sound archives are more concerned than most oral historians with sound quality—and for good reason, given the poor quality of so many of the recorded interviews they receive. Too many oral historians think that they have succeeded so long as the voice on the tape is audible enough to transcribe, but poor recordings reduce the possibility of any uses that go beyond simply conveying factual information, such as contributions to exhibits and documentaries.

Archives can either disperse oral history interviews among the collections from which they were drawn or centralize the sound recordings and transcripts in a special oral history section. Whatever the option chosen, if the interviews are separated from their original agency records, or if the tapes, disks and transcripts are stored in separate areas, then cross-references must alert researchers to these divisions and show where to locate the material. Never underestimate a researcher's ability to misunderstand archival cataloging systems. Unless the signposts are obvious, researchers may devote themselves entirely to manuscripts and neglect oral history and other types of non-print documentation.

Transcripts, easily skimmed and photocopied, are so often the research tool of choice in the United States that the preservation of original sound recordings has not received its deserved attention. Since archives, especially those in large institutions, often separate audio from printed materials, archivists responsible for preserving sound recordings often work separately from other archivists and tend to be more technologically oriented, belong to different professional associations, and read different literature—all the ingredients for failures of communication. Although print-oriented archivists have adapted to film and photographic sources, they all too often have largely ignored sound recordings, as is reflected in the thin literature about sound in archival publications. One sound archivist complained that "the silence of the archival community on the subject is deafening."[16]

Audiovisual archivists deal with music, speeches, radio and television broadcasts, and other materials that they often do not distinguish from oral history. An audio archivist once commented, in all sincerity, that if interview tapes were preserved, he could not understand the purpose of also keeping a transcript. To him, the tape and transcript were duplicate copies of the same record. His view was as erroneous as those of print-oriented archivists who, in their devotion to the transcript, went so far as to record over the tapes once the transcripts were completed. As Louis Starr, then director of the Columbia Oral History Research Office, reported in 1962:

> We erase most of our tapes for re-use. This is largely because we permit our victims to edit their transcripts. While the editing, we urge, should be done with accuracy alone in mind, there is nothing to prevent a man from changing his own words—particularly in view of the fact that we regard the material as his, and ourselves as merely the custodians. Thus if we kept the tapes, we'd be saving a first draft, which would make a lot of our people unhappy.
>
> Cost is another factor, and so is storage—the problem of "feed back" has yet to be solved. Finally, we are inclined to doubt the practicality of saving, for example, 200 hours of Madame Perkins on tape, assuming

she permitted us to do so. It would have to be indexed to be of much use, and that in itself would be pretty expensive. Only one scholar among the hundreds who have used the Oral History Collection has ever asked us for a tape, incidentally.

Fortunately, by the late 1960s Columbia had reversed this policy and has since been saving its tapes. Oral historians and archivists began to view both the sound recording and transcript as "primary" in their own mediums and to deem both worthy of preservation.[17]

Should sound recordings be preserved any differently than other documentation?

Although there are enough similarities in the preservation of paper and audio documentation to permit their storage together, sound recordings confront archivists with problems unique to their medium. Paper, particularly if low in acidity, can sit unattended for years without much damage, but sound recordings need constant care. Tape, if left unplayed for long periods or not rewound regularly, undergoes a process by which the sound on one layer of the tape is imprinted on the next layer, a condition, called "print through" or "voice over," that creates an echo on the tape. Fungus can attack certain types of sound recordings, quickening their deterioration. Furthermore, tape can be erased accidentally, and records and disks can be damaged and become unplayable.

The development of digital electronic recording in the 1990s confronted oral historians with a difficult choice: digital recorders provided superior sound quality, permitted copying without loss of clarity, and facilitated digital editing and placing interviews on the World Wide Web. But archivists had serious concerns about the long-term preservation of digital audio tape and compact discs. Since the first Digital Audio Tape (DAT) recorders were expensive and needed frequent repairs, many oral history projects were reluctant to adopt them. The first mini-disk recorders had their own problems; but when redesigned and introduced they were greatly improved, less expensive, and more popular. Digital audio tape recorders use tape, which like any tape can wear with use. Mini-disks record digitally on disks and can be transferred to CD-ROM or hard drives for storage. Some archivists copy digital recordings onto magnetic tape, a prudent combination pending further advances in digital technology. Although mini-disks are growing more prevalent among oral historians, users have warned of catastrophic failure if there is a sudden loss of power, when all material that has not been saved can be lost.[18]

Evolving technology that has made it easier to do oral history has also made its preservation more difficult. Many interviews were recorded on machines that no longer exist, outside of museums. One archives found a set of interviews done on an obsolete belt-type recorder from the 1950s, but being unable to locate such a machine, even from its manufacturer, could not play back the tapes. Interviews on wax cylinders, wire recorders, belt recorders, and dictaphones have been copied onto reel-to-reel and cassette tape, and are now being digitized. Reel-to-reel recorders have become harder to locate even though they remain the recommended form of tape for long-term archival preservation. The catalog of horrors is enough to suggest that oral history archives that are not regularly caring for their tapes and making transcripts are probably playing Russian Roulette with their interviews.[19]

The literature on the preservation of sound recordings is alarming—but may also be alarmist. Archivists have reported receiving tapes that had been stored in people's attics and basements under the worst possible conditions for decades and yet were still playable, at least enough to be rerecorded. But no sound recording is permanent. Oral history archivists cannot afford to allow technological problems to tie their hands and make them quit the enterprise, any more than they can go about blindly ignoring the problems. We search for a responsible middle ground.

How long will most audio tapes last?

The type of magnetic tape used for most oral history interviews has an approximate shelf-life of twenty-five years. But estimates vary widely and have become progressively more pessimistic. Magnetic tape has existed only for the past half-century, and experts can only speculate about how well it will maintain its sound quality into the future. With each new development in recording, whether magnetic tape, videotape, or digital audio tape, the initial predictions of longevity have always been more confident than justified by assessments. Older oral history programs have encountered some real crises with tape preservation. The George C. Marshall Research Foundation in Lexington, Virginia, discovered that the wire recordings Forrest C. Pogue had conducted with General Marshall in the early 1950s had deteriorated badly. With the help of an NEH grant, these wire recordings were copied onto cassettes, transcribed, and published, so that both the sound and the substance have been saved.[20]

If kept under hot and dry conditions, standard audio tape will become brittle and crack after a decade of storage. Some tape will begin to stick between layers or shed the coating from its backing after a few years in storage. On the other hand, if stored under proper conditions, decades-old tape has sounded very near the original recording quality. To ensure that an oral history archives has enduring value, that its interviews are accessible so that researchers can listen to them in later years, and that the recorded voices can be used for future exhibits and documentaries, the tapes must be processed and maintained carefully.

What's the best way to preserve tapes?

Start by conducting interviews on good-quality tape, with a good microphone, and as little background noise as possible. Folklorists, anthropologists, and ethnomusicologists prefer to capture ambient noises, but even they must be careful not to let the background obscure the interview. Most interviewers record on sixty-minute cassette tapes—certainly on nothing longer than ninety minutes. (Anything longer than ninety minutes would be too thin and likely to stretch, twist, or break.) Archives generally accept cassette tapes, although for longer preservation they may prefer that cassettes be copied onto reel-to-reel tape. To avoid the problem of accidental rerecording, remove the two small square tabs on the edge of the cassette case.

Magnetic tape is coated with millions of magnetic particles that can change their magnetic strength under the influence of heat, humidity, magnetic fields, radiation, and physical stress. Keep magnetic tape away from exposure to such magnetic fields as power lines, motors, generators, and transformers, and store them on nonconductive shelves and containers.[21]

Tapes generally survive well under "people conditions," that is, with air conditioning and air filtering at a constant temperature of around seventy degrees Fahrenheit and a constant humidity of about 45 percent. Some archives file their tapes, transcripts, notes, clippings, and deed of gift for each interviewee in a single acid-free archival storage box. If adopting this filing system, make sure that any documents in the container are also on acid-free paper. For instance, save photocopies of newspaper articles rather than the original clippings, since newsprint will deteriorate and affect the rest of the contents of the box. Transcripts should always be printed on acid-free paper. Remember that storing all records in the same location runs the risk of having everything damaged or lost together should a fire or tornado or similar disaster occur. Keep tapes away from windows and heat sources. Be careful of insects, rodents, mold, and other elements that can damage tape as well as paper. Archivists admit that they cannot eliminate the causes of decay, but they can slow down the deterioration.

"Constant" is the key word for preserving sound recordings. Archives need to avoid wide fluctuations in heat and humidity because, at different temperatures, air holds different amounts of moisture that, in turn, affect the tapes. Moisture from the air is absorbed into the tape binder (which holds the magnetic particles to the tape), causing the tape to lose its strength and break down. High temperatures and humidity will cause irreversible damage to the tape, as anyone who has heard the sound distortion caused by leaving a music tape inside a car during hot weather can testify.

The original recording is kept as the master copy (or even better, the original cassette may be copied onto reel-to-reel tape, which then becomes the master copy). For transcribing and research, always use copies of the tape rather than the master. Avoid eating, drinking, or smoking around tapes. (Ashes are the chief contaminant from smoking.) Oils from fingers can damage tapes, which should not be handled directly. Store tapes in their original container or their equivalents. Some archives seal master tapes in polyethylene bags. Given all the potential dangers to tapes from fires, floods, and other hazards, it is advisable to store the master tape and its copies in separate places.

To avoid print-through, tapes should be rewound at play speed every few years. This is a time-consuming and expensive procedure that large collections often follow less than diligently. But rewinding is essential to maintain distinct sound on the tapes and is all the more important for interviews that have not been transcribed.

The development of digital audio tape, mini-disks, CD-ROMs and other forms of digital electronic recording will eventually replace magnetic audio tape. As reel-to-reel and cassette tape recorders become outdated, archivists must decide whether to maintain obsolete equipment or convert large collections to newer technologies; either course can be expensive. Adopting new technology involves an element of risk, as those who invested in Beta over VHS can attest. For an oral history archives, it is advisable to approach new technology warily until it has been assessed for its usefulness in long-term preservation. Whatever equipment you choose, make sure that it can be serviced conveniently and replaced if necessary. Being on the "cutting edge" with new technology is not always the best![22]

How reliable are mini-disks and CD-ROMs for archival purposes?

Digital recordings tend to be clear and free from distortion. Because the sound is represented by a series of digits, each copy should sound as clear and sharp as the previous one, suggesting that the original sound on digital recordings could theoretically last forever as long as it was routinely copied. CDs employ a laser reading mechanism; there is no wear on them during use and no degrading of the sound. Yet for all these advancements in sound technology, digital recording raises troublesome issues for archival preservation. As practitioners have learned, digital failures can be catastrophic. If the disk is damaged, the entire recording may be lost (as opposed to magnetic tape, which if damaged can be repaired). CD-ROMs are flimsy and have an estimated life span of ten years or less.[23]

Some oral historians have experimented with recording directly onto a laptop, which with a larger memory and hard drive permits extended recording times as well as easy editing and conversion for Internet access. However, the process is risky. A good quality microphone is as essential for both mini-disk and laptop recording as for a conventional tape recorder. But microphone inputs on laptops may not be the highest quality, and laptops themselves are noisy machines. Interviewers need to keep the microphone positioned well away from the computer. Backup copies should be made promptly on disks, given that hard drives can crash.

A few sound archives have begun converting their oral history recordings from analog to digital format and are preserving the recordings on CDs and mass digital storage systems. These systems compress the collection and make it easier for restoring and enhancing damaged or poorly recorded sound.

What if the sound recordings are damaged?

Archivists always have to be prepared for fire, flood, and other natural disasters. Damaged tapes need to be copied onto clean tapes, but they may not initially be able to be copied. In 1989, when Hurricane Hugo struck the South Carolina coast, among the many items submerged under water were the tapes of the interviews that Theodore Rosengarten conducted for his award-winning book *All God's Dangers*. Forty-eight reels of magnetic tape were soaked in water and caked with mud and sand. After a month's delay, the tapes were turned over to the Southern Folklife Collection at the University of North Carolina at Chapel Hill, where each tape was wound by hand through a bath of distilled water and then up in a cardboard tube filled with air warmed by a hair dryer. The dried tapes were then wound onto new reels and were playable enough to be copied onto new master tapes. This procedure was funded by a grant from the North Carolina Arts Council. Rosengarten deposited his tapes with the Southern Folklife Center so "the voices and experience of Ned Cobb ["Nate Shaw" in the book] and his family. . . will be heard again." Other archives have sent damaged tapes to private companies that specialize in audio-visual restoration.[24]

Is it appropriate to edit sound recordings?

For preservation reasons a master tape should never be spliced, and for ethical and methodological reasons the master recording should never be edited. It is even easier to edit digital recordings, but the temptation to "clean up" an interview could affect its meaning. What was said was said and should not be altered to make it seem different. Although recordings are edited and condensed for documentary purposes, the original must remain true to the actual circumstances of the interview so that researchers can have confidence that it has not been tampered with. Interviewees' restrictions must always be honored, but if either the interviewee or the project decides—for reasons of privacy or to avoid a libel action—to close portions of the interview for a period of time, then a copy of the tape can be made with the portions in question deleted, to be used for research until the entire tape can be opened safely. Even though the transcript has been edited to improve the meaning of the interview, the spoken word, with all its imprecisions, should remain intact as a primary record or document.

If an archives does not transcribe its interviews, what alternatives are available?

The problems of preserving recordings of unknown durability, deterioration of sound quality, and potential obsolescence of equipment, all reinforce the value of transcribing for long-term preservation of oral history interviews. But transcribing is also expensive and time-consuming. If an archives lacks the funds to transcribe, plans to transcribe only selectively, or anticipates long delays before it can transcribe, then it needs to index its recordings to identify the major subjects discussed on them. Researchers need guidance and should not have to listen to entire tapes to locate specific information. An index may be a simple list of topics in the order that they are mentioned on the recording, or it may offer a schedule of the playing time, indicating the approximate location of each name or subject discussed.[25]

Archivists should keep in mind, however, that if transcripts are not made, they must maintain adequate equipment for researchers to play back the recordings for making notes, and have enough equipment that several researchers can work at the same time. Just as archives need to consider whether to allow researchers to photocopy all of an interview, they should have a policy on making copies of all or portions of their recordings and establish requirements for copying, quoting, and publishing excerpts.[26]

DIGITIZING ORAL ARCHIVES

What advantages does digital technology offer oral history collections?

Digital electronic technology is transforming every aspect of oral history, from research and interviewing, to transcription, preservation and dissemination. As digital recorders and transcribers become more commonplace, beginning projects can adopt the new technology from the start. More established projects, having invested in previous technology and grown comfortable with it, face the challenge not only of deciding whether to replace their equipment but whether to convert existing collections into digital format. Almost all oral history projects now transcribe on computer, and pre-computer-era typescripts can be scanned into electronic format. Sound and video recordings can also be recorded digitally or converted from analog to digital for editing, preservation and research use on CD-ROM and the Internet.

Oral historians first approached personal computers as glorified typewriters. But the benefits became obvious as transcribers discovered that they could work faster on computer, edit more easily, and no longer had to retype a second "clean" copy of the transcript after editing. They could preserve transcripts electronically and reproduce them on demand. In 1980 the futurist Alvin Toffler enthused that computers could "capture an original, correct it, duplicate it, send it, and file it in what amounts to a single process. Speed increases. Costs go down." The technophile Toffler argued that making paper copies was a primitive use of computers that "violates their very spirit." Even those unwilling to abandon paper could concede the merits of computers for retrieving, searching, transmitting and printing.[27]

As the digital revolution progressed, it opened diverse possibilities for oral historians, helping them organize, manipulate, and make available their interviews and also offering solutions for many of the problems of cataloging and indexing collections. Word searching capabilities and indexing software also enabled users to search the full text of oral histories and to pull up specific names and subjects from any of the interviews in the computer.[28]

Archivists at the University of Alaska at Fairbanks were among the first to experiment with the storage of oral history interviews on compact discs (CDs) a process that enabled them to include not only the recordings but the transcripts, release forms, and related photographs and maps on the same CD. As project director William Schneider explained: "An interview with a dog musher may be accompanied by photographs of him racing the dogs, a map showing where he lives, a copy of the release form he signed at the time of the interview, and even a short article about him." CD storage provided greater archival control over their materials and made the interviews far more accessible for research.[29]

The archivist of the U.S. Marine Corps inherited a collection of six thousand interviews conducted in Vietnam on open-reel tape, and three thousand for later operations, mostly on audio cassette tape. In evaluating the collection, the archivist noted that the interviews had been recorded on a variety of machines at different speeds, that there had never been a systematic program to run the tapes periodically for preservation purposes, that the tapes had not been stored under adequate temperature control, and that some of the tapes had either been misfiled or had disappeared. Approximately two thousand of the interviews had been transcribed, while the rest had data sheets. Some had been transcribed on such old word-processing programs that current computers could no longer read the disks (which came in three sizes). The open-reel tape was still playable but showed signs of deterioration, and the archives had only a single open-reel tape deck. To gain control over the collection, the archivist started by bringing all the tapes, transcripts, disks, and data sheets together in one storage area, and making preservation copies of all open-reel tapes. Then he persuaded the Pentagon to underwrite a massive project to digitize everything.[30]

The Marine Corps archivist turned to digital recordings to prevent further loss and to provide for easier reference and distribution. Once converted to digital format, the interviews could be stored on a hard drive, so long as there was sufficient space, or copied onto CD-ROM. By using compression software, many interviews could be stored on a single CD. Backup copies were essential, and sets of the disks could be distributed to multiple locations. The archives could also preserve the original magnetic tape with assurance that even if deterioration continued, the original information on the tapes would not be lost.

Digital electronic technology makes possible searchable databases that permit researchers to locate specific information, to read whole transcripts online, or to listen to the sound recordings. Rather than listen to an entire interview, researchers can follow topical themes throughout the collection, with more assurance of having seen all of the relevant information on a specific topic, and having instant access either at the archives or on the Internet.[31]

Are digital recordings suitable for archival preservation?

The up-front financial investment and staff time required to convert an analog oral history collection into digital formal will be costly, and archivists still have doubts about the durability of digital media over long periods of time. Software programs swiftly grow obsolete. Electronic records can migrate to new hardware and software without appreciable loss of sound quality, but the process still requires the monitoring of new data storage technology and software programs, and the conversion of data to new formats when necessary.

Each migration—or "media refreshment"—adds to the cost of digital preservation, although archivists point to "Moore's Law" as a factor that promises to reduce those costs. In 1965 the Silicon Valley pioneer Gordon Moore speculated that computing power would double every eighteen months, at the same time that computers became smaller and cheaper. His seemingly improbable prediction held true for the rest of the twentieth century. Presuming that it continues, digital storage density will increase while costs decrease with each re-copying. As a result, archivists calculate that any medium "needs to be reliable only for the length of time that it is economically advantageous to keep the data on it." If a digital medium is estimated to be reliable for only a few years, but storage costs can be cut in half during that time, then that medium can be judged sufficiently durable for an archives's preservation strategy. (But someone will still have to handle the migration of the data.)[32]

Is digitizing an oral history collection worth the expense and the effort?

Archival staffs and budgets have been stretched thin by the magnitude of handling burgeoning electronic records and of converting existing records to digital formats. There are costs involved in reformatting audio recordings and in cataloging collections, and staff training. Archivists are also troubled by the lack of established standards for digital preservation and the rapid technological development that threatens to make current systems obsolete before long.

Yet archivists increasingly confront users who expect their collections to be available electronically, at no cost. Virginia Danielson, curator of the Archive of World Music at Harvard University, has found it "variously hilarious, pitiable, or depressing" to hear library patrons insist that her collections will have to be digitized someday. She points out that cataloguing a collection and putting the catalog online is less expensive than digitizing the entire collection, and yet: "As a nation we have not managed to catalog our collections. We have not managed to complete online conversion of the catalogues that do exist." Those failings suggest that expectations for wholesale digitization of primary materials are unrealistic.

Not everything in a collection requires the same degree of access. Catalogs should receive top priority for online dissemination. Selected interviews of more general appeal can be incrementally digitized and placed on the web site. More sensitive material can be dealt with later when the restrictions have lifted.[33]

Is there an online database on oral history?

Archives have been inconsistent in cataloging their interviews for the national online computer databases. A few larger oral history collections report their interviews on the Research Libraries Information Network (RLIN). Others have adopted the Online Catalog Library Center (OCLC) form of cataloging. Many smaller archives and libraries have not catalogued their collections at all. Researchers have had to rely instead on published guides to oral history, which quickly become out-of-date.[34]

The Society of American Archivists has published an oral history cataloguing manual to assist oral history projects in cataloging, so that their oral histories can be incorporated into their library or archives' main catalogs. The Southwest Oral History Association (SOHA) has also developed a database system that offers descriptions of projects and interviews (although not the text of interviews) within its region, "for efficient input, organizational storage, and retrieval of up-to-date information." SOHA's experience is a lesson in how critical the accuracy of the data is to the creation of an automated system. Those inputting information must first verify it for accuracy and consistency. Data security also needs to be established, to prevent not only accidental deletions, but unauthorized tampering with the information. SOHA recommends that in choosing a system, an archives or library seeks to be compatible with and link into other systems.[35]

The inclination of more oral history projects to post portions or full-texts of their interviews on their web sites has also provided some ad hoc, haphazard, but remarkably useful finding aids. Using Internet search engines, researchers have stumbled across far-flung interviews by the name of the interviewee, the subjects of the interview, and even—if the transcripts are posted in full—by the names of people, events, issues and other key words mentioned in the interview. The online search may lead the researcher to the verbatim transcript, to the sound recording, to excerpts, or simply to a citation. Having located the transcript the researcher can travel to the archives, purchase a photocopy or CD, or borrow the transcript on interlibrary loan. As helpful as the Internet search engines have become, however, they remain far from comprehensive, because many archival repositories provide only the barest descriptions of their holdings, along with their access policies and hours of operation, on their web sites.[36]

Can a digital audio archives substitute for transcription?

Archives that have not systematically transcribed interviews have turned to the new digital technology to make their collections more accessible, especially for researchers who cannot visit the archives or do not have the time to listen to hours of recordings. The California State University at Long Beach had originally made summary sheets of its interviews, breaking them into three-minute segments to help researchers locate specific information. Director Sherna Berger Gluck explained that their intention was to allow researchers to "tap into the full richness of the orality of the interview, with its meaning derived not merely from the words uttered, but from all the nuances of pace, pitch, and performance—and even listen to what sometimes sounded like poetry." In the past, even with summaries, researcher use was limited by the cumbersome process of running the analog tape to find the desired segments. The university later sponsored a

Virtual Oral/Aural History Archives to make its sound recordings available online. Time-segmented summaries were assigned keywords, enabling users to find the information they sought either by reading the summaries or by entering the appropriate search term. The online version had the added advantage of photographs of the interviewees and other relevant visual materials. The archives made CD copies of the full interviews for preservation and made selected portions of the audio recordings available over the Internet. Despite the costs, the archives estimated that digitizing still amounted to less than what it would take to transcribe and edit all of its interviews.[37]

Exclusive reliance on sound recordings, however, shifts the burden of transcription onto users who may wish to reproduce portions of an interview in print, and increases the chance of misinterpretation and error, since neither the interviewer nor the interviewee will have any role in reviewing the transcript. Accents, jargon, and foreign languages further complicate the issue. The Long Beach archives, for instance, contains many hours of interviews with the former residents of the Japanese fishing village on Terminal Island conducted in Japanese. The University of Alaska's Project Jukebox, by contrast, provides recordings in the various languages of Native Alaskans along with transcriptions in English, preserving orality while extending the accessibility of the interviews.

Isn't it risky for an archives to post complete interviews on the Internet?

Some archivists express reservations about putting interviews online. Their reasons range from the need to protect interviewees' privacy to the danger of misuse and manipulation of sound recordings and transcripts. They seek hardware sufficient to accommodate their users while at the same time keeping the interviews well protected from hackers. They worry that the "unmonitored access" of the Internet suggests the loss of archival control of the interviews. They question whether deeds of gift that had not anticipated electronic reproduction and distribution would permit the posting of the interviews on the Internet without the express permission of the interviewees or their next of kin. Ethical questions of this nature have caused some oral historians to hesitate before proceeding into the minefield of the World Wide Web.

Having talked earnestly about returning interviews to the community, we need to ask: what constitutes the boundaries of that community? How broadly or narrowly do we want to define our audience? Did interviewees expect their life stories to remain relatively unused except by the occasional scholar, or did they hope to leave something of themselves for posterity, where their memories might be published, exhibited, and otherwise not forgotten? Given the democratic impulses of the oral history movement, it seems contradictory for oral historians not to avail themselves of the most universal and cost-effective means of mass communication and dissemination of information yet devised. "If we are to remain communicators," Paul Thompson has warned, "we must move with the technology of communication."[38]

Researchers who consult interview transcripts online will want the product to resemble as much as possible the original document. Some of the early attempts at downloading oral histories did not include the original pagination. Although researchers can scan the text by word on the screen, they will need page numbers for their citations as well as to make use of the prepared indexes if they print out a copy of the interview. To avoid abuse of an interview's copyright status, some projects have added a copyright symbol on all pages in a site.[39]

Should interviewees be contacted before posting their interviews on the Internet?

Even though broadly written deeds of gift that assign copyright to the archives or public domain will permit the posting of interviews online, it is imperative that oral historians grapple with the ethical issue of the Internet and avoid exploitation of their interviewees. Unless the possibility was made clear to interviewees from the outset, projects should notify living interviewees before placing their interviews on the Internet (although it seems excessive to consult the next of kin, whose intentions may conflict with those of the interviewee.) "What's the Internet?" some elderly interviewees ask when informed of plans to post their interviews. Explanations can be offered on the phone and printouts of how the interviews will appear online can be sent by mail. Several elderly interviewees later reported that grandchildren helped them find their interviews on the Internet— and were impressed to see their grandparents' life stories online.

Projects that have relied exclusively on audio recordings or that plan to make the recordings as well as the transcriptions available online have been the most diligent about prior notification. Hearing a voice seems more personal and intrusive than simply reading their transcripts. The University of Alaska at Fairbanks, which pioneered in putting audio interviews on CD-ROM, hesitated going on the Internet before contacting each of the interviewees directly. The oral history program sent out letters to some two hundred people interviewed over the past ten years, explained the possible Internet access, included a copy of the original signed release form, and the Site Use Agreement that it would post with their interviews, requiring the user to read a statement and click a button to agree not to use the material for commercial purposes, not to re-post or link to the site without permission, and to follow the Guidelines for Respecting Cultural Knowledge established by the Assembly of Alaska Native Educators and the Principles and Standards of the Oral History Association. The mailing revealed that some of the interviewees had died or could not be located, and of the rest, only about twenty-five people responded. Of those who responded, some favored broader exposure of their culture and community as a way of educating people; others worried about the potential for misuse, having their statements taken out of context, and a misunderstanding of their culture and community. The limited response suggested to the oral historians that personal contact rather than written communications would have been more useful in informing their interviewees.[40]

The California State University at Long Beach's archives went to similar lengths to contact the interviewees or their next of kin before putting interviews on its web site. Surviving family members not only approved, but provided many of the photographs that archives used online. Still concerned about adequately safeguarding their interviewees, the archives has developed a program that would enable users to hear the streamed sound but not to be able to download the sound files from the Internet. Those who wanted copies had to request permission from the university archives, identifying how they planned to use the recording. For a small fee, the archives would prepare a CD of the requested material and send it to the researcher.[41]

Oral history projects should build the Internet into their operating plans, fully informing participants of the project's intentions and of the interviewees' options, making sure that deeds of gift permit reproduction of the interviews, and preparing transcripts in formats convenient for downloading. For long-established oral history archives, the task of digitizing a large collection of transcripts and sound recordings might appear so daunting as to paralyze. A reasonable strategy would be to start by making any finding aids available on the Internet. That will alert researchers as to what exists where. Projects can next turn to interviews already transcribed on disk, or scan older transcripts, and post a sample of their interviews to display the richness of the collection. Researchers will pay virtual visits to the archives, searching the finding aids, reading the transcripts, listening to some of the recordings, and consulting with the archivists electronically.[42]

Is it necessary for a project to revise its deed of gift to put oral histories on the Internet?

Most deeds of gift were written to grant the researcher who conducted the interviews or the archives that received them broad latitude for their eventual use, anticipating articles, books, documentaries and exhibit materials. In those cases where the interviewees have relinquished copyright and turned their interviews over to the researcher, the archives, or the public domain without restriction, then no additional agreement should be necessary, although it would be a good faith effort to notify interviewees in advance of any major change in the access to their interviews. In those cases where the interviewee has retained copyright, requires permission to cite or quote, and otherwise restricts the use of their interviews, then an additional written agreement should be negotiated specifying that portions of all of the interview can be posted in electronic format on the Internet.

If an oral history archives redesigns its deed of gift to make sure that it covers the new technology, it should be careful not to define that technology too specifically. Even the Internet will be overtaken by unforeseen technology and will eventually pass into obsolescence. Rather than outlining particular forms of distribution, the Oral History Association recommends that deeds of gift grant permission for interviews to be "quoted from, published or broadcast in any medium" that the archives deems appropriate.[43]

DONATED INTERVIEWS

Even if an archives does not conduct oral history itself, is it likely to receive some donated interviews?

Yes, even without seeking them out, archives are likely to receive oral histories as donations from individual researchers and community groups, or as part of a larger accession of corporate, associational, or government agency records. The oral history may be an extensive collection or a random transcript filed among other records. There are so many forms and conditions in which donated oral histories may arrive that, to exercise any archival control, an archives cannot afford to be a passive recipient. Instead, an archives should establish its own standards and work with oral historians—whether individuals or representatives of an agency—to meet those standards.

The likelihood of all archives receiving oral history donations increased exponentially in 1989 when the American Historical Association (AHA) adopted its statement of principles on oral history interviewing, stipulating that "interviewers should arrange to deposit their interviews in an archival repository that is capable of both preserving the interviews and making them available for general research. Additionally, the interviewer should work with the repository in determining the necessary legal arrangements."[44]

The historical profession was responding to the laxity with which many authors had been treating oral sources. When books include citations to "interviews in author's possession," other historians will want the opportunity to examine them for verification and further research use. Through their professional associations, historians also wanted to create a greater awareness among researchers that they may have the only the interview with individuals who have died. And even if the interviewee was also interviewed by another oral history program, each interviewer's questions shed a different light on the interviewee's experiences. Other scholars who examine an author's oral source material may draw different conclusions from those of the original interviewer, just as researchers disagree over the meaning of written documentation.

Many academics, freelance writers, graduate advisers, and graduate students had simply never considered giving their interviews to an archives before the AHA promulgated its standards. The historian David Oshinsky conducted many interviews for his biography of Senator Joseph R. McCarthy, particularly for McCarthy's early life, about which little had been published. Although he taped most of his interviews, he did not collect any release forms because it never occurred to him to deposit them in an archives. After reading the AHA rules, Oshinsky became determined to adopt archival-quality standards. For his next book, he taped all of his interviews, obtained releases, produced written transcripts, and deposited tapes and transcripts in Rutgers University library, where they have already been used by other researchers.[45]

The Columbia Oral History Research Office both conducts its own interviews and regularly receives interviews from writers who have published their books. The Walt Disney Archives conducted no formal oral history program of its own but received an extensive collection of interviews with Disney, his family, studio animators, park planners, and other employees, donated by various authors who did the interviews in the course of their research. The University of Kentucky archives estimated that nearly 80 percent of the two hundred interviews added annually to the university's oral history collection are generated outside the archives by faculty from history, political science, anthropology, and sociology, and from graduate students and independent researchers. The archives also found that, however valuable the contributions of these "associate interviewers" their interviews often arrived untranscribed, unindexed, unabstracted, and with no legal release forms. The University of Kentucky archivist Terry Birdwhistell has noted that "the preservation of personal interviews generated by historians is a two-way street. For every historian who for one reason or another fails to place his or her interviews in an archives, there is likely an archivist who does not want to add an historians' recorded interviews and transcripts to his collections. Overcoming these biases will take the cooperation of both historians and archivists."[46]

Archivists must avoid even the appearance of favoritism when dealing with researchers. When offered donations of interviews from a researcher, they must balance what they do against what the researcher is giving. It would be questionable for an archives to invest large amounts of its staff time and financial resources in transcribing and preserving an oral history collection if it was to be closed for an excessively long period of time to all but the original researcher. If an archives provides equipment and invests its resources in a collection of oral histories, then it should avoid open-ended agreements and seek to negotiate with the donor a reasonable time for releasing the materials for general research.

What should archives do to get some control over donated interview recordings and transcripts?

Ideally, archivists work with researchers from the onset of an oral history project, rather than coming in at the end. But when researchers appear at the archives' door at the end of a project, carrying their interview recordings and no release forms—or having followed other guidelines—the archives needs to determine whether the material meets its standards. If the archives agrees to accession the interviews it can provide the researcher with deeds of gift to take back to interviewees for their signatures. Again, the interviews can be restricted until the book is published.

Archivists need to publicize their willingness to serve as repositories for individual and group oral history projects, whether conducted at their university, in their community, or on subjects complementary to their larger collections. By attracting such donations they can build their oral history holdings in the most cost-effective manner. But even more important, interviews will be "out of the desk drawers, closets, and basements" of the interviewers and made available to scholarship in general.[47]

Should an archives treat donated oral histories the same as those it commissions or conducts itself?

Donated interviews can be treated like those sponsored by the archives in terms of paperwork and filing agreements. Once archivists receive donated recordings, they should immediately make a security copy and store the originals in an environmentally controlled and secure area. In anticipation of receiving oral history donations, archives should establish guidelines for accession of oral documentation, including sample legal releases, recommended tape for long-term preservation, and other processing standards. A good model is the guideline that the National Archives and Records Administration issued for accessioning federal oral history projects.[48]

LEGAL CONSIDERATIONS

If only portions of an interview are restricted, can the rest of the interview be made available for research?

Emphatically, yes. There is no reason to hold back the bulk of an interview for the sake of a few pages of restricted material. Remove the restricted pages and place them in a sealed envelope identified with the name of the interviewee and the date the restriction will be lifted. Insert a note in the transcript: "Pages x to y have been restricted until [date]." Or, "A portion of the interview at this point in the transcript has been restricted." Be sure to remove and store separately any restricted material from transcripts that have been produced and stored electronically.

Some archives do not announce that they even possess an oral history until the restriction has passed, in part to avoid legal challenges. But researchers want to know if they have seen all the relevant material and what lies beyond their research. Some will delay publication of their own work if they know that the restriction will be lifted soon. By not announcing the existence of closed interviews, the archives favors those who happen to be present when the records open, a circumstance that too often has made researchers suspicious that favoritism was being shown.

If an archives does not advertise that it had a certain interview, even though restricted, then another oral history project may interview the same person and duplicate the information. One flattered interviewee never bothered to tell the second interviewer that he had already given a lengthy life review interview. If an interview is closed, researchers may seek to interview that person themselves and would be entirely within their rights to do so. But when the interviewee is deceased, only the archival oral history will be available.

In the government, are oral histories official public records?

They can be, but not necessarily. If an interview is done as a job requirement of a government employee, such as a debriefing, it is clearly an official record and should be treated as other government records. But simply because interviewees work for the government does not mean that they automatically waive rights to their interviews. Under federal copyright laws, anyone whose words are recorded and reproduced retains copyright over the recording. If a private citizen or government employee voluntarily gives an interview to a government oral history project, they should be asked, like anyone else, to sign a deed of gift assigning their copyright in the interview to the agency's repository and stipulating any restrictions on its use. The federal government recognizes the gift of restricted oral histories as an exemption to the Freedom of Information Act (FOIA). That is, researchers' FOIA requests for transcripts do not supersede interviewee's stipulated restrictions.[49]

Oral history is underway throughout the three branches of the federal government. Every military service has conducted oral history, as have historians at the Energy and Labor Departments, the Nuclear Regulatory Commission, the National Park Service, NASA, the CIA, and the FBI. Over the decades, they have produced oral histories in the tens of thousands, most of which are open for research. The Smithsonian Institution is an outstanding example of the diversity of oral history. The Air and Space Museum has interviewed aviation pioneers; on the occasion of its fiftieth anniversary, the National Gallery of Art interviewed those who built and operated the gallery (and continued it as an ongoing project); the Natural History Museum has interviewed early curators who brought back specimens; the American History Museum has interviewed African Americans who migrated "from field to factory." The Smithsonian archives has also conducted extensive video interviews with old-time curators throughout the Smithsonian's many museums.[50]

Is an archives liable for any potentially libelous or defamatory remarks in an oral history?

Libel and defamation are false statements that can injure a person's reputation, holding them up to public ridicule and contempt. Fortunately, the dead cannot be defamed, or else history could not be written. But should an interviewee defame a living person in an oral history, then the interviewee, interviewer, and archives could share liability for the statements. A defamatory statement would have to mention a person specifically by name, be published, and damage the person's reputation. Courts have been more protective of average citizens than of public figures in defamation cases.

Generally, libel and defamation cases have involved mass-circulation books, newspapers, and magazines rather than archival oral histories. Although there is no body of case law specifically involving oral history, no oral history archives relishes the possibility of becoming the first case, and most of them recognize that discretion is the better part of valor. Since most oral history projects cannot afford to have a lawyer read every interview for potentially libelous statements, they have used their common sense instead. Confronted with a potentially libelous portion, an archives can delete the specific names or close that portion for a period of time, perhaps ten or twenty years, until the remarks are no longer controversial.[51]

If interviews or other records are closed for a seemingly vague reason, researchers may well challenge why and by whose authority such restrictions have

been made. In anticipation of such questions, most archives list their own institutional restrictions in a document that researchers can read when they arrive
at the archives. Such information sheets establish that the archivist has the
authority to impose restrictions, if needed, to protect privacy, to guard against
libel, and to meet other general criteria set by the archives's governing board.

Should an archives release restricted interviews that have been subpoenaed?

Prosecutors in Mississippi subpoenaed three sealed oral history interviews with
an Imperial Wizard of the KKK indicted for the murder of a civil rights leader
decades earlier. Despite objections from the state's department of archives and
records, the court ordered that the interviews be turned over to the district
attorney. Since the defendant did not take the stand, the interviews were not used
in the trial but the incident shows the vulnerability of otherwise restricted material to subpoenas.[52]

Archivists are responsible for honoring and protecting donor restrictions.
The premature release of an oral history interview not only could embarrass the
individual but could have a "chilling effect" on other interviewees, making them
more reluctant to speak candidly on tape. Archivists therefore are faced with a
legal and ethical dilemma when restricted oral histories are subpoenaed for use
in a court proceeding. The few cases that have arisen have usually not focused
specifically on oral history but have been blanket requests, or "fishing expedi-
tions," for any and all archival materials regarding an individual, organization,
or issue. Archivists and their attorneys have negotiated more limited release of
materials, arguing that the type of information sought can be obtained from
sources other than the closed oral histories. Submitting the deeds of gift under
which interviewees donated restricted interviews, archives have also invoked
their "fiduciary privilege" to protect such sealed materials they hold in trust.

PUBLIC PROGRAMS

How can an archives use oral history for public outreach?

Public programs sometimes get lost in the archival shuffle of accessioning,
maintaining, and preserving collections and dealing with researchers and reference questions. But outreach is an important function that can heighten the
interest and appreciation for historical records and increase public support for
libraries and archives. Oral history offers unique opportunities for reaching
members of a community who might not otherwise use a library or archive.

After the first contacts have been made by conducting interviews in the community, the connection is reinforced through public programs that display the finished product.[53]

In California, the San Joaquin Valley library system sponsored an oral history with first- and second-generation Japanese Americans in the valley who had lived through the Second World War. The project aimed not only to create a resource for scholars, but to influence the community's thinking about its ethnic heritage. The collected oral histories enabled the library system to published three volumes and create a videotape (*Success Through Perseverance*) and a slide-tape show (*Improving Library Services to Japanese-Americans in the Valley*), which they publicized broadly on radio and television and in newspapers. Librarians rated the programs a great public relations success and noted that they resulted in greater utilization of the local libraries by the Japanese-American patrons.[54]

Archivists also have found public outreach benefits closer to home. Many archives are housed in universities and other institutions and are supervised by a board of trustees or executive board that determines whether the archives gets more space, staff, and equipment. The members of these governing boards can be directly involved in an oral history program, making recommendations over potential interviewees, getting copies of the interviews, discussing their use in public relations, and even being interviewed themselves. This contact helps make the work of the archives more tangible and immediate to those who influence its policies and its budgets. Similar public outreach can be directed toward the administrators, staff, faculty, students, and alumnae of a university and toward management and workers in a corporation.

Another return of such community awareness are the donations of photographs, manuscripts and other memorabilia from those who have given oral histories or who have attended the public programs. Archives should not hesitate to ask oral history interviewees to consider making such gifts; most will be honored by the request and will be pleased to have family keepsakes preserved. A word of caution, however: libraries and archives need to establish and communicate their collecting policies to ensure that their public programs do not generate inappropriate gifts.

Oral histories make good subjects for press releases. Local newspapers have reprinted portions of interviews, as single articles, or special supplements. Consider also using the tapes to create public service announcements for local radio and television stations. Some archives have used oral history interviews in curriculum packets for schools.[55]

Archives and historical societies have also posted oral history interviews on their web sites as a "springboard" to attract users to their larger collections. The

Idaho Historical Society, for instance, devoted a web page to the Smokejumping and Forest Fire Fighting oral history conducted by the one of its divisions, the Idaho Oral History Center. The project started by interviewing parachuting fire fighters who jumped from Idaho camps in the 1940s and gradually expanded it to include men and women who fought blazes across the U.S. West. The web page gave narrators' names, some basic information about them, a link to indices to each interview, and a few sound clips. The dramatic nature of these interviews helped capture browsers' attention and served as an advertisement for the historical society. At Virginia Tech, the university archivist developed a web site about the first black students at the university. Records in the archives enabled her to identify the first black undergraduates, while the Internet helped her to locate "missing" students, former faculty, staff, and alumni, whom she interviewed. They in turn provided photographs, memorabilia, and additional information to update the site, turning it into a growing exhibition.[56]

Such public programs are fine for larger, well-funded archives, historical societies, and library systems, but how could a local library afford to do that kind of outreach?

Some oral history has been well funded, but a lot more has operated on a shoestring, using volunteers, borrowed equipment, and surviving on modest donations. The local library often houses a local history collection, which is not only the local repository for community oral histories but the best research source for those conducting the interviews. Local librarians know the community and have a sense of who uses the facility and who does not. The librarian may not have the time to do the interviews but can coordinate volunteer interviewers, indexers, and transcribers. The librarian can also work with local students or with the state or local historical society, which may be eager to conduct oral history interviews. The library can serve as the sole repository for the interviews, or copies of the tapes and transcripts can be shared with the cooperating schools and historical societies. If guided, volunteers from the community often enjoy doing interviews and making a contribution to preserving community history. Remind them that creating the oral documentation is not an end in itself but just a first step toward the use of local oral histories in research, publications, and public programs. The best reward for volunteers is to include them in any public exhibits, performances, and receptions, where they can see the product of their labor.[57]

The Martin Luther King, Jr., Public Library in Washington, D.C., sought to enhance its Washingtoniana collection with oral histories of the people, neighborhoods, institutions, and events that had fostered public understanding of the history of the District of Columbia. Interviewers were invited to register their ongoing projects with the library so that others could be informed of their activities. Registrants were asked for the name of project, the name, address, and telephone number of the project director, a brief description of project's focus, and an estimated date for completion. The library also agreed to accept donations of tapes and transcripts so long as they were accompanied by formal legal agreements between interviewers and interviewees releasing the donated materials to unrestricted public use, were recorded with good sound quality, and were time-indexed or transcribed. The library provided copies of sample legal release forms; promised periodic workshops and seminars on oral history for those who requested them; offered to make referrals to university oral history classes in the metropolitan area; and promoted itself as a clearinghouse for local oral history projects and bibliographic references to oral history materials that were part of its collection. This Washington library's efforts exemplify the mutually beneficial relationship that can be established between libraries, archives, and interviewers to preserve the oral history of our time for the future.

CHAPTER 7

Teaching Oral History

At what level is oral history best used in the classroom?

Teachers have implemented oral history at every level from grade school to graduate school and in continuing and community education programs, including workshops for senior citizens. Interviewing techniques can be taught to students of all levels of ability. In secondary schools, oral history more often has been directed towards honors, gifted and talented, and advance-placement students, but has demonstrated that it can motivate slow learners and otherwise indifferent students as well. Doing oral history helps students break loose from their textbooks and become their own collectors of information and students remember best what they researched themselves.

Oral history works for teachers who, frankly, have grown tired of lecturing and want to engage their students more actively in learning. Instead of teachers telling students what is important, oral history projects require students to find out for themselves, by interviewing people and then by processing and analyzing the information gathered. Students often prove innately able to establish the necessary rapport, since many older interviewees feel a special need to make young people understand the events of the past. In many ways the ideal oral history relationship occurs when the interviewer plays student to the interviewee as teacher.[1]

It sounds too good to be true. What's the catch?

School oral history projects frequently encounter a lack of funds and equipment, school boards that are unsympathetic to new student electives, and department chairs and colleagues who are dubious about anything outside the standard curriculum. A teacher can grow discouraged over the time and commitment that oral history requires. Some lack training and personal experience in using oral history and have no mentor to turn to for advice. Teachers complain about the difficulty of completing oral history projects within the limited confines of a semester; others complain of students who do not prepare adequately for their interviews. Teachers also recognize the need for more structured assistance to help student projects succeed.

Admittedly, oral history is hardly a panacea for all that ails modern education, and not every student readily adopts to it. But those teachers who have used oral history offer enthusiastic assessments of its pedagogical advantages and attest that its rewards are worth the effort.[2]

Does oral history work in other classes besides history?

With "history" in its name, oral history has shown up most often in history and social studies programs; teachers can use it to study family, culture, community, and government. But interviewing has also flourished in English, journalism, drama, folklore, science, and other disciplines. The innovative *Foxfire* program sprang from an English composition course designed to get students to develop content and grammar skills by writing about what they saw and did. A composition or language skills class can assign students not only to conduct interviews and to write descriptions of the experience, but to do transcription, which is an exercise that calls for language skills in sentence structure, syntax, and punctuation.[3]

Students may never have associated their own everyday language with the standard English of textbooks and classroom assignments. One English teacher was surprised when her inner-city black students complained that Alice Walker's novel, *The Color Purple* (1982) sounded odd and was hard to read, despite the teacher's observation that Walker's prose perfectly captured her students' own "black English." None of them, she concluded, "had ever learned how to read and write their own verbal system of communication." An oral history project that had students recording and transcribing their own speech patterns would offer rare opportunities for self-revelation. Interview transcriptions similarly provide students a means of examining regional dialects, colloquialisms, and jargon.[4]

What is *Foxfire?*

Familiar to mass audiences through the stage play, television movie, and series of best-selling books, *Foxfire* is the pioneering secondary school project that combined oral history and folklore as instructional devices. It began in 1966, when a teacher at the Rabun Gap-Nacoochee high school, in an Appalachian community in Georgia, realized that his lectures were just not getting through to his students, who were deficient in language skills and uncomfortable expressing themselves in writing. "How would you like to throw away the text and start a magazine?" he asked. Soon, *Foxfire* proved so effective in motivating students that it spawned countless other school interviewing and journal-writing projects across the country.[5]

A typical *Foxfire* class lasts one semester. Before students begin interviewing, they listen to a short story read aloud and try to write down everything they heard. A sample reading of these papers easily demonstrates why the original is richer and fuller than any of the remembered versions. Then the same story is read again, slowly, with the students trying to take it down as dictation—a task they quickly find impossible. These exercises demonstrate the problems involved in listening and also make clear the need for recording interviews. But this leaves the question of how to get the story off the tape, a discussion that in turn leads to an explanation of transcribing, followed by students attempting practice transcripts. Other class sessions cover the varying sound quality of different recorders, tapes, microphones, with demonstrations on how to set up equipment properly. *Foxfire* classes include sessions on cameras as well, since students are encouraged to take photographs of the people they interview and to collect other items related to the subject matter.

Foxfire seeks to involve students in all phases of the oral history project. The class picks the theme of the project, whom to interview, and what questions to ask. Before going out to conduct interviews, students watch a practice in-class interview, in which someone—perhaps another teacher, a school administrator, cafeteria worker, or a parent—is invited to the class to be interviewed. The in-class interview is not a drill but an actual interview designed to impress on the students the seriousness of their responsibilities as interviewers.

In-class interviews give students the chance to analyze not only the interviewing process but also the transcription and the effects of different transcription styles on the content of the interview. Students begin to realize how easily a careless transcriber can alter the meaning of an interview. With all this in-class experience and discussion absorbed, the students finally go out to interview for themselves.[6]

Foxfire spread its message to other schools, recommending a "fieldwork enterprise" that mixes research, interviewing training, and community-school relationships. A term's project might be a slide-tape or PowerPoint presentation or a video, but quite often it has resulted in publication of a school journal. Since the publication of the first *Foxfire Book* in 1972, numerous schools have produced similar magazines combining oral history, folklore, and local history. Two of its off-spring, in Kennebunkport, Maine, and Lebanon, Missouri, similarly made the transition from local school magazines to nationally published books: *The Salt Book* (1977) and *Bittersweet County* (1978). *Long, Long Ago,* an intermediate school student magazine in Bell Gardens,

California, contains interviews with local community members, while seventh graders in Northern California's Anderson Valley published *Voices of the Valley*. Students with learning disabilities in Littleton, Colorado, published *Aspen Glow*, while the children of migrant farmworkers in Boulder produced *El Aguila. Bloodlines* is the student oral history journal in Holmes County, Mississippi, one of the poorest counties in the nation.

Many school oral history magazines have not lasted long. Some were identified with a particular teacher who moved on, and others were eliminated by school budget cuts. One well-regarded publication was canceled when its budget allotment went to pay for the school's heating oil. Its director bemoaned the project's death from "administrative ineptitude." Yet new oral history journals and newsletters continue to appear, facilitated by the greater availability of school computers for in-house publications.[7]

Where can a teacher get personal training in oral history?

If a teacher did not have an opportunity to take an oral history course in graduate school, courses and workshops are regularly available at universities and community colleges and in adult education programs. Between school years, summer institutes and week-long oral history workshops are conducted around the country. The web sites of several oral history archives contain bibliographies, sample deeds of gift, and other useful information that amount to "workshops on the web." State historical societies whose collections contain oral history interviews often can be enlisted to help.

The Oral History Association and its several affiliated state and regional oral history associations regularly run workshops and offer sessions aimed at teachers. They publish such practical-minded pamphlets as *Oral History in the Secondary School Classroom* and *Oral History Projects in Your Classroom*, with an accompanying video, *History from the Living: The Organization and Craft of Oral History. Talking Gumbo: An Oral History Manual for Secondary School Teachers*, a how-to-do-it guide for using oral history in history, English, and social studies classes, also has a companion thirty-minute video, *You've Got to Hear This*, designed to teach students how to conduct interviews.[8]

The National Council for the Social Studies offers its own pamphlet, *Oral History in the Classroom*, in its "How to Do It Series"; and the Teachers and Collaborative Workshop published *Like It Was: A Complete Guide to Writing Oral History* for junior and senior high school. The Smithsonian Center for Folklife and Cultural Heritage has produced *Discovering Our Delta: A Learning Guide for Community Research*. Its video component follows five students from the Mississippi Delta as they do fieldwork research largely through interviewing in their communities. Available for downloading from the Center's web site are useful student and teacher guides that accompany the video.[9]

Many of these organizations have recognized that overworked teachers are too busy preparing lessons, grading papers, and dealing with their supervisors to attend many extracurricular programs. Some have made their oral history workshops more attractive by offering certificates or qualifying as "in-service" teacher training during scheduled release time. Although these occasional workshops are usually brief and unable to cover much ground, they provide teachers with basic models for their own classroom projects. Teachers have also recognized oral history as a highly positive way of meeting state mandates and performing evaluations of students' advancement.

Where can a school get oral history equipment?

It was the availability of low-cost, lightweight, easy-to-operate cassette tape recorders that made oral history feasible as a teaching device in the first place, but acquiring equipment on limited school budgets still calls for creativity. Some school audiovisual departments will sometimes have recorders, microphones, video cameras, and computers, but in general teachers can expect anything from a complete lack of equipment to a severe limitation on its availability. Poll your students to see how many can use their own tape recorders and mini-disks. Some have access to family camcorders. Local merchants have cooperated with school projects by lending equipment. One California camera store annually lends a local high school all the equipment it needs for filming and editing its History Day media entries. Local support groups, from parent-teacher associations to alumni, should also be tapped for funds and equipment. With its objective of publishing a magazine of its interviews, the *Foxfire* program sent its students out to solicit contributions from local merchants and townsfolk. They listed gifts of any amount in the magazine, and each donor received a copy signed by all of the students.[10]

What is the single most important ingredient for starting an oral history project in a school?

Every classroom oral history project needs a teacher who is sincerely committed to it. "It's not all fun and games," as Barbara Gallant, a high school teacher in Gainesville, Florida, reported. "It has to be part of the curriculum and not something extra. I don't think you need the money to start, because I think that can be found. I do think there has to be a person who cares and wants to do it; who feels that there is some real value in it." Gallant began supervising an oral history project at a time when federal courts had ordered racial integration of her school system. Teachers and administrators at her school felt it essential to get white and black students communicating with each other and to build stronger ties with the community. Using borrowed tape recorders, she assigned her students to interview family members about how the county had changed over the past fifty years and brought local historians and anthropologists into class to talk to the students. The project worked well although she discovered that after a while her students grew bored with using school integration as the only subject. She subsequently allowed her classes to branch out into other areas. Still, the interviews they conducted helped the students through a time of dramatic changes and created a useful resource for future research on their school.[11]

ORAL HISTORY IN ELEMENTARY AND SECONDARY SCHOOLS

Can oral history really be tried in elementary school classes?

At the elementary school level, oral history is used not for teaching subject matter but for helping students become more aware of their surroundings. Recognizing that children wonder about themselves before they begin to appreciate others, elementary school teachers have had students interview their parents on the theme, "What was I like when I was younger?" Elementary school students have collected anecdotes about their families and learned about their neighborhoods. Educators note that children "grow socially" when they interview adults.[12]

In one elementary school project, students were asked to describe the route they typically took to school. They recorded what types of buildings they passed, such as businesses, churches, and other schools. Accompanied by an adult, students interviewed someone identified with one of the buildings on their daily route. They asked shop owners why they chose the location, how long they had been doing business there, and whether most of their customers came from the local community. Drawing from such programs, the District of Columbia school system published *Earth Waves,* a newsletter that reported on oral history in elementary schools, offered sample projects and questions, and reproduced portions of student interviews. Fourth graders in Middlebury, Vermont, published a similar journal, called *Village Green.*[13]

Oral history has become a recognizable part of children's popular culture. In the movie version of *The Grinch,* little Cindy Lou conducts oral histories to uncover the reasons for the Grinch's anti-holiday prejudices. The children's book *The Berenstain Bears and the Giddy Grandma* recounts a school assignment in which Sister Bear must interview a member of her family. She chooses her grandmother, but has second thoughts when she learns that others in her class have interviewed famous relatives. "And Gram is just . . . well, just Gram." The interview, however, uncovers surprising facts about Grandma's past as a circus bear, lures her out of retirement for a school talent show, and produces "the best oral history in the history of oral history." For younger readers, the book's message is that history can be found at home, and that oral history can help them discover things they never knew about their own families.[14]

Young children can focus their interviews on what their parents and grandparents did when they were children. What types of games did they play when they were young? What did they ever do before television? Was their schooling different? What types of songs were popular then? How had household technology changed during their lifetimes? Children seem most comfortable interviewing grandparents perhaps, as has been said, because they share a common enemy.

Do the objectives change when using oral history with middle or junior high school students?

Both the objectives and levels of sophistication in oral history advance as students move towards adolescence. For middle and junior high school students, oral history has been more used for dealing with the "affective domain," or issues pertaining to emotions and feelings. Since adolescents are struggling with their personal identity, oral history helps to refocus their attention from themselves to their families and the community in which they live. Middle and junior high school social studies curricula often emphasize local history, and provide local history texts that can be the basis for doing a locally oriented oral history where students get to practice social studies, "almost without realizing it." [15]

Schools in Quincy, Massachusetts, involved sixth-, seventh- and eighth-grade students in a Family Ties program. Students visited the Quincy Museum and studied Eliza Susan Quincy, who throughout the nineteenth century had recorded all of the furnishings and objects in the Quincy family home and had collected reminiscences of other family members. Returning home, students were asked to list what items their own families counted as "treasures" and to prepare their own family inventories in album form. The albums documented the students' families, homes, and times, with the idea that the albums could someday be passed along to their own children.

As part of this project, the museum staff helped train the students to interview family members. The interviews assisted in creating their family inventories by helping students understand not only what the items were, but their emotional significance. Little noticed bric-a-brac took on new meaning as mementos of the past. For students who were first or second generation immigrants, family treasures were cherished reminders of a former life in a different culture. The experiment helped the students to use primary source materials, gave them experience in different kinds of writing, and raised their curiosity about local historical resources. Students completed the project with a stronger sense of both of being "rooted in the past" as well as an "active part of the present." An unexpected by-product of the class discussions, students' increased consciousness of the different backgrounds of their classmates, was one the project directors trusted would foster greater tolerance in a multicultural environment.[16]

Would an oral history project be any different at the high school level?

In high school, oral history tends to be more closely connected to the subject matter being taught in the classroom. Students learn the same oral history techniques but apply them to a wide range of subjects. Often the interview subjects are particularly relevant to the local region, but have national significance as well and fit into a curriculum that includes world and U.S. history. Topics that high school students have tackled include native villages of the Aleutian Islands, Japanese-American relocation during the Second World War, the Buffalo Soldiers, the Three Mile Island incident, the Baltimore Air Show of 1910, multiculturalism in Hawaii, and the changing Lower East Side of Manhattan. One high school student evaluating an oral history course reported: "It helped me understand the human causes, not just 'the war began because' . . . but why it began, who was involved and most importantly how they felt."[17]

School administrators in Northern California's Anderson Valley experimented with a variety of ways of incorporating their *Voices of the Valley* oral history project into the high-school English curriculum. At first they offered it as a regular class, with students in alternating years selecting a theme and conducting the interviews and those in the following year transcribing them and producing a compact disc. As that plan allowed none of the students to experience the whole project from beginning to end or receive the same learning skills, the school revised the curriculum to offer *Voices of the Valley* as an elective course for ninth through twelfth graders. With the valley's large Mexican-American population, the interviewing and transcribing requirements helped many students in learning English. "When I got here, I didn't know any English," one student in the program reported. "But now that I'm doing this [project] I'm getting better at it. I know how to transcribe faster and to translate Spanish to English or English to Spanish."[18]

How should you prepare high school students to do oral histories?

A good way to start is to have the students read other oral histories before they do their own interviews. If previous classes at the school have done interviews that are available in the school library, students can read a sampling of the best ones. Many oral history recordings and transcripts can also be accessed on the Internet, including interviews conducted by high school students. Especially good sources are *History Matters,* a web site maintained by George Mason University, which includes first-person narratives and oral histories; and *Ordinary People Living Extraordinary Lives: The Civil Rights Movement in Mississippi,* which includes audio clips and transcripts. Since the spoken word is less formal than written text, published oral histories are usually easy to read and their stories can be gripping. Reading these oral histories stimulates classroom discussion, engages students' interest, and gives them some of the needed background to conduct their own interviews. By reading other oral histories, students get a better idea of the type of information that interviewing can elicit, and they see that interviewees often present contradictory accounts.[19]

The class textbook can also become a research tool; it provides the broad outline and some of the specifics for the subject being studied, and sometimes bibliographies suggesting further reading. When interviewees cover information outside the scope of the text or contradict something in the text, students must weigh the conflicting evidence and consider the complexity of the issue. Old magazines, newspapers, memoirs, and histories are all standard sources, but research can also include photographs, music, physical artifacts, and any number of other sources. There is a story behind most every photograph in a family photo album. The same items that provide inspiration for doing the interviews can also serve as illustrations for the transcripts, videos, exhibits, and other projects that grow out of the interviews.[20]

Pre-interview research is absolutely essential. An unprepared student is likely to conduct a poor interview and will miss most of the learning experience that oral history offers. If student interviewers have not done their homework, they will not know all the questions to ask, will not be able to assist interviewees with faulty memories, will not recognize new leads that require follow-up questions, and will neither fully understand nor appreciate what they are hearing.

Whom should students interview?

Students generally start with their own families. Oral history gives them a chance to collect more systematically the many stories they have already heard at the dinner table or at family reunions. They can interview one person in depth as a full life history, or several members of the same family in a family history. Their interviews might cover many generations, since grandparents can tell stories about their own parents and grandparents. Questions can include: When did their family immigrate to America? When did they move to the state they are now living in? How long have they lived in their community? What wars have family members fought in (or against)? What types of jobs have they held?

But the oral history experience is enhanced when students use it to interview people whom they normally would not have met and talked with. Working with the students, teachers can suggest likely places to seek interviewees. A class working on a group project can contact the local historical society for advice about potential interviewees. Local newspapers and informed citizens, nearby colleges, senior citizens' centers, veterans hospitals, and such national organizations such as Veterans of Foreign Wars (VFW) and the American Legion are all potential sources of interviewees.[21]

Whether they interview their family, neighbors, or members of the community at large, students will discover how historical events affected people like themselves, a revelation that will expand their historical consciousness and make their classwork more meaningful. A school oral history project can also lead students to reexamine their own communities and to break down the walls between the classroom and the "real world" outside.[22]

Student oral history projects can examine great national and international events and their impact on the local community events of the magnitude of the Great Depression, the war in Vietnam, the 1970s energy crisis, the environmental movement, the civil rights movement, and the women's rights movement. Churches and other religious centers in the community, a housing development, a manufacturing plant, an event like a flood, or tornado, can be documented through oral history.

The humorist Garrison Keillor once wrote a spoof about students living in a housing development so new that it had no cultural heritage to document. The only demonstrable craft was that of placing boards across stacks of bricks to make bookcases. But most communities have existed long enough to have a history. Possible subjects are neighborhood organizations, civil rights groups, local charities, newspapers, radio and television stations and their personnel, as well as local entertainers. Students can even document their own school by interviewing current and past administrators, teachers, and graduates. Student oral histories have recorded local folklore, crafts, skills, trades, occupations, and customs. Students have studied local government by interviewing political candidates, office holders, and civil associations. The purpose of these interviews is to record what people and organizations did (and why), and how people, events, and practices changed over time. The result will not be simply a snapshot of how things are today but a record of how they used to be, and how and why they evolved.[23]

Students can be quite unpredictable in choosing whom to interview. One student noticed an elderly man at her local library. After introducing herself, she asked him to give her an interview for her oral history project. The man replied, "I'm honored by so charming a young lady, but . . . no! I don't like publicity." Undeterred, the student approached her subject again a week later and persuaded him to give an interview about how different their city was during his childhood.[24]

Some students have no hesitation in going to the source. They will read a name in the newspaper or a book and call or write for an interview without any trepidation. In 1993 a group of students from North Carolina interviewed the eminent historian John Hope Franklin for a documentary they produced on slave spirituals as a History Day project. When asked how they came to interview Professor Franklin, they explained, "Oh, Coretta Scott King recommended that we call him."

Other students will be too shy to go next door and interview a neighbor. To help them overcome their shyness, teachers should encourage students to interview someone they feel comfortable with, a family member or a friend. Students may also feel more at ease if someone else, a family member or a fellow student, accompanies them. There is no reason why students should not work in teams, with one asking the questions and the other operating the recorder and perhaps taking photographs, an arrangement that helps to maximize the use of the equipment. Sometimes team interviewing works when each student handles a specific set of questions, although it requires a certain degree of practice and coordination to the keep the interviewers from interrupting each other. Instead of interviewing, other students prefer preparing and editing transcripts or writing up the results. Even veteran interviewers get butterflies before starting a new interview, but the experience of doing interviews can help students build their self-confidence.[25]

What can oral history teach students about historical research in general?

There is a good deal of historical detective work involved in doing oral history that can help students identify the ways in which historians operate. Interviewing turns the student into the primary historical investigators; they learn how to choose a topic, find people to interview, do the research, and prepare the questions. The more students prepare, the more they recognize what they do not know, as well as how much more they need to learn in order to ask meaningful questions and understand the answers. Student interviewers are likely to be confronted with contradictory evidence: different people give versions of the same event, and an interviewee's story can differ noticeably from the textbook and other sources of information. In short, students begin to appreciate how history is collected and interpreted and perhaps even begin to think like historians themselves.[26]

Once they have done their interviews, students, in class discussions or in written papers, analyze the varying responses and inevitably realize that historical events do not affect all people the same way. Seeing pictures of breadlines and widespread poverty during the Great Depression, for instance, students might assume that everyone suffered equally. But interviews with family members reveal that, although one grandfather was unemployed, the other kept his job and saw his real income rise as prices fell.

Oral history teaches students about cause-and-effect relationships, communications skills, and historical concepts. Interviewing may also give them a greater political awareness as they listen to interviewees discuss the role of the government and political issues in their lives. Could the unemployed grandfather have gotten work through the Works Progress Administration (WPA), or was he barred from the federal relief roles in his local jurisdiction because of his political affiliation?

Doing oral history helps students not only to see at firsthand what historians do but to better appreciate the jobs of journalists and other professional interviewers. Educators have found that oral history teaches students "how to learn," as well as what to learn. Students develop problem-solving skills and come away with an understanding that history, like any other pursuit of "the truth," is trickier than they expected. Writing papers about oral history experience further sharpens analytical and composition skills.[27]

Oral history fits the modern trend in teaching, away from an emphasis on political history toward social history. More than ever before, schools study everyday life over time, looking at the past several generations of immigrants, ethics, racial minorities, and women. Textbooks have struggled to keep up with these new trends, and teachers incorporate more outside materials into their classes. The historian Peter Stearns noted that high school experiments with social history had "generated enthusiasm among students who were intrigued with issues also familiar in their own lives, and some teachers, extending these same experiments, were able to move toward more sophisticated analytical training on issues of periodization or causation." But Stearns concluded that too many school assignments continued to require merely factual research. In family history projects, students gathered information about their own families but rarely analyzed the material or tried to relate their families to the larger generalizations of family behavior in different time periods. Stearns wants high school students to go beyond the recording of facts and discover not only "how it happened" but "what is the meaning of what happened?" They can do this only by learning how to handle various types of primary evidence, from documents and statistics to oral sources, to compare the activities, beliefs, and behaviors of their own lifetime to past eras.[28]

Oral history can deal with families and communities, but can it also be used to study the issues that are covered in the social studies curriculum?

Teachers who use oral history report that it is an especially powerful tool for addressing such social issues as racism, the civil rights movement, human rights, the nuclear arms race, war, and environmental issues. As a teaching device it allows students to meet, hear from, and engage in discussion with people who have played a personal role in these social issues; it also presents students with different points of view and demonstrates the individual beliefs, opinions, and experiences that underline people's social concerns.

Students and other researchers can be impressed and swayed by a single strong-minded interviewee. But they need to be made aware that social issues are inherently complex, and that the opinions from a single interview will not represent all sides of the issues. To obtain as complete a picture as possible, they must interview a variety of people representing different, conflicting points of view.[29]

Is oral history primarily an engaging extracurricular activity, or can it help improve students' learning skills?

Oral history is certainly no more than an educational accessory, but studies have shown that students respond more positively to it than from traditional methods of learning, and take more from it. One analysis of the entire eleventh grade in a Baltimore County, Maryland, high school including honors, average and basic-ability students compared oral history and traditional methods of instruction. Half the students considered immigration and black history using oral history, the other half studied these subjects using regular teaching methods. Tests given at the beginning and end of the four-week curriculum revealed that the oral history students at all levels of ability showed greater instructional gains than students taught by the traditional methods.

Those students using oral history felt that it had made their historical instruction more realistic. Particularly in the honors program, oral history students were more motivated to continue their learning about a topic even after the unit of study had been completed. Students appreciated oral history as a change of pace; as a highly creative activity; for making history seem more believable by associating real people with historical events; as an activity open to a great deal of input; and as a project with "a real purpose." They also showed an appreciation for learning from fellow students rather than from their teachers.[30]

Does an oral history project have to be done by the whole class?

There are definite benefits that accrue from having all the students experience and discuss oral history, but interviewing can also be done by a single student, or a small group, as part of their own project. With the increasing popularity of cooperative learning, oral history offers ideal strategies for getting students to work together in teams (and many state performance assessments are concerned with cooperative efforts). Oral history can be a onetime project or an ongoing series of projects. Many individuals and groups of students use oral histories as part of their History Day projects.

Should a practice interview be conducted in class before students do their own interviews?

Sometimes called a "fish bowl" approach, in-class interviews offer a good way to demystify oral history for the students. The teacher can conduct an in-class interview, or one or more students might serve as the interviewers. Invite someone connected with the school, an administrator, another teacher, a support staff member, or a parent to be interviewed. Be sure to conduct the interview as seriously as possible. To be most effective, the in-class interview should be a real experience rather than playacting. As the class watches the interview, students observe how to conduct an interview, and what types of questions elicit the fullest answers. They should be encouraged to ask additional questions after the initial interview is finished. Although adolescents adapt more easily than adults to using the technology of oral history, they still need experience in setting up the recorder and microphone to ensure the best sound quality and a reminder that there is no third side on a cassette tape. (Many a good interview has been recorded over by a nervous interviewer.) [31]

Before conducting the in-class interview, have the class as a whole plan the questions. Teachers find that students have more interest in the interview because their questions will be asked. After the interview is finished, the class can discuss the effectiveness of different questions. Which questions encouraged the interviewee to open up and talk? Which questions gathered new information? Which questions proved to be dead ends or were poorly phrased? Did the interviewer follow up on unexpected leads? Record the in-class interview, so that portions can be replayed in the discussion.[32]

As the class scrutinizes the in-class interview, it should consider whether the interviewer interrupted the answers or failed to pay attention or to follow up on information. The hardest thing to teach a student, or any interviewer for that matter, is to sit and listen to the interviewee's answers and not be too quick to ask the next question. Too many student interviews become a long string of questions followed by short, sometimes one-sentence answers, suggesting that the questions are too narrow, not open-ended, or that the interviewer has moved on to the next question too quickly.[33]

What is the teacher's responsibility for the student's actual conduct of the interview?

Even though they probably will not accompany students to the interviews, teachers need to impress upon students the responsibilities and ethics of conducting interviews, especially in someone's home or office. Like any other interviewer, students need to schedule an appointment in advance and then keep it. Interviewers must appear on time, act courteously, and be careful not to damage people's property. Interviewers have an obligation to explain to their interviewees the purpose of the interview, and to respect any wish they may express not to talk about certain subjects. Students should have their interviewees sign release forms. Finally, they need to remember to thank interviewees for their cooperation, either verbally or in writing, and should give them a copy of any transcript that might be made. If the school produces a magazine, exhibit, slide-tape or PowerPoint presentation, video documentary, or stage production based on the interviews, invite the interviewees to the performances or functions; doing so ties the student, the project, and the school more firmly to the community, and makes for good public relations.

Two schools in Maryland have experimented with public exhibitions of their oral histories. In Baltimore, the Loch Raven Academy features an oral history open house where its eighth-grade students display their oral history projects to other students, their parents and the community, while the St. Andrew's Episcopal School in Potomac runs an annual evening "coffeehouse" for student interviewers, their interviewees, and members of their families. At St. Andrew's, teacher Glenn Whitman requires students to communicate their interviews to a general audience in the form of an exhibition, a one-act play, or a Power Point presentation, designed to celebrate the students' work and showcase the history they uncovered.[34]

Writing for the National Educational Association, John A. Neuenschwander strongly recommended that students be made to realize that oral history interviewees "are not simply talking books" but require special handling. "The interviewer must always be sensitive to the interviewee's personal stake in the interview and avoid any psychological harm." Students, of all people, should not make their oral histories a test of older people's memories. The interviewee may not be able to recall specific names and dates or answer other detailed factual questions, and the experience may leave them feeling depressed.[35]

Should students process the interviews as well as conduct them?

Interviewing is only one step in teaching through oral history. While the interview is still fresh in their minds, students should review the entire recording to make sure it recorded properly and to prepare a summary of the remarks. Students can distribute these summaries to the class, relating their experiences and playing a portion of their recording. The class can analyze the sound quality of the recording, the types of questions asked, the quality of the content, the way the student opened and closed the interview, any distorted or slanted material, and how engaged the interviewer and the interviewee were in the interview. Some teachers ask students to review and evaluate each other's interviews.[36]

Transcription is arduous work, but it is not beyond the capabilities of most high school students. Students should attempt to transcribe at least a portion of their interviews, an exercise that will allow them to consider the amount of interpretation involved in converting spoken words into written form. Do people speak in full sentences or fragments? How do they determine punctuation and paragraphs? Does the transcript accurately reflect both what was spoken and the way it was spoken? How do transcripts deal with words that are spoken differently from the way they are written? What meanings are expressed when people use slang and street talk? The decisions that go into creating a transcript will force students to reexamine both the spoken and written word, and help them develop their own writing skills. The completed transcripts can be included in student portfolios in those schools that assess and grade portfolios of student writing as a substitute for examinations.

How closely should the teacher monitor each student's interviews?

Teachers need to supervise individual students closely as they begin their projects. As useful and motivating an experience as oral history can be, without appropriate preparation it can be a total failure. Even well-prepared students will feel apprehensive about conducting interviews. Throughout the course, the teacher should return to discussions of interviewing techniques, to keep their minds focused, provide useful suggestions, and reinforce the lessons. After the students have done their first interviews, the teacher should try to meet with each one individually to review at least a portion of their interviews. Students will be anxious to know how well they performed and will need guidance on what they did right, and what needs improvement, before they do their next interviews.[37]

How should student interviews be evaluated?

No two interviews will be alike, but all interviews depend on the interviewer's skills, which can be graded. In monitoring the interviews, consider whether the student really engaged in an informed dialogue or merely read scripted questions. Did the questions elicit thoughtful rather than perfunctory lines of inquiry? Did the interview collect useful information? It becomes clear after listening to a few recordings or reviewing a few transcripts how much the preparation, interview technique, and demeanor invoked a responsive chord in the interviewee.

From long experience in using oral history in the classroom, Frank Fonsino devised criteria that teachers can use to evaluate student interviews. These include:

1. What was the topic or focus of the interview?

2. Does the introduction to the recording provide sufficient information for the listener?

3. Does the interviewer use leading questions or make biased comments?

4. How capable was the interviewing style?

5. How good was the sound quality of the recording?

6. What is the historical value of the interview?[38]

When the class is over, what should we do with the completed oral histories?

Give the recordings and transcripts to the school library. If the interviews are of particularly good quality and deal with the community, consider giving copies to the local public library as well. Collected oral histories in a nearby library will provide a valuable resource not only for future students preparing to do their own interviews, but for researchers interested in the community's history. Since oral history is often conducted with the elderly, they may no longer be alive when others seek to interview them, and your students' interviews could be the only record they left. The librarian may prefer not to receive the poorer examples, but students will value their work all the more if they know it will be permanently preserved in a library collection.[39]

Consider using the Internet to promote the oral history projects. School projects have posted transcripts of their interviews along with photographs, essays, and some audio excerpts. Students at the South Kingsport, Rhode Island, high school conducted interviews on *The Whole World Was Watching: An Oral History of 1968*, and *What Did You Do During the War, Grandma?* on women and World War II. Nearby Brown University's Scholarly Technology Group helped the high school students display the interview transcripts and audio recordings on the university's web site. High school students in Richfield, Utah, similarly conducted interviews with community residents on their experiences during the Great Depression, which were posted on the New Deal Network.[40]

Many high school students participate in National History Day contests. How have they used oral history in their entries?

National History Day is not a specific date, but a series of contests held on the local, state, and national level that provide opportunities to see what students from schools across the nation are capable of doing. Modeled after science fairs, History Day contests are held in most states and several territories for students in grades six through twelve. Annually, some 400,000 students and 20,000 teachers participate in local and state contests, and the winners advance to national competition. Students do projects, media presentations, papers, and dramatic performances based around a common theme ("Change and Continuity," "Turning Points in History," "Communication in History"). About one-third of the entries each year contain some use of oral history interviews.

Judges at History Day competitions have viewed some memorable projects based on oral history. Students from Asheville, North Carolina, videotaped an interview with the survivor of a Nazi concentration camp who was living in their community. Students in El Dorado, Kansas, discovered that their town had once housed a camp for German prisoners of war during the Second World War, and they interviewed one of the former prisoners who had returned to live in the town after the war. Elementary and secondary school students in Toms River, New Jersey, interviewed shopkeepers to document the rise and fall of their Main Street. One junior high school student from Philadelphia studied the history of a chemical plant where his father worked, basing much of his information on interviews. The student made an appointment with the company vice president for public relations but told the man he seemed "too young" to be interviewed for a history project. The vice president located a ninety-year-old retired employee, who agreed to be interviewed, and whose answers indeed gave the project a long historical perspective.

Two students from Billings, Missouri, produced a slide-tape show, "Like Losing a Member of the Family," recounting the story of a century-old general store, The Mercantile, which had been demolished to make way for a convenience store. The students conducted a dozen interviews with people who had worked or shopped in the store, collecting their memories of Saturday shopping days, fires, depressions, bankruptcies, celebrations, and other memories to produce a touching tribute to a small-town institution that had fallen victim to the forces of modernization. They used photographs, newspaper ads, and other items submitted by their interviewees that captured the store as a patriotically decorated backdrop for parades from World Wars I and II and other town celebrations; indeed the store had long been witness to all the town's daily business. The project won first prize in the senior media division, and the town's public library planned to accession the slide-tape show into its local history collection. "Our media presentation began as a local library project, hopefully to leave some record of the building when it was gone," the students reported. "But between our project's beginning and ending we have made so many new friends among the elderly in our town, and learned so much more about the history of the community that our research has seemed more fun than chore."[41]

History Day students have interviewed Japanese Americans who were relocated and interred during World War II, farm protestors from the 1930s, and civil rights demonstrators of the 1950s and 1960s. They most often interview people in their own communities but have also interviewed over the phone, compensating for their lack of travel funds. A high school student in South Carolina sought to interview Rosa Parks about her role in the Montgomery bus boycott. Parks agreed but stipulated that the student and other members of his school history club read her autobiography before the interview.[42]

How supportive of oral history projects are school administrators?

Since oral history lies outside the standard curriculum, some administrators look upon it with suspicion, questioning the amount of class time necessary to prepare for, conduct, and process the interviews. It is advisable to submit a proposal to the school administration, before starting an oral history project. The proposal should detail the project's objectives and methods of evaluation and indicate how oral history supports the regular curriculum and how it develops skills and teaches computer literacy. Buttress your case with manuals and published articles on oral history in the classroom. School administrators are also attracted by the argument that oral history projects can benefit the school's public relations with the community, both through the collection and the exhibition of the interviews and memorabilia.[43]

ORAL HISTORY IN UNDERGRADUATE
AND GRADUATE EDUCATION

How widely is oral history taught in colleges and universities?

The number of college-level oral history methodology courses is difficult to measure, since course offerings have fluctuated and appear in different departments. Oral history may be offered as a separate course or as part of larger methodology courses that deal with conducting research and analyzing historical sources or that address theoretical issues of history and memory. Most applied and public history programs include an oral history component. Anthropology and other social sciences offer their own forms of instruction in fieldwork interviewing. Oral history is as likely to appear in the course offerings of library schools, journalism departments, or American Studies programs as in history departments.

Courses in oral history tend to be offered more consistently at colleges and universities with established oral history archives. Directors of the oral history archives often teach the course, and class projects contribute to the larger oral history collection. In schools without oral history archives, finding departments and teachers interested in oral history is usually more difficult than signing up students.

Community colleges have also found oral history highly applicable for adult-education or transitional studies between secondary school and the university. Conducting and processing interviews can develop and tap skills at all levels, even for those students approaching English as a second language. Classroom discussions can draw not only from the substance of the interview, but from the many styles of speaking.

Several newly established universities with student bodies drawn largely from working-class, immigrant communities, have incorporated oral history into their curriculum at the start. The California State University at Monterey, with many students of Mexican heritage, requires all its undergraduates to take an oral history course. One project was centered on the theme "First in My Family to Go to College," which offered much of the student body as potential interviewees. Sweden's Malmö University likewise built a history curriculum that would be relevant to both the region's traditional inhabitants and its many newcomers. After taking the basic methodological courses, students at Malmö do research projects based on primary sources, which must include biographical material based on personal interviews. Since a large share of the history students at Malmö intend to teach in primary and secondary schools, officials reasonably assume that many will utilize their oral history training in the classroom.[44]

Are methods courses in interviewing really necessary?
Isn't it better for students to learn simply by
going out and doing interviews?

Disciplines that employ fieldwork have periodically debated whether to teach interviewing as a methods course or to just send students out to experiment for themselves. Some argue that since all field situations will be different, students need to learn on their own and that the only methods necessary are "sensitivity and creativity." Others concede that fieldwork requires more than simply mastering a textbook but contend that students still have to prepare themselves to do it right. Even though oral history interviewing is best learned by doing, students can learn much in the classroom, both before and after conducting their interviews.

The anthropologist John Forrest believes that before students go out to interview, they need to learn about the complexity of human interaction. In his methods course, he stipulated that "students had to *care* about what they were documenting" because their projects would take them into other people's lives. "If they were insensitive they knew that at best they would end up with no data, and at worst they would have hurt a fellow human." Finding subjects that genuinely mattered to them also helped motivate the students and made it less necessary for the instructor to "drone on about why fieldwork and data collection are important, or to show how good data leads on to appropriate social theory."[45]

The social sciences have been more consistent than the humanities in teaching fieldwork methodology. It undoubtedly is safe to assume that the majority of history undergraduates and graduate students who use interviews as part of their research have never taken an oral history course. Interviews are done seat-of-the-pants style sometimes tape-recorded, more often captured in handwritten notes only; usually devoid of deeds of gift; and almost never conducted with the thought of depositing the completed interviews in an archives. Such interviews can still generate valuable information, despite needless mistakes, improper planning, and unnecessarily limiting procedures. The chief problem is that few graduate advisers have had any training themselves in oral history; they assume that anyone can interview and do not hold their students' oral sources to the same documentation standards as their written ones.[46]

Graduate-level courses in oral history deal more with theory and methodology than do undergraduate courses. The growing literature in the field has increased the amount of background reading for these courses; although most students do interviews, some classes have permitted students to write papers on theory and interpretation in lieu of interviewing. Some theoretical literature could also be introduced into undergraduate courses; the historian James

Hoopes has observed that college students "should have a more ambitious goal than the *Foxfire* students' objectives of merely collecting information on customs, folklore, and habits." College students should be better able to interpret the material they collect, to place it into historical context, and to apply theory to their fieldwork interviewing.[47]

What problems are encountered in teaching oral history in undergraduate college classes?

Instructors find that their biggest problem is the uneven abilities and prior experience of their students. Although it is true that students of every ability level can benefit from doing oral history, teachers who seek to develop an oral history as a research methodology prefer students with some training in a particular area of study, such as ethnic, labor, cultural, economic history, or the social sciences. Students who lack such backgrounds often feel frustrated over the demands placed upon them. They discover that oral history is a tool for study, not an end in itself, and that there is more to the process than just interviewing someone. In both the research before the interview and the interpretation afterwards, they must be able to place the material in its larger social or historical context. Some instructors have recommended offering oral history classes only as advanced electives or, at the minimum, requiring students to have taken the basic survey classes in history to ensure some control over students' levels of preparation.[48]

Some teachers worry that unless properly monitored, oral history projects often amount to little more than a conversation and a paper. At Indiana University Southwest, A. Glenn Crothers requires survey course students to conduct oral history to heighten their understanding of how the broader historical events they study actually affected their community, and to appreciate how historians use primary and secondary sources and move from evidence to interpretation. Crothers uses advanced history majors to tutor those with little prior preparation in history, and further pairs students in two-member interviewing teams where they can mentor each other and share the burdens of transcription. Project reports led him to conclude that oral history made "a profound impression" on the first-year students, whose knowledge of history and of the community was clearly enriched, and also on the advanced students who gained "concrete experience as teachers and public historians."[49]

When using oral history in her undergraduate classes at Villanova, Mary Schweitzer found that the hardest part of the process was getting students to weigh evidence and apply historical interpretation. Students assumed that their assignment was simply to collect a variety of opinions and string them together into an interesting story. Schweitzer warns students not to take all evidence at face value. As researchers, they need to analyze the varying perspectives of the witnesses, consider conflicting viewpoints, and fit first-person observations together with other forms of evidence. By expanding the interviewing process to include interpretation, students began to "think about the particularity and generality of all experience."[50]

How should a college course on oral history be structured?

Structure and objectives will depend on the department in which oral history is taught and on whether it is an undergraduate or graduate level course. Library science courses, for instance, will focus more on the use of interviews in research libraries and archives, on developing standards for the acquisition and preservation of oral history materials, on integrating oral history materials into library and archival collections, and on using automated databases for the storage, retrieval, and cataloging of interviews. In other departments, oral history courses may concentrate more on the methodological literature of oral history, on designing and running oral history projects, or on the techniques of interviewing and the content and analysis of the interviews.

Because much supervision and review of student work will be required, it is advisable to keep classes small and manageable. Students may need help in finding people to interview, especially if the campus is geographically or culturally detached from their surrounding community. Because they operate best in a practical, "hands-on" manner, oral history classes should be taught as seminars or laboratories rather than in lecture halls.[51]

Consider having the students monitor their own progress by maintaining a log in which they make regular notes on their impressions of the course, their readings, their interview objectives and preparations, and their observations of the actual interview situations. What unexpected leads and information developed? Did the interviews differ from what they expected? How did they rate themselves as interviewers, and did they feel they improved over time? Students might submit these logs at the end of the term for extra credit.

Regardless of the discipline in which oral history or fieldwork interviewing is taught, students should be introduced to the use of oral techniques in other fields, from folklore to anthropology and social psychology. They should understand the different interview standards and objectives in different fields. Consider inviting some guest lecturers from other disciplines to discuss how they use interviews in their research. Similarly, oral history courses often study the most common forms of interviews that students have watched on television or read in newspapers and magazines, requiring them to monitor the interviewing style of media interviewers.

Review the literature in the field—particularly dealing with the ethical responsibilities of interviewing. Familiarize the students with the equipment, and plan for practice interview sessions in the classroom. If the students plan to interview around a common theme, have them discuss the questions that might be asked of all interviewees, to provide for comparisons, and to balance the detail and complexity of individual stories with generalizations about the historical experience. Because experiences vary so widely from interview to interview, students should be required to interview more than one person. (When one instructor discovered that his students were conducting short interviews as a means of reducing the amount of transcribing they had to do, he set a three-hour minimum for interviews.)[52]

After students have conducted their interviews, they should compose a brief paper not only about the interview, and the subject covered, but the interviewee's place in local, regional, and national events. Students also should be required to transcribe at least portions of their interviews. Students are necessarily interested in the interview itself and impatient with learning the techniques of interviewing and processing interviews. It is imperative, however, to stress that poorly conducted interviews seriously undermine the end product—the information gathered by interview that the students hope to use themselves and to leave behind as an archival legacy.[53]

Finally, students should be encouraged to analyze the type of information generated by oral history, the interviewer-interviewee relationship, and the validity of oral sources versus written sources. They should consider the ways in which oral history can be integrated into the larger historiographies of the subject matter, as well as the ultimate uses of oral history in research, publication, and public presentation. More and more oral history classes also include discussion of video interviews.

Can oral history be incorporated into classes other than methodology?

In her seminar on women's history at the University of North Carolina at Chapel Hill, Jacqueline Dowd Hall has students conduct oral histories with three generations of women in their families. Such personal perspectives enrich "and sometimes contradict" popular views of history, as well as help students put their own lives into larger historical context. At Kent State University, Renata Prescott has used oral history interviews to examine the impact of the Vietnam War on her students' own families. Their experiences demonstrate the dual value of oral history both as a teaching tool and as source of historical content. As historians have widened their investigations beyond the public arena, oral history has helped students grapple with the more private spheres of family and community.[54]

Women's studies programs early adopted oral history in their curricula. At the University of Massachusetts at Boston, for instance, the women's studies program had students conduct interviews with individuals outside the university about sex-role stereotyping, women's roles in the workplace, family relationships, and women's movement organizations. Summaries of these interviews form the basis of class discussions. Many of the students had known surprisingly little about their mothers' lives and began to reexamine and appreciate the strength of other "unnoticed, unrewarded female relatives." Women's history programs at Boston University and Simmons College also provided useful generational studies, requiring students to interview two or more women in the same family, such as mother and daughter or an aunt and niece. These interviews show cultural change over time, most notable in the case of immigrant families. One student was astonished to learn that her Irish-Catholic grandmother had been a vociferous supporter of birth-control advocate Margaret Sanger. In another set of interviews, a father stated that he and his wife had as many children as "God had sent them," while the mother admitted using a diaphragm. Women students reported seeing the source of many of their own ideas and beliefs when they interviewed family members.[55]

College oral history classes have seized upon developing events within their own communities as subjects for student projects. When school integration became an issue in suburban Montgomery County, Maryland, nearby George Washington University launched an oral history. The first stage in the project was compiling newspaper clippings on the issue, to prepare students to interview school officials, parents, and teachers. As it developed, the project uncovered a story that was far more complex than the newspaper reports had suggested. The students discovered, for instance, that the initiative for the most original element in the integration plan had come from teachers at the school rather than from the school board. The interviews also revealed that, although men held most of the formal leadership positions in the various organizations involved, women had been most active in the grassroots movement, "ringing doorbells, making phone calls, and using their organizational know-how to promote their respective causes." The transcripts of the interviews were deposited at the university library, where they became instructional material for courses in political science and education.[56]

After functioning for over forty years primarily as a research institution, the Regional Oral History Office at the University of California at Berkeley began integrating its work more firmly into the campus' teaching mission. Under its new director, Richard Candida Smith, who held a joint appointment as director of the oral history program and professor of history, ROHO sponsored advanced oral history institutes for faculty, post-doctoral fellows, graduate students, and independent scholars. ROHO also offered undergraduate courses focused on oral history, such as "American Lives: Oral History and the Understanding of Social Change," with students either developing their own interview projects or participating in an ongoing ROHO project.

Would a college itself be a suitable subject for an oral history?

Students, faculty, and alumni have participated in recording the histories of their schools, often in connection with school anniversaries. For the University of Kentucky oral history project, interviews have been conducted with former and current presidents, administrators, faculty, and graduates. Interviews on the subject of campus life and history conducted by students from Bryn Mawr to Stanford have been compiled not only as archival collections but as highly profitable books and videos marketed to the alumnae.[57]

When the Northern Virginia Community College reached twenty years of age, five historians in the system began interviewing those who had started the community college system, built it, taught in it, and attended its first classes. They published twenty-seven interviews with these "prime movers" and pioneers. "At the end of our labors as oral historians, some of us working within the methods of this subdiscipline for the first time, we have come to feel great pride in what we have been privileged to compile—this history of our college—as well as renewed pride in the college itself," they concluded. "We often felt ourselves in the presence of that admixture of pragmatism and idealism characteristic of so many of our once and current colleagues who have stamped these traits onto our colleges." The recordings and transcripts were housed at one of the college's library, where they would form the nucleus of a research collection on the institution's beginnings. Some of the interviews have also been posted on the college web sites.[58]

Istanbul's Boğaziçi University, founded as Roberts College in 1863 as the first American college outside of the United States, was transferred to the Turkish government as a state university in 1971, after which its history department underwent a major reorganization. Thirty years later the department began an oral history project to document the surviving "founders," along with the second and third generations of faculty who followed. These interviews documented the original and evolving philosophies that shaped the department's development, and recorded how larger events in Turkey had influenced academic life. Although initially designed to commemorate an anniversary, the oral history unexpectedly provided a beneficial self-analysis, and the department has used the interviews in evaluating the curricula, methods of teaching, and standards of historical research, and for charting its future development.[59]

Doing oral history of one's own college or university is not always a celebratory practice. In May 1968, when student demonstrators took over Columbia University, the Columbia Oral History Research Office hired three advanced fellows from the School of Journalism to interview students, faculty, administrators, and mediators. Within a month's time they had collected more than 1,500 pages of testimony. Interviewers from Cornell University conducted oral histories connected with the killings of two Jackson State University students by Mississippi state police very shortly after the incident. Cornell similarly conducted interviews related to the dramatic 1968 demonstrations at its own campus.[60]

Ultimately, what do undergraduates get out of taking oral history courses?

Undergraduates take oral history for any number of reasons, usually because it sounds interesting and easy. Once enrolled, they find the subject much more complex than they imagined. Oral history challenges their preconceived notions and makes them rethink how they research and analyze.

One prelaw student in an oral history class chose a topic on the impact of judges on the law, assuming that it was "a very easy way to get a good grade." Nothing came simply, however. The busy lawyers he interviewed kept taking phone calls, disrupting their answers, and straining his efforts to build rapport. Some answered precisely and briefly, quibbled over words, or evaded his questions. A circuit judge insisted on having his three rather obnoxious law clerks sit in on the interview. Despite these obstacles, the student collected valuable perspectives. What surprised him most was how often their answers disagreed with his written research. From his interviews, the student concluded that "the way a practitioner looks at the corpus of law differs greatly from the way a scholar investigates the law," a finding he suspected was true of other fields as well.[61]

Willa Baum, the former director of the Regional Oral History Office at the University of California, Berkeley, has observed that even in graduate school, oral history helps students learn "to go and ask people for information." She noted that graduate students excelled at doing library research and using transcripts of Berkeley's oral history interviews, "but they are appalled when we suggest that they should just go out and ask a person for information we don't have on our tapes or transcripts."[62]

What is the difference between an oral history class and a workshop?

Time, essentially. A class might extend over a fourteen-week semester; a workshop might last for only a single day. Many state and regional oral history organizations hold annual and semiannual workshops to serve as introductions for those just beginning and as refresher courses for those in midcareer. When oral history projects begin, they often seek an experienced oral historian to conduct a workshop to train volunteer interviewers and processors to ensure consistency in their product.

What role does oral history play in continuing education programs?

Oral history courses are offered in adult education programs and as summer institutes. People take such continuing education courses to aid them in changing careers, refreshing their knowledge, doing freelance interviewing, or interviewing family members or longtime community residents. A variety of such courses are publicized in the newsletters of the Oral History Association and its many state and regional affiliates.

Some of the most active oral historians are those who came to the field as a second career, often after raising families or retiring early, sometimes simply because they were looking for something interesting to do. Some study interview techniques and return to conduct oral histories within their previous profession. Others shift within a career, such as librarians and archivists seeking training to start or continue an oral history collection within their institution. If you want to do oral history, it is never too late to get some formal training.

INSTITUTIONAL REVIEW BOARDS

What are Institutional Review Boards and why do they review oral history proposals?

On college campuses, Institutional Review Boards (IRBs), or Human Subjects Review Boards, date back to the 1980s, although most oral historians did not encounter them for another decade. The review boards grew out of the public outrage following revelations of a forty-year syphilis experiment in Tuskegee, Alabama, where researchers had allowed a curable disease to go untreated. In 1979 *The Belmont Report* of the National Commission for the Protection of Human Subjects of Biomedical and Behavioral Research recommended rules to govern federally funded research involving human subjects, based on three basic principles: respect for people's ability to make decisions about their own behavior; beneficence, or the minimizing of harm and maximizing of benefits from research projects; and justice, as in the equitable selection of research subjects. Colleges and universities that received federal funds were required to establish Institutional Review Boards to review faculty and student research protocols and make sure they complied with the federal code. At first these regulations applied only to medical and behavioral science research funded by federal agencies that specifically subscribed to them, such as the National Science Foundation and National Institutes of Health, but not the National Endowment for the Humanities.[63]

Given the serious harm to physical and mental health that the IRBs were created to police, it seems peculiar that they have diverted their attention to the social sciences and humanities, where interviews pose far less risks if any at all. But a 1991 revision of the federal regulations broadened the definition of human subject research to include any "interaction with living individuals." Reasoning that research standards should not differ simply because of a project's source of funding, government officials encouraged universities to regulate *all* research, regardless of whether it received federal funding and warned that an entire campus could lose all federal funding if *any* research involving human interaction failed to undergo review. Universities wanted to protect human subjects but also wanted to protect themselves, and campus IRBs stepped up their vigilance accordingly. They turned first to the social sciences, where quantitative methods most closely resembled scientific research. Peculiar situations developed on team interviewing projects, with the sociologists and anthropologists on the team submitting their interviewing protocols to the campus IRB, while the historians went ahead interviewing without review, unaware of the very existence of the review boards.[64]

In a stunning move in 1995, the University of Delaware declined to accept a doctoral dissertation that its history department had approved until the graduate student obtained retroactive exemption from the IRB for interviews she had conducted. Other graduate students in the department had used oral history before without incident, and the history department had no prior notice of any IRB requirements. Now the university announced a compulsory review of all faculty and student research conducted with human participants, regardless of the discipline or source of funding. After some anxious moments, the graduate student received her exemption and her degree. Graduate students in general are most vulnerable to review, since their work will eventually be read at the graduate level, where IRBs are generally located, and their degrees can be withheld pending compliance.[65]

Since IRBs devoted their primary attention to biomedical research, they naturally recruited most of their board members from the sciences. A few larger universities established separate IRBs to deal with other forms of research, to which they appointed members from the social sciences and humanities; but most college campuses have only a single board (some have none). Board members trained in scientific methodologies often assumed that everyone used the same research practices, such as standard questionnaires that record anonymous interviewees for quantitative analysis, rather than the qualitative, free-flowing, open-ended interviews that oral historians conduct.

IRBs have returned an estimated 85 percent of all research proposals for further fine-tuning before authorization. In the process they have asked oral historians to submit the questions they intended to ask, and at times have rejected questions that might place the interviewees in an embarrassing light. Boards have recommended, even insisted, that interviewees be anonymous. Some boards have ordered that recordings be erased at the project's completion. Boards have also cautioned interviewers against asking any questions about illegal activity (even though some interviewers, such as civil rights activists, are quite proud of acts of civil disobedience that led to their arrests). A few IRBs have even required researchers to obtain permission from third parties who were mentioned during an interview. Boards have also instructed faculty advisers who supervised theses and dissertations using oral histories to take a standardized test on research ethics related to human subjects, despite its pharmacology and medical orientation.

Believing that people have a right to be identified with their own stories, and that researchers have a right to verify their sources, oral historians have argued against the inapplicability of many of these requirements. Usually, they have won reprieve, or at least some modification of more restrictive rulings, once the boards better understood the goals of the project and the informed consent of the interviewees. Appeals take time, however, and the review process has delayed scholarly projects, theses, and class work. It could well discourage researchers from tackling sensitive subjects.[66]

How can oral history projects meet IRB requirements?

The key to winning IRB approval is establishing "informed consent." Once interviewees have been informed the purpose of the project and what rights they have, they sign consent forms that demonstrate the voluntary nature of the interview. Interviewees have the right to decline to answer questions or to terminate an interview at will, and often receive advance copies of the transcripts for revision. Informed consent affords more protection than an easily penetrated "anonymity." Standard oral history protocols aim to avoid the type of misunderstanding that developed when fieldworkers disguised their objectives. For her dissertation, a sociologist interviewed fishermen in the Chesapeake Bay, providing each family with pseudonyms to protect their identities, but did not tell them that she was secretly recording their conversations for her research. She justified this deception as an effort to keep people from becoming suspicious of her, but the practice violated their trust. In response to complaints from the offended community, the American Sociological Association adopted new guidelines for conduct in fieldwork. They recognized, in the words of Kai Erikson, that it "jeopardizes the reputation of all the rest of us when some of us sneak around."[67]

Federal statues and regulations deal specifically with mental and bodily harm and stipulate that research should not "place the subjects at risk of criminal or civil liability" or be damaging to their "financial standing, employment, or reputation." Some IRBs have tried to dissuade researchers from asking questions that might invoke painful memories of traumatic events. Yet oral history frequently deals with sorrowful recollections about the Holocaust, wartime experiences, floods and natural disasters, in which interviewees have suffered grievous losses. Confronting memories that may have been long suppressed can have a cathartic and therapeutic effect. Oral history interviewers seek to be sympathetic listeners, and interviewees usually express gratitude for the opportunity of telling their personal stories, even after the most emotional sessions. Although oral history is not an adversarial form of interviewing, it does require asking the difficult and sometimes embarrassing questions that are part of serious scholarly inquiry. Responses will range from direct to evasive and denial, providing further areas for analysis. It is vital that interviewers remain free to pursue any line of inquiry that interviewees are willing to discuss.

In testifying before the National Bioethics Advisory Commission, the oral historian Linda Shopes pointed out that historians "do not dispute the importance of high ethical standards governing research that involves human beings, the review of research protocols involving human beings, and the principle of informed consent." What they object to is the evaluation of their projects "by standards and protocols not appropriate for historical research." Shopes noted that IRBs had asked how their narrators would be chosen, when patterns of recruitment was not an issue. Oral historians usually choose interviewees who can make a unique contribution to their particular project. IRBs had also asked about the consequences if someone declined to be interviewed. "Again, this simply isn't an issue in oral history research," she explained, "unless of course, one considers the consequence of not having a particular person's version of events on record, though obviously that's not what the regulations refer to." [68]

The purpose of an Institutional Review Board is not to prevent research but to make sure that research involving living human beings does not inflict physical or emotional harm. To do this job properly, the review board must have some understanding of the scholarly disciplines they are regulating. Many IRBs have demonstrated sufficient appreciation for historical research to expedite oral history interviewing with a minimum of delay or bureaucratic intrusion. But all too often IRBs have demonstrated a woeful ignorance of oral history methodology.[69]

Is it possible to win exemption from IRB review?

Federal regulations exempt certain categories of research from review. Information that is already on the public record, such as newspaper articles and official documents, is not subject to review. Interviews with political candidates and elected or appointed public officials are also specifically exempt. Interviews that do not place identifiable individuals "at risk of criminal or civil liability" or damage their "financial standing, employment, or reputation" are also exempt. These broad categories cover most oral history research, yet many IRBs still require that projects file for review anyhow, on the reasoning that the board rather than the researcher should determine whether the project is exempt. In these cases, boards will generally provide expedited review, which entails less delay and does not require annual review. Expedited review usually involves having the chair of the IRB or an experienced reviewer designated by the chairman examine the proposed oral history project, rather than having the full board conduct the review. Oral historians who follow the Oral History Association's evaluation guidelines should be able to qualify for exemption, since federal regulators have found that the guidelines exceed the federal regulations.[70]

Oral history may also qualify for exemption because it usually does not meet the government's basic definition of regulated "research," which is "a systematic investigation, including research development, testing and evaluation, designed to develop or contribute to generalizable knowledge." Interviewing a group of anonymous sources with a questionnaire fits that definition, while open-ended, individualistic interviewing does not. Oral history does not constitute a lesser form of research, simply a different form of research than the federal regulations contemplated. Oral history interviewing usually seeks to gain unique perspectives rather than to develop a generally applicable theory.[71]

Teachers may also seek exemption for interviews conducted for pedagogical reasons rather than for research. Some have achieved blanket exemptions for students' assignments by demonstrating the classroom review procedures for interviews and the informed consent forms to be used. However, if students later use the interviews for a thesis or dissertation, they may need to submit them for review at that time. University-based oral history archives have also been able to establish IRB-approved standard protocols for interviewing that eliminate the need to seek separate clearance for individual interviews.

Can IRB rulings be appealed?

No formal appeals process exists, but students and faculty who have confronted unreasonable rulings have successfully managed to have those rulings modified or reversed. Those who feel that an Institutional Review Board was excessively restrictive or applied inappropriate standards to their work should enlist graduate advisers and department chairs to help explain oral history methodology, and its safeguards, to the IRB's members or compliance officer. A little rational discussion goes a long way.

If a board's policies continue to inhibit free inquiry, appeal can be made to the university official (usually the president or provost) who is specifically responsible for enforcing federal regulations on the campus. If all else fails, report the problem to the Office for Human Research Protection in the U.S. Department of Health and Human Services.

No matter how well-intentioned, IRBs run the risk of becoming modern versions of Anthony Comstock, the overzealous postal inspector who a century ago crusaded against pornography, prostitution, gambling, and other "traps for the young." While protecting home and family and defending decency were noble missions, Comstock's inability to distinguish between pornography and art, or obscenity and science led him to ban books on human anatomy and sexual primers for newlyweds, attempt to shut down the Art Student's League for displaying pictures of nudes, and denounce George Bernard Shaw's play *Mrs. Warren's profession* as depraved. Shaw retaliated by labeling American censorship as "Comstockery."[72]

Comstock frightened university administrators. To avoid offending him when he spoke at Princeton in 1888, the university draped a red velvet garment over its nude statute of *The Gladiator* and had to hire the local fire department later to undrape it. Comstock's biographer, Anna Bates, was drawn to the subject as a feminist historian who assumed that pornography degraded all women and should be illegal. Yet in grappling with Comstock's motivations, she changed her mind. "Now, I see that although some obscenity does insult women, laws that define women according to their biological composition and ascribe their social roles accordingly have historically done far more harm to women than pornographic pictures," she wrote. "During the ten some-odd years I worked on this project, I grew increasingly committed to free speech, which I consider a liberty above price."[73]

Oral historians stand committed to free speech and critical inquiry. Good intentions alone are insufficient for effective regulation. Discernment and common sense are equally essential ingredients for protecting human subjects without imposing censorship. Inappropriate rulings by IRBs suggests that federal regulators have inadequately defined the regulations to make clear what types of research they cover. By concentrating on the protection of human subjects from actual physical and mental harm, rather than from the benign interaction of interviews, federal regulators and Institutional Review Boards can best steer clear of further "Comstockery."

CHAPTER 8

Presenting
Oral History

After the interviewing is done, how can oral histories best be put to use?

Early practitioners of oral history set out primarily to create archives that authors would use for writing books and articles. Relatively few of the pioneers also appreciated the value of the sound recordings. Over time, more creativity has blossomed and an array of new uses for oral histories, sound, video, and transcripts have emerged. A half century after the first oral history archives were established, an oral historian surveyed the types of "products" that emerged from their work, looking for broad categories of traditional and innovative historical and interpretive works. The following list emerged from the responses she collected:

1. Books (histories, biographies, poetry, and published transcripts)
2. Storytelling cassette tapes, oral history tapes, audio books and CDs
3. Movies in various formats
4. Training videos and books
5. Museum and multimedia exhibits, and art installations
6. Cultural preservation and heritage projects
7. Driving audio tours
8. Radio programs
9. Educational material for children and teachers
10. Theatrical works (plays, operas, drama, and comedy)
11. Dance choreography
12. Internet web sites
13. Legal briefs and other law-related documentation[1]

As this list indicates, the options for using oral history interviews have grown remarkably varied, limited chiefly by imagination and financial resources. Previous chapters have discussed the creation of oral history archives, the use of oral history for scholarly research, and the production of video documentaries.

What follows are additional uses that recognize the accessibility of oral history—literally the words of the people—and the ease with which oral history interviews can be used in a number of arenas: in public presentations, in community and family history projects, on radio broadcasts, in stage productions, on the Internet, and even for therapeutic purposes. They reflect the concern of oral historians that, having taking their interviews from the community, they should share the results with the community.[2]

COMMUNITY HISTORY

What exactly is "community history," and how does oral history apply to it?

A community can be defined loosely as a group of people who share a common identity, whether based on location, racial or ethnic group, religion, organizational affiliation or occupation. Obviously, communities differ considerably. One group may be fiercely proud of its collective identity, and another needs to be convinced that its heritage is worth preserving. Oral historians have helped to broaden traditional notions of what constitutes a community's history by looking not only at its political and institutional structures, but at its economic development and the ethnic and occupational composition of its population. Some oral history projects have tried to preserve lost communities, conducting interviews about buildings that were demolished or institutions that disappeared in all respects except in people's memories.[3]

Residents of the rural, mountain community of Ivanhoe, Virginia, initiated an oral history project to help save their rapidly disappearing history and revitalize their community. Their "participatory research" project combined outside researchers, educators, grassroots community groups and community members, who collectively designed the project and analyzed the results. Their "history group" of volunteers interviewed people at the post office, in the Civil League office, on the street, and in stores, collecting, transcribing and editing fifty-three interviews and gathering over eight hundred photographs. Project director Helen Lewis noted that through the process of gathering its history, "Ivanhoe has looked to its elders and has carefully recorded times past, seeking lessons from traditions which may be creatively applied to present realities."[4]

In inner-city Philadelphia, Temple University developed the Discovering Community History Project to encourage residents of different neighborhoods to document their pasts through oral history, manuscripts, and photographs. The project staff wanted to aid and encourage the neighborhoods rather than do the work themselves. They started with a slide show to introduce the project to the community but discovered that merely stating the importance of the community's heritage was not very convincing. Neighbors initially hesitated to share memories and photographs they believed outsiders would consider commonplace. Slowly over time, and after repeated staff visits, residents eventually came to realize how their community looked to the outside, and how they could contribute to recording its history.

Temple's experience demonstrated that such projects cannot expect the same response from every community. The most significant differences in neighborhood response to the project were based on neither race nor class but on the neighborhood's recent history and demographics—that is, on whether it was stable, declining, or undergoing gentrification. The project achieved its greatest successes in those neighborhoods with strong community organizations—civic associations, clubs, churches and synagogues, especially those that cared for the elderly—that were willing to take charge of contacting potential interviewers and interviewees, "assigning tasks, checking up, and following through." Communities that lacked organizations with such clout, or where community associations were distracted by more pressing concerns, proved the hardest to convince of the merits of oral history.[5]

Noting that people who live in the same area can actually be quite distant from each other, the D.C. Community Humanities Council sponsored the City Lights Program to bring scholars, storytellers, and other performers to senior citizens living in public housing to talk about their common culture and history. At the predominantly African-American Potomac Gardens, these discussions focused on religious traditions, migration from the South to the city, work as domestics, living through the Depression, and the Washington riots of 1968. The elderly residents of Potomac Gardens had attended school at a time when, except for references to slavery, black people did not exist in the history textbooks, which gave them little sense of having contributed anything worthwhile to society. The City Lights Program emphasized how important their experiences were, and how much they had in common with each other. "We were strangers before," said Thelma Russell, a member of the community. "Now we understand that our common ground is the African American heritage that we share."

Senior citizens at Potomac Gardens collected the stories of their struggles and accomplishments to leave as a record for their descendants. Supported by a Humanities Council grant, they conducted a door-to-door survey in their building and collected data about the residents. Drawing from this information, they scheduled weekly meetings, focusing each week on a different birthplace and encouraging residents to share their personal memorabilia and stories of home and migration. With the assistance of the local historical society, the seniors learned how to interview each other. A local video production company video-taped the interviews, from which they produced a documentary video, *In Search of Common Ground* (1993). A curator from the Anacostia Neighborhood Museum helped residents develop an exhibit from their project. Both the video and the exhibit were displayed at schools, public housing sites, and other neighborhood organizations throughout the city and will be preserved as a legacy for the future. "We may not be rich," Thelma Russell concluded, "but we are rich in history."[6]

Can oral history be used to aid historic preservation?

Preservationists have tapped the memories of still-living informants to recon-struct the material culture of the past—furnishings, tools, structures, vehicles, and many other physical objects—and to determine how these items were used, by whom, and how they fit into the broader social and economic patterns of the community. Oral history has helped gather the details of day-to-day life in his-toric buildings—to re-create period furnishings and decorations—through interviews with those who visited the house during the era in question, often when it was associated with a particular family or prominent individual. Their memories bring color to the black-and-white photographs of the past and pro-vide context for otherwise sketchy and incomplete documentary evidence.

In seeking to save San Diego's older architecture during a period of massive redevelopment, the Downtown San Diego Project found gaps in the official records that only oral history could fill. Project members interviewed con-struction crews and demolition company employees to determine the extent to which bulldozers and backhoes had penetrated certain areas. The California Office of Historic Preservation called for interviews with the state's architects and engineers and advocated interviews with those in the building trades, those who established the utility networks, transportation planners, bridge builders, and officials of the development agencies in local government.[7]

On the national level, the National Historic Preservation Act of 1966 has required federal agencies to consider how such federally funded projects as high-way construction, dams, reservoirs, airports, and parks affect local cultural resources. To carry out this mandate, culture resource management (CRM) teams have applied the insights of archaeology, architectural history, folklore, and oral history to urban planning, resource conservation, public works proj-ects, and commercial development. While archaeologists were working on a CRM crew in Irion County, Texas, they uncovered hundreds of what appeared to be prehistorical petroglyphs in a limestone outcropping. But they also found the carved name of Burt Smalley, dated 1921; by then, Smalley was deceased. The mystery was solved through oral history interviews with surviving family members and old-timers in the community. These interviews developed a portrait of a recluse who spent his life carving petroglyphs in the rocks near his ranch.

Oral history interviews have helped CRM projects locate unmarked gravesites and abandoned farmhouses, as well as the otherwise unrecorded names of sharecroppers. Interviews have helped reconstruct farmers' living patterns, including the layout of yards and houses, gardens, fields, wells, barns, and privies. "Oral history can turn a prairie foundation into Hansford County's one-room Palo Duro Schoolhouse," noted Dan Utley, an oral historian who works with CRM teams. "Oral history can transform seemingly unrelated artifacts—a Model T transmission, a scatter of bricks, and welded metal barrels—into an irrigation system used to pump Concho River water up a steep bank and across a ravine to what was a parched cotton field in the 1950s."[8]

Does it matter whether the interviewer on a community project is an "outsider"?

Just as the race and gender of the interviewer and interviewee may affect the interview, whether the interviewer comes from the subject's community will influence what is said. The Temple Discovering Community History Project found that its best interviews often came from enthusiastic amateurs in the community. Because "spontaneity and candor naturally extended between friends, neighbors and people of the same background," it was easier for those insiders to establish rapport. But with thorough research, persistent effort, and the right personality, interviewers from outside a community can also build the kind of rapport that facilitates interviewing. In fact, all oral historians constantly find themselves shifting between the roles of "insider-outsider, historian-listener, participant-observer, minority-majority, student-teacher, apprentice-mentor." What is important is that interviewers become conscious of these varying relationships and how they influence the interviews. Those who have engaged in extensive fieldwork interviewing in communities in which they are outsiders strongly recommend that interviewers keep a journal of their impressions of the community and their changing relations within it.[9]

Won't a community volunteer only information that will make it look good?

Communities naturally seek to preserve and present their best image. Interviewers often find themselves being steered toward those who tell "success" stories; they must attempt to record the dissatisfied as well. Interviewers also need to avoid being seduced by the democratic impulses of oral history to just "let people speak for themselves." Unquestioned and unchallenged memory can veer toward nostalgia. The oral historian's job is not to celebrate the past but to explore and document its diversity and complexity.[10]

At the same time, people's privacy becomes an issue when recording a community's oral history. Interviewers must consider what right they have to raise questions that embarrass the community, especially if they are outsiders who will not remain there to live with the consequences. When dealing with a community's denial or a difficult or traumatic event or issue, interviewers ask challenging questions and then give people an opportunity to respond, but they must also honor interviewees' refusal to address certain issues. Clearly, it is essential to interview as broadly as possible. Some people cannot or will not reflect on painful issues of the past, but others have just as strong an impulse to bring the same issues out into the open.

Stories and opinions within a community will probably vary widely. When oral historians try to determine which versions are more reliable, they seek patterns—another reason to interview more than one type of person in a community. Rather than simplifying the past, oral historians complicate the history by collecting counterevidence and challenging simple answers. The picture of the community that emerges from the interviews is thus most likely to be neither all good nor all bad.

What if the community will not cooperate at all?

Interviewers usually assume that the community will be pleased, flattered, and empowered by being the focus of an oral history project. But some communities want no attention and consider any project suspicious and intrusive.

In New York City, the public historian Joe Doyle studied the Chelsea neighborhood on Manhattan's West Side. Situated along the Hudson River docks, Chelsea had a history as a longshoremen's and seamen's community. During the 1940s the Longshoremen's Union had expelled its Communist members, badly splitting the neighborhood. Then, during the 1950s, newspapers had published lurid exposés of organized crime on the waterfront. A "code of silence" developed in the neighborhood, and Chelsea residents would not talk to the police or to outsiders. In later years the neighborhood residents had no desire to reminisce about those troubled years. "As for talking at the present time to young historians eager for 'oral history,' it still does not quite sit right with old-timers," Doyle concluded. Uncomfortable with its history, the National Maritime Union destroyed all of its noncurrent records; nor were its members interested in recreating those records through oral testimony. Far more willing to talk about the past were the members of the Marine Workers Historical Association, many of them battle-scarred "Reds" who had been ejected from the union. Pragmatically aiming his project toward the most cooperative segment of the community, Doyle shifted the focus of his interviews to the Communist party on the waterfront. But even that subject was still so sensitive that people had second thoughts about speaking on the record. When Doyle organized an "oral history day" for residents, none of the invited speakers appeared. Doyle then gave the oral history a "breathing space" of two years, after which he opened a second round of public meetings. By that time some of the tensions and opposition to studying waterfront history had begun to decrease. His persistence even encouraged local Longshoreman's Union officials to speak more openly. Doyle's experiences suggest that interviewers facing uncooperative communities need to give them time rather than to give up on their projects.[11]

How do you return community oral history to the community?

A project's immediate goal may simply be to record the recollections of key members of a community, but it should consider long-term objectives as well. The ultimate goal may be a book, play, exhibit, videotape, or other public presentation that depicts the patterns and themes of importance to the community.

Excerpts from oral histories can be published in local newspapers or broadcast over local radio stations or community-access television channels. The oral historian Charles Hardy produced a series of radio programs, "Goin' North: Tales of the Great Migration," based on interviews with African Americans who left their homes in the South to relocate in Philadelphia. The *Philadelphia Inquirer* ran a special education supplement to serve as a companion to the series and to encourage listeners—particularly students—to collect similar information about their own families. Journalism students at the University of Texas created the U.S. Latinos and Latina WWII Oral History Project. Working in collaboration with the *San Antonio Express-News,* they have published a tabloid newspaper, *Narratives,* that includes student articles and interview excerpts drawn from the project. Available both on paper and online, *Narratives* offers its interviewees "a wonderful way of sharing their stories with a broader audience."[12]

Community oral historians have found outlets for their work in brochures distributed by the local chamber of commerce to promote the area and as source material for secondary social studies classes studying local history. Oral history has been incorporated into exhibits, walking tours, and dramatic productions. Popular oral history exhibits drawn from the community have encouraged many people to visit museums that they had never before entered, although they had lived in the area all their lives. But often the challenge is to display the material in places where people will actually see it. As eager as they are to participate, local historical societies or museums may not attract many viewers. Instead, consider displaying the exhibit at a shopping mall, senior citizens' center, public library, school, union hall, church, or civic organization to reach a broader cross-section of the community. Find out where people congregate in the community and put your exhibit there. Hold a reception to show the exhibit, invite the interviewees, and allow the rest of the community to view the product.[13]

In Idaho, a county museum director used oral history to catch the attention of the area's schoolchildren and to attract them to the museum. She conducted interviews on women's rural life and their roles in the county during the early decades of the twentieth century and turned the interviews into a 45-minute presentation that combined a slide show, period music, museum props, and a narration by a character in costume. The production traveled to every school in the county, as well as to many senior citizens' organizations.[14]

The Montana Historical Society encouraged the collection of historical materials on Montana's many women's clubs by producing a booklet, *Molders and Shakers: Montana Women as Community Builders: An Oral History Sampler and Guide* (1987) that detailed how clubs could collect their histories through club records, minute books, financial records, yearbooks, luncheon programs, newspaper clippings, and craftwork. From these archives, interviewers from the clubs could gain a better sense of what topics to cover and what questions to ask in club oral histories. *Molders and Shakers* urged club members to be imaginative in getting the stories generated from the oral histories back to the community, recommending that the clubs consider publishing newspaper articles drawn from the interviews, creating a booklet on the club's history featuring excerpts from the interviews and accompanying photographs, or producing slide-tape shows with interview excerpts as narration. The oral histories were incorporated into lesson plans on women's experience for local history classes. Transcripts also provided scripts for readers' theaters—club members presenting dramatic readings of the interviews. *Molders and Shakers* reminded women's club members that the results of oral history can be shared with the club's own membership or made more widely available as a public program in a community center.[15]

The Friends of Patapsco Valley and Heritage Greenway, near Baltimore, Maryland, organized a traveling exhibit of an oral history project to display in local galleries and libraries. The project conducted fifty-six oral histories in four small towns in the valley, while a photographer took portraits from which framed museum-quality prints were made. The exhibit was mounted in various local galleries and libraries, with excerpts from the oral histories accompanying each portrait. An excerpt of audiotape was played between two rocking chairs, while a mural created from one of the prints served as a backdrop. At some "narrative stage

events," the interviewer publicly drew out stories from those previously interviewed. At others, a script based on the interviews was performed. The combination provided depth and texture. Scriptwriter Sally Voris reported that "They have
been performed in the galleries while the exhibits have been on display so that people can see the images, read the text, hear the stories and see them enacted."[16]

What role can oral history play in folklife festivals?

A staple of folklife festivals, oral histories have been conducted before audiences: interviewees tell their story, play their music, or demonstrate their craft.
In 1981, with little in the way of funds, staff, or publicity, the Center for Southern
Folklore turned a previously commercial crafts festival, the Sorghum Days Folk
Festival, into a folklife festival by arranging for people to demonstrate their
techniques and talk about their lives and work. The festival brought together
white and black crafts workers and presented the differences and similarities in
their heritage; it drew large and appreciative audiences of local residents and out-
of-town visitors. Similarly, the Mid-South Folklife Festival invited blues musicians to perform and then to participate in oral history workshops, in which they
were interviewed by professional historians and discussed how the conditions
of the rural, segregated South influenced their music.

Oral history has been prominently featured at the Smithsonian Institution's
annual folklife festivals on the Mall. One event in the mid-1980s blended generations as well as races and genders by bringing together sleeping-car porters
and airline stewardesses to compare their jobs before an audience that had never
before fully appreciated what went into their work. The festival celebrated the
bicentennial of the White House by inviting White House workers, from stone
cutters to table setters, to reflect on their careers and the many occupants of the
White House whom they had served. Their behind-the-scenes testimony was supported by photographs, menus, and other memorabilia, which the Smithsonian
recorded in a video documentary, *Workers in the White House*.[17]

FAMILY INTERVIEWING

Can oral history be used to collect family history?

There always seems to be at least one relative who retains the family lore, who
can identify every obscure photo in the family album, and who corresponds with
far-flung kin. Or there is a family member with an interesting past that we have
always wanted to ask about. They make logical candidates to interview, but
somehow no one has gotten around to it. Suddenly they are gone, taking with

them all that unrecorded family history. Christopher Columbus's son Fernando admitted to a hazy knowledge of his father's early life and voyages, "for he died before I made so bold as to ask him about such things; or to speak more truly, at the time such ideas were farthest from my boyish mind."[18]

The traditional means of tracing one's family tree through census reports, city directories, and ship manifests can be supplemented with the recorded memories of living relatives. Older family members are repositories of stories about their childhood and of stories their parents and grandparents told them about the family's past, about immigration, about former residences, and about changes in the family name over time. They often feel a responsibility for passing along the family traditions to the following generations—who are not always appreciative or responsive. Grandparents are usually willing to talk, but their children and grandchildren, feeling they have heard these stories too often before, have never taken the trouble to record them. Then, too, it is hard to admit that older relatives will not always be around to be interviewed later.

Families can do their own interviews—a number of useful guidebooks include sample questions—or they can hire professional interviewers. Many family interviewing services have developed; they conduct interviews and produce tapes, CDs, transcripts, videotapes, and book-length family histories. The interviews become family keepsakes to be passed along, and copies can be given to alma maters, church libraries, or local public libraries.[19]

Is doing a family oral history any different from doing other oral histories?

To get a good interview, family oral histories should follow the same standards and procedures that apply to any other oral history. Prepare a family history questionnaire that includes some standard questions to ask all the family members to be interviewed as well as specific questions for each interviewee. Even for a family interview a legal release is advisable, so that the tapes and transcripts might someday be deposited in a suitable library.

Family oral histories need not be just a series of anecdotes. They can tell not only the "who" and "what" in a family but the "why" as well—the motives and attitudes that research in traditional genealogical sources would not necessarily bring to light. Sometimes the interviews provide clues that lead the interested family researcher to other sources of family documentation, such as the name of a town where family members once lived, or the location of a cemetery where birth and death dates appear on tombstones, dates that in turn help in locating newspaper obituaries. Traditional sources of family history provide preliminary research for the interviews. Family Bibles often contain dates of births, deaths, and marriages. In addition, school diplomas, letters, and local newspaper clippings provide basic information about family members.

Families reflect their times and communities. Questions can be directed at family life during the Depression, the Second World War, the cold war, the turbulent 1960s, the civil rights movement, the women's rights movement, and other sociohistorical periods. Family interviewers pursuing such questions should familiarize themselves with some of the history of these larger events, perhaps through reading basic history textbooks; such preparation generates questions to ask and frames the interviewee's story against a larger backdrop.

But do not limit your family history to a simple collection of pleasant memories. Family pasts may include stories of feuds or deaths that may be painful to revisit but are important for understanding family relationships. Some family members may be reluctant to dredge up unhappy memories, and others will want to use the interviews to settle a few scores.[20]

When Corinne Krause interviewed three generations of ethnic American women in Pittsburgh, she found that grandmothers, mothers, and daughters offered dissimilar versions of the same family's shared history. Their stories suggest how family members experience the same events and react to the same individuals in different ways, depending on their age, attitudes, and expectations. Krause recorded the conflicts between generations, but she also tracked their deep bonds and persistent values. She conducted her initial round of interviews during the 1970s, a time when the granddaughters were in open rebellion against old traditional family ways. When she returned a decade later, most of the grandmothers had died and their granddaughters had married and had their own children, in whom they were trying to instill the traditional values of their families.[21]

Bill Fletcher, whose book *Recording Your Family Roots* (1986) offers a multitude of sample questions to ask family members, has noted that the geographic spread and mobility of modern society has led to less frequent interaction between the generations of many families. Grandchildren often see grandparents only on holidays or during vacations and other limited encounters. Fletcher views taping an oral history as an excuse "to talk across the generational lines." Similarly, Linda Shopes has argued that doing family oral history "can be the impetus for developing and deepening relationships with other family members. Even more important, it can enhance one's own sense of identity."[22]

Will my family oral history be of any use to anyone outside my family?

Yes, because family history is part of popular culture and has become a subject of scholarly study. Researchers are increasingly interested in the lives of everyday people and open to looking at family oral histories for valuable information. The details a family wants from oral history interviews—treasured stories, data on births, deaths, weddings, divorces, graduations, jobs, and trips—are the same subjects that social historians now study.

Oral history can record a family's daily pattern of living, how the household was organized, how the family spent money, who sat where at the dining table, and what types of meals were served. As these topics are common to all families, researchers use data from one family to compare with others as they compile aggregates from which to make generalizations about social patterns. "From classroom projects to family efforts to large research projects, the possibilities for such family history are endless," the historian Carl Ryant noted. "What is required is a greater scholarly sensitivity to the possibilities of oral history and family history. This should result not only in more extensive scholarly analysis of existing data but also better quality data being generated for future analysis."[23]

THERAPEUTIC USES OF ORAL HISTORY

What therapeutic value do the elderly get from recording their oral histories?

Near the end of his life, the journalist Henry Fairlie commented that "in growing old, one has a stocked attic in which to rummage and the still passing show and pageant of life to observe, not only at a more leisurely pace, but with the convincing satisfaction and interest of having lived through many of the changes, even from their beginnings, that have brought us from there to here." The object of oral history interviews with elderly people is to collect their recollections for the record, but the elderly themselves also gain something from the process. Aristotle observed that the elderly "are continually talking of the past, because they enjoy remembering." Some in a family may scoff that older relatives are "living in the past," but as the gerontologist Robert Butler noted, elderly people naturally pass through a period of life review. As people take stock of their lives, they may reveal information that they have long suppressed, even from their families.[24]

Oral historians often comment on the eagerness with which many older people agree to be interviewed. The elderly seem to return to their youth while talking about it. They act more animated and treat their knowledgeable interviewer as a contemporary. Their children and grandchildren have heard snatches of these stories for so long that they no longer ask them about them; the interviewee's closest friends may be deceased. The folklorist Patrick Mullen thought that it was "as if elderly persons are waiting for someone to come along and ask for the stories, and the folklorist had better be a good listener." Henry Glassie also noted that "old tellers of tales are not astray in a wilderness of nostalgia. . . . They fill a crucial role in their community. They preserve its wisdom, settle its disputes, create its entertainment, speak its culture. Without them, local people would have no way to discover themselves."[25]

Those involved in reminiscence therapy have observed an increase in self-esteem among the nursing home residents who participated, and some overt changes in body language. One therapist noted that during the early sessions her interviewee sat hunched in his wheelchair, his head hanging low and displaying almost no eye contact as he spoke. As they continued to meet, the interviewee felt increasing confidence in his ability to recall memories and some assurance that she would listen to him. "His back became more upright, he focused his eyes on those of his listener and his face became much more animated." She found such changes in body language typical in both men and women who participated in the therapy sessions, and that the process brought older people out of their shells.[26]

Nursing homes have encouraged and sometimes hired oral historians to record the reminiscences of their residents. The Larksfield Place retirement community in Wichita, Kansas, established an oral history program in cooperation with Wichita State University and Emporia State University to collect life stories and encourage residents to use those interviews as starting points for other autobiographical projects. The Parker Jewish Geriatric Institute in New Hyde Park, New York, videotaped interviews with its residents. These interviews provided families with "a lasting record of treasured stories," but also had therapeutic value for the storytellers, who came away from the experience feeling more positive about themselves and their lives. "It reaffirms for them that their lives were valuable and productive," concluded Edith Shapiro, the institute's director of therapeutic recreation.[27]

For others, the experience of being interviewed for an oral history stimulates a cathartic release of long-pent-up emotions. Ronald Marcello has interviewed hundreds of Americans who were prisoners of war during the Second World War. "One byproduct has been some therapeutic value for the men," said Marcello. Many had been encouraged by their wives and children to participate in the taping. "Some say to me, 'I wouldn't have talked to you about this in 1946. The scars were too recent.'" Yet oral historians should keep in mind that the recall of painful memories can have traumatic as well as therapeutic effects. Those who have interviewed Holocaust victims, for instance, report that some interviewees express a felt duty to leave a record for future generations, but that doing the interviews triggered recurring nightmares.[28]

Are there any special considerations for interviewing in nursing homes?

Nursing homes have been described as places "where biography ends," since the residents so often have no knowledge of their neighbors' past lives before they became old and infirm. Yet when Tracy Kidder researched his book *Old Friends* (1993), he was always welcomed because older people enjoyed having someone to talk with. "Old people have nothing to do but try to make meaning out of their lives," he concluded.[29]

A video interviewer who works in nursing homes has suggested that the interviewer try to put the person in a comfortable setting, "preferably a favorite place—with soft, flattering light." As a starting place for her interviews, she usually asks about such enjoyable family occasions as weddings and bar mitzvahs to give the interviewee a chance to introduce all the characters of the story "in a celebratory manner."

Those working with the elderly recommend asking about a particular event or occasion more than once. The chances are that the second time the question is asked it will receive a more thorough answer, since the interviewee will have had time to remember it more vividly. Memory cues become increasingly useful with older interviewees. Sometimes an old photograph or song will bring back the past to them. Photo albums are even more helpful, since they are usually arranged in chronological order. A company in Madison, Wisconsin, called Bi-Folkal Productions sells "reminiscence resources" to nursing homes and libraries. The company produces a dozen different kits that use slides, tapes of sing-alongs, poetry, and photographs and are based on topics like pets, summertime, train rides, and the Depression. The company reasoned, for instance, that playing radio clips from a particular time would elicit memories that no question could ever tap.

The American Association of Retired Persons (AARP) has acknowledged the therapeutic value of oral history and storytelling among the elderly and established its own reminiscences program to train interviewees. AARP also publishes a guide to help volunteers elicit life stories. In Minneapolis, the Retired Senior Volunteers Program did oral histories of local senior citizens on such subjects as desegregating hotels and restaurants in the city, wartime experiences, and caring for the hungry and homeless. The project was cosponsored by a local radio station, which edited the tapes for weekly broadcast and then deposited them at the Minnesota Historical Society.[30]

Is there therapeutic value in oral history
for anyone other than the elderly?

Any group that has gone through a troublesome common experience can benefit from documenting impressions and memories through oral history interviews. The Women Miners Project has recorded the lives of women coal miners,
many of whom are still young or middle-aged women. They began collecting
interviews during the 1980s, a period of crisis for women miners because jobs
were disappearing rapidly and the miners' union was battling for survival. Many
of the women had been thrown into indefinite unemployment and faced a bleak
economic future.

During a particularly difficult period, the women miners were able to use the
oral history program "as a means of emotional support." The project developed
an exhibit out of the personal collections, writings, artwork, and other historical materials related to women miners and conducted videotaped interviews.
According to Marat Moore, the project's director, the interviews helped establish "an affirming context" for the women miners: "Our questions involve how
we have fared, do we go on from here, and whatever happened to affirmative
action in mining and other high-skilled, high-paying industries."[31]

Northwestern University Medical School instituted an oral history of AIDS
patients to learn how hospital personnel could care for them more effectively.
Interviews with nurses and other AIDS caregivers at the medical school and associated clinics identified the characteristics, values, training, and behavior
needed to treat AIDS patients. Interviewers reported that interviewees frequently commented that the project made them stop and reflect for the first
time on what they do in response to having AIDS. Social workers at the
Durham, North Carolina, Early Intervention Clinic conducted a similar oral history project with HIV-positive men to help them "give form and meaning" to
their past and to leave a record to help others grappling with issues of sex and
drugs.[32]

Realizing that the AIDS crisis in Africa was leaving a staggering number of
orphans, deprived of the emotional support of parents whose memories were
fading, the School of Theology at the University of Natal established the Memory
Box Project, which encouraged ailing parents to record their life stories "as a way
of keeping alive the family's memories." Project directors posited that children
who knew their roots would grow more resilient. For each family interviewed,
the project created a box that could be decorated with photos and drawings and
that would contain the recorded family stories to help the child cope with the
loss of parents and retain their family identities. The surviving caregivers were
asked to preserve the Memory Boxes and update them from time to time as new

events occurred. In the event of loss or misappropriation, the project retained copies of the interviews, but limited their access only to family members. Researchers would require family permission to consult the interviews.[33]

MUSEUM EXHIBITS

How has the use of oral history influenced museum exhibits?

Historical museums are sensitive to "the vanishing act of the past." In the words of the historian Joyce Appleby, "people, buildings and institutions disappear swiftly, first from sight and then from memory, taking along with them the sights, smells, sensibilities and styles that distinguish a time and a place." Historical exhibitions therefore serve as retrieval operations that arrange and explain the items and images in a manner that will "evoke a lost context" for the museum visitor. All too commonly in the past, historical museums were dimly lit halls, seemingly designed for nothing more than the veneration of objects, which were grouped together without much sense of how people had used them. Lights could be low since there were few captions to read. Museums are better illuminated now, allowing visitors to read longer, more informative captions for items that are woven together to tell a story of a time, place, event, or people. "History is not the old walking plow but the person who walked behind it," as one museum curator asserted. Many historical museums have incorporated oral history tapes and excerpts from transcripts into their exhibits, which allow visitors to hear the voices of the people who used the objects on display or lived through the events depicted. Interviews not only enhance a museum's displays and exhibits but provide material for public talks and media presentations.[34]

The deindustrialialization of the American Rust Belt has generated a number of industrial heritage museums that use oral historians to capture the memories of workers, whether of the preunion era or the heyday of unionization. The labor historian James B. Lane recommended that interviews focus on a wide range of attitudinal studies "about such matters as safety conditions and ecological standards, labor organizing and union-management relations, workplace folktales and corporate customs, and the bureaucratization process in both unions and businesses." Oral historians need to interview not only employees and employers but competitors and customers, and the topics covered should include the machinery, the foremen, and the relationships between workers, especially in industries that have grown obsolete.[35]

Nearly every museum in the vast Smithsonian complex has collected oral history interviews and integrated them into their exhibits. From the Smithsonian's

Anacostia Neighborhood Museum to the National Air and Space Museum, interviews are displayed to visitors in audio and visual form and as part of the text of exhibits. The National Museum of American History has long collected and displayed artifacts of American advertising. In the 1980s it realized that its collection consisted of newspaper advertisements, trade cards, tearsheets, and other static objects, but that it had no representations from modern multimedia advertising campaigns. The Smithsonian did interviews with executives of BBD&O (Batten, Barton, Durstine & Osborn) to collect memories and obtain films of television advertisements, jingles, and other memorabilia relating to its "Pepsi Generation" ad campaign—interviews that revealed how much of the campaign was spontaneous, not planned. Created as an archival collection, with descriptive brochures and finding aids, the taped interviews and television commercials became part of an audiovisual exhibit at the museum. Historians, archivists, and curators working on the project discovered that they had not only created new material for scholarly research and museum use, but had "established a healthy working relationship between a private corporation and a public research institution. This relationship went beyond financial support, in that employees of the company identified and contacted potential interviewees and encouraged their cooperation."[36]

As befitting a museum devoted to journalism, Washington's Newseum makes much use of interviews, including a studio where live interviews with news makers and news reporters take place regularly. One floor features traditional museum items, from Tom Paine's writing desk to Edward R. Murrow's microphone. On the floor below, visitors can film their own news broadcasts, and can "question" prominent journalists, appropriate portions of whose prerecorded interviews are replayed on computer screens. The variety of options have different generational appeals. Older visitors tend to linger longer in the museum-like News History Gallery, while younger students crowd the interactive videos below.[37]

Computers assist in tailoring the museum-going experience to individual needs and interests. At Ellis Island in New York harbor, oral historians conducted over 1,600 interviews with immigrants who had been processed there, along with military and civilian personnel who worked there. Many of the exhibits incorporated extracts from the interviews, as did a documentary film, and theatrical performance. The museum also makes the audio recordings and transcripts accessible online in its Oral History Listening Room, where visitors can accession interviews by the name of the interviewee, country of origin, ship of passage, or the year of arrival in America. Visitors seeking information about a relative, or about the common experiences of others who migrated about the same time from the same region, can call up the appropriate audio recordings and transcripts, to hear and read separately or simultaneously.[38]

What are the problems of using oral history in museum displays?

Museum curators use oral history to "bridge the gap between representation and reality." Oral history can be inserted as sound or video played at stations throughout an exhibit, or transcripts can be excerpted in captions and other text to inform visitors. Some exhibits incorporate interviews in documentaries shown in small theaters, usually before or after the exhibit; others intersperse the oral history material throughout the collection on various monitors and interactive videos. Because usually only a fraction of the interviews can be used, selection, editing, and brevity of remarks are all-important. As David Lance has noted, such display tapes are "most effective when they combine a variety of speakers and a range of subject content in short and pithy juxtaposition."

Curators also note that it is important for visitors to understand that individual opinions expressed in the interviews may not be held by the majority—a concept that confuses people who expect museums as sources of factual information. To distinguish between the subjectivity of the speakers and the objectivity of the curatorial text, some museums have printed quotations in different typeface, and have made sure that the speaker's names follow their words.[39]

The extensive use of audio and visual playback machines can escalate the costs of mounting an exhibit, and there is always the risk that machines will break down. It can be a depressing experience to walk through an exhibit with darkened gaps in its presentation owing to malfunctioning machines. Too often the equipment has been "adapted for exhibition purposes rather than designed for it" and breaks down because of the strain of continuous playback. Showing documentary films and video with sound or having audio broadcasts requires a careful positioning of speakers "and a fairly elaborate arrangement of equipment and wiring that takes careful planning and craftsmanship to conceal." Using loudspeakers so that all may hear can be distracting; listening to repeated playback of the same tape becomes unnerving, and many museums have opted to use headsets for individual listening. Tape-recorded tours that are played individually can also include oral history excerpts.[40]

What advantage does oral history offer museums in dealing with controversial subjects?

The cultural wars in recent years have spilled over into the once quiet world of historical museums. An explosion of bad publicity followed the Smithsonian's

Air and Space Museum mounting of an exhibit on the *Enola Gay*, the military plane that dropped the atomic bomb on Hiroshima. Veterans' organizations protested against the exhibit in the media and on Capitol Hill. The veterans and the curators of the exhibit had starkly different ways of analyzing and explaining the same event. One side argued that dropping the bomb ended the war with Japan without American troops having to invade, while the other side saw Hiroshima as the dawn of the age of nuclear anxiety. The result of their battle was an unhappy compromise in which the museum exhibited parts of the plane with a minimum of explanatory text and a prominently placed apology from the Secretary of the Smithsonian. Some visitors felt profoundly moved by seeing the plane and considering the destruction that it caused, but many others found it possible to view the fuselage as an artifact of aviation without pondering its role in the atomic age.[41]

After *Enola Gay*, the Smithsonian's National Museum of American History attempted to take no side at all in an aptly titled exhibit *Between a Rock and a Hard Place: A Dialogue on American Sweatshops, 1820–Present.* Curators sought to diffuse criticism by offering evidence and letting visitors draw their own conclusions. But when the exhibit opened, the *Washington Post* commented that it "treads the line between hot-button advocacy and cold, precise historical facts. Outrage, which should be the heartbeat of the show about human exploitation and illegality, is present only in the weighty collection of details."[42]

Oral history offers a middle way between these two poles. Institutions like the Newseum, which bills itself as the "only interactive museum of news," and the U.S. Holocaust Memorial Museum have relied successfully on audio and videotaped narratives and interactive computers to engage their visitors. This approach allows a museum to offer multiple viewpoints in different voices. Interactive technology makes it possible for museum-goers to "ask questions" of those who participated in historic events. Interviews that have been videotaped and edited so that the interviewee will answer a series of pre-selected questions offered on the screen. By incorporating multiple voices, the exhibits teach the public that history may be interpreted in different ways. Rather than the authoritative, and sometimes condescending, single voice of the historian/curator lecturing the visitor on what it all means, the mélange of voices of participants and commentators can argue with each other to re-create the complexity of the past. The *Enola Gay*'s curators could have spared themselves much grief by including the voices of both the military veterans and the anti-nuclear activists, as well as diverse scholars in the field, to frame the exhibit as a debate rather than to try to settle the issue by themselves.[43]

RADIO AND ORAL HISTORY

How has oral history been used in radio broadcasts?

As both involve recorded human speech, oral history is "custom built for radio," according to David Dunaway, an oral historian who has produced radio documentaries. Radio production is less costly than producing video documentaries, and radio studios operate in all kinds of communities throughout the nation, from inner cities to rural counties, and on the campuses of many universities. The growth of national and local radio stations has especially stimulated interest in producing and broadcasting historical documentaries over the radio, and funding agencies have underwritten some ambitious projects. "The craft of radio production rises to art in the hands of someone fashioning a program from disparate interviews, ambient noise, and historical recordings such as speeches and old radio broadcasts," Dunaway notes. "By juxtaposing these elements the expert producer creates a textural tapestry of sound, complete with the built-in punctuation of pauses and music."[44]

Oral history-based radio broadcast have included "Living Atlanta," an urban history of Atlanta, Georgia; "First-Person America," reminiscences of the Great Depression; "New Yorkers at Work: Oral Histories of Life, Labor, and Industry"; and the life and times of New York City's colorful mayor Fiorello LaGuardia. The University of Alabama funded an oral history of Alabama blacks who worked as coal and iron ore miners, sharecroppers, union organizers, domestics, teachers, ministers, lawyers, and small-business operators. Focusing on Birmingham, Alabama, which in the 1920s had the largest black population of any major U.S. city, the project resulted in a dozen half-hour radio programs, *Working Lives,* that were broadcast on National Public Radio (NPR).[45]

The Blues Archives at the University of Mississippi worked with Media Production International of Memphis, Tennessee, to produce *The Original Down Home Blues Show,* a regular NPR series. The program combines blues music with interviews with the musicians. Each interviewee is asked to select the records played on the show, a practice that the producers feel reveals "a deeper insight into their sense of memory of place and time." Recognizing that music is their livelihood, and that blues is a particularly marketable form of oral history, the producers feel a moral obligation not only to secure the rights of interviewees for their copyrighted material but to pay them a fee for their contributions to the show. In return, such programs provide outstanding publicity for oral history archives and stimulate use of its own collection.[46]

Will the Circle Be Unbroken? a thirteen-hour, twenty-six part radio series about the civil rights movement, was broadcast over Public Radio International in 1997. Initiated by the Southern Regional Council, an Atlanta based civil rights organization, the programs contained more than 250 reflective voices of blacks and whites from five Southern cities: Atlanta, Little Rock, Jackson, Montgomery and Columbia. "What makes it work well is the medium itself," wrote Alan Bunce, a reviewer for the *Christian Science Monitor*. The television series *Eyes on the Prize* had already covered much of the same territory. "Yet by revisiting the story on the radio, through the reminiscences of people who have lived through the history, without seeing the speakers, you are able to experience the individuals in a special way—to savor the tone of voice, to sense the emotional meaning."[47]

The oral historian Gene Preuss was a high school student working at his hometown radio station in 1983 when it launched a weekly oral history program. The station manager, an old newsman, interviewed older residents of the community about changes around them and local traditions. "I found the interviews fascinating, and listened to every single one of these programs for almost three years, almost 120 different programs!" he commented. Preuss credited the program with convincing him to change his college major to history, and his use of oral history in his work. Years later he noted that the radio station was still doing interviews, some one thousand of them, and was working with the town's archive to preserve them.[48]

If radio and oral history are so compatible, why has there not been more oral history on the radio?

Oral history archivists often feel frustrated that radio producers do not make greater use of their collections as raw material for documentaries. More often trained as journalists than historians, and working under tight deadlines and budget constraints, radio producers are often loath to spend the time needed to review long archival tapes. Too often they find the sound quality of archival tapes inadequate for broadcast use (although poor sound quality can now be enhanced digitally). Radio documentary producers may find it easier simply to do their own interviewing, using broadcast studio equipment and asking questions specific to the project—an alternative that is possible, of course, only if there are survivors left to interview.[49]

To expand use of their collections, oral historians need to recognize the differences between their type of interviewing and radio interviewing and to try, when possible, to accommodate radio's needs. "Radio producers work with action, sensation, emotion, and audio presence as their palette, the oral historian with objectivity and verisimilitude," Dunaway argued. "Both pursue truth on different roads." Oral historians must improve the sound quality of their recording and preserve them under optimal archival conditions for future use. Radio producers pick and choose from many different interviews, editing and rearranging them, adding music and sound effects, and rarely using more than a fraction of a single interview. Interviews therefore need to be abstracted or indexed for easy retrieval. Oral historians can work with radio producers to identify the most colorful dialogue, revealing anecdotes, emotional interludes, and those moments of verbal eloquence that can give spark to a documentary. Interviewers can also explain the themes and historical framework of the interviews. They need to take some care that the rights of the interviewees are protected, and that in the editing and excerpting of the interviews for broadcast, the meaning is not distorted and the interviewees are not held up to ridicule.[50]

ORAL HISTORY ON STAGE

If an oral history project has already resulted in an archival collection or a book, what is the advantage of trying to turn it into a stage production?

Oral historians want to return their material to the community from which it came, but they recognize that the community may never read their books and articles. The six authors who collaborated on the highly acclaimed book *Like a Family: The Making of a Southern Cotton Mill World* (1987) recognized that, as a university press publication, it reached a predominantly academic audience. They had collected the life stories of the mill workers, then processed, edited, interpreted, and published them, but the authors wanted to do even more to "keep the stories alive and keep history ongoing." Recognizing how much interviews involve storytelling, and that those stories were already in a sense a performance, the speech communications department at the University of North Carolina at Chapel Hill offered an independent study course in which eleven undergraduates read through the interview transcripts and pulled characters and dialogue from the book to produce a script. In 1988 they took the play to many mill towns throughout North and South Carolina. The producers observed that audiences, seeing their own lives performed on stage, responded instinctively, "imitating what was going on and talking about it." At the end of each performance, the cast would talk with the audience, who contributed additional stories and argued with the case over interpretation, keeping alive the collaborative process between history and performance.[51]

In Baltimore and St. Paul, Minnesota, groups have used oral histories to produce stage plays about local history for local audiences. The Baltimore Voices oral history was initiated in 1978 to explore and present in popular forms the social history of Baltimore's six oldest neighborhoods. A team of professional historians, graduate students, and community historians interviewed over two hundred people, transcribed the interviews, and divided them into such common topics as family, neighborhoods, ethnicity, religion, work, income, wages and expenditures, education, immigration, race, prejudice, and the Great Depression. From these, they produced hundreds of one-page stories, with different ethnic groups, broken down by neighborhoods. The Baltimore Theatre Project organized these excerpts into a play, also named *Baltimore Voices* (1981), which was presented in the various Baltimore neighborhoods and videotaped as a documentary. The same year the Baltimore Voices project started, the St. Paul History Theatre in St. Paul, Minnesota, produced the first in a series of oral history-based plays. In the 1970s and 1980s its repertoire included *The Deadly Decades,* dealing with the effects of Prohibition on the city; *You Can't Get to Heaven through the U.S.A.,* about Swedish and Italian immigrants; *We Win or Bust,* about a railroad strike; and *Nina! Madam to a Saintly City,* the story of police corruption and a famous operator of a local bordello. The playwright Arthur Miller turned Studs Terkel's oral history *Working* into a stage play, *An American Clock* (1982).[52]

In the 1990s students at Cuyahoga Community College conducted oral histories in ethnic and minority neighborhoods in Cleveland, Ohio, from which *The People of Cleveland: Building Community* was drawn. Accompanying dialogue from the life histories were slides and music and dance performances. The *People of Cleveland* played to more than 100 audiences in churches, schools, and neighborhood organizations. Another play, *Growing Up and Growing Old,* drew from interviews about life cycles and sought to overcome negative stereotypes of the elderly. The Center for Oral History at the University of Hawaii mixed interviews with 1940s swing music in its "living history performances" of *An Era of Change: Oral Histories of Civilians in World War II Hawaii,* for presentation at libraries and senior citizens centers.[53]

The John Jay College of Criminal Justice in New York, which lost more than one hundred of its students, faculty and alumni in the terrorist attacks on September 11, 2001, conducted interviews with a cross-section of New Yorkers caught in the chaos of the collapse of the World Trade towers. Drawing from forty of those interviews with police, firefighters, emergency personnel and citizen bystanders, they prepared *What Happened? The September 11th Testimony Project,* a ninety-minute, one-act documentary drama designed to be performed with a cast from six to fifteen actors. Offering the script for commemorative performances, project directors described it as "a collective narrative that follows events and personal experiences from early that beautiful morning through impact, escape, rescue and recovery, grieving, and reflection on how our lives have changed."[54]

CD-ROM AND THE INTERNET

What advantages do CD-ROM and the Internet offer oral historians?

Despite their dependence on technology, oral historians tend to approach technological innovations cautiously. In adopting any new equipment, they seek assurances of its reliability, durability, and affordability. Archivists will be especially concerned with the long-term preservation of audio and visual recordings. Established oral history projects that have invested a great deal in a particular type of technology will shudder at the expense of transferal to the new, including the cost of staff retraining. Oral historians will question whether new technology will affect the interview process, hinder the development of rapport and candor, and turn the interview more into a form of public performance. The first interviewers worried whether tape recorders inhibited interviewees from speaking freely; some later grew concerned that video would induce interviewees to play to the camera. More recently, others have conjectured that people might speak more guardedly if they knew their interviews would be posted on the Internet. There is always the danger that the type of medium used would affect the selection of people to be interviewed and the type of responses collected, and Paul Thompson has posited that the digital revolution might make oral history "a different animal." But he argues that "we need all these different animals" to get more people to read and use our interviews. In seeking to attract a new generation of oral historians from among today's students, practitioners must be prepared to investigate digital technology thoroughly.[55]

Among the first to utilize the new medium were Roy Rosenzweig, Steve Brier, and Josh Brown, who incorporate oral history reminiscences into a CD-ROM "electronic book," *Who Built America? From the Centennial Celebration of 1876 to the Great War of 1914* (1993). They combined audio and film clips, six hundred pictures, and five thousand pages of text with computer-based search features to help students see and hear the history they were studying. Although the project began with the late nineteenth century, Rosenzweig and his colleagues discovered that many of the earliest oral histories were conducted with people who grew up in the 1880s and 1890s. Some projects did

not save their tapes, and the sound quality of other tapes was not repro-
ducible, but the authors of *Who Built America?* nevertheless were able to collect first-person recollections to accompany the photographs and written
documentation. "Readers" of the their electronic book could actually hear the
sounds of history, through oral history, music and newsreels. "Our larger
motivation in experimenting with this new technology has been toward
democratizing historical understanding," the authors explained. The electronic book turned users into "active participants in the process of constructing historical interpretations rather than merely passive consumers of
historical 'facts.'"[56]

In 1992 the National Park Service installed Project Jukebox as a workstation
at the Yukon-Charley National Preserve in Alaska. Called a "jukebox" because
users select recordings from an automated system of stacked compact discs, it
allows computer searching and retrieval of information. Project Jukebox combined oral histories of people who had lived, fished, hunted, and worked in the
Yukon-Charley Preserve. It provided recordings on historical themes about the
Yukon River, the administrative history of the preserve, and experiences of
people who settled there. Visitors to the park, local students, and new park
rangers used the workstations to select topics and pull up recordings, transcripts,
and illustrations at their own speed, to follow their own interests. The opening screen provided a general map of the area, from which viewers could click
on specific areas and listen to portions of the interviews relating to those sites.
When interviewees spoke in their own native languages, English translations
were available on-screen.[57]

These innovations on CD-ROM suggested to oral historians that advances in
digital technology might solve their problem of making completed interviews
more readily accessible to scholars, teachers, and the larger community. By the
mid-1990s the Internet became universally available, and educational institutions were among the first to recognize that CD-ROM and the Internet would
be more than tools but "a new way of thinking and viewing the world." Students
often mastered the new digital technology more readily than adults and showed
more creativity in its applications. Schools found creating web sites inexpensive,
effective, and attractive ways of publishing the results of student oral history projects. Archives began to post their catalogs, transcripts, and sound recordings.
New projects got underway with Internet-access as a built-in goal. Oral history
organizations at the local, national, and international level found the Internet
an ideal means of networking and communication. All of this stimulated new
discussions of the legal and ethical ramifications of the new medium as well as
of its creative uses.[58]

What sort of oral history is available online?

To their great relief, researchers found a wide variety of oral history collections coming online on the Internet, from long-established archives to brand-new projects, large and well-funded to small, shoestring operations, government agencies, universities, high schools, religious and community groups. Presidential libraries, faced with decisions about what to digitize among the mountains of records in their holdings, turned first to their oral history transcripts, as more manageable, self-contained, and appealing to the broadest audience of users. When the Washington Press Club Foundation sponsored interviews with pioneering women journalists, it planned from the start to post them on its web site, if the interviewees agreed. The pioneering oral history archives at Columbia, Berkeley and UCLA have gone online along with university and community college archives from Honolulu to Chapel Hill.

The Library of Congress has initiated the American Memory Project, one of the largest and most ambitious efforts to digitize research materials. Among the collections available online through the American Memory Project are the WPA Federal Writers' Project Life Stories, most notably its many interviews with former slaves. The United States Holocaust Memorial Museum in Washington and the Survivors of the Shoah Visual History Foundation have used the Internet for worldwide dissemination of their materials. Working with Brown University, sophomores at the South Kingsport high school in Providence, Rhode Island turned a school project into a web page on "The Whole World Was Watching: An Oral History of 1968."

Many of the oral history web sites have an educational objective. The United Indian Traders Association, whose members run trading posts on American Indian reservations, underwrote efforts by the Northern Arizona University to conduct interviews on the history of trade relations and cultural interactions in the Four Corners region of the Southwest. From the start, they intended it to be an Internet site. "Traders: Voices from the Trading Post" contains transcripts and short audio clips of the traders and the Native Americans who trade with them, tribal leaders, attorneys, accountants, sales personnel, artisans and trading post employees. Placing the collection on the Internet made it available to public school teachers throughout the region and elsewhere, with an accompanying teachers' guide and lesson plans. A CD-ROM that replicated the web site was also distributed to local schools, libraries, and museums.[59]

An endowment in 1998 enabled the Regional Oral History Office at Berkeley to document the history of the campus Free Speech Movement of the 1960s. The project built a digital archive of interviews with the movement's leaders, participants, and witnesses, paying particular attention to areas that had not been covered in depth before, such as the participation of women and minority students, faculty-student relationships, legal counsel, and the press. The interviews were then made available on ROHO's web site together with an extensive archives of newsletters, newspaper and journal articles, leaflets, speeches, minutes of meetings and other supporting evidence.[60]

Although not exclusively an oral history site, the free online *Journal of MultiMedia History* regularly makes use of interviews in its articles and "aural essays." A creative effort to exploit the possibilities of electronic publishing, the journal seeks to help historians "radically re-imagine" how to communicate their work digitally. Presenting articles that demonstrate how the new media can influence the practice of history in archives, museums, and the classroom, the journal has offered such "essays in sound" as "I Can Almost See the Light of Home—A Field Trip to Harlan County, Kentucky," by Charles Hardy, III and Alessandro Portelli, that follow the researcher and his research in Appalachia. Similarly, "Miner's Son, Miner's Photographer" by Tom Dublin and Melissa Doak profiled a documentary photographer and combined his photographs with oral history interviews.[61]

The Internet blurred international borders. Researchers can virtually visit the British Library National Sound Archive, read interviews from the Imperial War Museum in London, keep up with the work of the Centre for Popular Memory at the University of Cape Town in South Africa, check the Oral History and Folklore Collection at the National Library of Australia in Canberra, or the Sound Recordings in the National Archives of Singapore, all without visas, passports, or airline tickets. They can also keep contact with others who share similar interests on a daily basis via the oral history listserv, H-Oralhist. Sponsored by the Oral History Association, H-Oralhist uses e-mail to provide an interactive forum for anyone interested in using or doing oral history. They can pose questions, provide solutions, and share experiences, research interests, current projects, teaching methods and the latest literature. They can also post announcements of conferences, fellowships and jobs. (Subscription to H-Oralhist is free and can be obtained by sending an e-mail to: listserv@h-net.msu.edu with the following text: SUBSCRIBE H-ORALHIST, first name, last name, and affiliation.)[62]

Should an oral history project plan to post all of its oral histories online, or would a sampling suffice?

Ideally, researchers want full-text access to all available documentation. However, there are a number of reasons why an oral history project may choose not to post all of its interviews. Issues of copyright and personal privacy may be at stake, and the staff time needed to scan and download collections may be prohibitive. Whether for copyright, cost, or concern over retaining more control over their collections, some archives have adopted mixed programs of making interviews selectively available on the Internet and the rest on CD-ROM that researchers purchase, usually at a minimum price.

Sampling interviews on web sites or on CD-ROM can serve as an advertisement for the wealth of resources in an oral history collection. Before the Columbia Oral History Office, the oldest and largest oral history archives, made any of its interviews available on the Internet, it issued a CD-ROM called *Stories from the Collection: Columbia University Oral History Research Office,* which included highlights of a half-century of interviews, ranging from Justice Thurgood Marshall discussing his appointment to the Supreme Court to Fred Astaire discussing his Hollywood dancing career. The University of Kentucky Oral History Program similarly commemorated its thirtieth anniversary with a CD-ROM, *Voices from the Collection.*[63]

The Regional Oral History office at the University of California at Berkeley provides access to several of its oral history collections, from projects on women's suffrage, former Governor Earl Warren, the disabilities rights movements, and Berkeley's Black Alumni. Berkeley's site provides complete interview transcripts with background information on the circumstances of the interviews, the interviewers and the topics covered. Its posted interviews range from those with suffrage leaders like Alice Paul and Jeanette Rankin to the first physicians to treat AIDS patients. Reviewers have noted that it is a straightforward textual site with no multimedia presentation, that "looks and reads an awful lot like a book."[64]

What kind of oral history guidance is available online?

For those seeking models for their own interviews, there is nothing better than reading online transcripts. Quite a few oral history web sites also provide helpful advice—especially for students and teachers—on everything from interviewing tips to sample deeds of gift.

Part of the National Endowment for the Humanities' web site, "My History is America's History," contains a guide on how to do an interview. "The most important piece of advice is simple: get started," the site recommends. "Your family history isn't getting any younger." It urged users—both children and adults— to create "balanced portraits of family members in a logical collection of good-quality recordings that your grandchildren can make sense of fifty years from now." The guide contains steps to consider before the interview, types of questions to ask, how to conduct the interview, and what to do after the interview to help "save America's stories."[65]

Specifically designed to help middle school and high school students conduct oral histories in their communities, "Discovering Our Delta" provides online learning guides for both students and teachers. An accompanying video that follows five students from the Mississippi Delta as they conduct research on their communities must be ordered through the site, but the student and teacher guides are available online. They provide tips for locating community members to interview, preparing for the interviews, transcribing the recorded interviews, interpreting the gathered material, and a sample letter to parents of participating students explaining the project and its procedures. A related site, Cultural Arts Resources for Teachers and Students (CARTS), carries information on upcoming oral history summer institutes for teachers, and links to other educational guides for using interviewing and fieldwork to explore communities and traditions.[66]

History Matters, which describes itself as a "U.S. Survey Course on the Web," provides a teacher syllabus using oral history, information about online resources, interactive exercises, talking history forums, and online assignments. Created by American Social History Project/Center for History and New Media at George Mason University, *History Matters* offers itself as a starting point for history students to explore the Internet, and as a storehouse of teaching resources grounded in the latest scholarship, including an annotated guide to web sites. The site offers Linda Shopes' helpful essay and guide, "What Is Oral History?" that includes information on other oral history web sites and "tips for evaluating oral history online."[67]

In 2001 the United States Congress voted to authorize the American Folklife Center at the Library of Congress to organize a Veterans Oral History Project. Its sponsors intended the project to be a "living memorial" to all war veterans from World War I to the Persian Gulf, along with civilian volunteers and war industry. With more than 19 million war veterans still living in the United States (including over three thousand from World War I), there was an abundance of potential interviewees. The project has encouraged the public to conduct the interviews and submit them to the Folklife Center. To coordinate these efforts and improve the standards of interviewing, the Center sponsored workshops and guides, including a booklet on *Helpful Guidelines for Conducting and Preserving Interviews and Other Project Materials.* The project directors saw their task to be as much about "process" as "product," making sure that people of all ages participate in the program, and that the participating public learn about wartime, veterans, and about oral history as a methodology for better understanding their culture and society.[68]

Many oral history associations, international, national, and regional, maintain web sites to announce meetings and workshops and to provide guidance for members. These sites further the networking efforts of oral historians, from academics to freelancers, to maintain contact, share information, and keep current with new developments in oral history.

From the most remote rural territories to inner-city neighborhoods, on audio- and videotape, over the Internet, on radio and on stage, in museums and community centers, oral history has proven to be a multifaceted tool, usable in a seemingly limitless number of ways, in many disciplines. Beyond their immediate purposes, oral historians seek to leave a better historical record, to preserve what would otherwise be lost or more obscure. In a sense, oral history has turned upside down George Santayana's famous dictum that "those who cannot remember the past are condemned to repeat it." Now oral historians are making sure that those who *can* remember the past must repeat it for the record.[69]

Principles and Standards of the Oral History Association

The Oral History Association promotes oral history as a method of gathering and preserving historical information through recorded interviews with participants in past events and ways of life. It encourages those who produce and use oral history to recognize certain principles, rights, technical standards, and obligations for the creation and preservation of source material that is authentic, useful, and reliable. These include obligations to the interviewee, to the profession, and to the public, as well as mutual obligations between sponsoring organizations and interviewers.

People with a range of affiliations and sponsors conduct oral history interviews for a variety of purposes: to create archival records, for individual research, for community and institutional projects, and for publications and media productions. While these principles and standards provide a general framework for guiding professional conduct, their application may vary according to the nature of specific oral history projects. Regardless of the purpose of the interviews, oral history should be conducted in the spirit of critical inquiry and social responsibility and with a recognition of the interactive and subjective nature of the enterprise.

Responsibility to Interviewees:

1. Interviewees should be informed of the purposes and procedures of oral history in general and of the aims and anticipated uses of the particular projects to which they are making their contributions.
2. Interviewees should be informed of the mutual rights in the oral history process, such as editing, access restrictions, copyrights, prior use, royalties, and the expected disposition and dissemination of all forms of the record, including the potential for electronic distribution.
3. Interviewees should be informed that they will be asked to sign a legal release. Interviews should remain confidential until interviewees have given permission for their use.

4. Interviewers should guard against making promises to interviewees that the interviewers may not be able to fulfill, such as guarantees of publication and control over the use of interviews after they have been made public. In all future uses, however, good faith efforts should be made to honor the spirit of the interviewee's agreement.

5. Interviews should be conducted in accord with any prior agreements made with the interviewee, and such agreements should be documented for the record.

6. Interviewers should work to achieve a balance between the objectives of the project and the perspectives of the interviewees. They should be sensitive to the diversity of social and cultural experiences and to the implications of race, gender, class, ethnicity, age, religion, and sexual orientation. They should encourage interviewees to respond in their own style and language and to address issues that reflect their concerns. Interviewers should fully explore all appropriate areas of inquiry with the interviewee and not be satisfied with superficial responses.

7. Interviewers should guard against possible exploitation of interviewees and be sensitive to the ways in which their interviews might be used. Interviewers must respect the rights of interviewees to refuse to discuss certain subjects, to restrict access to the interview, or, under Guidelines extreme circumstances, even to choose anonymity. Interviewers should clearly explain these options to all interviewees.

8. Interviewers should use the best recording equipment within their means to accurately reproduce the interviewee's voice and, if appropriate, other sounds as well as visual images.

9. Given the rapid development of new technologies, interviewees should be informed of the wide range of potential uses of their interviews.

10. Good faith efforts should be made to ensure that the uses of recordings and transcripts comply with both the letter and spirit of the interviewee's agreement.

Responsibility to the Public and to the Profession:

1. Oral historians have a responsibility to maintain the highest professional standards in the conduct of their work and to uphold the standards of the various disciplines and professions with which they are affiliated.

2. In recognition of the importance of oral history to an understanding of the past and of the cost and effort involved, interviewers and interviewees should mutually strive to record candid information of lasting value and to make that information accessible.

3. Interviewees should be selected based on the relevance of their experiences to the subject at hand.

4. Interviewers should possess interviewing skills as well as professional competence and knowledge of the subject at hand.

5. Regardless of the specific interests of the project, interviewers should attempt to extend the inquiry beyond the specific focus of the project to create as complete a record as possible for the benefit of others.

6. Interviewers should strive to prompt informative dialogue through challenging and perceptive inquiry. They should be grounded in the background of the persons being interviewed and, when possible, should carefully research appropriate documents and secondary sources related to subjects about which the interviewees can speak.

7. Interviewers should make every effort to record their interviews using the best recording equipment within their means to reproduce accurately the interviewee's voice and, if appropriate, image. They also should collect and record other historical documentation the interviewee may possess, including still photographs, print materials, and other sound and moving image recordings, if appropriate.

8. Interviewers should provide complete documentation of their preparation and methods, including the circumstances of the interviews.

9. Interviewers and, when possible, interviewees should review and evaluate their interviews, including any summaries or transcriptions made from them.

10. With the permission of the interviewees, interviewers should arrange to deposit their interviews in an archival repository that is capable of both preserving the interviews and eventually making them available for general use. Interviewers should provide basic information about the interviews, including project goals, sponsorship, and funding. Preferably, interviewers should work with repositories before conducting the interviews to determine necessary legal Guidelines arrangements. If interviewers arrange to retain first use of the interviews, it should be only for a reasonable time before public use.

11. Interviewers should be sensitive to the communities from which they have collected oral histories, taking care not to reinforce thoughtless stereotypes nor to bring undue notoriety to them. Interviewers should take every effort to make the interviews accessible to the communities.

12. Oral history interviews should be used and cited with the same care and standards applied to other historical sources. Users have a responsibility to retain the integrity of the interviewee's voice, neither misrepresenting the interviewee's words nor taking them out of context.

13. Sources of funding or sponsorship of oral history projects should be made public in all exhibits, media presentations, or publications that result from the projects.

14. Interviewers and oral history programs should conscientiously consider how they might share with interviewees and their communities the rewards and recognition that might result from their work.

Responsibility for Sponsoring and Archival Institutions:

1. Institutions sponsoring and maintaining oral history archives have a responsibility to interviewees, interviewers, the profession, and the public to maintain the highest technical, professional, and ethical standards in the creation and archival preservation of oral history interviews and related materials.

2. Subject to conditions that interviewees set, sponsoring institutions (or individual collectors) have an obligation to: prepare and preserve easily usable records; keep abreast of rapidly developing technologies for preservation and dissemination; keep accurate records of the creation and processing of each interview; and identify, index, and catalog interviews.

3. Sponsoring institutions and archives should make known through a variety of means, including electronic modes of distribution, the existence of interviews open for research.

4. Within the parameters of their missions and resources, archival institutions should collect interviews generated by independent researchers and assist interviewers with the necessary legal agreements.

5. Sponsoring institutions should train interviewers. Such training should: provide them basic instruction in how to record high fidelity interviews and, if appropriate, other sound and moving image recordings; explain the objectives of the program to them; inform them of all ethical and legal considerations governing an interview; and make clear to interviewers what their obligations are to the program and to the interviewees.

6. Interviewers and interviewees should receive appropriate acknowledgment for their work in all forms of citation or usage.

7. Archives should make good faith efforts to ensure that uses of recordings and transcripts, especially those that employ new technologies, comply with both the letter and spirit of the interviewee's agreement.

Sample Legal Release Forms

SAMPLE DEED OF GIFT

[From John Neuenschwander, *Oral History and the Law* (2003)]

I, [name of interviewee] of [address], herein permanently give, convey, and assign to [name of archive, program or individual], which is currently in possession of my interview (or oral memoir) consisting of [description]. In so doing I understand that my interview (or oral memoir) will be made available to researchers and may be quoted from, published or broadcast in any medium that the [archive, program or individual] shall deem appropriate.

In making this gift I fully understand that I am conveying all legal title and literary property rights which I have or may be deemed to have in my interview (or oral memoir) as well as my rights, title and interest in any copyright which may be secured under the laws now or later in force and effect in the United States of America. My conveyance of copyright encompasses the exclusive rights of: reproduction, distribution, preparation of derivative works, public performance, public display as well as all renewals and extensions.

I, [agent for the duly appointed representative of] accept the interview (or oral memoir) of [name of interviewee] for inclusion into the [archive or program].

_____   _____
[signature of donor]   [signature of agent/representative]

_____
[date]

Provisions for Control of Access and/or Sealing of Interview

No researcher shall be allowed access to my oral history without my written permission.

No researcher will be permitted to quote from my interview unless he or she has submitted the quotes to me and received my written approval.

My oral history interview will remain closed to all researchers until [date] or my death, whichever occurs first.

My oral history interview cannot be made available to researchers unless all references from which my identity could be known are edited out and a pseudonym is assigned. After my death, all portions of my oral history interview which were held back, as well as my true identity, shall be made available.

DEED OF GIFT FOR HEIR OR HEIRS OF INTERVIEWEE

[From John Neuenschwander, *Oral History and the Law* (2003)]

In accordance with the willing participation of [name of interviewee] in the [name of oral history project or program] on [date], in which he/she voluntarily gave to the [name of receiving group or individual] an interview (or oral memoir) in the form of [number of tapes or transcripts], I/we, [names] as legal heir or heirs, herein do permanently give, convey and assign same to [name of archive, program, or interviewer]. In doing so, I/we understand that [name of interviewee]'s interview (or oral memoir) will be made available to researchers and may be quoted from, published and broadcast in any medium that [the archive, program or individual] shall deep appropriate.

I/we further acknowledge in making this gift that I/we are conveying all legal title and literary property rights which I/we as heir/heirs to [name of interviewee]'s interview (or oral memoir) as well as all rights, title, and interest in any copyright which may be secured now or under the laws later in force and effect in the United States of America. My/our conveyance of copyright encompasses the exclusive rights of reproduction, distribution, preparation of derivative works, public performances, public display as well as all renewals and extensions.

I, [name], agent for or duly appointed representative of [the archive, program or individual], accept the interview (or oral memoir) with [name of interviewee] for inclusion into the [archive or program].

_____   _____
[signature of agent/representative]   [signature of heir/heirs]

_____
[date]

DEED OF GIFT RELEASE FOR INTERVIEWER

[From John Neuenschwander, *Oral History and the Law* (2003)]

I, [name of interviewer], who served as an interviewer for the [name of project or sponsoring program or archive] and who conducted an interview or interviews with [name of interviewee] on or about [date] for which no legal releases were executed, do herein permanently give, convey and assign to [name of program or archive]. In doing so I understand that the interview (or oral memoir) with [name of interviewee] will be made available to researchers and may be quoted from, published or broadcast in any medium that the [name of program or archive] shall deem appropriate.

In making this gift I fully understand that I am conveying all legal title and literary property rights which I have or may be deemed to have in this interview or interviews (or oral memoir) as well as all my right, title and interest as joint author in any copyright which may be secured under the laws now or later in force and effect in the United States of America. My conveyance of copyright encompasses the exclusive rights of reproduction, distribution, preparation of derivative works, public performance, public display as well as all renewals and extensions.

I, [name], agent for or duly appointed representative of [the archive or program], accept the interview (or oral memoir) with [name of interviewee] for inclusion into [the archive or program].

_____   _____
[signature of interviewer]   [signature of agent/representative]

_____
[date]

DEED OF GIFT TO THE PUBLIC DOMAIN
[Senate Historical Office]

I, [name of interviewee], do hereby give to the [archives or organization] the recordings and transcripts of my interviews conducted on [dates].

I authorize the [archives or organization] to use the recordings and transcripts in such a manner as may best serve the educational and historical objectives of their oral history program.

In making this gift, I voluntarily convey ownership of the recordings and transcripts to the public domain.

_____   _____
Agent of Receiving Organization   Donor

_____
Date

INTERVIEWEE RELEASE FORM
[St. Andrew's Episcopal School, Potomac, Maryland]

I, [name of interviewee], do hereby give to the Saint Andrew's Episcopal School all right, title or interest in the tape-recorded interviews conducted by [name of interviewer] on [dates]. I understand that these interviews will be protected by copyright and deposited in Saint Andrew's Library and Archives for the use of future scholars. I also understand that the tapes and transcripts may be used in public presentations including but not limited to audio and visual documentaries, slide-tape presentations, exhibits or articles. This gift does not preclude any use that I myself want to make of the information in these recordings.

CHECK ONE:

____ Tapes and transcripts may be used without restriction

____ Tapes and transcripts are subject to the attached restriction

_____   _____
Signature of Interviewee   Date

_____
Address

_____
Telephone Number

Notes and References

CHAPTER 1: AN ORAL HISTORY OF OUR TIME

1. Charles T. Morrissey has grappled persuasively with the definition of oral history in his essays, "Why Call It 'Oral History'? Searching for Early Usage of a Generic Term," *Oral History Review* 8 (1980), 20–48; "Introduction," in *Oral History: An Interdisciplinary Anthology,* ed. David K. Dunaway and Willa K. Baum (Nashville: American Association for State and Local History, 1984, 1st ed.), xix–xxiii; and "Beyond Oral Evidence: Speaking (Con)structively about Oral History," *Archival Issues* 17 (November 2, 1992), 89–94.
2. See the Principles and Standards of the Oral History Association, which are reprinted as an appendix to this volume.
3. William W. Moss, "Oral History: What Is It and Where Did It Come From?" in, *The Past Meets the Present: Essays on Oral History,* ed., David Stricklin and Rebecca Sharpless (Lanham, Md: University Press of America, 1988) 5; Thucydides, *History of the Peloponnesian War* (New York: Penguin, 1972), 48. See also William W. Moss and Peter C. Mazikana, *Archives, Oral History and Oral Tradition: A RAMP [Records and Archives Management Programme] Study* (Paris: UNESCO, 1986), 2.
4. Iván Jaksíc, "Oral History in the Americas," *Journal of American History* 79 (September 1992), 590.
5. Paul Thompson, "Britain Strikes Back: Two Hundred Years of 'Oral History,'" *Oral History Association Newsletter* 15 (Summer 1981), 4–5; Paul Thompson, *The Voice of the Past: Oral History* (New York: Oxford University Press; 1978), 19, 25–26; Fritz Stern, ed., *The Varieties of History: From Voltaire to the Present* (New York: Vintage Books, 1973), 39.
6. David Hackett Fischer, *Paul Revere's Ride* (New York: Oxford University Press, 1994), 327–28; Dean Albertson, "Remembering Oral History's Beginning," *The Annual of the New England Association of Oral History* 1 (1987-88), 2.
7. Thompson, *Voice of the Past,* 46–47; Peter Novick, *That Noble Dream: The 'Objectivity Question' and the American Historical Profession* (Cambridge: Cambridge University Press, 1988), 21–46.
8. Donald A. Ritchie, *Press Gallery, Congress and the Washington Correspondents* (Cambridge: Harvard University Press, 1991), 81–83.
9. Donald A. Ritchie, "Oral History in the Federal Government," *Journal of American History* 74 (September 1987), 587–595; Ira Berlin, Marc Favreau, and Steven F. Miller, eds., *Remembering Slavery: African Americans Talk About Their Personal Experiences*

of Slavery and Emancipation (New York: New Press, 1998); Norman R. Yetman, "'Born in Slavery': An Introduction to the WPA Slave Narratives," *Library of Congress Information Bulletin* 60 (April 2001), 86–95. Many of the WPA interviews are accessible online via the Library of Congress' American Memory Web site: http://memory.loc.gov.

10. Stephen E. Everett, *Oral History Techniques and Procedures* (Washington: Center of Military History, 1992), 5–11; Forrest C. Pogue, *Pogue's War: Diaries of a WWII Combat Historian* (Lexington: University Press of Kentucky, 2001); H. Lew Wallace, "Forrest C. Pogue: A Biographical Sketch," *Filson Club Historical Quarterly* 60 (July 1986), 373–402; see also John Douglas Marshall, *Reconciliation Road: A Family Odyssey of War and Honor* (Syracuse, N.Y.: Syracuse University Press, 1993), for some of the controversies concerning S. L. A. Marshall's interviews and the conclusions he drew from them.

11. Joseph L. Mitchell, *Joe Gould's Secret* (New York: Viking Press, 1965), reprints the two *New Yorker* essays from 1942 and 1964, and was the basis for the motion picture *Joe Gould's Secret*. Winslow C. Watson referred to "oral history" in an address to the Vermont Historical Society in 1863, but Watson lacked the national audience and notoriety that the *New Yorker* gave to Gould. See Charles T. Morrissey, "Why Call It 'Oral History'?" 20–48.

12. Allan Nevins, *The Gateway to History* (Boston: Appleton-Century, 1938), iv; Ray Allen Billington, ed., *Allan Nevins on History* (New York: Charles Scribner's Sons, 1975), 209–10, 281–83, 288–93; Elizabeth I. Dixon, et al, "Definitions of Oral History," *Oral History at Arrowhead: The Proceedings of the First National Colloquium on Oral History* (Los Angeles: Oral History Association, 1969), 14.

13. Willa K. Baum, "A Brief History of Oral History," Address delivered at California State University, Fullerton, April 22, 1972; David Lance, *An Archive Approach to Oral History* (London: Imperial War Museum and International Association of Sound Archives, 1978).

14. Wolfgang Weber, *"Mass of Trash" or "Veins of Gold"? An Investigative Report on the Relationship Between Oral History and Archives* (Regensburg, Austria: S. Roderer Verlag, 2000), 21–24; Irina Sherbakova, "The Gulag in Memory," in Robert Perks and Alistair Thomson, eds., *The Oral History Reader* (New York: Routledge, 1998), 235–45.

15. Thompson, *Voice of the Past*, 55–59; Studs Terkel, *Hard Times; An Oral History of the Great Depression* (New York: Pantheon, 1970); *Working; People Talk About What They Do All Day and How They Feel About What They Do* (New York: Pantheon, 1974); and *"The Good War": An Oral History of World War Two* (New York: Pantheon, 1984); Alex Haley, *Roots: The Saga of an American Family* (Garden City, N.Y.: Doubleday, 1976); and "Black History, Oral History, and Genealogy," in David K. Dunaway and Willa K. Baum, eds., *Oral History: An Interdisciplinary History*, 2nd ed. (Walnut Creek, Calif.: AltaMira, 1996), 258–79.

16. Sally Adams with Wynford Hicks, *Interviewing for Journalists* (New York: Routledge, 2001); Ronald J. Grele, "Why Call It 'Oral History'?" Some Ruminations from the Field," *Pennsylvania History* 60 (October 1993), 506–9.

17. Scott Sherman, "Caro's Way," *Columbia Journalism Review* (May/June 2002), 68.

18. Reporting on an oral history project in three Philadelphia neighborhoods, Charles Hardy noted, "We have found that the best interviewers often come from the enthusiastic amateur. . . . The historian generally comes from or has been trained in academic culture and academic style which raises the problem of establishing rapport,

particularly when the time with the interviewee is limited." Charles Hardy, "The Urban Archives' 'Discovering Community History Project,'" *Oral History Association Newsletter* 15 (Winter 1981), 4-5; Jean Lester, *Faces of Alaska from Barrow to Wrangell: A Glimpse of History Through Paintings, Photographs, and Oral Histories* (Ester, Alaska: Poppies Publishing, 1992); Dr. Junichi Saga, *Memories of Wind and Waves: A Self-Portrait of Lakeside Japan* (New York: Kodansha America, 2002), 13–17.

19. Susan Paterno, "The Question Man," *American Journalism Review* (October 2000), 52.

20. Marc Bloch, *The Historian's Craft* (New York: Knopf, 1953), 10; James MacGregor Burns, "The Truth of the Battlefield," *New York Times Book Review* (March 6, 1994), 34.

21. Gore Vidal, *Screening History* (Cambridge: Harvard University Press, 1992), 88. For an example of the blind spots in written history, see Lael Morgan, "Writing Minorities Out of History: Black Builders of the Alcan Highway," *Alaska History* 7 (Fall 1992), 1–13.

22. Louise A. Tilly, "People's History and Social Science History," "Between Social Sciences: Responses to Louise A. Tilly by Paul Thompson, Luisa Passerini, Isabell Bertaux-Wiame, and Alessandro Portelli," and "Louise A. Tilly's Response," *International Journal of Oral History* 6 (February 1985), 5–46; David Lodge, *Out of the Shelter* (New York: Penguin, 1989), 185.

23. Michael Burlingame, ed., *An Oral History of Abraham Lincoln: John G. Nicolay's Interviews and Essays* (Carbondale: Southern Illinois University Press, 1996), xv–xviii.

24. Alexander Stille, "Prospecting for Truth in the Ore of Memory: Oral History is Gaining New Respect Through Insights into Its Distortions," *New York Times,* March 10, 2001.

25. Dixon, et al, "Definitions of Oral History," 3–8; see also Martha J. Ross, "Interviewer or Intervener: Interpretation in the Oral History Interview," *Maryland Historian* 13 (Fall/Winter 1982), 3–6.

26. Joseph Roddy, "Oral History: Soundings from the Sony Age," *RF* [Rockefeller Foundation] *Illustrated* 3 (May 1977), 4; E. Culpepper Clark, Michael J. Hyde, and Eva M. McMahon, "Communication in the Oral History Interview: Investigating Problems of Interpreting Oral Data," *International Journal of Oral History* 1 (February 1980), 29; Saul Benison, "Oral History: A Personal View," in Edward Clark, ed., *Modern Methods in the History of Medicine* (New York: Oxford, 1971), 291; Ronald J. Grele, Introduction to the *International Annual of Oral History, 1990: Subjectivity and Multiculturalism in Oral History* (New York: Greenwood Press, 1992), 2; and Grele, ed., *Envelopes of Sound* (New York: Praeger, 1991).

27. Perry Blatz, "Craftsmanship and Flexibility in Oral History: A Pluralistic Approach to Methodology and Theory," *The Public Historian* 12 (Fall 1990), 7–22; Ross, "Interviewer or Intervener," 3–6; Michael Frisch, *A Shared Authority: Essays on the Craft and Meaning of Oral and Public History* (Albany: State University of New York Press, 1990), xx–xxiii; Donald A. Ritchie, "An Interview with Michael Frisch," *OHMAR Newsletter* 11 (Fall 1988), 4–9.

28. Eva McMahan, *Elite Oral History Interviewing* (Tuscaloosa: University of Alabama Press, 1989); Sherna Gluck and Daphne Patai, eds., *Women's Words: The Feminist Practice of Oral History* (New York: Routledge, 1991); Alessandro Portelli, *The Death of Luigi Trastulli and Other Stories* (Albany: State University of New York Press, 1991); and Terry L. Birdwhistell, "Re-Educating an Oral Historian: Putting Practice Into Theory," unpublished paper, April, 26 1990.

29. Herman Kahn, review, *American Historical Review* 73 (June 1968), 1471.

30. Gluck and Patai, eds., *Women's Words,* 226–227; see also Charles T. Morrissey, "Riding a Mule Through the 'Terminological Jungle': Oral History and the Problems of

Nomenclature," *Oral History Review* 12 (1984), 13–28.

31. Elizabeth Kolbert, "Memories Wanted for History of Ellis Island," *New York Times*, November, 24 1985.

32. Lawrence S. Ritter, *The Glory of Their Times: The Story of the Early Days of Baseball Told by the Men Who Played It* (New York: Macmillan, 1966), xvii–xviii, 62.

33. John Neuenschwander, "Oral Historians and Long-Term Memory," in Dunaway and Baum, eds., *Oral History*, 1st ed., 324–32; James W. Lomax and Charles T. Morrissey, "The Interview as Inquiry for Psychiatrists and Oral Historians: Convergence and Divergence in Skills and Goals," in *The Public Historian* 11 (Winter 1989), 17–24; William C. Davis, *Jefferson Davis: The Man and His Hour* (New York: HarperCollins, 1991) 687.

34. Robert N. Butler, "The Life Review: An Interpretation of Reminiscence in the Aged," in Robert Kastenbaum, ed., *New Thoughts on Old Age* (New York: Springer, 1964), 265–280.

35. "Memory has always proven difficult for historians to confront," Michael Frisch noted in his essay, "The Memory of History"(*A Shared Authority*, 15–27); see also David Thelen, "Memory and History," *Journal of American History* 75 (March 1989), 1117–29.

36. Diane Manning, *Hill Country Teacher: Oral Histories from the One-Room School and Beyond* (Boston: Twayne, 1990), xx–xxi.

37. Ruth Young Watt, chief clerk of the Senate Permanent Subcommittee on Investigations, interviewed by Donald A. Ritchie, 1979, transcripts, Senate Historical Office Oral History Project, Library of Congress, Washington, D.C.

38. On Kirk's memory, the historian Gordon Prange commented: "Pearl Harbor's happening the next day impressed the memory upon him." Gordon Prange, *At Dawn We Slept: The Untold Story of Pearl Harbor* (New York: McGraw-Hill, 1981), 719–20.

39. See Jean Piaget, *Memory and Intelligence* (New York: Basic, 1973); Edmund Blair Bolles, *Remembering and Forgetting: Inquiries into the Nature of Memory* (New York: Walker, 1988); and W. Walter Menninger, "Memory and History: What Can You Believe?" *Archival Issues: Journal of the Midwest Archives Conference* 21 (1996), 97–106.

40. Nigel Hamilton, *JFK, Reckless Youth* (New York: Random House, 1992), 532–33.

41. See Jaclyn Jeffrey and Glenace Edwall, eds., *Memory and History: Essays on Recalling and Interpreting Evidence* (Lanham, Md.: University Press of America, 1994).

42. David Brinkley, *Washington Goes to War* (New York: Knopf, 1988); and "The Conversation: Arthur Schlesinger, Jr. Interviews David Brinkley," *Washington Post Magazine* (April 10, 1988), 29.

43. See Jacklyn L. Jeffrey, "The Waco Tornado of 1953 as Symbol of Modernization and Rite of Initiation," *Sound Historian: Journal of the Texas Oral History Association* 1 (Fall 1993), 39.

44. Joyce Appleby, Lynn Hunt and Margaret Jacob reexamine memory and perspective in *Telling the Truth About History* (New York: W.W. Norton, 1994), 254–61.

45. William Allen White, *A Puritan in Babylon: The Story of Calvin Coolidge* (New York: Macmillan, 1938), vii.

46. David Cho, "N.Va. Exhibit Examines History at a Crossroads," *Washington Post*, May 19, 2002. See Charles T. Morrissey, "More Than Embers of Sentiment: Railroad Nostalgia and Oral History Memories of the 1920s and 1930s," *The Public Historian* 15 (Summer 1993), 29–35.

47. Joel Gardner, "An Interview with Linda Shopes," *OHMAR Newsletter* 15 (Fall 1992), 9, 11; Linda Shopes, "Beyond Trivia and Nostalgia: Collaborating in the Construction of a Local History," *International Journal of Oral History* 5 (November 1984), 151–158.

48. Ronald Steel, "Harry of Sunnybrook Farm," *The New Republic* (August, 10 1992) 34.

49. Jacquelyn Dowd Hall, James Leloudis, Robert Korstad, Mary Murphy, Lu Ann Jones, Christopher B. Daly, *Like a Family: The Making of a Southern Cotton Mill World* (Chapel Hill: University of North Carolina Press, 1987), xv; see also Selma Leydesdorff, "The Screen of Nostalgia: Oral History and the Ordeal of Working-Class Jews in Amsterdam," *International Journal of Oral History* 7 (June 1986), 109–115.

50. Barbara Erskine, "Loss and Grief in Oral History," *Oral History Association of Australia Journal* 18 (1996), 1–6; Ken Ringle, "People Were Drowning All Around Us," *Washington Post,* May 22, 1994; Rhoda G. Lewin, ed., *Witnesses to the Holocaust: An Oral History* (Boston: Twayne, 1990).

51. David Glassberg, "Public History and the Study of Memory," *Public Historian* 18 (Spring 1996), 7–23; John Bodnar, *Remaking America: Public Memory, Commemoration, and Patriotism in the Twentieth Century* (Princeton, N.J.: Princeton University Press, 1992);

52. See Robert R. Weyeneth, "History, He Wrote: Murder, Politics, and the Challenges of Public History in a Community with a Secret," *The Public Historian* 16 (Spring 1994), 51–73.

53. Portelli, *The Death of Luigi Trastulli and Other Stories,* 1, 15, 20, 51–52.

54. Barbara Allen, "Oral History: The Folk Connection," in Stricklin and Sharpless, eds., *The Past Meets the Present,* 15–26; see also William Lynwood Montell, *The Saga of Coe Ridge: A Study in Oral History* (Knoxville: University of Tennessee Press, 1970), vii–xxi.

55. Micaela di Leonardo, "Oral History as Ethnographic Encounter," *Oral History Review* 15 (Spring 1987), 1–20; Kathyrn Marie Dudley, "In the Archive, In the Field: What Kind of Documentation Is an 'Oral History'?" in Mary Chamberlain and Paul Thompson, eds., *Narrative and Genre* (New York: Routledge, 1998), 160–66; see also Peter Bartis, *Folklife & Fieldwork: A Layman's Introduction to Field Techniques* (Washington, D.C.: American Folklife Center, 1979); and Harry F. Wolcott, *Ethnography: A Way of Seeing* (Walnut Creek, Calif.: AltaMira, 1999).

56. Barbara Allen, "Story in Oral History: Clues to Historical Consciousness," *Journal of American History* 79 (September 1992), 606–11; William Schneider, *So They Understand: Cultural Issues in Oral History* (Logan: Utah State University Press, 2002), 37–52.

57. William Schneider, "Expanding the Definition of Oral History with Examples from Alaska and South Africa," in Philippe Denis and James Worthington, eds. *The Power of Oral History: Memory, Healing and Development* (Pietermaritzburg, South Africa: International Oral History Association, 2002), volume 2: 839–49; Schneider, *So They Understand,* 66.

58. "American Folklife Center Collects Reactions to the September 11, 2001, Terrorist Attacks," *Folklife Center News* 223 (Fall 2001), 3–4; *Wall Street Journal,* November 30, 2001; Mary Marshall Clark, "The September 11, 2001, Oral History Narrative and Memory Project: A First Report," *Journal of American History* 89 (September 2002), 569–79.

59. See James Hoopes, *Oral History: An Introduction for Students* (Chapel Hill: University of North Carolina Press, 1979), 33–40.

60. Rick Harmon, "Oral Histories of the Federal Courts: The Oregon Experience," *Western Legal History* 1 (Summer/Fall 1988), 277–284.

61. American Historical Association, "Statement on Interviewing for Historical Documentation," *Statement on Standards of Professional Conduct* (Washington, D.C.: American Historical Association, 1989).

62. See Daniel J. Walkowitz, "On Public History...," *Organization of American Historians*

Newsletter 12 (August 1984), 11; and James B. Gardner and Peter S. LaPaglia, eds., *Public History: Essays from the Field* (Malabar, Fla.: Krieger, 1999).

63. See Donald A. Ritchie, "The Oral History/Public History Connection," in *Public History: An Introduction,* ed. Barbara J. Howe and Emory L. Kemp (Malabar, Fla.: Krieger, 1986), 57–69.

64. "Oral History Survey," *The Federalist: Newsletter of the Society for History in the Federal Government* 4 (September 1983), 1, 7; Ritchie. "Oral History in the Federal Government," 587–95.

65. J. Todd Moye, "The Tuskegee Airmen Oral History Project and Oral History in the National Park Service," *Journal of American History* 89 (September 2002), 580–87; Public Law 106–380; Veterans' Oral History Project: http://www.loc.gov/folklife/vets/.

66. Hilary Stout, "Historians-for-Hire Chronicle Lives of Ordinary Folks," *Wall Street Journal,* December 29, 1998; L. Elizabeth Beattie, "The Advent of Independents: Oral Historians Who Stand Alone," *Oral History Association Newsletter* 26 (Summer 1992), 1.

67. Ibid., 3; Susan Q. Stranahan, "Lending an Ear to Corporate History," *Philadelphia Inquirer,* September 21, 1992; "COH Starts Pioneer Mill Company Project," *Oral History Recorder: Newsletter of the Center for Oral History, Social Science Research Institute, University of Hawaii at Manoa* 18 (Summer 2001), 1.

68. Enid Hart Douglass, "Corporate History: Why?" *The Public Historian* 3 (Summer 1981), 75–80.

69. "Oral History Supports Land Claims in West," *Oral History Association Newsletter* 17 (Fall 1983), 1, 8.

70. Charles T. Morrissey, "Public Historians and Oral History: Problems of Concept and Methods," *The Public Historian* 2 (Winter 1980), 22–29; see also Charles T. Morrissey, "Truman and the Presidency: Records and Oral Recollections," *The American Archivist* 28 (January 1965), 53–61.

71. James Morris, "The Historian's Craft," *The Woodrow Wilson Center Report* 4 (September 1992), 4–5.

72. Ritchie, "The Public History/Oral History Connection," 57–69; Donald A. Ritchie, *James M. Landis: Dean of the Regulators* (Cambridge: Harvard University Press, 1980).

73. Charles L. Sullivan, *Gathering at the River: South Mississippi's Camp Meetings* (Perkinston: Mississippi Gulf Coast Community College Press, 1990), 10–11.

CHAPTER 2: SETTING UP AN ORAL HISTORY PROJECT

1. If all else fails, a follow-up session may be conducted by telephone—although it is a poor substitute for a face-to-face oral history.

2. L. Elisabeth Beattie, "The Advent of Independents: Oral Historians Who Stand Alone," *Oral History Association Newsletter* 26 (Summer 1992), 6.

3. See Joe Rossi, "Who Was That Masked Interviewer?" *Oral History Recorder; Newsletter of the Center for Oral History, University of Hawaii at Manoa* 8 (Fall 1991), 1.

4. Debra Bernhardt, *Working Womenroots: An Oral History Primer* (Ann Arbor, Michigan: Institute of Labor and Industrial Relations, 1980); Stephen E. Everett, *Oral History Techniques and Procedures* (Washington, D.C.: Center of Military History, 1992); and Heather Huyck, David Nathanson and Blair Hubbard, *Oral History in the National Park Service* (Harper's Ferry, W.V.: National Park Service, 1984).

5. "Nuclear History Program Examines Past Policies of Nuclear Arms Management and Explores Assumptions About Nuclear Detente," *Oral History Association Newsletter* 23 (Spring 1989), 1, 8.

6. See, for example, Charles Scribner, Jr., *In the Company of Writers: A Life in Publishing,*

based on the oral histories by Joel R. Gardner (New York: Macmillan, 1990).

7. Dean Albertson, "Remembering Oral History's Beginning," *The Annual of the New England Oral History Association* 1 (1987/88), 3.

8. Linda Hoxit Raxter, H-Oralhist, May 29, 2002.

9. Charles Hardy, "Minidisk Versus Audio Cassette: Is It Time to Make the Leap?" *OHMAR Newsletter* 22 (Fall 2001), 6–7.

10. Kevin Mulroy, "Preserving Oral History Interviews on Tape: Curatorial Techniques and Managing Procedures," *International Journal of Oral History* 7 (November 1986), 189–197.

11. For the advantages and disadvantages of group interviewing, see Robert K. Merton, Marjorie Fiske, and Patricia L. Kendall, *The Focused Interview: A Manual of Problems and Procedures* (New York: Free Press, 1990), 135–69.

12. Michael Kenny, "The Patron-Client Relationship in Interviewing: An Anthropological View," *Oral History Review* 15 (Spring 1987), 75.

13. Dale Treleven, *TAPE (Time Access to Pertinent Excerpts) System: A Method For Producing Oral History Interviews & Other Sound Recordings* (Madison: State Historical Society of Wisconsin, 1979).

14. Deborah Reid, "Talk Ain't Cheap: How to Get a Perfect Transcript," Techni-Type brochure.

15. Elliot G. Mishler, *Research Interviewing: Context and Narrative* (Cambridge: Harvard University Press, 1986), 47–51; Henry H. Glassie, *Passing the Time in Ballymenone: Culture and History of an Ulster County* (Philadelphia: University of Pennsylvania Press, 1982), 40.

16. David Crystal, *The Cambridge Encyclopedia of the English Language* (New York: Cambridge University Press, 1995), 214.

17. David Henige, *Oral Historiography* (New York: Longman, 1982), 107; Raphael Samuel, "Perils of the Transcript," in Robert Perks and Alistair Thomson, eds., *The Oral History Reader* (New York: Routledge, 1998), 388–92; Kate Moore, "Perversion of the Word: The Role of Transcripts in Oral History," *Words and Silence: Bulletin of the International Oral History Association* 1 (June 1997), 14–35, and responses Michael Frisch and Rosemary Block, 26–35; Michael Agar, "Transcript Handling: An Ethnographic Strategy," *Oral History Review* 15 (1986), 209–19.

18. Carl M. Marcy, interviewed by Donald A. Ritchie, September 14 to November 16, 1983, transcripts, Senate Historical Office, 24–25, Library of Congress, Washington, D.C.

19. *The Chicago Manual of Style*, 14th ed. (Chicago: University of Chicago Press, 1993).

20. Shannon Page, "The Invisible Participant: The Role of the Transcriber in Interpreting Meaning in Oral History Research," in Philippe Denis and James Worthington, eds., *The Power of Oral History: Memory, Healing and Development* (Pietermaritzburg, South Africa: University of Natal, 2002), vol. 2: 825–38.

21. Katherine R. Martin and Charles E. Martin, "Transcription Style: Choices and Variables at the Appalachian Oral History Project," *International Journal of Oral History* 6 (June 1985), 126–128.

22. Nell Irvin Painter, *The Narrative of Hosea Hudson: His Life as a Negro Communist in the South* (Cambridge: Harvard University Press, 1979), 1–44.

23. John A. Neuenschwander, *Oral History and the Law*, rev. ed. (Albuquerque, N.M.: Oral History Association, 1993), 16–35; John A. Neuenschwander, "Legal Release Agreements: A Closer Look," *Oral History Association Newsletter* 32 (Spring 1998), 1, 4–5.

24. Neuenschwander, *Oral History and the Law*, 19–22.

25. Responses to an H-Oralhist request by Greta Reisel Browning, September 19, 2002.

26. John Noble Wilford, "Fun and Comradeship," *New York Times Book Review* (July 7, 1985), 3; George Tames, *Eye on Washington: The Presidents Who've Known Me* (New York: HarperCollins, 1990).

27. Alben Barkley, *That Reminds Me* (Garden City, N.Y.: Doubleday, 1954); Donald A. Ritchie, "Alben W. Barkley: The President's Man," in *First Among Equals: Outstanding Senate Leaders of the Twentieth Century,* ed. Richard A. Baker and Roger H. Davidson (Washington, D.C.: Congressional Quarterly, 1991), 127–62.

28. Neuenschwander, *Oral History and the Law,* 5–12.

29. Sherna Berger Gluck, Donald A. Ritchie, and Bret Eynon, "Reflections on Oral History in the New Millennium: Roundtable Comments," *Oral History Review* 26 (Summer/Fall 1999), 1–28.

30. "The Rocky Gap High School Oral History and Technology Project," 110; Tamara Kennelly, "Oral History on the Internet: Narratives from Pioneering Black Students," In Denis and Worthington, eds. *The Power of Oral History,* vol. 1: 86–99.

31. John A. Neuenschwander, "Legal Considerations in Electronic Publishing," *Oral History Association Newsletter* 28 (Fall 1994), 1, 3–4; John A. Neuenschwander, "Putting Interviews on the Internet? A Look at Key Issues," *Oral History Association Newsletter* 33 (Fall 1998), 4–6.

CHAPTER 3: CONDUCTING INTERVIEWS

1. Clifford Terry, "The Real Studs," *Chicago Tribune* (April 5, 1992); Ken Adelman, "The Voice in the Box," *Washingtonian* 35 (March 2000), 32.

2. Ruth Finnegan, "A Note on Oral Tradition and Historical Evidence," in David K. Dunaway and Willa K. Baum, eds., *Oral History: An Interdisciplinary Anthology* (Nashville: American Association of State and Local History, 1984), 113–114; see also Linda Shopes, "Beyond Trivia and Nostalgia: Collaborating in the Construction of a Local History," *International Journal of Oral History* 5 (November 1984), 151–58.

3. Donald A. Ritchie, "Beyond the *Congressional Record*: Congress and Oral History," *Maryland Historian* 13 (Fall\Winter 1982), 7–16.

4. John Brady, *The Craft of Interviewing* (New York: Vintage, 1977), 155.

5. Shirley Biagi, *Interviews That Work: A Practical Guide for Journalists* (Belmont, Calif.: Wadsworth, 1986), 56.

6. Paul Grabowicz, "Researching People on the Internet," *Online Journalism Review* (July 24, 2002), http://www.ojr.org.

7. See Edward D. Ives, *The Tape-Recorded Interview: A Manual for Field Workers in Folklore and Oral History* (Knoxville: University of Tennessee Press, 1980), 33–47.

8. David King Dunaway, "Field Recording Oral History," *Oral History Review* 15 (Spring 1987), 34.

9. Sherna Gluck, "What's So Special about Women? Women's Oral History," in Dunaway and Baum, eds., *Oral History,* 231.

10. Shirley Biagi, *Interviews That Work: A Practical Guide for Journalists* (Belmont, Calif.: Wadsworth, 1986), 82–85. A useful collection of sample questions for recording family history, and models for other types of interviewing, can be found in William P. Fletcher, *Recording Your Family History: A Guide to Preserving Oral History with Videotape, Audio Tape, Suggested Topics and Questions, Interview Techniques* (New York: Dodd, Mead, 1986.)

11. Charles T. Morrissey, "The Two-Sentence Format as an Interviewing Technique in Oral History Fieldwork," *Oral History Review* 15 (Spring 1987), 43–53.

12. Elliot G. Mishler, *Research Interviewing: Context and Narrative* (Cambridge: Harvard

University Press, 1986), 117–135; for the "human element" in fieldwork interviewing, see Robert A. Georges and Michael O. Jones, *People Studying People: The Human Element in Fieldwork* (Berkeley: University of California Press, 1980).

13. William Cutler III, "Accuracy in Oral History Interviewing," in David K. Dunaway and Willa K. Baum, eds., *Oral History: An Interdisciplinary Anthology* (Nashville: American Association of State and Local History, 1984), 82;. Although it is directed at pollsters, anyone asking questions should also consult Stanley L. Payne's classic and oft-reprinted account *The Art of Asking Questions* (Princeton, N.J.: Princeton University Press, 1951).

14. William W. Moss, *Oral History Program Manual* (New York: Praeger, 1974), 43.

15. Studs Terkel, *Talking to Myself: A Memoir of My Times* (New York: Pantheon, 1977), 64–70.

16. Professor Timothy P. Maga interviewed Secretary Muskie for his book on Jimmy Carter's foreign policies.

17. Ronald Steel, "The Biographer as Detective: What Walter Lippmann Preferred to Forget," *New York Times Book Review*, July 21, 1985.

18. Louis Achincloss, *The House of the Prophet* (Boston: Houghton Mifflin, 1980), 19.

19. Brian Lamb, *Booknotes: Stories from American History* (New York: Public Affairs, 2001), 257.

20. Ron Chernow, *Titan: The Life of John D. Rockefeller, Sr.* (New York: Random House, 1998), xiv–xv, xix–xxii, 615–19.

21. Brady, *The Craft of Interviewing*, 104; Oscar Wilde, *An Ideal Husband*, Act 1.

22. Percora's son, Louis, and nephew, Louis Stephens, recalled his acute memory and persistent reminiscing in interviews that I conducted while writing "The Pecora Wall Street Expose," in *Congress Investigates: A Documented History, 1972–1974*, ed. Arthur M. Schlesinger, Jr. and Roger Bruns (New York: R. R. Bowker, 1975), 4:2555–732.

23. For a case study, see Mary Elizabeth Aube, "Oral History and the Remembered World: Cultural Determinants from French Canada," *International Journal of Oral History* 10 (February 1989), 31–49.

24. Ives, *The Tape-Recorded Interview*, 74–79.

25. Pete Daniel, *Deep'n as It Come* (New York: Oxford University Press, 1977); Andrea Hammer, "Federal Visions/Regional Revisions: Oral History's Role in Revisiting FSA Portraits of Southern Maryland"(paper delivered to the Oral History Association meeting, October 1992, Cleveland, Ohio). Another creative merging of oral history and visual imagery is the work of the Alaskan portrait artist Jean Lester, who interviews her subjects as she paints them to learn more about their personalities and gain a deeper perspective. See Jean Lester, *Faces of Alaska* (Ester, Alaska: Poppies Publishing, 1988), and *Faces of Alaska from Barrow to Wrangell* (Ester, Alaska: Poppies Publishing, 1992).

26. "Twenty Years of Oral History," *Oral History Recorder* (newsletter of the Center for Oral History, University of Hawaii at Manoa) 13 (Spring 1996), 1.

27. James West Davidson and Mark Hamilton Lytle, *After the Fact: The Art of Historical Detection* (New York: Knopf, 1982), 169–204.

28. Oral History Association, *Evaluation Guidelines* (Carlisle, Penn.: Oral History Association, 2001), 2.

29. William M. Hammond, *Public Affairs: The Military and the Media, 1968–1973* (Washington, D.C.: U.S. Army Center of Military History, 1996), 479.

30. For an example of this type of strategic planning, see Mary Jo Deering, "Oral History and School Integration Research: A Case Study," *Oral History Review* 7 (1979), 27–41.

31. John T. Chirban, *Interviewing in Depth: The Interactive-Relational Approach* (Thousand Oaks, Calif.: Sage, 1996), xii, 90.

32. James Holstein and Jaber F. Gubrium, *The Active Interview* (Thousand Oaks, Calif.: Sage, 1995), 5; Mary J. Festle, "Qualifying the Quantifying: Assessing the Quality of Life of Lung Transplant Recipients," *Oral History Review* 29 (Winter/Spring 2002), 85.

33. *Washington Post,* February 20, 2001; Marc Pachter, ed., *Telling Lives: The Biographer's Art* (Philadelphia: University of Pennsylvania Press, 1981); see also Theodore Rosengarten, *All God's Dangers: The Life of Nate Shaw* (New York: Knopf, 1974).

34. Donald A. Ritchie, "Learning to Listen," *Southwest Oral History Association Newsletter* 13 (Summer 1987), 1–7; Kathryn Anderson and Dana C. Jack, "Learning to Listen: Interview Techniques and Analysis," in Sherna Berger Gluck and Daphni Patai, eds., *Women's Words: The Feminist Practice of Oral History* (New York: Routledge, 1991), 11–26.

35. See Martha J. Ross, "Interviewer or Intervener: Interpretation in the Oral History Interview," *Maryland Historian* 13 (Fall/Winter 1982), 3–6.

36. Moss, *Oral History Program Manual,* 39–40.

37. Gerald Posner, *Case Closed: Lee Harvey Oswald and the Assassination of JFK* (New York: Random House, 1993), 235.

38. Kate Darian-Smith and Paula Hamilton, eds., *Memory and History in Twentieth-Century Australia* (New York: Oxford University Press, 1994), 13; Judith Miller, "Erasing the Past: Europe's Amnesia about the Holocaust," *New York Times Magazine* (November 16, 1986), 3–15; Daon and Petrie Kladstrup, *Wine and War: The French, the Nazis, and the Battle for France's Greatest Treasure* (New York: Broadway, 2001), 7.

39. Sally Adams with Wynford Hicks, *Interviewing for Journalists* (New York: Routledge, 2001), 32–33; Amelia Fry correspondence with the author, August 1993.

40. Mike Walters, "Report on 'Siberia' Interviews," *Working Together: A Regional Approach to Community Traditions and History in Idaho, Newsletter* 5 (Fall 1982), 4.

41. Richard F. Fenno, Jr., "Observation, Context, and Sequence in the Study of Politics," *American Political Science Review* 80 (March 1986), 2–15.

42. Ives, *The Tape-Recorded Interview* 79–81.

43. Walter Liniger, "The Original Down Home Blues Show," *Oral History Association Newsletter* 22 (Spring 1988), 1.

CHAPTER 4: USING ORAL HISTORY
IN RESEARCH AND WRITING

1. "Statement on Interviewing for Historical Documentation," *Statement on Professional Conduct* (Washington: American Historical Association, 1990), 25–27; *Perspectives: The American Historical Association Newsletter* 27 (October 1989), 8.

2. Barbara Tuchman, "Distinguishing the Significant from the Insignificant," in David K. Dunaway and Willa K. Baum, eds., *Oral History: An Interdisciplinary Anthology,* 2nd ed. (Walnut Creek, Calif.: AltaMira, 1996), 96–97; Shirley Biagi, *Interviews That Work: A Practical Guide for Journalists* (Belmont, Calif.: Wadsworth, 1986), 16–19.

3. Barth Healey, "'I'm Not One of Those Who Say Kissinger Is Paranoid,' Mr. Nixon Said," *New York Times Sunday Book Review* (September 6, 1992), 20.

4. Martha Ross has cited this incident frequently in oral history workshops.

5. Donald A. Ritchie, Holly Cowan Shulman, Richard S. Kirkendall, and Terry L. Birdwhistell, "Interviews as Historical Evidence: A Discussion of New Standards of Documentation and Access," *The History Teacher* 24 (February 1991), 226–228.

6. The interview with Sen. Fong was conducted by Michaelyn P. Chou of the University of Hawaii. See Donald A. Ritchie, "Beyond the *Congressional Record*: Congress and

Oral History," *The Maryland Historian* 13 (Fall/Winter 1982), 7–16.

7. See Ronald J. Grele, "Why Call It Oral History? Some Ruminations from the Field," *Pennsylvania History* 60 (October 1993), 506–9.

8. Philip Brooks's remarks are included in Elizabeth I. Dixon, et al, "Definitions of Oral History," *Oral History at Arrowhead: The Proceedings of the First National Colloquium on Oral History* (Los Angeles: Oral History Association, 1969), 6–7; see also Ronald J. Grele, "Introduction," *International Annual of Oral History, 1990: Subjectivity and Multiculturalism in Oral History* (Westport, Conn.: Greenwood, 1992), 1–8.

9. Lewis L. Gould, ed. *Watching Television Come of Age: The New York Times Review by Jack Gould* (Austin: University of Texas Press, 2002).

10. See for example Robert W. Cherny, "Constructing a Radical Identity: History, Memory, and the Seafaring Stories of Harry Bridges," *Pacific Historical Review* 70 (November 2001), 571–99.

11. Emmanuel LeRoy Ladurie, *Montaillou: The Promised Land of Error* (New York: Vintage, 1979).

12. John C. Dann, *The Revolution Remembered: Eyewitness Accounts of the War for Independence* (Chicago: University of Chicago Press, 1977), xv–xxi; see also Elizabeth A. Perkins, *Border Life: Experience and Memory in the Revolutionary Ohio Valley* (Chapel Hill: University of North Carolina Press, 1998); and Charles T. Morrissey, "Beyond Oral Evidence: Speaking (Con)structively about Oral History," *Archival Issues* 17 (November 2, 1992), 90.

13. "Stewart E, McClure, Chief Clerk, Senate Committee on Labor, Education, and Public Welfare," interviewed by Donald A. Ritchie for the Senate Historical Office, December 1982–May 1983, transcripts, Library of Congress, 118.

14. John A. Neuenschwander, *Oral History and the Law,* 3rd ed. (Carlisle, Penn.: Oral History Association, 2002); Joan Fairweather, "Stories Matter: Oral History and Land Claims in Canada and South America" in Philippe Denis and James Worthington, eds., *The Power of Oral History: Memory, Healing and Development* (Pietmaritzburg, South Africa: University of Natal, 2002), 611–26.

15. Bongani Finca, "Learning to Bless Our Memories," in Philippe Denis, ed., *Orality, Memory and the Past: Listening to the Black Clergy under Colonialism and Apartheid* (Pietermaritzburg, South Africa: Cluster Publications, 2000), 16.

16. Ritchie, et al, "Interviews as Historical Evidence," 223–38.

17. Dan K. Utley, "From the Ground Up: Oral History and Historical Archaeology," *Sound Historian: Journal of the Texas Oral History Association* 1 (Fall 1993), 24.

18. See T. G. Ashplant, "Anecdote as Narrative Resource in Working-Class Life Stories: Parody, Dramatization and Sequence," in Mary Chamberlain and Paul Thompson, eds., *Narrative and Genre* (New York: Routledge, 1998), 99–113.

19. Donald A. Ritchie, "Learning to Listen," *Southwest Oral History Association Newsletter* (Summer 1987), 1, 3–7.

20. Blair Worden, "Lyrical Historian," *New York Review of Books* 40 (July 15, 1993), 12; Johnson quoted in Christopher Matthews, *Hardball: How Politics Is Played—Told by One Who Knows the Game* (New York: Summit, 1988), 133.

21. "Southern History and the Politics of Recent Memory: Responses to the C. Vann Woodward Interview," *Radical History Review* 38 (1987), 143–51.

22. Kathleen M. Blee, "Evidence, Empathy, and Ethics: Lessons from Oral Histories of the Klan," *Journal of American History* 80 (September 1993), 143–51.

23. Allan Nevins, "Oral History: How and Why It was Born," in Dunaway and Baum, eds., *Oral History,* 34.

24. See Ronald J. Grele, "On Using Oral History Collections: An Introduction," *Journal of American History* 74 (September 1987), 570–78; and Allen Smith, *Directory of Oral History Collections* (Phoenix: Onyx, 1988).

25. See the appendix on *Internet Resources.*

26. Mark A. Stoler, *George C. Marshall: Soldier-Statesman of the American Century* (Boston: Twayne, 1989). A part from his four-volume biography of Marshall, Pogue's interviews were published in Larry I. Bland, et al, eds., *George C. Marshall Interviews and Reminiscences for Forrest C. Pogue* (Lexington, Va.: George C. Marshall Research Foundation, 1991).

27. Arthur M. Schlesinger, Jr. *Robert Kennedy and His Times* (Boston: Houghton Mifflin, 1979), I:xv.; Lynn A. Bonfield, "Conversations with Arthur M. Schlesinger, Jr.: The Use of Oral History," *The American Archivist* 43 (Fall 1980), 466.

28. Sherna Berger Gluck, "We Will Not Be Another Algeria: Women's Mass Organizations, Changing Consciousness, and the Potential for Women's Liberation in a Future Palestinian State," *International Annual of Oral History,* 1990, 225.

29. William W. Moss, "Anonymity of Sources in Oral History," *Oral History Association Newsletter* 23 (Fall 1989), 1, 8.

30. Oral History Association, *Evaluation Guidelines* (Los Angeles: Oral History Association, 1992), 2.

31. Howard E. McCurdy, *Inside NASA: High Technology and Organizational Change in the U.S. Space Program* (Baltimore: Johns Hopkins University Press, 1993), 189.

32. Joseph Roddy, "Oral History: Soundings from the Sony Age," *RF [Rockefeller Foundation] Illustrated,* 3 (May 177); Charles T. Morrissey, "Oral History and the Boundaries of Fiction," *The Public Historian* 7 (Spring 1985), 42.

33. Morrissey, "Oral History and the Boundaries of Fiction," 43; Robert H. Ferrell and Francis H. Heller, "Plain Faking?" *American Heritage* (May/June 1995), 14, 16.

34. Cullom Davis, "Success and Excess: Oral History at High Tide," in *The Past Meets the Present: Essays on Oral History,* ed. David Stricklin and Rebecca Sharpless (Lanham, Md.: University Press of America, 1988), 77–85.

35. Elizabeth Hardwick, "The Teller and the Tape," *New York Review of Books* (May 30, 1985), 3–5.

36. Henry Fairlie [review of *Robert F. Kennedy and His Times,* by Arthur Schlesinger, Jr.], *The New Republic* 179 (September 9, 1978), 32.

37. Unlike other reviewers who praised *Hard Times'* uplifting, inspirational spirit, Frisch thought it depressing that even thirty years after a massive breakdown in the economic system Americans still could not bring themselves to examine their culture and institutions. Reading the other views, he decided that most had been more concerned with the celebratory message of the interviews for the dispirited America of the 1970s than with the reality of the 1930s. Donald A. Ritchie, "An Interview with Michael Frisch," *OHMAR Newsletter* 11 (Fall 1988), 5; Michael Frisch, *A Shared Authority: Essays on the Craft and Meaning of Oral and Public History* (Albany: State University of New York Press, 1990), 5–13.

38. Bonfield, "Conversations with Schlesinger," 33.

39. Diane Johnson, "I, The Jury: Why This Novelist Can't Resist a Good Book Panel," *New York Times Book Review* (April 10, 1994), 14; see also Ina Yalof's rebuttal, "Thinking Is Required," *New York Times Book Review* (May 8, 1994), 27.

40. Timothy Foote, "Battle Stars: Recollections of the Pacific War," *Washington Post Book World* (May 8, 1994), 27.

41. Linda Shopes, "Developing a Critical Dialogue about Oral History: Some Notes

Based on an Analysis of Book Reviews," *Oral History Review* 14 (1986), 9–25.

42. Ritchie, et al, "Interviews as Historical Evidence," 223–224.

43. Kate L. Turabian, *A Manual for Writers of Term Papers, Theses, and Dissertations* 6th ed., revised by John Grossman and Alice Bennett (Chicago: University of Chicago Press, 1996), 150, 206–7.

CHAPTER 5: VIDEOTAPING ORAL HISTORY

1. Henry Glassie, *Passing the Time in Ballymenone: Culture and History of an Ulster County* (Philadelphia: University of Pennsylvania Press, 1982), 40; Richard Sweterlitsch, "Oral History and Myth-Making: Confessions of a Researcher Turned Producer," *Annual of the New England Oral History Association* 1 (1987–88), 10–17.

2. Pamela M. Henson and Terri A. Schorzman, "Videohistory: Focusing on the American Past," *Journal of American History* 78 (September 1991), 620; Joel Gardner, "Oral History and Video in Theory and Practice," *Oral History Review* 12 (1984), 105–11; Brad Jolly, *Videotaping Local History* (Nashville: American Association for State and Local History, 1982), 75–87; "History Leaves the Page: Videotaping Oral History," *HAIpoints* [History Associates, Inc. Newsletter] (Winter/Spring 1997), 2–3; Legacy program.

3. See Thomas L. Charlton, "Videotaped Oral Histories: Problems and Prospects," *American Archivist* 47 (Summer 1984), 228–36.

4. Gardner, "Oral History and Video," 108–9.

5. See "The Mirror with a Memory," in James West Davidson and Mark Hamilton Lytle, *After the Fact: The Art of Historical Detection* (New York: Knopf, 1982), 205–31.

6. L. Elizabeth Beatime, "Video: The Saving Face," *Oral History Association Newsletter* 25 (Winter 1992), 6.

7. W. Richard Whitaker, "Why Not Try Videotaping Oral History?" *Oral History Review* 9 (1981), 120.

8. Charlton, "Videotaped Oral Histories," 235.

9. Joseph Wilson, "The Afro-American Labor Leadership Oral/Video History Series," *Oral History Review* 14 (1986), 27–33.

10. Henson and Schorzman, "Videohistory," 620; Pamela Henson, "Excerpts from an Interview with John Schuchman," *OHMAR Newsletter* 8 (Fall 1990), 6–10.

11. Henson and Schorzman, "Videohistory," 623.

12. Jim Small, "A Visual Recording," *CRM Bulletin* [National Park Service] 13 (1990), 1, 4–5.

13. Henson and Schorzman, "Videohistory," 622; Beattie, "Video: The Saving Face," 6.

14. Jolly, *Videotaping Oral History,* 109–21; this section also draws on a video workshop conducted by the producer Brien Williams, OHMAR meeting, St. Mary's College, St. Mary's City, Md., April 1992.

15. Dennis Curtin, "A Short Course on Digital Video": http://www.shortcourse.com.

16. Whitaker, "Why Not Try Videotaping Oral History?" 115–24.

17. Documentary filmmaker William Gazecki, "Breaking into Documentary Filmmaking," *Digital VideoEditing*: http://production.digitalmedianet.com/2002/01_jan/features/gazecki_advice.htm.

18. David H. Mould, "Composing Visual Images for the Oral History Interview," *International Journal of Oral History* 7 (November 1986), 198–205; Jolly, *Videotaping Local History,* 50–51.

19. Richard Campbell, "Don Hewitt's Durable Hour," *Columbia Journalism Review* (September–October 1993), 26.

20. Terri A. Schorzman, ed., *A Practical Introduction to Videohistory: The Smithsonian*

Institution and Alfred P. Sloan Foundation Experiment (Malabar, Fla.: Krieger, 1993), 59–65, 210–15.

21. Dan Arden, "Producing Videos: Reports from the Field," presentation at the 1996 meeting of the Oral History Association.

22. William Gazecki, "Breaking into Documentary Filmmaking," *Digital VideoEditing*: www. digitalvideoediting.

23. Charlton, "Videotaped Oral Histories," 234.

24. See John A. Neuenschwander, *Oral History and the Law,* rev. ed. (Albuquerque, N.M.: Oral History Association, 1993), 16–34; and Schorzman, *Practical Introduction to Videohistory,* 41–42, 206–8.

25. William W. Moss and Peter C. Mazikana, *Archives, Oral History, and Oral Tradition, a RAMP [Records and Archives Management Programme] Study* (Paris: UNESCO, 1986), 44; Jolly, *Videotaping Local History,* 19–37.

26. Verena Alberti, "How to Deal with Sound Archives: Dilemmas on the Technical Preservation of Oral History Archives," *Crossroads of History: Experience, Memory, Orality* (Istanbul: International Oral History Association, 2000), vol., 1, 1–8.

27. William J. Staples, "Videotape Is Dead," *Industrial Photography* (March 1993), 14–15.

28. "The Film and Video Archive Project," *Oral History Recorder* [Newsletter of the Center for Oral History, University of Hawaii at Manoa] 6 (Spring 1989), 2–3, 8.

29. Henson and Schorzman, "Videohistory," 625.

30. E. John B. Allen, "A Sporting Chance: Oral History and Films," *Annual of the New England Oral History Association* 1 (1987–88), 23.

31. Dean Albertson, "Remembering Oral History's Beginnings," *Annual of the New England Oral History Association* 1 (1987–88), 7–8.

32. "Film Documents Kentucky's Civil-Rights Movement," *Louisville Courier-Journal,* January 21, 2002.

33. Michael Frisch, "Oral History, Documentary, and the Mystification of Power: A Critique of Vietnam: A Television History," in *A Shared Authority: Essays on the Craft and Meaning of Oral and Public History* (Albany: State University of New York Press, 1990), 159–78.

34. Sweterlitsch, "Oral History and Myth-Making," 12; see also Brien Williams, "Recording Videohistory: A Perspective," in Schorzman, *Practical Introduction to Videohistory,* 138–54.

35. http://www.pbs.org/wgbh/pages/frontline/shows/clinton/

36. Daniel Schorr, *Clearing the Air* (New York; Berkeley, 1978), 18.

37. Sweterlitsch, "Oral History and Myth-Making," 15–16; Allen, "A Sporting Chance," 19–20.

38. Allen, "A Sporting Chance," 23-24; Robert Brent Toplin, "The Filmmaker as Historian," *American Historical Review* 93 (December 1988), 1219–27.

39. "The Rights and Responsibilities of Historians in Regard to Historical Films and Video," *Perspectives: American Historical Association Newsletter* 30 (September 1992), 15, 17.

40. Jolly, *Videotaping Local History,* 77.

41. Mary Rose Bosewell [review of "The Boott Cotton Mills Museum,"] *Oral History Review* 20 (Spring–Fall 1992), 88–89.

42. Whitaker, "Why Not Try Videotaping Oral History," 123; Shaw, "Public Access Television," 7.

43. "Oral History and the Arts," plenary session, OHMAR conference, April 18, 1982, transcript, OHMAR papers, George Washington University.

44. Lynn A. Bonfield, "Conversations with Arthur M. Schlesinger, Jr.: The Use of Oral History," *The American Archivist* 43 (Fall 1980), 471.
45. Beattie, "Video: The Saving Face," Shaw, "Public Access Television," 7.

CHAPTER 6: PRESERVING ORAL HISTORY
IN ARCHIVES AND LIBRARIES

1. Donald A. Ritchie, "A Sense of Collective Responsibility: An Interview with Ronald J. Grele," *OHMAR Newsletter* 16 (Fall 1993), 7; Elizabeth I. Dixon, et al, "Definitions of Oral History," *Oral History at Arrowhead: The Proceedings of the First National Colloquium on Oral History* (Los Angeles: Oral History Association, 1969), 5–7.
2. Barbara Tuchman, "Distinguishing the Significant from the Insignificant," in David K. Dunaway and Willa K. Baum, eds., *Oral History: An Interdisciplinary Anthology,* 2nd ed.(Walnut Creek, Calif.: AltaMira, 1996), 96; see also Wolfgang Weber, *"Mass of Trash" or "Veins of Gold"? An Investigative Report on the Relationship Between Oral History and Archives* (Regensburg, Austria: S. Roderer Verlag, 2002), 33–37.
3. Donald A. Ritchie, "Oral Histories May Help Scholars Plow Through the Rapidly Accumulating Mass of Federal Paper," *The Chronicle of Higher Education* (November 2, 1988), A44.
4. James E. Fogerty, "Filling in the Gap: Oral History in the Archives," *American Archivist* 46 (Spring 1983), 148–157.
5. Ibid., 151; see also Ronald L. Filippelli, "Oral History and the Archives," *American Archivist* 39 (October 1976), 479–483.
6. Fogerty, "Filling in the Gap," 153–154; William W. Moss and Peter C. Mazikana, *Archives, Oral History and Oral Tradition: A RAMP Study* (Paris: UNESCO, 1986), 4, 25–26, 29.
7. Ritchie, "A Collective Sense of Responsibility," 7.
8. John T. Mason, Jr. interviewed by Benis M. Frank, July 16, 1983, transcripts, Marine Corps Oral History Program, Marine Corps Historical Center, Washington, D.C.
9. *Oral History Evaluation Guidelines* (Los Angeles: Oral History Association, 1992), 1–2.
10. Cary C. Wilkins, ed., *The Guide to Kentucky Oral History Collections* (Frankfort: Kentucky Oral History Commission, 1991); "California Legislature Creates State OH Program," *Oral History Association Newsletter* 20 (Fall 1986), 3.
11. The National Historical Publications and Records Commission has shied away from giving grants for oral histories, with the single exception: the commission concluded that oral traditions were so integral in Native American historical consciousness that efforts to preserve its documentation would be incomplete without oral sources.
12. Moss and Mazikana, *Archives, Oral History and Oral Tradition,* 60. Federal copyright law stipulates that a transfer of ownership "is not valid unless an instrument of conveyance, or a note or memorandum of the transfer, is in writing and signed by the owner of the rights conveyed." See John A. Neuenschwander, *Oral History and the Law,* rev. ed. (Albuquerque, N.M.: Oral History Association, 1993), 18–19.
13. Ibid., 34–35, 48–49, 56; William W. Moss, *Oral History Program Manual* (New York: Praeger, 1974), 46–49, 64–68.
14. Marion Matters, *Oral History Cataloging Manual* (Chicago: Society of American Archivists, 1995).
15. For archival finding aids, see Moss and Mazikana, *Archives, Oral History and Oral Tradition,* 62–63; for library finding aids, see Cullom Davis, Kathryn Back, and Kay MacLean, *Oral History from Tape to Type* (Chicago: American Library Association, 1977), 87–101.

16. Christopher Ann Paton, "Whispers in the Stacks: The Problem of Sound Recordings in Archives," *American Archivist* 53 (Spring 1990), 274–280.

17. Louis Starr, letter to David Wallace, February 16, 1962, reprinted in *Oral History Association Newsletter* 24 (Spring 1990), 2.

18. "In the Trenches" [an interview of Charles Hardy by Elaine Eff], *OHMAR Newsletter* 23 (Spring 2002), 2–8.

19. Paton, "Whispers in the Stacks," 276–277; Moss and Mazikana, *Archives, Oral History and Oral Tradition*, 43–45.

20. Larry I. Bland, ed., *George C. Marshall Interviews and Reminiscences for Forrest C. Pogue* (Lexington, VA: George C. Marshall Research Foundation, 1991).

21. Stacey Roth, "The Care and Preservation of Sound Recordings," *Conservation Administration News* 23 (October 1985), 5.

22. Moss and Mazikana, *Archives, Oral History and Oral Tradition*, 43–45; "Magnetic Tape Recording: Forever?" *3M Technical Bulletin* (St. Paul, Minn.: 3M Magnetic Media Division, 1984), 1–3.

23. David H. Mould, "Digital Archival Storage for Oral History," *International Journal of Oral History* 10 (February 1989), 59–63; Schneider and Grahek, *Project Jukebox*, 5; Frederick J. Stielow, "Archival Theory and the Preservation of Electronic Media: Opportunities and Standards Below the Cutting Edge," *American Archivist* 55 (Spring 1992), 332–43.

24. "Nate Shaw Tapes Damaged in Hurricane, Restored by UNC Southern Folklife Collection," *Oral History Association Newsletter* 24 (Fall 1990), 3; Theodore Rosengarten, *All God's Dangers: The Life of Nate Shaw* (New York: Knopf, 1974).

25. The best guide to tape indexing is Dale Treleven, *TAPE (Time Access to Pertinent Excerpts) System: A Method For Producing Oral History Interviews & Other Sound Recordings* (Madison: State Historical Society of Wisconsin, 1979); see also Dale E. Treleven, "Oral History, Audio Technology and the TAPE System," *International Journal of Oral History* 2 (February 1981), 27–45.

26. Elizabeth P. Jacox, "Making an Oral History Collection Available to the Public," *Idaho Oral History Center Newsletter* 4 (Summer 1982), 3–4.

27. Alvin Toffler, *The Third Wave* (New York: Bantam, 1980), 189.

28. Roy Rosenzweig, "Automating Your Oral History Program: A Guide to Data Base Management on a Microcomputer," *International Journal of Oral History* 5 (November 1984), 174–187.

29. Kenneth Thibodeau , "Overview of Technological Approaches to Digital Preservation and Challenges in Coming Years," *The State of Digital Preservation, An International Perspective* (Washington, D.C.: Council on Library and Information Services, 2002); William Schneider and Daniel Grahek, *Project Jukebox: Where Oral History and Technology Come Together* (Anchorage: Center for Information Technology, University of Anchorage, 1992), 1–8.

30. Frederick J. Graboske, "Digitizing the United States Marine Corps Oral History Collection," in Philippe Denis and James Worthington, eds. *The Power of Oral History: Memory, Healing and Development* (Pietermaritzburg, South Africa: International Oral History Association, 2002), vol. 1: 72–85.

31. Ibid; Schneider and Grahek, *Project Jukebox*.

32. John Naughton, "Gordon E. Moore: No Goodbyes for World's Mr. Chips," *The Observer* (August 8, 1999); Thibideau, "Overview of Technological Approaches to Digital Preservation and Challenges in Coming Years."

33. Virginia Danielson, "Stating the Obvious: Lessons Learned Attempting to Access

Archival Audio Collections," *Folk Heritage Collections in Crisis* (Washington, D.C.: Council on Library and Information Resources, 2000).

34. Bruce H. Bruemmer, "Access to Oral History: A National Agenda," *American Archivist* 54 (Fall 1991), 494–501; Meg Bellinger, "Understanding Digital Preservation: A Report from OCLC," *The State of Digital Preservation, An International Perspective* (Washington, D.C.: Council on Library and Information Services, 2002).

35. Matters, *Oral History Cataloging Manual*; Cathryn A. Gallacher and Dale E. Treleven, "Developing an Online Database and Printed Directory and Subject Guide to Oral History Collections," *Oral History Review* 16 (Spring 1988), 33–68.

36. Helen R. Tibbo and Lokman I. Meho, "Finding Finding Aids on the World Wide Web," *American Archivist* 64 (Spring/Summer 2001), 61–77.

37. Sherna Berger Gluck, "Pace, Performance, Pitch—and Even Poetry: The CSULB Virtual Oral/Aural History Project," *Oral History Association Newsletter* 36 (Spring 2002), 4–5; see www.csulb.edu/voaha.

38. Donald A. Ritchie, "www.oral history.infinity," *Oral History Review* 26 (Summer/Fall, 1999), 13–15; Paul Thompson, "Sharing and Reshaping Life Stories: Problems and Potential in Archiving Research Narratives," in Mary Chamberlain and Paul Thompson, eds. *Narrative and Genre* (New York: Routledge, 1998), 180.

39. Mary Ann Larson, "Guarding Against Cyberpirates," *Oral History Association Newsletter* 33 (Fall 1999), 4–5.

40. Karen Brewster, "Oral Recordings on the Internet: Finding the Issues," paper delivered at the American Folklore Society, October 17–21, 2001, Anchorage, Alaska.

41. Sherna Berger Gluck, "Brief Note on CSULB Project Methodology and Procedures," *Oral History Association Newsletter* 36 (Spring 2002), 6.

42. Ritchie, "www.oralhistory.infinity," 13–15.

43. Neuenschwander, *Oral History and the Law,* 3rd ed.

44. "Statement on Interviewing for Historical Documentation," *Perspectives: The American Historical Association Newsletter* 27 (October 1989), 8.

45. David M. Oshinsky, "Oral History: Playing by the Rules," *Journal of American History* 77 (September 1990), 609–614; Oshinsky, *A Conspiracy So Immense: The World of Joe McCarthy* (New York: Free Press, 1983).

46. Jon Wiener, "The Alger Hiss Case, the Archives, and Allen Weinstein," *Perspectives: Newsletter of the American Historical Association* 30 (February 1992), 12; Donald A. Ritchie, "Interviewers and Archivists," *Society of American Archivists Newsletter* July 1990, 13; Donald A. Ritchie, Holly Cowan Shulman, Richard S. Kirkendall, and Terry L. Birdwhistell, "Interviews as Historical Evidence: A Discussion of New Standards of Documentation and Access," *The History Teacher* 24 (February 1991), 234.

47. Ritchie, et al, "Interviews as Historical Evidence," 235–36.

48. Frederick J. Stielow, *The Management of Oral History Sound Archives* (New York: Greenwood, 1986), 36; Ritchie, "Interviewers and Archivists," 13; National Archives and Records Administration, "Procedures for Initiating Cooperative Oral History Projects," typescript report available from the National Archives and Records Administration, Washington, D.C., 20408.

49. "National Archives Adopts Oral History Plan," *The Federalist: Newsletter of the Society for History in the Federal Government* 8 (Fall 1987), 7–8.

50. Pamela Henson, "Smithsonian Leads the Way Among Federal Agencies," *Oral History Association Newsletter* 13 (Winter 1979), 1, 6; Carol Dreyfus and Thomas Connors, "Oral History and American Advertising: How the 'Pepsi Generation' Came Alive," *International Journal of Oral History* 6 (November 1985), 191–197.

51. Neuenschwander, *Oral History and the Law,* 3rd ed.

52. Ibid.

53. Ann E. Pederson and Gail Farr Casterline, *Archives & Manuscripts: Public Programs* (Chicago: Society of American Archivists, 1982), 8.

54. Joseph W. Palmer, *Oral History in Public Libraries* (Urbana: University of Illinois Graduate School of Library and Information Service, 1984), 8–9, 10.

55. Pederson and Casterline, *Archives & Manuscripts: Public Programs,* 9, 15, 23–24.

56. http://www2.state.id.us/ishs/smokejumper.html; Troy Reeves, H-ORALHIST, May 23, 2002; Tamara Kennelly, "Oral History on the Internet: Narratives from Pioneering Black Students," In Denis and Worthington, eds. *The Power of Oral History,* vol. 1: 86–99.

57. Willa K. Baum, "Building Community Identity Through Oral History—A New Role for the Local Library," *California Librarian* (October 1970), 271–284.

CHAPTER 7: TEACHING ORAL HISTORY

1.   Richard P. Onderdonk, "Piaget and Oral History: Cognitive Development in the Secondary Studies Class," *Oral History Review* 11 (1983), 77.

2.   John A. Neuenschwander, *Oral History as a Teaching Approach* (Washington, D.C.: National Education Association, 1976), 9; John A. Neuenschwander, "Oral History in the High School Classroom," *Oral History Review* 3 (1975), 61; Barry A. Lanman, "The Use of Oral History in the Classroom: A Comparative Analysis of the 1974 and 1987 Oral History Association Surveys," *Oral History Review* 17 (Spring 1989), 223–24.

3.   Eliot Wigginton, *Sometimes a Shining Moment: The Foxfire Experience* (Garden City, NY: Doubleday, 1985), 325–86.

4.   June Jordan, "Nobody Means More to Me Than You and the Future Life of Willie Jordan," in *From the Hip: Documentary Team Guidebook* (Durham, N.C.: From the Hip, 1993), 14–15.

5.   Eliot Wigginton, ed., *The Foxfire Book* (Garden City, N.J.: Doubleday, 1972), 9–14.

6.   Wigginton, *Sometimes a Shining Moment,* 329–30, 343–46, 352, 354; Thad Sitton, "The Descendants of *Foxfire,*" *Oral History Review* 6 (1978), 20-35; see also the *Foxfire* series published by Doubleday since 1972.

7.   During the 1970s, Thad Sitton identified some eighty secondary school oral history magazines, in thirty-one states, the District of Columbia, Guam, Samoa, the Virgin Islands and the Dominican Republic. See Sitton, "The Descendants of *Foxfire,*" 20–35; George L. Mehaffy, "Foxfire Comes of Age," *Oral History Review* 13 (1985), 145–49; "Cultural Journalism Shares Oral History Through Schoolchildren," *Oral History Association Newsletter* 20 (Summer 1986), 3; Pamela Wood, ed., *The Salt Book* (Garden City, N.J.: Doubleday, 1977); Ellen G. Massey and Ruth E. Massey, eds., *Bittersweet County* (Garden City, N.J.: Doubleday, 1978); and "Minds Stayed on Freedom: Movement Veterans Speak to Holmes County Youth," *Bloodlines* 2 (Spring 1990).

8.   Barry A. Lanman and George L. Mehaffy, *Oral History in the Secondary School Classroom* (Los Angeles: Oral History Association, 1988); Linda P. Wood, *Oral History Projects in Your Classroom* (Carlisle, Penn.: Oral History Association, 2001); *History from the Living: The Organization and Craft of Oral History,* (video, Newport, R.I.: Grin Productions, 1998); Pamela Dean, Toby Dispat, and Petra Munro, *Talking Gumbo: An Oral History Manual for Secondary School Teachers* (Baton Rouge: Louisiana State University, 1998), and *You've Got to Hear This,* video (Baton Rouge: Louisiana State University, 1998).

9.   George L. Mehaffy, Thad Sitton, and O. L. Davis, Jr., *Oral History in the Classroom* (Washington: National Council for the Social Studies, 1979); Cynthia Stokes Brown,

Like It Was: A Complete Guide to Writing Oral History (New York: Teachers and Writers Collaborative, 1988); http://www.folklife.si/edu/MississippiDelta/discoveringourdelta.htm.

10. Lanman and Mehaffy, *Oral History in the Secondary School Classroom,* 11–12; Wigginton, ed., *The Foxfire Book,* 12.

11. William Cutler, et al., "Oral History as a Teaching Tool," *Oral History Review* 1 (1973), 38–43.

12. George Mehaffy, "Oral History in Elementary Classrooms," *Social Education* (September/October 1984), 470–73; Stephen Lehane and Richard Goldman, "Oral History: Research and Teaching Tool for Educators," *Elementary School Journal* 77 (January 1977), 173–81; Laura Wendling, "Oral History...It's Elementary!" *The Oral History Educator* 1 (Fall 1999), 5–7; and Alistair Ross, "Children Becoming Historians: An Oral History Project in a Primacy School," in Robert Perks and Alistain Thomson, eds., *The Oral History Reader* (New York: Routledge, 1998), 432–47.

13. "Cultural Journalism," 3.

14. Stan and Jan Berenstain, *The Berenstain Bears and the Giddy Grandma* (New York: Random House, 1994).

15. George Mehaffy and Thad Sitton, "Oral History: A Strategy That Works," *Social Education* 41 (May 1977), 378–82; Barbara A. Levy and Karen Marshall, "Kids Making History," *History News* (March/April 1990), 20; Michael Brooks, "'Long, Long Ago': Recipe for a Middle School Oral History Program," *Organization of American Historians Magazine of History* 11 (Spring 1997), 32–35.

16. Levy and Marshall, "Kids Making History," 18–20; see also Alan J. Singer, "Oral History and Active Learning," *Social Science Record* 31 (Fall 1994), 4–20; and John Marshall Carter, "'Grandma Book': Writing to Discover Your Past: Classroom Teachers Idea Notebook," *Social Education* 59 (February 1995), 92–94.

17. Lanman and Mehaffy, *Oral History in the Secondary School Classroom,* 1–6, 8; see also Donald A. Ritchie, "Teaching the Cold War through Oral History," *History Teacher* 8 (Winter 1994), 10–12; and the special oral history issue edited by Cliff Kuhn and Marjorie L. McLellan, *Organization of American Historians' Magazine of History* 11 (Spring 1997).

18. Mitch Mendosa, "Reflections on Voices of the Valley," in *Tell Us How It Was: Stories of Rural Elders Preserved by Rural Youth* (Washington, D.C.: Rural School and Community Trust, 2002), 15–22, 25.

19. Roy Rosenzweig, "www.historymatters.gmu.edu: The U.S. Survey Course on the Web," *Organization of American Historians Newsletter* (November 1998), 13; "Ordinary People Living Extraordinary Lives:" http://www.dept.usm.edu/~mcrohb; Samuel Totten, "Using Oral Histories to Address Social Issues in the Social Studies Classroom," *Social Education* 53 (February 1989), 114.

20. Joel R. Gardner, "Using Oral History and Folklore in the Classroom," *New Jersey Folklore Society* 11 (Spring/Fall 1990), 1–16; Brown, *Like It Was,* 31–47.

21. Lanman and Mehaffy, *Oral History in the Secondary School Classroom,* 14; Totten, "Using Oral Histories to Address Social Issues," 115.

22. Neuenschwander, *Oral History as a Teaching Approach,* 11–13.

23. Garrison Keillor, *Happy to Be Here* (New York: Atheneum, 1982), 194–95; Mehaffy, et al, *Oral History in the Classroom,* 3; Thad Sitton, "Oral History: From Tape Recorder to Typewriter," *The Social Studies* 72 (May/June 1981), 122–23.

24. Interview with G. R. F. Key, *Earth Waves* 3 (1982), 6.

25. Gardner, "Oral History and Folklore," 1–15.

26. Mehaffy and Sitton, "Oral History: A Strategy That Works," 378–82; James West Davidson and Mark Hamilton Lytle offer a valuable case study in *After the Fact: The Art of Historical Detection* (New York: Knopf, 1982), 169–204.

27. Lehane and Goldman, "Oral History: Research and Teaching Tool for Educators," 181; Onderdonk, "Piaget and Oral History," 77–85.

28. Peter N. Stearns, *Meaning over Memory: Recasting the Teaching of Culture and History* (Chapel Hill: University of North Carolina Press, 1993), 15, 63, 155–56, 170, 175–76.

29. Totten, "Using Oral Histories to Address Social Issues," 114–16, 125

30. Barry A. Lanman, "Oral History as an Educational Tool for Teaching Immigration and Black History in American High Schools: Findings and Queries," *International Journal of Oral History* 8 (June 1987), 122–35.

31. Paula J. Paul, "Fish Bowls and Bloopers: Oral History in the Classroom," *Organization of American Historians Magazine of History* 11 (Spring 1997), 43–46; Nicholas P. Ciotola, "Recording Wartime Reminiscences: Using Oral History to Teach World War II," *Organization of American Historians Magazine of History* 16 (Spring 2002), 59–61.

32. Totten, "Using Oral Histories to Address Social Issues," 115.

33. Mehaffy, Sitton, and Davis, *Oral History in the Classroom*; Gardner, "Using Oral History and Folklore in the Classroom," 5.

34. Barbara Ruden, "Living History Lessons," *Washington Post*, March 11, 1999; Glenn E. Whitman, "Teaching Students How to be Historians: An Oral-History Project for the Secondary School Classroom," *The History Teacher* 33 (August 2000), 469–81.

35. Neuenschwander, *Oral History as a Teaching Approach*, 21.

36. George L. Mehaffy and Thad Sitton, "Oral History Tells Its Own Story: The Development of the Loblolly Project," *Social Studies* 68 (1977), 231–35.

37. Neuenschwander, *Oral History as a Teaching Approach*, 9, 22.

38. Frank J. Fonsino, "Criteria for Evaluating Oral History Interviews," *The History Teacher* 2 (1980), 239–43.

39. Mehaffy, Sitton, and Davis, *Oral History in the Classroom*, 1; Willa K. Baum, "Looking at Oral History," *ERIC/CHESS* (September 1975), 2.

40. Marjorie L. McLellan, "Oral History in the Classroom and on the World Wide Web," *Oral History Association Newsletter* 31 (Fall 1997), 9; Anne Ray, "Resources Make Oral History Work," *The [National History Education] Network News* 7 (Summer 1999), 1, 3; "What Did You Do in the War, Grandma?" Oral histories of Rhode Island women in World War II by students of South Kingstown High School, 1989: http://www/stg.brown/edu/projects/1968; http://www.stg.brown.edu/projects/WWII_Women; and http://newdeal.feri.org.

41. "Observations on National History Day," *OHMAR Newsletter* 8 (Fall 1984), 14–15.

42. McGregor McCance, "Learning History from its Source," *Greenville* (South Carolina) *News*, (June 13, 1993).

43. Lanman and Mehaffy, *Oral History in the Secondary School Classroom*, 19.

44. Rina Benmayor, "Digital Technologies and Life Stories," vol. 1: 60–71, and Mats Greiff, "Oral History at Malmö University," in Philippe Denis and James Worthington, eds., *The Power of Oral History: Memory, Healing and Development* (Pietermaritzburg: South Africa: University of Natal, 2002), vol. 3:1510–23.

45. John Forrest and Elisabeth Jackson, "Get Real: Empowering the Student Through Oral History," *Oral History Review* 18 (Spring 1990), 29–44.

46. See Stacy Erickson and Troy Reeves, eds., *A Field Notebook for Oral History* (Boise: Idaho Oral History Center, 2001).

47. James Hoopes, *Oral History for Students* (Chapel Hill: University of North Carolina

Press, 1979), 49; Donald A. Ritchie, "A Sense of Collective Responsibility: An Interview with Ronald J. Grele," *OHMAR Newsletter* 16 (Fall 1993), 6–8.

48. Michael H. Ebner, "Students as Oral Historians," *The History Teacher* 9 (February 1976), 196–201.

49. A. Glenn Crothers, "'Bringing History to Life': Oral History, Community Research, and Multiple Levels of Learning," *Journal of American History* 88 (March 2002), 1446–51.

50. Mary M. Schweitzer, "Oral History in the Classroom," *Pennsylvania History* 60 (October 1993), 496–99.

51. See Tracy E. K. Meyer, "'It's Not Just Common Sense': A Blueprint for Teaching Oral History," 35–56, and Marjorie L. McLellan, "Case Studies in Oral History and Community Learning," *Oral History Review* 25 (Fall 1998), 81–112.

52. Edward Ives, untitled subsection of Cutler, et al., "Oral History as a Teaching Tool," 45; see also Louisa Schell Hoberman, "The Immigrant Experience and Student-Centered Learning: An Oral History Video Project," *Perspectives* 32 (March 1994), 1, 13–16.

53. See Ebner, "Students as Oral Historians," 198. Much of the discussion of oral history on the college level is drawn from the course syllabi of Terry L. Birdwhistell at the University of Kentucky, Thomas L. Charlton at Baylor University, and Wendell Wray at the University of Pittsburgh.

54. Elizabeth Gibbens, "Jacqueline Dowd Hall," *Humanities* 20 (Nov./Dec. 1999), 22–23; Renata W. Prescott, "The Vietnam War and the Teaching and Writing of Oral History: The Reliability of the Narrator," *Oral History Review* 26 (Summer/Fall 1999), 47–64.

55. Jean M. Humenz and Laurie Crumpacker, "Oral History in Teaching Women's Studies," *Oral History Review* 7 (1979), 53–69.

56. Mary Jo Deering, "Oral History and School Integration Research: A Case Study," *Oral History Review* 7 (1979), 27–41.

57. For example, see Dan Riordan, ed., *Reminiscences: An Anthology of Oral History* (Stout, WI: University of Wisconsin-Stout, 1980); *As I Remember Fordham: Selections from the Sesquicentennial Oral History Project* (New York: Fordham University, 1991); and Charles H. Martin and Rebecca M. Craver, eds., *Diamond Days: An Oral History of the University of Texas at El Paso* (El Paso: University of Texas at El Paso, 1991).

58. Beverly Blois, et al., *Northern Virginia Community College: An Oral History, 1965–1985* (Annandale, Va.: Northern Virginia Community College, 1987).

59. Günham Danisman, "The Oral History of a History Department," in Denis and Worthington, eds., *The Power of Oral History,* vol. 3:1477-92.

60. Charles T. Morrissey, "Oral History on Campus: Recording Changes in Higher Education," *Dartmouth College Library Bulletin* 11 (April 1971), 75–76.

61. John Rothstein, "Oral History: A Student's View," *The Journal of the New England Association of Oral History* 2 (1988/89), 38–44.

62. Baum, "Looking at Oral History," 2.

63. The recommended regulations were codified in Title 45, Code of Federal Regulations, Part 46 (usually cited as 45 CFR 46). National Commission for the Protection of Human Subjects of Biomedical and Behavioral Research, *The Belmont Report: Ethical Principles and Guidelines for the Protection of Human Subjects Research* (Washington: Department of Health and Human Services, 1979), 4–5; Linda Shopes, "Historians and Human-Subjects Research," *Recent Science Newsletter* 2 (Spring 2001), 6–7, 15.

64. "Panelists Defend, Criticize Campus IRB Process," *Oral History Association Newsletter* 35 (Winter 2001), 6.

65. Gary May to author, November 4, 1995; Michael A. Gordon, "Historians and Review Boards," *Perspectives* (September 1997), 35–37.

66. Jeffrey Brainard, "The Wrong Rules for Social Science?" *Chronicle of Higher Education* (March 9, 2001), A21–23; Christopher Shea, "Don't Talk to the Humans: The Crackdown on Social Science Research," *Lingua franca* 10 (September 2000) 26–34.

67. Charlotte Allen, "Spies Like Us: When Sociologists Deceive Their Subjects," *Lingua Franca* 7 (November 1997), 31–39.

68. Linda Shopes, "Institutional Review Boards Have a Chilling Effect on Oral History," *Perspectives* (September 2000), 54–7.

69. "Protecting Human Beings: Institutional Review Boards and Social Science Research," *Academe: Bulletin of the American Association of University Professors* 87 (May–June 2001), 55–67.

70. "OHA Involved in New Rules Affecting Academic Oral Historians," *Oral History Association Newsletter* 33 (Winter 1999), 3.

71. National Commission for the Protection of Human Subjects of Biomedical and Behavioral Research, *The Belmont Report*, 35.

72. Anna Louise Bates, *Weeder in the Garden of the Lord: Anthony Comstock's Life and Career* (Lanham, Md.: University Press of America, 1995), 1–2, 10–11, 15, 62–63; 177–78, 192–94

73. Ibid, vii, 185.

CHAPTER 8: PRESENTING ORAL HISTORY

1. Elizabeth Gremore Figa, "Products of Oral History Work—Follow-Up," H-Oralhist, June 22, 2000.

2. The public history uses of oral history are discussed in chapter 1. For the use of oral history in video documentaries, see chapter 5.

3. Laurie Marcier and Madeline Buckendorf, *Using Oral History in Community History Projects* (Los Angeles: Oral History Association, 1992), i; Rose T. Diaz and Andrew B. Russell, "Oral Historians: Community Oral History and the Cooperative Ideal," in James B. Gardner and Peter S. LaPaglia, eds., *Public History: Essays from the Field* (Malabar, Fla.: Krieger, 1999), 203–16.

4. Helen M. Lewis, "Community History," *Organization of American Historians Magazine of History* 11 (Spring 1997), 20–22.

5. Charles Hardy, "The Urban Archives' 'Discovering Community History Project,'" *Oral History Association Newsletter* 15 (Winter 1981), 4–5.

6. Thelma Russell, "The Humanities Belong to All of Us: A Voice from Public Housing," *Humanities* (Newsletter of the D.C. Community Humanities Council) 6 (Summer 1993), 1–2; "In Search of Common Ground Video to Premier at Public Humanities Award Program," *Humanities* 6 (Fall 1993), 1, 3.

7. Knox Mellon, "Oral History, Public History, and Historic Preservation: California Birds of a Feather," *Oral History Review* 9 (1981), 85–95.

8. Dan J. Utley, "From the Ground Up: Oral History and Historical Archaeology," *Sound History: Journal of the Texas Oral History Association* 1 (Fall 1993), 18–28.

9. Hardy, "Discovering Community History Project," 4; Michelle Palmer, Marianne Esolen, Susan Rose, Andrea Fishman, and Jill Bartoli, "'I Haven't Anything to Say': Reflections of Self and Community in Collecting Oral Histories," *International Annual of Oral History, 1990: Subjectivity and Multiculturalism in Oral History* (Westport, Conn.: Greenwood, 1992), 175.

10. Linda Shopes, "Oral History and the Study of Communities: Problems, Paradoxes, and Possibilities," *Journal of American History* 89 (September 2002), 588–98.

11. Joe Doyle, "Community History in a Community That Doesn't Want It," *Public History:*

The Newsletter of New York University's Program in Public History 1 (1984), 6–9.

12. Jerry Carrier, ed., "Goin' North: Tales of the Great Migration," *Philadelphia Inquirer*, February 4, 1985; "Fourth Issue of Narratives Builds on a Strong Start," *Narratives* 2 (Spring 2001), 2.

13. Donald Hyslop, "From Oral Historians to Community Historians: Some Ways Forward for the Use and Development of Oral Testimony in Public Institutions," *Oral History Association of Australia Journal* 17 (1995), 1–8; Mercier and Buckendorf, *Using Oral History*, 16–19.

14. Ibid, 30–31.

15. Laurie Mercier, Mary Murphy, Linda Peavy, Diane Sands, and Ursula Smith, *Molders and Shapers: Montana Women as Community Builders: An Oral History Sampler and Guide* (Helena: Montana Historical Society Office, 1987), 9–19.

16. Sally Voris, "Oral History in Museum Exhibits," H-Oralhist, November 13, 2001.

17. George McDaniels, "Folklife Festivals: History as Entertainment and Education," in *Public History: An Introduction*, ed. Barbara J. Howe and Emory L. Kemp (Malabar, Fla.: Krieger, 1986), 277–91; http://www.folklife.si.edu/education/started1.htm.

18. Fernando Columbus, *The Life of the Admiral Christopher Columbus* (New Brunswick, N.J.: Rutgers University Press, 1959), 10.

19. See Ellen Robinson Epstein and Rona Mendelsohn, *Record and Remember: Tracing Your Roots Through Oral History* (New York: Monarch, 1978), 2, 16; Robert Bowden, "Recording Your Family Roots," *St. Petersburg Times*, February 24, 1985.

20. Linda Shopes, "Using Oral History for a Family History Project," in David K. Dunaway and Willa K. Baum, eds., *Oral History: An Interdisciplinary Anthology* (Walnut Creek, Calif.: AltaMira, 1996), 231–240.

21. Corrine Azen Krause, *Grandmothers, Mothers, and Daughters: Oral Histories of Three Generations of Ethnic American Women* (Boston: Twayne, 1991). See also Tamara Haraven, "The Search for Generational Memory," in David K. Dunaway and Willa K. Baum, eds., *Oral History: An Interdisciplinary Anthology*, 241–56.

22. William P. Fletcher, *Recording Your Family History: A Guide to Preserving Oral History with Videotape, Audiotape, Suggested Topics and Questions, Interview Techniques* (New York: Dodd, Mead, 1986); Shopes, "Using Oral History," 239.

23. Ingrid Winther Scobie, "Family and Community History through Oral History," *The Public Historian* 1 (Summer 1979), 38–39; Carl Ryant, "Oral History and the Family: A Tool for the Documentation and Interpretation of Family History," *Annual of the New England Oral History Association* 2 (1989–1990), 30–37.

24. Henry Fairlie, review, *New Republic* 204 (March 28, 1988), 20; Robert B. Butler, "The Life Review: An Interpretation of Reminiscence in the Aged," in *New Thoughts on Old Age*, ed. Robert Kastenbaum (New York: Springer, 1964), 265–80.

25. Patrick B. Mullen, *Listening to Old Voices: Folklore, Life Stories and the Elderly* (Urbana: University of Illinois Press, 1992), 7, 11; Henry Glassie, *Passing the Time in Ballymenone* (Philadelphia: University of Pennsylvania Press, 1982), 63.

26. Sandy Forster, "'Reminiscence Is Wonderful Therapy for Older People and Their Care-Givers,'" *Oral History Association of Australia Journal* 18 (1996), 9.

27. Terrl M. Asia, "'I Witness to History' Sparks Retirement Community Interest," *Oral History Association Newsletter* 33 (Fall 1999), 6–7; Denise Flaim, "Oral History Preserves the Past for Future," *Kenosha [Wis.] News*, June 7, 1993.

28. *Kenosha News*, June 7, 1993; see also Joanna Bornat, "Oral History as Social Movement: Reminiscence and Older People," in Robert Perks and Alistair Thomson, eds. *The Oral History Reader* (New York: Routledge, 1998), 189–295.

29. Tracy Kidder, *Old Friends* (Boston: Houghton Mifflin, 1993); Marie Arana-Ward, "Tracy Kidder," *Washington Post Book World* (September 5, 1993), 10.

30. American Association of Retired People, *Reminiscence: Researching Back, Moving Forward* (Washington, D.C.: American Association of Retired People, 1990); "Oral History and the Elderly in Minnesota," *Oral History Association Newsletter* 24 (Winter 1991), 3.

31. Marat Moore, "Oral History: An Organizing Tool and a Healing Art for Labor Union Women," *Oral History Association Newsletter* 26 (Fall 1992), 1–2.

32. "Oral History Used to Enhance Care for AIDS Victims," *Oral History Association Newsletter* 21 (Fall 1993), 1; Wendy Rickard, "HIV and AIDS Testimonies in the 1990s," in Joanna Bornat, Robert Perks, Paul Thompson and Jan Walmsley, eds., *Oral History, Health and Welfare* (New York: Routledge, 2000), 227–48; "Whole Lives: Reflections on Living with HIV," *NC Crossroads: North Carolina Humanities Council* 3 (November/December 1999).

33. Philippe Denis and Nokhaya Makiwane, "Stories of Love, Pain and Courage: The Memory Box Project of the School of Theology, University of Natal," in Philippe Denis and James Worthington, *The Power of Oral History: Memory, Healing and Development* (Pietermaritzburg, South Africa: University of Natal, 2002), 1376–90.

34. Joyce Appleby, "Rattling Skeletons in the Nation's Attic," *Washington Post,* February 10, 2002; "Voices' Preserving Minnesota History," *Oral History Association Newsletter* 21 (Fall 1987), 7.

35. James B. Lane, "Oral History and the Industrial Heritage Museum," *Journal of American History* 80 (September 1993), 607–18; Emory L. Kemp, "A Perspective on Our Industrial Past through Industrial Archaeology," in Howe and Kemp, *Public History,* 188.

36. Carol Dreyfus and Thomas Connors, "Oral History and American Advertising: How the 'Pepsi Generation' Came Alive," *International Journal of Oral History* 6 (November 1985), 191–97.

37. Donald A. Ritchie, review of the Newseum, *The Public Historian* 19 (Fall 1997), 98–100.

38. Paul E. Sigrist, Jr., "Ellis Island Project Captures Unique Slice of American History," *Oral History Association Newsletter* 32 (Winter 1998), 10.

39. Linda Clark and Elspeth Wishart, "The Frozen Face: Using Oral Histories in Museum Exhibitions," *Oral History Association of Australia Journal* 18 (1996), 60–62.

40. David Lance, *An Archive Approach to Oral History* (London: Imperial War Museum and International Association of Sound Archives, 1978), 55–57.

41. "History and the Public: What Can We Handle? A Round Table about History after the *Enola Gay* Controversy," *Journal of American History* 82 (December 1995), 1029–1144,

42. *Washington Post,* April 22, 1998.

43. Donald A. Ritchie, review of the Newseum, *Public Historian* 19 (Fall 1997), 98–100; Ritchie, "When History Goes Public: Recent Experiences in the United States," *Oral History* (Spring 2001), 92–97.

44. David Dunaway, "Radio and the Public Use of Oral History," in Dunaway and Baum, *Oral History,* 306–320.

45. "Black Workers' History Airing on Radio," *Oral History Association Newsletter* 18 (Spring 1985), 1.

46. Walter Liniger, "The Original Down Home Blues Show," *Oral History Association Newsletter* 22 (Spring 1988), 1–2.

47. Alan Bunce, "Radio Series Evokes Powerful Images with Accounts of Civil Rights," *Christian Science Monitor,* March 31, 1997; "The Making of *Will the Circle Be*

Unbroken?: Beyond the Printed Word," *Southern Changes: Southern Regional Council, Atlanta* 19 (Spring 1997), 22–27.

48. Gene Preuss, H-Oralhist.

49. Lance, *An Archive Approach to Oral History,* 53.

50. Dunaway, "Radio and the Public Use of Oral History," 312.

51. Kathryn Nasstrom, "Performing *Like a Family,*" *Oral History Association Newsletter* 23 (Spring 1989), 3.

52. "Urban Oral Histories Dramatized," *Oral History Association Newsletter* 15 (Summer 1981), 4.

53. Edward M. Miggins, "Communities of Memory," *Oral History Association Newsletter* 26 (Spring 1992), 1, 3; "World War II Living History Performances Scheduled," Center for Oral History, *Oral History Recorder* 18 (Fall 2001), 1.

54. Amy Green, "New Oral-History Based Play Available for September 11 Memorials," H-Oralhist, July 23, 2002.

55. Donald A. Ritchie, "At the Crossroads: Oral History in the 21st Century," *Oral History Association Newsletter* 35 (Winter 2001), 3.

56. Roy Rosenzweig, "Why Read a History Book on a Computer? Putting *Who Built America?* on CD-ROM," *History Microcomputer Review* (Fall 1993), 1–2, 6, 11; Thomas J. DeLoughry, "History Post-Print," *Chronicle of Higher Education* 40 (January 12, 1994), A19–20; Roy Rosenzweig and Steve Brier, "Historians and Hypertext, Is It More Than Hype?" *American Historical Association Perspectives* 32 (March 1994), 3–6.

57. William Schneider and Daniel Grahek, *Project Jukebox: Where Oral History and Technology Come Together* (Anchorage: Center for Information Technology, University of Alaska, Anchorage, 1992), 1–9; William Schnider, *So They Understand: Cultural Issues in Oral History* (Logan: Utah State University Press, 2002), 27–28.

58. "The Rocky Gap High School Oral History and Technology Project," 110.

59. Bradford R. Cole, "'Voices from the Trading Post': The United Indian Traders Association Legacy Project," *Western Historical Quarterly* 33 (Summer 2002), 205–11; http://www.nau.edu/library/speccol/exhibits/traders.

60. http://bancroft.berkeley.edu/FSM/

61. http://www.albany.edu/jmmh

62. H-ORALHIST@H-NET.MSU.EDU.

63. *Stories from the Collection: Columbia University Oral History Research Office,* produced by Charles Hardy III (New York: Columbia University, 1998), CD-ROM; *The University of Kentucky Oral History Program: Voices from the Collection,* produced by Doug Boyd (Lexington: University of Kentucky, 2002).

64. See Susan Levine review of Oral Histories Online, Berkeley, Calif., in *Oral History Review* 28 (Summer/Fall 2001), 139–40; http://www.lib.berkeley.edu/BANC/ROHO/ohonline

65. http://www.myhistory.org

66. http://www.folklife.si.edu/MississippiDelta/discoveringourdelta.htm; http://www.carts.org

67. http://historymatters.gmu.edu/

68. *Congressional Record,* 105th cong., 1st sess., S5605; David Darlington, "Veterans History Project Launched," *Perspectives: Newsletter of the American Historical Association* 40 (May 2002), 14–15; Gail Fineberg, "Veterans History Project Enlists Powerful Allies," *Folklife Center News* 24 (Winter 2002), 8–11.

69. See Charles T. Morrissey, "The Santayana Watch," *Organization of American Historians Newsletter* 20 (February 1992), 8.

Selected
Bibliograpy

HANDBOOKS AND METHODOLOGICAL STUDIES

Allen, Barbara, and Lynwood Montell. *From Memory to History: Using Oral Sources in Local Historical Research.* Jackson: University of Mississippi Press, 1991.

Baum, Willa K. *Oral History for the Local Historical Society.* Walnut Creek, Calif.: AltaMira, 1995.

———. *Transcribing and Editing Oral History.* Nashville, Tenn.: American Association for State and Local History, 1991.

Caunce, Stephen. *Oral History and the Local Historian.* New York: Longman, 1994.

Chamberlain, Mary, and Paul Thompson, eds. *Narrative and Genre.* New York: Routledge, 1998.

Chirban, John T. *Interviewing in Depth: The Interactive-Relational Approach.* Thousand Oaks, Calif.: Sage, 1996.

Dunaway, David K., and Willa J. Baum. *Oral History: An Interdisciplinary Anthology.* Walnut Creek, Calif.: AltaMira, 1996.

Eff, Elaine, ed. *You Should Have Been Here Yesterday: A Guide to Cultural Documentation in Maryland.* Crownsville, Md.: Maryland Historical Trust, 1995.

Epstein, Ellen Robinson, and Jane Lewit. *Record and Remember: Tracing Your Roots Through Oral History.* Lanham, Md.: Scarborough House, 1994.

Erickson, Stacy, and Troy Reeves. *A Field Notebook for Oral History.* Boise: Idaho Oral History Center, 2002.

Everett, Stephen E. *Oral History: Techniques and Procedures.* Washington, D.C.: Center of Military History, 1992.

Fletcher, William P. *Recording Your Family History: A Guide to Preserving Oral History with Videotape, Audio Tape, Suggested Topics and Questions, Interview Techniques.* New York: Dodd, Mead, 1986.

Frisch, Michael. *A Shared Authority: Essays on the Craft and Meaning of Oral History and Public History.* Albany: State University of New York Press, 1990.

Greene, Bob, and D. G. Fulford. *To Our Children's Children: Preserving Family Histories for Generations to Come.* New York: Doubleday, 1993.

Greenspan, Henry. *On Listening to Holocaust Survivors: Recounting and Life History.* Westport, Conn.: Praeger, 1998.

Grele, Ronald J., ed. *Envelopes of Sound: The Art of Oral History.* New York: Praeger, 1991.

Henige, David. *Oral Historiography.* New York: Longman, 1982.

Holstein, James, and Jaber F. Gurbrium. *The Active Interview.* Thousand Oaks, Calif.: Sage, 1995.

Howarth, Ken. *Oral History: A Handbook.* Stroud, England: Sutton, 1998.

Huen, P. Lim Pui, James H. Morrison, and Kwa Chong Guan. *Oral History in Southeast Asia: Theory and Method.* Singapore: National Archives of Singapore and Institute of Southeast Asian Studies, 1998.

Ives, Edward D. *The Tape-Recorded Interview: A Manual for Field Workers in Folklore and Oral History.* Knoxville: University of Tennessee Press, 1995.

———. *An Oral Historian's Work.* [Video] Blue Hills Falls, Me.: Northeast Historic Film, 1988.

Jackson, Bruce. *Fieldwork.* Urbana: University of Illinois Press, 1987.

Jeffrey, Jaclyn, and Glenace Edwall, eds. *Memory and History: Essays on Remembering and Interpreting Human Experience.* Lanham, Md: University Press of America, 1994.

Kammen, Carol, ed. *The Pursuit of Local History: Readings on Theory and Practice.* Walnut Creek, Calif.: AltaMira, 1996.

Kornbluh, Joyce, M. Brady Mikusko, and Debra Bernhardt. *Working Womenroots: An Oral History Primer.* Ann Arbor, Mich.: Wayne State University, 1980.

Lance, David. *An Archive Approach to Oral History.* London: Imperial War Museum and International Association of Sound Archives, 1978.

Lichtman, Allen J. *Your Family History; How to Use Oral History, Family Archives, and Public Documents to Discover Your Heritage.* New York: Vintage, 1978.

Lummis, Trevor. *Listening to History: The Authenticity of Oral Evidence.* Totowa, N.J.: Barnes & Noble, 1988.

Martin, Ruth R. *Oral History in Social Work: Research, Assessment, and Intervention.* Thousand Oaks, Calif.: Sage, 1995.

McMahan, Eva M. *Elite Oral History Discourse: A Study of Cooperation and Coherence.* Tuscaloosa: University of Alabama Press, 1989.

McMahan, Eva, and Kim Lacy Rogers, eds. *Interactive Oral History Interviewing.* Hillsdale, N.J.: Lawrence Erlbaum Associates, 1994.

Neuenschwander, John A. *Oral History and the Law.* Carlisle, Penn.: Oral History Association, 2002.

Oral History Association. *Evaluation Guidelines.* Carlisle, Penn.: Oral History Association, 2002.

Perks, Robert, and Alistair Thomson, eds. *The Oral History Reader.* New York: Routledge, 1998.

Perks, Robert. *Oral History: Talking About the Past.* London: Historical Association, 1995.

Portelli, Alessandro. *The Death of Luigi Trastulli and Other Stories: Form and Meaning in Oral History.* Albany: State University of New York Press, 1991.

———. *The Battle of Valle Giulia: Oral History and the Art of Dialogue.* Madison: University of Wisconsin Press, 1997.

Robertson, Beth M. *Oral History Handbook.* Adelaide: Oral History Association of Australia, 2000.

Rosenbluth, Vera. *Keeping Family Stories Alive: A Creative Guide to Taping Family Life and Lore.* Point Roberts, Wash.: Hartley and Marks, 1990.

Rosenzweig, Roy, and David Thelen. *The Presence of the Past: Popular Uses of History in American Life.* New York: Columbia University Press, 1998.

Samuel, Raphael. *Theatres of Memory.* London: Verso, 1994.

Schneider, William. *Project Jukebox: Where Oral History and Technology Come Together.* Anchorage: University of Alaska Anchorage, 1992.

———. *So They Understand: Cultural Issues in Oral History.* Logan: Utah State University Press, 2002.

Shedden, David B. *Preserving a Newspaper's Past: A Guide to Developing a Newspaper Oral History Program.* St. Petersburg, Fla.: Poynter Institute for Media Studies, 1992.

Sommer, Barbara W., and Mary Kay Quinlan. *The Oral History Manual*. Walnut Creek, Calif.: AltaMira, 2002.

Stave, Bruce M. *The Making of Urban History: Historiography Through Oral History*. Beverly Hills, Calif.: Sage, 1977.

Stave, Bruce M., and John F. Sutherland, eds. *Talking About Connecticut: Oral History in the Nutmeg State*. Storrs: University of Connecticut, 1985.

Stielow, Frederick J. *The Management of Oral History Sound Archives*. Westport, Conn.: Greenwood Press, 1986.

Stricklin, David, and Rebecca Sharpless. *The Past Meets the Present: Essays on Oral History*. Lanham, Md.: University Press of America, 1988.

Sturdevant, Katherine Scott. *Bringing Your Family History to Life Through Social History*. Cincinnati: Betterway, 2000.

Thelen, David, ed. *Memory and American History*. Bloomington: Indiana University Press, 1990.

Thompson, Paul. *The Voice of the Past: Oral History*. New York: Oxford University Press, 2000.

Tonkin, Elizabeth. *Narrating Our Pasts: The Social Construction of Oral History*. New York: Cambridge University Press, 1992.

United States Holocaust Memorial Museum. *Oral History Interview Guidelines*. Washington, D.C.: U.S. Holocaust Memorial Museum, 1998.

Vansina, Jan. *Oral Tradition as History*. Madison: University of Wisconsin Press, 1985.

Ward, Alan. *A Manual of Sound Archive Administration*. Brookfield, Vt: Gower, 1990.

Weber, Wolfgang. *"Mass of Trash" or "Veins of Gold"? An Investigative Report on the Relationship Between Oral History and Archives*. Regensburg, Austria: S. Roderer Verlag, 2000.

Yow, Valerie Raleigh. *Recording Oral History: A Practical Guide for Social Scientists*. Thousand Oaks, Calif.: Sage, 1994.

VIDEOTAPING

Fuller, Barry, et al. *Single-Camera Video Production*. Englewood Cliffs, N.J.: Prentice-Hall, 1982.

Hartman, Geoffrey H. *Preserving Living Memory: The Challenge and Power of Videotestimony*. Washington, D.C.: United States Holocaust Memorial Museum, 1995.

Jolly, Brad. *Videotaping Local History*. Nashville, Tenn.: American Association for State and Local History, 1982.

Schorzman, Terri A., ed. *A Practical Introduction to Videohistory: The Smithsonian Institution and Alfred P. Sloan Foundation Experiment*. Malabar, Fla.: Krieger, 1993.

Winston, Brian, and Julia Keydel. *Working With Video: A Comprehensive Guide to the World of Video Production*. London: Mobius International, 1986.

ORAL HISTORY FOR TEACHERS AND STUDENTS

Brown, Cynthia. *Like It Was: A Complete Guide to Writing Oral History*. New York: Teachers & Writers Collaborative, 1988.

Dean, Pamela, Toby Daspit, and Petra Munro. *Talking Gumbo: A Teacher's Guide to Using Oral History in the Classroom*. Baton Rouge: Louisiana State University, T. Harry Williams Center, 1998.

Flynn, Robert. *When I Was Just Your Age*. Denton: University of North Texas Press, 1992.

Gebhard, Krzysztof M. *Community as Classroom: A Teacher's Practical Guide to Oral History*. Regina, Canada: Saskatchewan Archives Board, 1985.

Hickey, M. Gail. *Bringing History Home: Local and Family History Projects for Grades K–6*. Boston: Allyn and Bacon, 1999.

History from the Living: The Organization and Craft of Oral History [Video]. Newport, R.I.: Grin Productions, 1998.

Hoopes, James. *Oral History: An Introduction for Students.* Chapel Hill: University of North Carolina Press, 1979.

Kuhn, Cliff, and Marjorie L. McLellan, eds. Oral History Issue of the *Organization of American Historians' Magazine of History.* June 1996.

Lanman, Barry A. and George L. Mehaffy. *Oral History in the Secondary School Classroom.* Los Angeles: Oral History Association, 1988.

Mehaffy, George L., Thad Sitton, and O.L. Davis, Jr. *Oral History in the Classroom.* Washington, D.C.: National Council for the Social Studies, 1979.

Metcalf, Fay D., and Matthew T. Downey. *Using Local History in the Classroom.* Nashville: American Association for State and Local History, 1982.

Oxford, Rebecca. *Language Learning Strategies: Conversation Skills Through Oral Histories.* New York: HarperCollins, 1989.

Sitton, Thad, George J. Mehaffy, and O. L. Davis, Jr. *Oral History for Teachers (and Others).* Austin: University of Texas Press, 1983.

Stone, Frank A. *Using Oral History in Educational Studies.* New York: I N Thut World Education Center, 1989.

Wigginton, Eliot. *Sometimes a Shining Moment: The Foxfire Experience.* Garden City, N.Y.: Doubleday, 1985.

You've Got to Hear This Story [Video]. Baton Rouge: Louisiana State University, T. Harry Williams Center, 1998.

ORAL HISTORY BIBLIOGRAPHIES

Ekrish, A. H. *Oral History and Oral Tradition: A Selective Bibliography.* Pittsburgh: University of Pittsburgh School of Library Science, 1985.

Flekke, Mary M. *Telling Our Stories, Oral & Family History: A Bibliography.* 4th ed. Lakeland, Fla.: M. M. Flekke, 1999.

Havlice, Patricia Pate. *Oral History: A Reference Guide and Annotated Bibliography.* Jefferson, N.C.: McFarland, 1985.

Perks, Robert. *Oral History: An Annotated Bibliography.* London: The British Library, 1990.

ORAL HISTORY DIRECTORIES AND CATALOGS

Alan Paton Centre. *Guide to the Oral Sources in the Alan Paton Centre, University of Natal, Pietermaritzburg.* Pretoria: National Archives of South Africa, 2000.

Albert F. Simpson Historical Research Center. *USAF Oral History Catalog.* Washington, D.C.: Office of Air Force History, 1977.

Allen, Susan E., and Terry L. Birdwhistell. *The Frontier Nursing Service Oral History Project: An Annotated Guide.* Lexington: University of Kentucky, 1987.

Anderson, Terry H. *A Guide to the Oral History Collection of Texas A&M University.* College Station: Texas A&M University, 1988.

Archives of American Art. *The Card Catalog of the Oral History Collections of the Archives of American Art.* Wilmington, Del.: Scholarly Resources, 1984.

Bertrando, Betsy. *History Comes Alive: Catalog of Oral History Holdings in San Luis Obispo County.* San Luis Obispo, Calif: San Luis Obispo Oral History Organization, 1980.

Bibliographical Center of the Institute of Contemporary Jewry. *Oral History of Contemporary Jewry: An Annotated Catalogue.* New York: Garland, 1990.

Bloom, Jonathan, and Paul Buhle, eds. *Guide to the Oral History of the American Left.* New York: New York University Libraries, 1984.

Borneman, Patricia. *Directory to Montana Oral History Resources.* Helena: Montana Oral History Association, 1985.

———. *Speaking of Montana: A Guide to the Oral History Collection at the Montana Historical Society, Through 1996.* Helena: Montana Historical Society Press, 1997.

Brown, Jeffrey P., Andrew O. Wiget and Colleen M. O'Neil, eds. *Oral History Collections Catalog for New Mexico.* Las Cruces: New Mexico State University, 1989.

Buckendorf, Madeline, and Elizabeth P. Jacox. *Directory of Oral History Resources in Idaho.* Boise: Idaho State Historical Society, 1982.

Calabretta, Fred. *Guide to the Oral History Collections at Mystic Seaport Museum.* Mystic, Conn.: The Mystic Seaport Museum, 1992.

Catalogue of Memoirs of the William E. Wiener Oral History Library. New York: American Jewish Committee, 1978.

Champagne, Anthony, Cynthia Harrison, and Adam Land, eds. *A Directory of Oral History Interviews Related to the Federal Courts.* Washington, D.C.: Federal Judicial Center, 1992.

Charles Babbage Institute. *Guide to CBI Oral History Collection.* Minneapolis: Charles Babbage Institute, 1986.

Chepesiuk, Ron, ed. *A Guide to the Manuscript and Oral History Collections in the Winthrop College Archives and Special Collections.* Rock Hill, S.C.: Winthrop College, 1978.

Collection Catalog of the Oral History Program. Reno: University of Nevada, 1987.

Cook, Patsy A. *Directory of Oral History Programs in the United States.* New York: Microfilming Corporation of America, 1982.

A Directory of Oral History Projects in South Africa. Pretoria: National Archives of South Africa, 1999.

Ethnic Studies Oral History Project. *Catalog of the ESOHP Collection, 1976–84.* Honolulu: University of Hawaii at Manoa, 1984.

Forrest C. Pogue Oral History Institute. *Voices from the Past: A Catalog of Oral History Interviews from the Land Between the Lakes.* Murray, Ky.: Murray State University, 1982.

Fortier, Normand. *Guide to Oral History Collections in Canada.* Ottawa: Canadian Oral History Association, 1993.

Frank, Benis M. *Marine Corps Oral History Collection Catalog.* Washington, D.C.: History and Museums Division, U.S. Marine Corps, 1989.

Gallacher, Cathryn, ed. *Oral History Collections in the Southwest Region: A Directory and Subject Guide.* Los Angeles: Southwest Oral History Association, 1986.

Goff, Lila Johnson, and James E. Fogerty, eds. *The Oral History Collections of the Minnesota Historical Society.* St. Paul: Minnesota Historical Society Press, 1984.

Grathwold, Robert P., and Donita Moorhus, and Douglas J. Wilson. *Oral History and Postwar German-American Relations: Resources in the United States.* Washington, D.C.: German Historical Institute, 1997.

Guide to Archival and Oral History Collections. Berkeley, Calif: Western Jewish History Center, 1987.

Heintze, James R. *Scholars' Guide to Washington, D.C. Audio Resources: Sound Recordings in the Arts, Humanities, and Social, Physical, and Life Sciences.* Washington, D.C.: Smithsonian Institute, 1985.

Hill, Ruth Edmonds, and Patricia Miller King, eds. Guide to the Transcripts of the *Black Women Oral History Project Sponsored by the Arthur and Elizabeth Schlesinger Library of the History of Women in America.* Westport, Conn.: Meckler, 1990.

Historical Materials in the Lyndon Baines Johnson Library. Austin, Tex.: Lyndon Baines Johnson Library, 1988.

Hoffman, Alice M., ed. *The Pennsylvania State University Oral History Projects*. University Park: Pennsylvania State University, 1985.

Humphreys, Hubert. *Louisiana Oral History Collections: A Directory*. Shreveport: Louisiana State University, Shreveport, 1980.

Jimenez, Rebecca Sharpless, Jane Frances Healey, and Harriet Hull Fadal. *Baylor University Institute for Oral History: A Guide to the Collection, 1970–85*. Waco, Tex.: Baylor University, 1985.

Johnson, Coburn R., and Karen A. Hatcher, eds. *People Will Talk: Oral History Collection of the Mansfield Library, University of Montana*. Missoula: University of Montana, 1987.

Josias, Anthea, Norman Kaplan, and André Odendaal, eds. *Mayibuye Centre Oral History Collections*. Bellville, South Africa: University of the Western Cape, 1994.

Julin, Suzanne. *Index to the American Indian Research Project*. Pierre: South Dakota Oral History Center, 1979.

Kayanti, Vimala, ed. *The UCLA Oral History Program: Catalog of the Collection*. Los Angeles: University of California, 1992.

Kendrick, Alice M., and Helen M. Knubel, eds. *The Oral History Collection of the American Lutheran Church, Association of Evangelical Lutheran Churches and Lutheran Church in America*. New York: Lutheran Council in the USA, 1987.

Key, Betty McKeever, and Larry E. Sullivan, eds. *Oral History in Maryland: A Directory*. Baltimore: Maryland Historical Society, 1981.

Kidwell, Peggy A., and Juanita Y. Morris, eds. *A Combined Index to Oral Histories Open to Readers*. Washington, D.C.: Smithsonian Institution, 1986.

Knight, Margot H., ed. *Directory of Oral History in Washington State*. Pullman: Washington State University, 1981.

Koontz, Christopher N., and Ronald E. Marcello, eds. *Heroes: Oral History Interviews with World War II Veterans*. Denton: University of North Texas, 2002.

Langlois, W. J., ed. *A Guide to Aural History Research*. Victoria: Provincial Archives of British Columbia, 1976.

Lunt, C. Richard K., ed. *The Maine Folklife Index*. Orono: University of Maine, 1982.

Marcello, Ronald E., ed. *University of North Texas Oral History Program, Revised Catalog, 1997*. Denton: University of North Texas, 1997.

Martell, Charles R., and Kitty W. Shek. *A Guide to the Oral History Collection of Cambodians in California*. Sacramento: California State University, 1992.

Mason, Elizabeth B., and Louis M. Starr, eds. *The Oral History Collection of Columbia University*. New York: Oral History Research Office, 1979.

McInerny, Carmel Frances. *Parliamentary Voices in History: A Guide to the Location of Federal Parliamentarians' Personal Papers and Oral History Interviews*. Canberra: Australian Government Publications Service, 1991.

Meckler, Alan M., and Ruth McMullin, eds. *Oral History Collections*. New York: R. R. Bowker, 1975.

Miller, Cynthia Pease. *A Guide to Research Collections of Former Members of the United States House of Representatives, 1789–1987*. Washington, D.C.: Government Printing Office, 1988.

Nowicke, Carole Elizabeth, David K. Allison, and Peter S. Buchanan, eds. *Index of Oral Histories Relating to Naval Research and Development*. Bethesda, Md.: David W. Taylor Naval Ship Research and Development Center, 1985.

Oral History Collection of the Federation of Jewish Philanthropies. New York: Federation of Jewish Philanthropies, 1985.

Oral History Collection on the Performing Arts in America. Dallas: Southern Methodist University, 1984.

Oral History Guide: A Bibliographic Listing of the Memoirs in the Micropublished Collections. Glen Rock, N.J.: Microfilming Corp. of America, 1976-1983.

Palmer, Joseph W. *A Directory of Oral History and Audio Visual Local History Resources in Public Libraries of New York States.* Buffalo: State University of New York Buffalo, 1985.

Palmer, Joseph W. *Oral History in Public Libraries.* Urbana: University of Illinois Graduate School of Library and Information Service, 1984.

Palmer, Michele, Janet Nolan, and Brian O'Connor, eds. *Catalog of Interviews: Connecticut Workers and a Half Century of Technological Change, 1930–1980, Oral History Project.* Storrs: Center for Oral History at the University of Connecticut, 1983.

Riess, Suzanne B., and Willa K. Baum, eds. *Catalogue of the Regional Oral History Office, 1954–1979.* Berkeley: University of California, Berkeley, 1980.

Ringelheim, Joan Miriam. *A Catalogue of Audio and Video Recollections of Holocaust Testimony.* New York: Greenwood, 1992.

Rune, Ann. *Oral History Index: Washington State Oral/Aural History Program, 1974–1977.* Olympia: State of Washington, Division of Archives and Records Management, 1977.

Smith, Allen. *Directory of Oral History Collections.* Phoenix. Ariz.: Oryx, 1988.

Stephenson, Shirley E., ed. *Oral History Collection.* Fullerton: California State University, Fullerton, 1985.

Todd, Joe L., ed. *Catalogue of Oral Histories.* Oklahoma City: Oklahoma Historical Society, 1984.

———. *Native American Interviews.* Oklahoma City: Oklahoma Historical Society, 1987.

United Jewish Appeal. *The Oral History Collection.* New York: UJA—Federation of Jewish Philanthropies of New York, 1998.

University of Vermont Library. *Folklore and Oral History Catalogue.* Burlington: University of Vermont, 1991.

Wasserman, Ellen S. *Oral History Index: An International Directory of Oral History Interviews.* Westport, Conn.: Meckler, 1990.

Whealan, Ronald E., ed. *Historical Materials in the John Fitzgerald Kennedy Library.* Boston: John Fitzgerald Kennedy Library, 1990.

Whittaker, David J., and Bryan Dixon, eds. *African Oral History Project: Interviews by E. Dale LeBaron: MSS 1937.* Provo, Utah: Brigham Young University, 1996.

Wilkins, Cary C., ed. *The Guide to Kentucky Oral History Collections.* Frankfort: Kentucky Oral History Commission, 1991.

Wilton, Janis. *Oral History in Australia: A List.* Sydney: Oral History Association of Australia, (New South Wales Branch), 1996.

Wood, Thomas J., ed. *Guide to the Oral History Collections at the University of Illinois at Springfield.* Springfield: University of Illinois at Springfield, 1996.

ORAL HISTORY IN FAMILY AND COMMUNITY STUDIES

Archibald, Robert R. *A Place to Remember: Using History to Build Community.* Walnut Creek, Calif.: AltaMira, 1999.

Brown, Robert F. *The New Englanders.* Worcester, Mass.: Commonwealth, 1980.

Coles, Robert. *The Old Ones of New Mexico.* Albuquerque: University of New Mexico Press, 1973.

Cooper, Leland, and Mary Lee Cooper. *The People of the New River: Oral Histories from the Ashe, Alleghany, and Watauga Counties of North Carolina*. Jefferson, N.C: McFarland, 2001.

Egerton, John. *Generations: An American Family*. Lexington: University Press of Kentucky, 1983.

Ellison, Elaine Krasnow. *Voices from Marshall Street: Jewish Life in a Philadelphia Neighborhood, 1920–1960*. Philadelphia: Camino, 1993.

Fee, Elizabeth, Linda Shopes, and Linda Zeidman. *The Baltimore Book: New Views on Local History*. Philadelphia: Temple University Press, 1991.

Frommer, Myrna Katz, and Harvey Frommer. *It Happened in Manhattan: An Oral History of Life in the City during the Mid-Twentieth Century*. New York: Berkley, 2001.

Ginns, Patsy Moore. *Snowbird Gravy and Dishpan Pie: Mountain People Recall*. Chapel Hill: University of North Carolina Press, 1982.

Goldberg, Linda S., ed. *Here on This Hill: Conversations with Vermont Neighbors*. Middlebury: Vermont Folklife Center, 1991.

Green, Howard. *Family and Community Life*. Trenton: New Jersey Historical Commission, 1990.

Hall, Jacqueline Dowd, James Leloudis, Robert Korstad, Mary Murphy, Lu Ann Jones, and Christopher B. Daly. *Like a Family: The Making of a Southern Cotton Mill World*. Chapel Hill: University of North Carolina Press, 1987.

Kisseloff, Jeff. *You Must Remember This: An Oral History of Manhattan from the 1890s to World War II*. Baltimore, Md.: Johns Hopkins University Press, 1999.

Kuhn, Cliff, Harlon E. Joye, and E. Bernard West. *Living Atlanta: An Oral History of the City, 1914–1948*. Athens: University of Georgia Press, 1990.

Mercier, Laurie, and Madeline Buckendorf. *Using Oral History in Community History Projects*. Los Angeles: Oral History Association, 1992.

Montell, William Lynwood. *The Saga of Coe Ridge*. Knoxville: University of Tennessee Press, 1970.

Naske, Claus M. *Alaska Statehood, the Memory of the Battle and the Evaluation of the Present by Those Who Lived It: An Oral History of the Remaining Actors in the Alaska Statehood Movement*. Fairbanks: Alaska Statehood Commission, 1981.

Oblinger, Carl. *Interviewing the People of Pennsylvania: A Conceptual Guide to Oral History*. Harrisburg: Pennsylvania Historical and Museum Commission, 1978.

Ransel, David. *Village Mothers: Three Generations of Change in Russia and Tataria*. Bloomington: Indiana University Press, 2000.

Sitton, Thad, and Dan Utley. *From Can See to Can't: Texas Cotton Farmers on the Southern Prairies*. Austin: University of Texas Press, 1997.

Slim, Hugo, and Paul Thomson. *Listening for a Change: Oral Testimony and Community Development*. Philadelphia: New Society, 1995.

Strickland, Ron., ed. *Whistlepunks & Geoducks: Oral Histories from the Pacific Northwest*. New York: Paragon House, 1990.

Warren, Mame. *Then Again . . . Annapolis, 1900–1965*. Annapolis, Md.: Time Exposures, 1990.

ETHNIC ORAL HISTORY

Benmayor, Rina. *Stories to Live By: Continuity and Change in Three Generations of Puerto Rican Women*. New York: City University of New York, 1987.

Bruchac, Joseph. *Lasting Echoes: An Oral History of Native American People*. San Diego, Calif.: Silver Whistle, 1997.

Cash, Joseph H., and Herbert T. Hoover. *To Be An Indian: An Oral History*. St. Paul: Minnesota Historical Society Press, 1995.

Cowan, Neil M. *Our Parents' Lives: The Americanization of Eastern European Jews.* New York: Basic, 1989.

Davis, Marilyn P. *Mexican Voices/American Dreams: An Oral History of Mexican Immigration to the United States.* New York: Holt, 1990.

Dubrow, Gail. *Sento at Sixth and Main: Preserving Landmarks of Japanese American Heritage.* Seattle: University of Washington Press, 2002.

Frommer, Myrna Katz, and Harvey Frommer, eds. *Growing Up Jewish in America: An Oral History.* Lincoln: University of Nebraska Press, 1999.

Kim, Elaine H., and Eui-Young Yu. *East to America: Korean American Life Stories.* New York: New Press, 1996.

Lee, Joann Faung Jean. *Asian Americans: Oral Histories of First to Fourth Generation Americans from China, the Philippines, Japan, India, the Pacific Islands, Vietnam, and Cambodia.* New York: W.W. Norton, 1992.

Leviatin, David. *Following the Trail: Jewish Working-Class Radicals in America.* New Haven, Conn.: Yale University Press, 1989.

Martin, Patricia P. *Images and Conversations: Mexican Americans Recall a Southwestern Past.* Tucson: University of Arizona Press, 1983.

Masumoto, David Mas. *Country Voices: The Oral History of a Japanese American Family Farm Community.* Del Rey, Calif.: Inaka Countryside, 1987.

McCunn, Ruthanne Lum. *Chinese American Portraits: Personal Histories 1828–1988.* San Francisco: Chronicle, 1988.

Mormino, Gary R., and George E. Pozzetta. *The Immigrant World of Ybor City: Italians and Their Latin Neighbors in Tampa City, 1885–1985.* Urbana: University of Illinois Press, 1987.

Morrison, Joan, and Charlotte Fox Zabusky. *American Mosaic: The Immigrant Experience in the Words of Those Who Lived It.* New York: Dutton, 1980.

Namias, June. *First Generation: In the Words of Twentieth-Century American Immigrants.* Boston: Beacon, 1978.

Perdue, Theda. *Nations Remembered: An Oral History of the Cherokees, Chickasaws, Choctaws, Creeks, and Seminoles in Oklahoma, 1865–1907.* Norman: University of Oklahoma Press, 1993.

Rothschild, Sylvia. *A Special Legacy: An Oral History of Soviet Jewish Emigrés in the United States.* New York: Simon and Schuster, 1985.

Rottenberg, Dan. *Middletown Jews: The Tenuous Survival of an American Jewish Community.* Bloomington: Indiana University Press, 1997.

Stave, Bruce M., and John F. Sutherland, with Aldo Salerno. *From the Old Country: An Oral History of European Migration to America.* New York: Twayne, 1994.

Tamura, Linda. *The Hood River Issei: An Oral History of Japanese Settlers in Oregon's Hood River Valley.* Urbana: University of Illinois Press, 1993.

Tateishi, John. *And Justice For All: An Oral History of the Japanese American Detention Camps.* Seattle: University of Washington Press, 1999.

Vecoli, Rudolph, ed. *Voices from Ellis Island: An Oral History of American Immigration: A Project of the Statue of Liberty-Ellis Island Foundation.* Frederick, Md.: University Publications of America, 1990.

Wolman, Ruth. *Crossing Over: An Oral History of Refugees from Hitler's Reich.* New York: Twayne, 1996.

Wright, Giles, ed. *Looking Back: Eleven Life Histories.* Trenton: New Jersey Historical Commission, 1986.

ORAL HISTORY, BLACK HISTORY AND CIVIL RIGHTS

Berlin, Ira, Marx Faveau, and Steven F. Miller, eds. *Remembering Slavery: African Americans Talk About Their Personal Experiences of Slavery and Emancipation.* New York: New Press, 1998.

Blauner, Bob, ed. *Black Lives, White Lives: Three Decades of Race Relations in America.* Berkeley: University of California Press, 1989.

Bullock, Paul, ed. *Watts: The Aftermath: An Inside View of the Ghetto, by the People of Watts.* New York: Grove, 1969.

Chafe, William, et. al. *Remembering Jim Crow: African Americans Tell About Life in the Segregated South.* New York: New Press, 2001.

Ellsworth, Scott. *Death in a Promised Land: The Tulsa Race Riot of 1921.* Baton Rouge: Louisiana State University Press, 1982.

Govenar, Alan B. *African American Frontiers: Slave Narratives and Oral Histories.* Santa Barbara, Calif.: ABC-CLIO, 2000.

Gwaltney, John Langston. *Drylongso: A Self-Portrait of Black America.* New York: New Press, 1993.

Hamburger, Robert. *Our Portion of Hell: Fayette County, Tennessee: An Oral History of the Struggle for Civil Rights.* New York: Link Books, 1973.

Hampton, Henry, Steve Fayer, and Sarah Flynn. *Voices of Freedom: An Oral History of the Civil Rights Movement from the 1950s through the 1980s.* New York: Bantam, 1990.

Holway, John. *Voices from the Great Black Baseball Leagues.* New York: Dodd, Mead, 1975.

Hurmence, Belinda, ed. *Before Freedom, When I Just Can Remember: Twenty-Seven Oral Histories of Former South Carolina Slaves.* Winston-Salem, N.C.: J. F. Blair, 1989.

Moon, Elaine Latzman. *Untold Tales, Unsung Heroes: An Oral History of Detroit's African American Community, 1918–1967.* Detroit, Mich.: Wayne State University Press, 1994.

Morris, Ann, ed. *Lift Every Voice and Sing: St. Louis African-Americans in the Twentieth Century: Narratives Collected by Doris A. Wesley.* Columbia: University of Missouri Press, 1999.

Morris, Gabrielle. *Head of the Class: An Oral History of African-American Achievement in Higher Education and Beyond.* New York: Twayne, 1995.

Perdue, L. Charles, Jr., Thomas E. Barden, and Robert K. Phillips, eds. *Weevils in the Wheat: Interviews with Virginia Ex-Slaves.* Bloomington: Indiana University Press, 1980.

Raines, Howell. *My Soul Is Rested: Movement Days in the Deep South Remembered.* New York: Putnam, 1977.

Rawick, George P., ed. *The American Slave: A Composite Autobiography.* Westport, Conn.: Greenwood, 1972–1973. Nineteen volumes of WPA interviews.

Rogers, Kim Lacy. *Righteous Lives: Narratives of the New Orleans Civil Rights Movement.* New York: New York University Press, 1993.

Rosengarten, Theodore. *All God's Dangers: The Life of Nate Shaw.* New York: Knopf, 1974.

Schultz, Debra L. *Going South: Jewish Women in the Civil Rights Movement.* New York: New York University Press, 2001.

Terkel, Studs. *Race: How Blacks and Whites Think and Feel about the American Obsession.* New York: New Press, 1992.

Thornbrough, Emma Lou. *Indiana Blacks in the Twentieth Century.* Bloomington: Indiana University Press, 2000.

ORAL HISTORIES OF WOMEN

Alexander, Maxine, ed. *Speaking for Ourselves: Women of the South.* New York: Pantheon, 1984.

Armitage, Susan H., with Patricia Hart and Karen Weathermon, eds. *Women's Oral History: The Frontiers Reader.* Lincoln: University of Nebraska Press, 2002.

Casey, Kathleen. *I Answer With My Life: Life Histories of Women Teachers Working for Social Change.* New York: Routledge, 1993.

Coles, Robert, and Jane Hallowell Coles. *Women of Crisis: Lives of Struggle and Hope.* New York: Delacorte, 1978.

Ewen, Elizabeth. *Immigrant Women in the Land of Dollars: Life and Culture on the Lower East Side, 1890–1925.* New York: Monthly Review Press, 1985.

Fenzi, Jewell, and Allida Black. *Democratic Women: An Oral History of the Woman's National Democratic Club.* Washington, D.C.: WNDC Educational Foundation, 2000.

Fenzi, Jewell, with Carl T. Nelson. *Married to the Foreign Service: An Oral History of the American Diplomatic Spouse.* New York: Twayne, 1994.

Fyfe, Judith. *The Matriarchs: A Generation of New Zealand Women Talk to Judith Fyfe.* Auckland, New Zealand: Penguin, 1990.

Gallagher, Dorothy. *Hannah's Daughters: Six Generations of an American Family, 1876–1976.* New York: Thomas Cromwell, 1976.

Glenn, Evelyn Nakano. *Issei, Nisei, War Bride: Three Generations of Japanese American Women in Domestic Service.* Philadelphia: Temple University Press, 1986.

Gluck, Sherna. *From Parlor to Prison: Five American Suffragists Talk About their Lives, An Oral History.* New York: Vintage, 1976.

Gluck, Sherna Berger, and Daphne Patai, eds. *Women's Words: The Feminist Practice of Oral History.* New York: Routledge, 1991.

Gurewitsch, Brana. *Mothers, Sisters, Resisters: Oral Histories of Women Who Survived the Holocaust.* Tuscaloosa: University of Alabama Press, 1998.

Hungry Wolf, Beverley. *The Ways of My Grandmothers.* New York: William Morrow, 1980.

Jones, Lu Ann. *Mama Learned Us to Work: Farm Women in the New South.* Chapel Hill: University of North Carolina Press, 2002.

Jones-Eddy, Julie. *Homesteading Women: An Oral History of Colorado, 1890–1950.* New York: Twayne, 1992.

Kahn, Kathy. *Hillbilly Women.* Garden City, N.Y.: Doubleday, 1973.

Kennedy, Elizabeth Lapovsky, and Madeline D. Davis. *Boots of Leather, Slippers of Gold: The History of a Lesbian Community.* New York: Routledge, 1993.

Kramer, Sydelle, and Jenny Masur, eds. *Jewish Grandmothers.* Boston: Beacon, 1976.

Krause, Corinne Azen. *Grandmothers, Mothers, and Daughters: Oral Histories of Three Generations of Ethnic American Women.* Boston: Twayne, 1991.

Leydesdorff, Selma, Luisa Passerini, and Paul Thompson, eds. *Gender and Memory.* New York: Oxford University Press, 1996.

Mercier, Laurie, Mary Murphy, Linda Peavy, Diane Sands, and Ursula Smith. *Molders and Shapers, Montana Women as Community Builders: An Oral History Sampler and Guide.* Helena: Montana Historical Society Oral History Office, 1987.

Moore, Marat. *Women in the Mines: Stories of Life and Work.* New York: Twayne, 1996.

Morin, Ann Miller. *Her Excellency: An Oral History of American Women Ambassadors.* New York: Twayne, 1995.

Newton, Esther. *Cherry Grove, Fire Island: Sixty Years in America's First Gay and Lesbian Town.* Boston: Beacon, 1993.

Personal Narratives Group. *Interpreting Women's Lives: Feminist Theory and Personal Narratives.* Bloomington: Indiana University Press, 1989.

Rogers, Carole Garibaldi. *Poverty, Chastity, and Change: Lives of Contemporary American Nuns.* New York: Twayne, 1996.

Rothschild, Mary Aickin. *Doing What the Day Brought: An Oral History of Arizona Women.* Tucson: University of Arizona Press, 1992.

Sharpless, Rebecca. *Fertile Ground, Narrow Choices: Women on Cotton Farms of the Texas Blackland Prairie, 1900–1940.* Chapel Hill: University of North Carolina Press, 1999.

Smith, Anne. *Women Remember: An Oral History.* New York: Routledge, 1989.

Summerfield, Penny. *Reconstructing Women's Wartime Lives: Discourse and Subjectivity in Oral Histories of the Second World War.* New York: St. Martin's Press, 1998.

Rousseau, Ann Marie. *Shopping Bag Ladies: Homeless Women Talk About Their Lives.* New York: Pilgrim, 1981.

Walker, Melissa. *All We Knew Was to Farm: Rural Women in the Upcountry South, 1919–1941.* Baltimore: Johns Hopkins University Press, 2000.

ORAL HISTORY OF WORKERS

Brecher, Jeremy, Jerry Lombardi, and Jan Stackhouse. *Brass Valley: The Story of Working People's Lives and Struggles in an American Industrial Region.* Philadelphia: Temple University Press, 1982.

Buhl, Paul M., ed. *Working Lives: An Oral History of Rhode Island Labor.* Providence: Rhode Island Historical Society, 1987.

Dunar, Andrew J., and Dennis McBride. *Building Hoover Dam: An Oral History of the Great Depression.* Reno: University of Nevada Press, 2001.

Erlich, Mark, and David Goldberg. *With Our Hands: The Story of Carpenters in Massachusetts.* Philadelphia: Temple University Press, 1986.

Evans, George Ewart. *Tools of Their Trade: An Oral History of Men at Work, c. 1900.* New York: Taplinger, 1970.

Friedlander, Peter. *The Emergence of a UAW Local, 1936–1939: A Study in Class and Culture.* Pittsburgh: University of Pittsburgh Press, 1975.

Friedman, Clara H. *Between Management and Labor: Oral Histories of Arbitration.* New York: Twayne, 1995.

Halpern, Rick, and Roger Horowitz. *Meatpackers: An Oral History of Black Packinghouse Workers and Their Struggle for Racial and Economic Equality.* New York: Twayne, 1996.

Hareven, Tamara K., and Randolph Langenbach. *Amoskeag: Life and Work in an American Factory City.* New York: Pantheon, 1978.

Kodama-Nishimoto, Michi, Warren S. Nishimoto, and Cynthia A. Oshiro. *Hanahana: An Oral History Anthology of Hawaii's Working People.* Honolulu: University of Hawaii at Manoa, 1984.

Korth, Philip A., and Margaret R. Beegle. *I Remember Like Today: The Auto-Lite Strike of 1934.* East Lansing: Michigan State University Press, 1988.

Kuhn, Clifford M. *Contesting the New South Order: The 1914–1915 Strike at Atlanta's Fulton Mills.* Chapel Hill: University of North Carolina Press, 2002.

Lynd, Alice, and Staughton Lynd. *Rank and File: Personal Histories by Working-Class Organizers.* Boston: Beacon, 1973.

Maurer, Harry. *Not Working: An Oral History of the Unemployed.* New York: Holt, Rinehart and Winston, 1979.

Perata, David B. *Those Pullman Blues: An Oral History of the African American Railroad Attendant.* New York: Twayne, 1996.

Rubin, Lillian Breslow. *Worlds of Pain: Life in the Working-Class Family.* New York: Basic, 1976.

Safier, Gwendolyn. *Contemporary American Leaders in Nursing: An Oral History.* New York: McGraw-Hill, 1977.

Santino, Jack. *Miles of Smiles, Years of Struggle: Stories of Black Pullman Porters.* Urbana: University of Illinois Press, 1989.

Terkel, Studs. *Working: People Talk About What They Do All Say and How They Feel About What They Do.* New York: Pantheon, 1974.

ORAL HISTORY AND THE PROFESSIONS

Abelove, Henry, Betsy Blackmar, Peter Dimock, and Jonathan Schneer, eds. *Visions of History: Interviews with E. P. Thompson, Eric Hobsbawm, Sheila Rowbotham, Linda Gordon, Natalie Zemon Davis, William Appleman Williams, Staughton Lynd, David Montgomery, Herbert Gutman, Vincent Harding, John Womack, C. L. R. James, and Mose Lewin by MARHO, the Radical Historians Organization.* New York: Pantheon, 1983.

Baer, Michael A., Malcolm E. Jewell, and Lee Sigelman, eds. *Political Science in America: Oral Histories of a Discipline.* Lexington: University Press of Kentucky, 1991.

Braden, Maria. *She Said What? Interviews with Women Newspaper Columnists.* Lexington: University Press of Kentucky, 1993.

Brennen, Bonnie. *For the Record: An Oral History of Rochester, New York, Newsworkers.* New York: Fordham University Press, 2001.

Brown, Kenneth A. *Inventors at Work: Interviews with 16 Notable American Inventors.* Redmond, Wash.: Tempus Books of Microsoft Press, 1988.

Casey, Kathleen. *I Answer with My Life: Life Histories of Women Teachers Working for Social Change.* New York: Routledge, 1993.

Duling, Gretchen. *Oral Life Histories of One-Room Schoolhouse Teachers: Voices from the Recitation Bench.* Lewiston, N.Y.: Edwin Mellen Press, 1997.

Etter-Lewis, Gwendolyn. *My Soul Is My Own: Oral Narratives of African American Women in the Professions.* New York: Routledge, 1993.

Garrity, John A. *Interpreting American History: Conversations with Historians.* 2 vols. New York: Macmillan, 1970.

Lightman, Alan, and Roberta Brawer. *Origins: The Life and Worlds of Modern Cosmologists.* Cambridge: Harvard University Press, 1990.

Lyle, Guy R. *The Librarian Speaking: Interviews With University Librarians.* Athens: University of Georgia Press, 1970.

Manning, Diane. *Hill Country Teacher: Oral Histories from the One-Room School and Beyond.* Boston: Twayne, 1990.

Rinehart, Alice Duffy. *Mortals in the Immortal Profession: An Oral History of Teaching.* New York: Irvington, 1983.

ORAL HISTORY OF MEDICINE, ILLNESS AND TRAUMA

Bayer, Ronald and Gerald M. Oppenheimer. *AIDS Doctors: Voices from the Epidemic.* New York: Oxford University Press, 2000.

Benison, Saul. *Tom Rivers: Reflections on a Life in Medicine and Science: An Oral History Memoir.* Cambridge, Mass.: MIT Press, 1967.

Bornat, Joanna, Robert Perks, Paul Thompson, and Jan Walmsley, eds. *Oral History, Health and Welfare.* New York: Routledge, 2000.

Fink, Mitchell. *Never Forget: An Oral History of September 11, 2001.* New York: Regan Books, 2002.

Lofton, J. Mack. *Healing Hands: An Alabama Medical Mosaic.* Tuscaloosa: University of Alabama Press, 1995.

Miller, Donald E., and Lorna Touryan Miller. *Survivors: An Oral History of the Armenian Genocide.* Berkeley: University of California Press, 1993.

Murphy, Dean E. *September 11: An Oral History.* New York: Doubleday, 2002.

Rabinowitz, Peter MacGarr. *Talking Medicine: Doctors Tell Their Stories.* New York: Norton, 1981.

Rogers, Kim Lacy, Selma Leydesdorff, and Graham Dawson, eds. *Trauma and Life Stories: International Perspectives.* New York: Routledge, 1999.

Vaucher, Andréa R. *Muses from Chaos and Ash: AIDS, Artists, and Art.* New York: Grove, 1993.

ORAL HISTORIES OF THE ARTS AND LEISURE

Balliett, Whitney. *American Musicians: 56 Portraits in Jazz.* New York: Oxford University Press, 1986.

Barkow, Al. *Gettin' to the Dance Floor: An Oral History of American Golf.* New York: Antheneum, 1986.

Cataneo, David. *Hornsby Hit One Over My Head: A Fans' Oral History of Baseball.* San Diego: Harcourt Brace, 1997.

Cook, John W., and Heinrich Klotz. *Conversations with Architects.* New York: Praeger, 1973.

Cooper-Clark, Diana. *Interviews with Contemporary Novelists.* New York: St. Martin's Press, 1986.

Cummings, Paul. *Artists in Their Own Words: Interviews.* New York: St. Martin's, 1979.

Cunnningham, Kitty, and Michael Ballard. *Conversations With A Dancer.* New York: St. Martin's, 1980.

Dance, Helen Oakley. *Stormy Monday: The T-Bone Walker Story.* Baton Rouge: Louisiana State University Press, 1986.

Davis, Francis. *In The Moment: Jazz in the 1980s.* New York: Oxford University Press, 1986.

Dunaway, David King. *How Can I Keep From Singing: Pete Seeger.* New York: McGraw-Hill, 1981.

Fink, Mitchell. *Off the Record : An Oral History of Popular Music.* New York: Warner, 1988.

Freedman, William. *More Than a Pastime: An Oral History of Baseball Fans.* Jefferson, N.C.: McFarland, 1998.

Gitler, Ira. *Swing to Bop: An Oral History of the Transition to Jazz in the 1940s.* New York: Oxford University Press, 1985.

Holway, John B. *Black Diamonds: Life in the Negro Leagues from the Men Who Lived It.* Westport, Conn.: Meckler, 1989.

Lally, Richard. *Bombers: An Oral History of the New York Yankees.* New York: Crown, 2002.

Perlis, Vivian. *Charles Ives Remembered: An Oral History.* New Haven, Conn.: Yale University Press, 1974.

Ritter, Lawrence S. *The Glory of Their Times: The Story of the Early Days of Baseball, Told By the Men Who Played It.* New York: Macmillan, 1966.

Sarris, Andrew, ed. *Hollywood Voices: Interviews with Film Directors.* Indianapolis: Bobbs-Merrill, 1968.

Schafer, William J. and Richard B. Allen. *Brass Bands and New Orleans Jazz.* Baton Rouge: Louisiana State University Press, 1977.

Smith, Joe. *Off the Record: An Oral History of Pop Music.* New York: Warner, 1988.

Smith, Richard Cándida. *Utopia and Dissent: Art, Poetry, and Politics in California.* Berkeley: University of California Press, 1995.

Steen, Mike. *Hollywood Speaks: An Oral History.* New York: G. P. Putnam's Sons, 1974.

Suid, Lawrence. *Guts and Glory: Great American War Movies.* New York: Addison-Wesley, 1978.

Tullius, John. *I'd Rather Be a Yankee: An Oral History of America's Most Loved and Most Hated Baseball Team.* New York: Macmillan, 1986.

ORAL HISTORIES OF THE GREAT DEPRESSION

Appel, Benjamin. *The People Talk: American Voices from the Great Depression.* New York: Simon and Schuster, 1982.

Banks, Ann. *First-Person America.* New York: Knopf, 1980.

Broadfoot, Barry. *Ten Lost Years, 1929–1939: Memories of Canadians Who Survived the Depression.* Toronto: Doubleday, 1973.

Couch, W. T., ed. *These Are Our Lives.* Chapel Hill: University of North Carolina, 1939.

Daniels, Roger, ed. *Eleanor Roosevelt: Oral Histories from the Collections of the Franklin D. Roosevelt Library.* New York: K.G. Saur, 1993.

Dunar, Andrew J., and Dennis McBride. *Building Hoover Dam: An Oral History of the Great Depression.* New York: Twayne, 1993.

Jellison, Charles A. *Tomatoes Were Cheaper: Tales from the Thirties.* Syracuse: N.Y.: Syracuse University Press, 1977.

Terkel, Studs. *Hard Times: An Oral History of the Great Depression.* New York: Pantheon, 1970.

Terrill, Tom E., and Jerrold D. Hirsch. *Such As Us: Southern Voices of the Thirties.* Chapel Hill: University of North Carolina Press, 1978.

Williams, T. Harry. *Huey Long.* New York: Knopf, 1969.

ORAL HISTORIES OF THE SECOND WORLD WAR

Adams, Judith Porter. *Peacework: Oral Histories of Women Peace Activists.* Boston: Twayne, 1991.

Barnwell, Janet, and Stanley E. Hilton, eds. *Louisiana Voices: Remembering World War II.* Baton Rouge: Louisiana State University, 1998.

Carlson, Lewis H. *We Were Each Other's Prisoners: An Oral History of World War II American and German Prisoners of War.* New York: Basic, 1997.

Fox, Stephen. *America's Invisible Gulag: A Biography of German American Internment & Exclusion in World War II: Memory and History.* New York: Peter Lang, 2000.

Fox, Stephen. *The Unknown Internment: An Oral History of the Relocation of Italian Americans During World War II.* Boston: Twayne, 1990.

Fraser, Ronald. *Blood of Spain: An Oral History of the Spanish Civil War.* New York: Pantheon, 1979.

Frazer, Heather T., and John O'Sullivan. *"We Have Just Begun to Not Fight": An Oral History of Conscientious Objectors in Civilian Public Service During World War II.* New York: Twayne, 1996.

Gerassi, John. *The Premature Antifascists: North American Volunteers in the Spanish Civil War, 1936–39: An Oral History.* New York: Praeger, 1986.

Gluck, Sherna B. *Rosie the Riveter Revisited: Women, the War, and Social Change.* Boston: Twayne, 1987.

Hoffman, Alice M., and Howard S. Hoffman. *Archives of Memory: A Soldier Recalls World War II.* Lexington: University Press of Kentucky, 1990.

Kessler, Lynne S., and Edmond B. Bart, eds. *Never in Doubt: Remembering Iwo Jima.* Annapolis, Md.: Naval Institute Press, 1999.

King, R. T., ed. *War Stories: Veterans Remember WW II*. Reno: University of Nevada Oral History Program, 1995.

La Forte, Robert S., and Ronald E. Marcello. *Remembering Pearl Harbor: Eyewitness Accounts by U.S. Military Men and Women*. New York: Bantam, 1991.

La Forte, Robert S., and Ronald E. Marcello. *Building the Death Railway: The Ordeal of American POWs in Burma, 1942–1945*. Wilmington, Del.: Scholarly Resources, 1993.

La Forte, Robert S., Ronald E. Marcello, and Richard L. Himmel. *With Only the Will to Live: Accounts of Americans in Japanese Prison Camps, 1941–1945*. Wilmington, Del.: Scholarly Resources, 1994.

Lanzmann, Claude. *Shoah: An Oral History of the Holocaust*. New York: Pantheon, 1985.

Lewin, Rhoda G. *Witnesses to the Holocaust, An Oral History*. Boston: Twayne, 1990.

Mason, John T., Jr. *The Atlantic War Remembered: An Oral History Collection*. Annapolis, Md.: Naval Institute Press, 1990.

Mason, John T., Jr. *The Pacific War Remembered: An Oral History Collection*. Annapolis, Md.: Naval Institute Press, 2003.

Mason, Katrina. *Children of Los Alamos: An Oral History of the Town Where the Atomic Age Began*. New York: Twayne, 1995.

Motley, Mary Penick, ed. *The Invisible Soldier: The Experience of the Black Soldier, World War II*. Detroit: Wayne State University Press, 1975.

O'Donnell, Patrick. *Into the Rising Sun: In Their Own Words, World War II's Pacific Veterans Reveal the Heart of Combat*. New York: Free Press, 2002.

Onorato, Michael P. *Forgotten Heroes, Japan's Imprisonment of American Civilians in the Philippines, 1942–1945, An Oral History*. Westport, Conn.: Greenwood, 1990.

Passerini, Luisa, ed. *Memory and Totalitarianism*. New York: Oxford University Press, 1992.

Petty, Bruce M. *Saipan: Oral Histories of the Pacific War*. Jefferson, N.C.: McFarland, 2002.

Satterfield, Archie. *The Home Front: An Oral History of the War Years in America, 1941–1945*. New York: Playboy Press, 1981.

Spiller, Harry, *Pearl Harbor Survivors: An Oral History of 24 Servicemen*. Jefferson, N.C.: McFarland, 2002.

Stannard, Richard M. *Infantry: An Oral History of a World War II American Infantry Battalion*. New York: Twayne, 1993.

Stave, Bruce M., and Michele Palmer, with Leslie Frank. *Witnesses to Nuremberg: An Oral History of American Participants at the War Crime Trials*. New York: Twayne, 1998.

Stillwell, Paul. *The Golden Thirteen: Recollections of the First Black Naval Officers*. Annapolis, Md.: Naval Institute Press, 1993.

Terkel, Studs. *The "Good War": An Oral History of World War Two*. New York: Pantheon, 1984.

Woolridge, E. T., ed. *Carrier Warfare in the Pacific: An Oral History Collection*. Washington, D.C.: Smithsonian Institution Press, 1993.

ORAL HISTORIES OF THE 1960S

Fraser, Ronald, et al. *1968: A Student Generation in Revolt: An International Oral History*. New York: Pantheon, 1988.

Gillette, Michael L. *Launching the War on Poverty: An Oral History*. New York: Twayne, 1996.

Joseph, Peter. *Good Times: An Oral History of America in the Nineteen Sixties*. New York: Charterhouse, 1973.

Kessler, Lauren. *After All These Years: Sixties Ideals in a Different World*. New York: Thunder's Mouth, 1990.

Makower, Joel. *Woodstock: The Oral History*. New York: Doubleday, 1989.

Morrison, Joan, and Robert K. Morrison. *From Camelot to Kent State: The Sixties Experience in the Words of Those Who Lived It*. New York: Times Books, 1987.

Sneed, Larry A. *No More Silence: An Oral History of the Assassination of President Kennedy*. Denton: University of North Texas Press, 2002.

Strober, Gerald S., and Deborah Hart Strober, eds. *Let Us Begin Anew: An Oral History of the Kennedy Presidency*. New York: HarperCollins, 1993.

Terkel, Studs. *Division Street, America*. New York: Pantheon, 1967.

ORAL HISTORIES OF THE VIETNAM WAR

Baker, Mark. *Nam: The Vietnam War in the Words of the Men and Women Who Fought There*. New York: William Morrow, 1981.

DeBonis, Steven. *Children of the Enemy: Oral Histories of Vietnamese Amerasians and Their Mothers*. Jefferson, N.C.: McFarland, 1995.

Gioglio, Gerald P. *Days of Decision: An Oral History of Conscientious Objectors in the Military During the Vietnam War*. Trenton, N.J.: Broken Rifle, 1988.

Hammel, Eric M. *Khe Sanh: Siege in the Clouds: An Oral History*. New York: Crown, 1989.

Lehrack, Otto J. *No Shining Armor: The Marines at War in Vietnam: An Oral History*. Lawrence: University Press of Kansas, 1992.

Marshall, Kathryn. *In the Combat Zone: An Oral History of American Women in Vietnam, 1966–1975*. Boston: Little, Brown, 1987.

McHugh, Siobhan. *Minefields and Miniskirts: Australian Women and the Vietnam War*. Sidney, Australia: Doubleday, 1993.

Norman, Elizabeth M. *Women at War: The Story of Fifty Military Nurses Who Served in Vietnam*. Philadelphia: University of Pennsylvania Press, 1990.

Santoli, Al. *Everything We Had: An Oral History of the Vietnam War by Thirty-Three American Soldiers Who Fought It*. New York: Random House, 1981.

Stacewicz, Richard. *Winter Soldiers: An Oral History of the Vietnam Veterans Against the War*. New York: Twayne, 1997.

Terry, Wallace. *Bloods: An Oral History of the Vietnam War by Black Veterans*. New York: Random House, 1984.

Tollefson, Jane W. *The Strength Not to Fight: An Oral History of Conscientious Objectors of the Vietnam War*. Boston: Little, Brown, 1993.

Walker, Keith. *A Piece of My Heart: The Stories of 26 American Women Who Served in Vietnam*. Nocato, Calif: Presidio Press, 1986.

Willenson, Kim. *The Bad War: An Oral History of the Vietnam War*. New York: New American Library, 1987.

Internet
Resources

As useful as the Internet has become, it is also an ephemeral media. Web sites permutate and material consulted on one visit may be "Not Found" on the next. Although these sites will undoubtedly change, most of them maintain links to other related sites that collectively provide a large network of oral history information.

ORAL HISTORY ORGANIZATIONS

Canadian Oral History Association: http://www.ncf.carleton.ca./oral-history
International Oral History Association: http://www.ioha.fgv.br
Michigan Oral History Association: http://www.h-net.msu.edu/~moha
Northwest Oral History Association:
    http://www.ohs.org/collections/oralhistory/nohahome.htm
Oral History Association (U.S.): http://www.omega.dickinson.edu/organizations/oha
Oral History Association of Australia: http://www.geocities.com/oha_australia/
Oral History in the Mid-Atlantic Region (OHMAR): http://www.ohmar.org
Oral History List Service: H-ORALHIST@H-NET.MSU.EDU
Oral History Society (Great Britain): http://www.oralhistory.org.uk/
Southwest Oral History Association: http://soha.fullerton.edu/

ORAL HISTORY COLLECTIONS

American Memory: Historical Collections at the Library of Congress:
    http://memory.loc.gov/
Billy Graham Archives: Many Voices Make One Story: Oral History Interviews:
    http://www.wheaton.edu/bgc/archives/exhibits/ohistory/oral01.htm
British Library National Sound Archive Oral History: http://www.bl.uk
California State University at Fullerton, Oral History Program:
    http://www.ohp.fullerton.edu/ohphome.html
California State University at Long Beach, Oral History Program:
    http://www.csulb.edu/depts/history/relprm/oral01.html
California State University at Monterey Bay, Oral History and Community Memory
    Institute and Archive: http://www.hcom.csumb.edu/oralhistory/
City University of New York, United Nations Intellectual History Project:
    http://www.unhistory.org/Oral.History.htm
Columbia University Oral History Research Office:
    http://www.columbia.edu/cu/lweb/indiv/oral/
Duke Center for Documentary Studies: http://cds.aas.duke.edu/

East Midlands Oral History Archive, Leicester, United Kingdom:
     http://www.le.ac.uk/emoha/
Florida State University, Oral History Program:
     http://www.fsu.edu/~ohp/index.html
Forest History Society, Oral History Program:
     http://www.lib.duke.edu/forest/ohguide.html
George Mason University Oral History Projects:
     http://www.gmu.edu/library/specialcollections/ohp.htm
Georgia State University: http://www.library.gsu.edu/spcoll/ggdp/index.htm
Goucher College: http://www.goucher.edu/harbel/
Imperial War Museum, London: Department of South Records:
     http://www.iwm.org.uk/lambeth/sound.htm
Indiana University Center for the Study of History and Memory:
     http://www.indiana.edu/~ohrc/
Iowa Women Artists Oral History Project: http://www.lucidplanet.com/IWA/
John F. Kennedy Library Oral History Project:
     http://www.cs.umb.edu/~serl/jfk/oralhist.htm
Kellogg African American Health Care Project:
     http://www.reuther.wayne.edu/ohkellog.htm
Legacy Program: www.dancelegacy.org
Louisiana State University: T. Harry Williams Center for Oral History:
     http://www.lib.lsu.edu/special/williams/
Lyndon B. Johnson Library Oral History Collection:
     http://www.lbjlib.utexas.edu
Minnesota State University Moorhead, Heritage Education Commission Oral History
     Project: http://www.mnstate.edu/heritage/
National Library of New Zealand Oral History Centre:
     http://www.natlib.govt.nz/en/services/1oralhistory.html
National Press Club: Women in Journalism:
     http://npc.press.org/wpforal/ohhome.htm#top
Northern Arizona University, Navajo Traders Project, Voices from the Trading Post:
     http://www.nau.edu/library/speccoll//exhibits/traders/
Ohio State University Archives: Byrd Polar Expedition Oral History Project:
     http://www.lib.ohio-state.edu/arvweb
Rutgers University World War II Oral History Project:
     http://fas-history.rutgers.edu/oralhistory/orlhom.htm
Smithsonian Institution Archives: http://www.siris.si.edu
Smokejumping and Forest Fire Fighting Oral History Project:
     http://www2.state.id.us/ishs/smokejumper.html
Survivors of the Shoah Visual History Foundation: http://www.vhf.org
United States Holocaust Memorial Museum, Washington: http://www.ushmm.org
United States Senate Historical Office Oral Histories:
     http://www.senate.gov/learning/learn_history_oralhist.html
University of Alaska Fairbanks Oral History Program:
     http://www.uaf.edu/library/libweb/oralhist/home.htm
University of California at Berkeley: Regional Oral History Office:
     http://www.lib.berkeley.edu/BANC/ROHO

University of California at Los Angeles (UCLA) Oral History Program:
   http://www.library.ucla.edu/libraries/special/ohp/ohpindex.htm
University of California at Monterey Bay:
   http://classes.monterey.edu/HCOM/HCOM314SL-01/world/spring98/
University of Cape Town, South Africa: Centre for Popular Memory:
   http://www.uct.ac.za/depts/cfpm/
University of Connecticut Center for Oral History: http://www.oralhistory.uconn.edu
University of Hawaii Center for Oral History:
   http://www2.soc.hawaii.edu/css/orahist/index.htm
University of Louisville Oral History Center:
   http://www.louisville.edu/library/uarc/ohc.htm
University of Mississippi: Center for the Study of Southern Culture:
   http://www.olemiss.edu/depts/south
University of North Carolina at Chapel Hill, Southern Oral History Program:
   http://www.unc.edu/depts/sohp
University of Texas at Austin: U.S. Latinos and Latinas in World War II:
   http://www.utexas.edu/projects/latinoarchives
University of Texas at San Antonio: Archives for Research on Women and Gender:
   http://www.lib.utsa.edu/Archives/arwg.html
Utah State University Oral History Program: http://www.usu.edu/oralhist/oh.html
World Bank Oral History Program: http://www.worldbank.org/archives
1968: The Whole World Was Watching: http://www.stg.brown.edu/projects/1968

ONLINE ORAL HISTORY GUIDES

American Bar Foundation Oral Histories:
   http://www.abf-sociolegal.org/oralhistory/index.html
Art Institute of Chicago, Chicago Architects Oral History Project:
   http://www.artic.edu/aic/collections/dept_architecture/oralhistory.html
Baylor University Institute for Oral History: http://www3.baylor.edu/Oral_History/
Claremont Graduate University, Oral History Program:
   http://www.cgu.edu/inst/oralhis.html
Conservation Online [A collection of online resources relating to the preservation of audio
   materials]: http://palimpsest.stanford.edu/bytopic/audio
Cultural Arts Resources for Teachers and Students: http://www.carts.org
Discovery Channel [features several sites focusing on oral history in the schools]:
   http://school.discovery.com
Discovering Our Delta: A Learning Guide for Community Research:
   http://www.folklife.si.edu/MississippiDelta/discoveringourdelta.htm
Doing Oral History [use of oral history for high school teaching]:
   www.doingoralhistory.org
Folk Heritage Collections in Crisis, Council on Library and Information Services [dis-
   cussions of digitizing audio recordings]:
   http://www.clir.org/pubs/reports/pub96/contents.html.
Getting Word: The Monticello African American Oral History Project:
   http://www.monticello.org/gettingword/
The History of Jim Crow [includes recommendations on teaching with oral history]:
   http://www.jimcrowhistory.org/

Michigan State University, Matrix—The Center for Humane Arts, Letters, and Social Sciences Online: http://www.historicalvoices.org/oralhistory

The Mississippi Civil Rights Movement: An Online Bibliography of Oral History [joint venture of the University of Southern Mississippi's Center for Oral History and Cultural Heritage, and the Tugaloo College Archives]: http://www-dept.usm.edu/~mcrohb

Mississippi Action For Community Education (MACE), Community Development Program Oral History: http://www.picced.org/advocacy/mace.htm

National Endowment for the Humanities: "My History is America's History": http://www/myhistory.org

National Institutes of Health, "In Their Own Words: NIH Researchers Recall the Early Days of AIDS": http://aidshistory.nih.gov

Oral History and Folklore Collection, National Library of Australia, Canberra, Australia: http://www.nla.gov.au/oh/

Oral History Program, University of New South Wales Archives, Sydney, Australia: http://www.oralhistory.unsw.edu.au/

Oral History Society, Practical Advice: http://www.oralhistory.org.uk/advice/

Smithsonian's Archives of American Art: http://www.archivesofamericanart.si.edu/oralhist/oralhist.htm

Sound Recordings in the National Archives of Singapore: http://aavis.nhb.gov.sg/

University of Southern Mississippi Center for Oral History and Cultural Heritage: http://www-dept.usm.edu/~ocach/msohp.html

U.S. Army Center for Military History: http://www.army.mil/cmh-pg/books/oral.htm

Veterans Oral History Project: http://www/loc.gov/folklife.vets

RELATED SITES

American Association for State and Local History: http://www.aaslh.org/

American Folklore Society: http://www.afsnet.org

American Historical Association: http://www.theaha.org/

The History Channel: http://www.historychannel.com

Indiana University Folklore Institute: http://www.indiana.edu/~folklore/index.html

Organization of American Historians: http://www.oah.org/

Index

As associate historian in the Senate Historical Office, Donald A. Ritchie conducts an oral history program with former Senate staff. A graduate of the City College of New York, he received his Ph.D. in history from the University of Maryland. He has edited the Twayne oral history series and published several American history textbooks. His other books include *James M. Landis: Dean of the Regulators* (1980), *Press Gallery: Congress and the Washington Correspondents* (1991), *American Journalists: Getting the Story* (1997) and *The Oxford Guide to the United States Government* (2001). He has conducted numerous oral history workshops, chaired the Organization of American Historians' committee on research and access to historical documentation, and helped establish the "Pioneers in Public History" interview series for *The Public Historian.* A past president of the Oral History Association and of Oral History in the Mid–Atlantic Region (OHMAR), he has also served on the council of the American Historical Association and the board of the Society for History in the Federal Government. He received the Organization of American Historian's Richard W. Leopold Prize and OHMAR's Forrest C. Pogue Award for significant contributions to the field of oral history.